THE
BOATING BIBLE
AN ESSENTIAL HANDBOOK
FOR EVERY SAILOR

79

013

THE
BOATING BIBLE
AN ESSENTIAL HANDBOOK
FOR EVERY SAILOR

JIM MURRANT

Angus&Robertson
An imprint of HarperCollins*Publishers*

FOR ANN REYNOLDS

The medical advice and procedures outlined in this book
should not be taken without first consulting a doctor
or a trained paramedic.

Angus&Robertson
An imprint of HarperCollins*Publishers*, Australia

First published in Australia in 1991
Reprinted in 1995

HarperCollins*Publishers*
25 Ryde Road, Pymble, Sydney, NSW 2073, Australia
31 View Road, Glenfield, Auckland 10, New Zealand

National Library of Australia Cataloguing-in-Publication data:

Murrant, Jim.
The boating bible:
an essential handbook for every sailor
Bibilography.
Includes index.
ISBN 0 207 16166 6.
1. Boats and boating.
2. Seamanship. 3. Navigation.
I. Title.
623.88

Typeset in Australia by Midland Typesetters, Maryborough, Vic.
Printed in Australia by Griffin Press, Adelaide

10 9 8 7 6 5 4 3 2   95 96 97 98 99

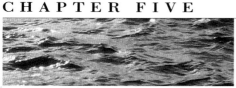

PREFACE

My sailing career has spanned almost five decades, and to try to distill those years into a book has taken nearly five years. Although the years of writing have come near the end of the years of learning, there is always more knowledge to be gained.

Since the end of World War II almost everything has changed radically. Political systems have collapsed, moonwalking is now commonplace, and we are planning to send astronauts to Mars, such has been the technological explosion.

The world of boats didn't escape. After hundreds of years of slow development, sailing vessels went through their own technological explosion: winged keels, sailcloth stronger than steel, low maintenance fibreglass, and electronic instruments from wind indicators to Global Positioning System navigation accurate to 20 feet.

Despite all this, sailing still has enough of 'man against the elements' about it to continue its attraction. It has given me many years of pleasure, and I hope many more. If this book can help any of those men and women who go down to the sea in ships get the same enjoyment I will be delighted.

JIM MURRANT
February 1991

CONTENTS

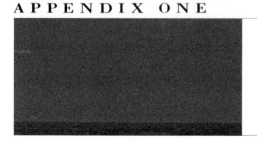

PARTS OF A SAILING BOAT

The purpose of this chapter is to give a cursory look at boat construction—not so that you would be able to build one, or even be expert in one, but to show some of the reasons why boats look as they do. Although there is a huge range of designs for boats they are basically the same whether they are a racing dinghy, a fishing smack, or an ocean racer or cruiser. They are as cars are—the design changes only with the purpose of the machine, and after that for cosmetic effect.

So boats, generally, are sharp at the end that goes through the water first, they have varying degrees of width (beam) and they are blunt at the trailing end. They will have a mast, either tall or short, and they will have sails. Because they have sails, they must have a keel, as we shall discuss later in this chapter.

If the boat is a fishing smack it will be slow, it will have a short mast, and it will be made of enormously strong timbers because it has to survive heavy weather, it has to carry a heavy catch, and it has to have great power to drag its nets.

If the boat is a racing dinghy, it will hold two, sometimes three people. It will be light enough to carry to the beach and trail home, and it will have a dish shaped bottom and a centreboard. This is because it usually sails in sheltered waters, the weight of the crew keeps it upright, and it wants as little wetted surface as possible so that it can travel as fast as possible.

An ocean racer won't have a doghouse (the bit of the cabin that sticks up above the deck), it will have a mast that seems ridiculously light for such a powerful vessel and it will have a wide range of sails to choose from.

The ocean cruiser will have a solid mast, often with steps up the side. It will have a big cockpit, and a big doghouse. The boat will tend to have more beam than the racer, although not necessarily so, and it will have sails that furl into the mast, or around themselves, with the controls running back to the cockpit.

The point I am making is that however the special purpose of a boat affects the design, it will still be within broad controlling factors. In the same way that design can change for special purposes, so has it changed in the last decade especially because new materials have come to hand.

In fact materials from which hulls are made have changed dramatically. Designers have moved from wood, fibreglass, aluminium and steel to specify foam and Kevlar sandwiches, end-grain balsa held by thin wooden skins inside and out, carbon fibre and other space-age materials. Also instead of being constructed in a style which had not changed much since Biblical times, hulls are now moulded, and are even baked in giant ovens to cook the exotic materials into a lightweight shape that is lighter than alloy and stronger than steel. Hull shapes have changed, too. The fat, shallow, modern boat sails to windward far better than the traditional styles by utilising lift from the keel. And, because they are light, the modern boats run far faster. The only advantage the older, heavier boat has over the modern boat is that it is not thrown sideways as much in big, breaking seas.

Diagram 1.1 *Wooden boat under construction, showing basic longitudinal and vertical components, tied together by the keel.*

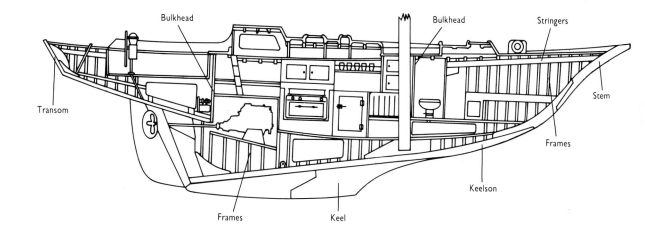

But however much shape and materials have altered, the skeleton of a boat is still much the same. To understand the structure of a hull is to understand the strain on it and to know when to take that strain off. It is outside the scope of this book to discuss design in the sense of which is the latest or which is the best. Every boat buyer decides that personal equation himself. We only want to understand enough about boat construction to see how the design and building absorb the stresses handed out by the sea. So we will discuss the elements of hull construction before talking about standing and running rigging, how to tune a mast, and sails.

H U L L   S H A P E

Hull shape has a profound effect on boat speed. Long narrow boats will be faster, given the same sail area, than short fat ones. The dish type hull with a spade keel and rudder and very little hull in the water will be faster again. A boat with a long keel will be steadier in directional stability than the modern dagger keel type.

Speed in yachts is a function of waterline length. It's generally accepted that the maximum boat speed that can be achieved—maximum hull speed—is to the formula **speed in knots = square root of the designed waterline x 1.5.**

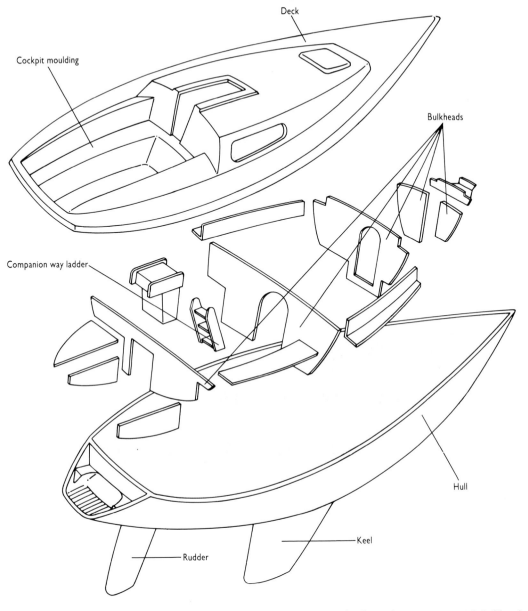

Deck

Cockpit moulding

Bulkheads

Companion way ladder

Hull

Keel

Rudder

This is a fairly rough method because some boats will be faster than the formula indicates and some slower, but not by very much in either case. The factors which prevent a boat travelling any faster than this are skin friction and wave-making resistance. You will sometimes in heavy conditions have boats staying alongside you which look so old-fashioned that you would have expected to have been able to outstrip them quickly. Their ugly longer hull is being pushed through the water at its maximum because it has reached an equilibrium with the skin friction and the wave-making resistance. Your boat, too, will have reached its maximum hull speed but because of your shorter waterline you are unable to break away from the ugly duckling. Also, as a boat's speed increases, the length between the bow wave and the stern wave becomes equal to the length of the boat, and the yacht tends to squat in this trough, so increasing the amount of hull that's in the water and the friction on it.

Diagram 1.2 *A fibreglass boat during construction. Although moulded, the same basic strengtheners are apparent as in the wooden boat.*

Diagram 1.3 *A long keeled boat.*

Diagram 1.4 *A bilge keeler, useful in shallow water.*

Diagram 1.5 *A fin keel, common in harbour racers, and in a developed form in powerful ocean racers.*

Diagram 1.6 *A lifting or drop keel, which combines the stiffness of a deep keel with the shallow water capability of a bilge keeler.*

The only way a sailing yacht can exceed its designed hull speed or its maximum hull speed, is by surfing. This is where modern lightweight construction has it all over the boats of even as recently as 15 years ago. They are so much lighter for the amount of sail they carry that they can get up on to a wave long before their heavier rivals, and so gradually outrun boats considerably bigger than themselves.

H U L L   S T R U C T U R E

Whatever material a boat is made of, it will have a keel, a stem, and a sternpost of some kind. The keel is the spine, the backbone of the boat. The stem rises from the keel at the front of the boat and is attached to it. The sternpost similarly rises from the keel at the back of the boat and is attached to it. At regular intervals, and at 90 degrees to the keel, are frames which determine the shape of the hull. They are joined across the top of the developing boat by cross-pieces which support the decking. The frames are held in place longitudinally by stringers—members which run from stem to stern. At each intersection of frame and stringer, and of frame and deck beam, knees tie them even more strongly together (see diagram 1.1). Where the frames join the keel, horizontal members called floors (floor timbers) bind them together. When the hull material is attached to the shape formed by this skeleton, it becomes enormously strong, but not so rigid that there isn't some movement in a seaway. A hull which could not twist slightly would soon be smashed to pieces—the shocks need to be absorbed.

Modern boats, particularly those made of fibreglass, have only very light stringers and frames because most of the strength is in the moulded hull— nevertheless they do have those members.

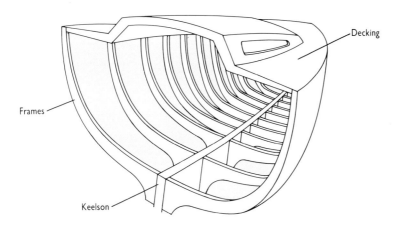

Diagram 1.7 *Shown are cross-members of the boat's hull, the ribs, beams and frames, and floors.*

Decking

Frames

Keelson

S T A N D I N G   R I G G I N G

Anybody who has sailed for even the shortest time will know the names of most of the rigging, but may not have that almost instinctive knowledge of the function that allows the right decision to be made when part of the rig is damaged and strain has to be transferred or removed.

The **forestay** prevents the mast falling backwards, determines the amount of permanent rake that is built into the rig and holds the luff of the headsails.

The **backstay** prevents the mast falling forward, pulls the top of the mast backwards when under pressure, and tightens the forestay so that it does not sag to leeward under the weight of the headsail.

The **shrouds** support the mast laterally and, when properly tuned, hold the mast upright. They also transmit the power of the sails to the hull through the chainplates.

The **inner forestay**, that is, the intermediate forestay or babystay, controls the amount of bend put into the mast between the crane and the deck, and is used to flatten the mainsail as wind increases.

The **runners (running backstays)**, or checkstays, take the pumping action out of the mast and are critical in preventing breakage. If properly set up they will help prevent the onset of vibration. The lower part of the stay is more important than the upper—according to the computer model discussed on pages 13–15.

The **boom vang** really counts as a control, but I believe it has a function under standing rigging as well as running rigging in that it flattens the mainsail, pulls the boom down as well as pushing it forward, and so affects the control of mast bend.

R U N N I N G   R I G G I N G

Before saying anything about running rigging there are two paramount, invariable, must-never-be-disobeyed rules: never put in a half-hitch when cleating a line, they jam and will not undo in a hurry, and they can cause severe danger. One complete turn around the base of the cleat (coming in

Diagram 1.8 *Standing rigging.*

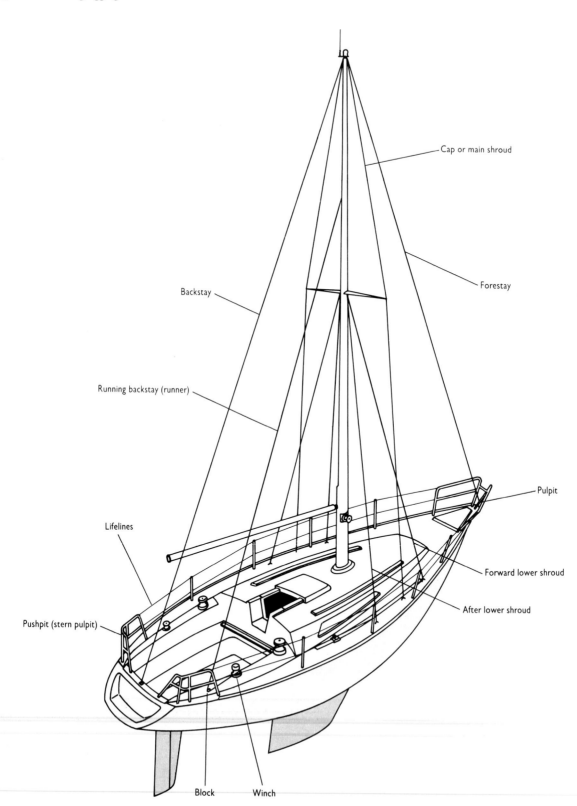

Cap or main shroud

Forestay

Backstay

Running backstay (runner)

Pulpit

Lifelines

Forward lower shroud

After lower shroud

Pushpit (stern pulpit)

Block   Winch

Diagram 1.9 *Running rigging.*

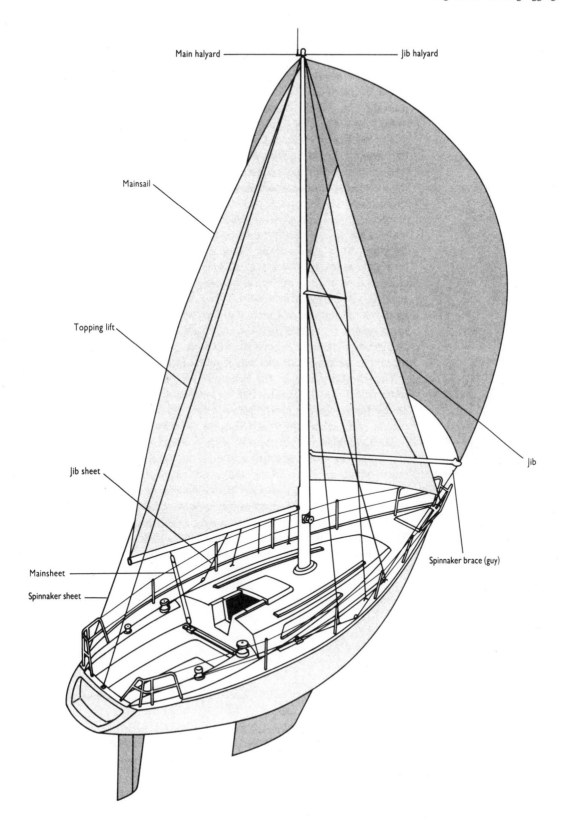

Main halyard

Jib halyard

Mainsail

Topping lift

Jib

Jib sheet

Spinnaker brace (guy)

Mainsheet

Spinnaker sheet

from the open side), followed by a figure of eight around the horns of the cleat and a finishing turn around the base of the cleat will provide all the friction you will ever need and will come free easily. Also, never put a stopper knot or a figure of eight knot into a sheet or halyard. When a sail is out of control and the boat is at risk, sometimes the only solution is to let the sheet or halyard run free—it cannot when the end is knotted.

The **halyards** haul sails up the mast to their effective positions and are then locked off on a cleat. The adjustment may be altered for light winds, by easing, or for heavy winds, by tightening.

The **mainsheet** controls the mainsail, and is also the longest component of the running rigging, a factor to remember when putting together a jury rig. The sheet is led through a car which can move up and down a track, called the traveller. The car is eased down the traveller as the first method of relieving weather helm. When this is no longer sufficient, the mainsail has to be reefed.

The only other controls of the main actually control the movement of the boom. One such control, the boom vang, is discussed above under Standing Rigging. When running, the boom is prevented from moving up and down by a **preventer** (usually a four to one purchase which attaches to a shackle along the boom) put in such a position that when the boom is right out, the shackle is directly above the toe rail. The preventer then clips to another shackle, or a slot, at the toe rail and is pulled on hard to hold the boom firm, and to prevent an accidental jibe. In some cases—usually when cruising—a **foreguy**, and/or an **afterguy** is rigged to stop a jibe. These consist of a line led from the end of the boom and cleated off either forward or aft.

The **jib sheets** control the headsails. On the wind they are led through a track which is well inboard. Off the wind they should be led through a block on the leeward rail. Control between these two positions is achieved through the use of a **barberhaul**, which pulls the sheet inboard.

The **spinnaker** is controlled by a sheet and a brace which are working and are called the **sheet** and **brace** (guy), but have attached another sheet and brace, which are not working and so are called the **lazy sheet** and **lazy brace** (guy). The brace (guy) attaches to the spinnaker at the outboard end of the spinnaker pole, and the sheet at the opposite clew. The lazy sheet is attached to the brace (guy) and the lazy brace (guy) to the sheet (see diagrams 1.10–1.11). The reason for the apparent doubling of the lines is that the lazy sheet and brace (guy) become the active controls after a jibe.

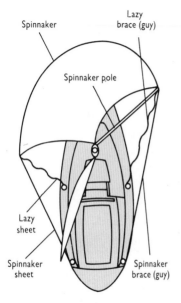

Diagram 1.10 *The double sheet and brace system. This system is needed to perform dip pole jibes and spinnaker peels.*

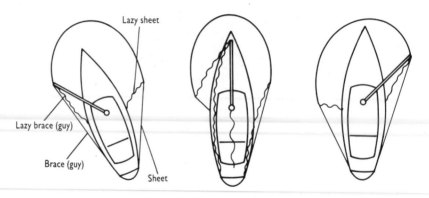

Diagram 1.11 *A spinnaker and its controls during a jibe.*

Another control of the spinnaker is the **snotter**, a whip or single open-sided block on the end of a line, which is hooked over the spinnaker sheet and/or brace and led through another block on the deck nearby, but in any case close to the spinnaker clew. When the line is tightened the sheet is hauled down tight, which prevents the death rolls. This system is used in heavy weather running.

All other sails are controlled by a halyard and a sheet, in the usual way.

Diagram 1.12 *Sloop.*

TUNING THE MAST

The first step is to tune the mast, a very complicated affair. There is no hope of tuning a boat for good performance until this has been done. First we'll deal with a single spreader rig, which will enable us to cover both racing dinghies and smaller keel boats. As the boats become larger and more powerful and the masts therefore have to be taller and relatively lighter, the rig has to be a double or even a triple spreader.

A mast rake is the easiest of the adjustments. I belong to the school that believes that a raked mast is almost always more efficient than one that's straight. Although most people believe the wind blows straight along the surface of the earth, it does not. It blows slightly downwards at an angle of about four degrees. A mast which is leaning back four to six degrees will be actually presenting a leading edge which is at right angles, or very nearly so, to the direction of flow of the wind. And it just seems logical that this will be more effective. You may have class regulations which govern what happens when you set up the mast, in which case you will have to follow those precisely or risk being disqualified or penalised in some other way. So let's assume that six degrees is about the angle of rake one should use in this first tuning. To achieve this rake, the fore and aft controls of the standing rigging—the forestay and the backstay—will be used. In the smaller boats the mast will most likely be stepped on deck and it may in some cases be possible for it to move forwards or backwards from the median position. Set it up for the moment in the median position and we'll talk later about why it may want to move forward or aft.

Diagram 1.13 *Ketch—the steering position is in front of the mizzen.*

As boats get larger and become keel boats rather than centreboarders, the mast may well still be stepped on deck but it will be in a fixed tabernacle and so the tuning will be slightly easier. The most reliable way of setting the mast up in the first place is to have the adjustment on the rigging screws for the forestay and backstay and for the cap shrouds (main shrouds) open to their full extent and attached in their respective positions. With smaller boats the mast can be supported by a crew member, or, if this is not practicable, halyards or other lines can be rigged to hold the mast in a rough temporary position while the permanent rigging is attached. First tighten the cap shrouds so that the mast is held firmly but not tightly in position and appears to be plumb as far as the eye can tell. Then tighten the forestay and backstay synchronously while somebody else observes by eye that the mast is raking slightly aft. Bring the forestay and backstay up to be firm, but not as tight as the cap shrouds. Since there's almost no compression load on the mast at this stage it should stand quite comfortably in approximately the position you want. It will be safe enough for someone to go up it to drop a plumb

Diagram 1.14 *Yawl—the steering position is behind the mizzen.*

Diagram 1.15 *Cutter—two headsails before the mast.*

Diagram 1.16 *Schooner—the second mast is higher than the first.*

Diagram 1.17 *Day sailer.*

bob to check the rake against a protractor or use an inclinometer if a bob was not rigged before the mast was raised. (Another method is to have a halyard rigged with a weight on it, which will determine the angle of the rake quite accurately.) To adjust the rake just let off the forestay or tighten it as required to bring the top of the mast to the point where the angle of rake is shown by the plumb bob and protractor as six degrees. In most smaller boats there will be one set of lower shrouds only, running from the base of the single spreaders to the gunwale slightly aft of the cap shrouds. The purpose of the lowers is to hold the mast firm against forward pressure from the boom. (They also hold the mast firm in its sideways direction where the pressure of the spreader pushes against the mast.) Larger boats or those boats which have extraordinarily high aspect ratios and therefore tall masts need runners to control that forward push and to keep the forestay tight. But with the simple one spreader rig with one set of lowers, mast tuning is relatively easy.

Now that the mast is in the right position the cap shrouds should be tightened to increase the compression on the mast. Tighten both at once for a fixed number of turns, and keep checking that the plumb of the mast is absolutely dead straight. It mustn't fall off at the top either to port or starboard, but be directly upright. When the mast seems absolutely dead straight across the boat and has the required take fore and aft, the lower shrouds can be tightened enough to take up the load.

Once your mast is set in approximately the right place, go for a sail. Take the boat out on one of those ideal days that provides a steady, moderate wind and therefore steady pressure. It is almost impossible to tune a mast properly in anything but flat waters and a steady wind, otherwise the pitching and the changes in the angle of heel change the forces too erratically and too often. Set the sails for median performance. Make sure the jib sheet leads are adjusted for the pressures of the day by moving them forward and aft until the telltales along the leading edge of the jib all break together when the boat is luffed into the wind.

Next check the jib halyard tension. Get enough tension so that there are no soft wrinkles flowing back horizontally along the sail or radiating from the position of each of the hanks. Pull the halyard tighter until you get to the other unwanted extreme which is a tight stretch and fold in the sail running parallel to the forestay for the whole length of the sail. When that point is reached, ease the tension off until all of that ridge disappears. The sail will then take on a nice even curve which will be pleasant to the eye. Note this pleasant-to-the-eye look because it's all that people who sail long enough and observe conditions enough, need to see when looking at a rig to know that it's properly tuned.

The jib is now in good trim for handling the conditions of the day, so next work on the mainsail. The same conditions of halyard tension apply to the main as to the headsail. The sailmaker will have built a certain amount of curve into the leading edge of the sail, the luff of the sail, to match the curve in the mast itself so that the sail looks smooth and powerful when it's properly set. If there's a ridge running up along the sail near the mast and parallel to it, then the tension is too tight and it should be eased off. If a cunningham eye is fitted, then the halyard tension should be just slightly soft so that it can be tightened by the cunningham as the conditions vary.

The other control that's needed on the mainsail, and this does not apply to a headsail, is the tension of the foot of the sail. Here most inexperienced sailors go wrong. They almost invariably pull the tension out (outhaul too tight) in the mistaken belief that more tension means more power, and they then flatten the sail—these are the boats you see at the back of a racing fleet where, although the conditions are moderate, they're set up as if there's a gale.

The rule for placing draught or camber into a mainsail is that the depth of the sail should be about in the proportion of one in ten to its width at any given point. This can best be gauged by looking at the sail from underneath and to leeward so that the belly can be seen to the top of the mast. If you were to hold a batten of wood three metres (10 feet) long from the mast to the edge of the sail, then the belly at its deepest point should be .3 metres (one foot). Further up, as the sail becomes narrower, the amount of depth in the sail becomes less. This again is something a really good sailor can appreciate simply by looking at the sail.

Now the boat is set up well enough for you to be able to check the mast in finer detail. Come on to a reach and see whether there are any horrible shapes or wobbles in the mast. If you've followed the earlier instructions it's highly unlikely that there will be any problems because basic tension will be taken care of. But it's just reasonable to be a little cautious. If there's nothing untoward in that first manoeuvre come hard on the wind. If you have a helmsman you can trust to steer accurately upwind (who doesn't pinch the boat) then go to the mast yourself and give it a thorough looking over. First check that it's not wobbling fore and aft. If the middle of the sail is bellying about, the lowers will need to be tightened a little at a time, working on the weather shroud and taking say two turns and then going on to the other tack and taking two turns on the other lower. Keep doing this until there's no wobble in the mast at all.

Diagram 1.18 *Catamaran.*

The next thing to look for is to see whether the top of the mast falls away to leeward at all above the spreaders. If this is the case obviously the cap shrouds have to be tightened. And the cap shrouds should in any case be tighter than the forestay and the backstay. Perform the same tightening operation going from tack to tack until the mast is dead upright under the pressure of the sail. In some cases where only one spreader rig exists on a mast, there are two lower shrouds called the forward and aft. The aft lower should be tighter than the forward lower as its function is to prevent the mast moving forward under the thrust of the main boom. Generally speaking the lowers will not be nearly as tightly screwed home as the cap shrouds because they're much shorter and don't get the same stretch, as well as of course being of lighter material than the caps. The rig is now tuned and from now on anything done to improve the rig will be fine tuning. Although these adjustments may be minute, the differences in speed may be quite dramatic.

Diagram 1.19 *Cat-rigged boat.*

Next we'll deal with the double rig which really is one mast sitting on top of the other. If you imagine that the first mast that you'd rig is cut off at the first spreaders and then another mast is set on top of it with one set of spreaders, and cap shrouds running through both sets of spreaders to the chainplates, then you know how simple it is to tune the double rig.

It's best to check for any falling off at the top of the mast first. If, when on the wind, the top of the mast does fall to leeward, the cap shrouds need to be tightened in just the same way as for a single spreader rig until the mast is dead upright. However, a double rig will almost invariably step through the deck and so another variable is introduced to the tuning process. In most

Diagram 1.20 *Racing dinghy.*

Diagram 1.21 *Heavy displacement hull.*

Diagram 1.22 *Light displacement hull.*

Diagram 1.23 *Motor sailer.*

boats with through-deck masts wooden chocks are used to hold the mast firmly in position where it goes through the deck. However, it is not always as easy as it sounds because there's far less space at the sides than there is at either end and chocks which are banged too firmly into position can very easily produce an 'S' in the lower part of the mast which is very difficult to get rid of. This chocking of the mast is done while the boat is tied up in its marina or alongside a dock or somewhere stable, before taking the boat out to be checked with the sails up. Tap the chocks into place and sight up the mast, or use a plumb bob, to see that no nasty curves are being forced in. But don't make the mistake of not allowing the chocks to go very firmly into place—they will be taking a fair amount of load and it's quite common with the flexing of rigs for the chocks to jump out, which can be dangerous.

Tighten the cap shrouds and the forestay and backstay to get the right rake into the mast as we did with the single spreader rig, but now we have to make sure that under load that same straightness and same rake and same athwartships position will hold. The same rules apply for the double spreader rig as did for the single spreader rig, so follow that procedure so that all the rigging is firm to the touch and the mast is straight.

The set of rigging which holds up the 'first' mast is known as the intermediates. And these should only be tightened until they are firm, but not really tight. If the mast is set up properly the cap shrouds are tightest of all, the lowers are firm, with the forward lower being tighter than the aft, and the intermediate shrouds are just firm. There should now be no bend and no twists and the mast should be free to move fore and aft slightly at the deck so that a controlled bend can be applied where wanted.

Most double spreader and triple spreader rigs need further support for the mast in the long stretches between the spreaders. This is provided by an intermediate forestay—or babystay as it's sometimes known—and runners (running backstays). An intermediate forestay comes from about the height of the second spreaders at a sharpish angle down to the deck probably about two metres (six feet) forward of the mast (if the boat is about 12 metres (40 feet) long).

The runners (running backstays) come from both spreader heights and join into one and then come back on to winches aft in the boat. The main purpose of the runners (running backstays) and the babystay is to take any pumping action out of the mast, particularly in heavy weather and when the seas start to get up a bit. On very powerful ocean racing boats these controls—backstay, inner forestay, boom vang and sometimes first reef—are all controlled by hydraulics and consequently the mast becomes an object of great concentration on the part of the crew. If great loads are being applied and not counteracted, in other words if the runners (running backstays) aren't on properly when 225 kilograms of pressure is on the inner forestay, the mast is actually in a more dangerous condition than if neither of these controls were there. The boom vang is particularly hazardous under a tight spinnaker reach where, if the boom is held down by the vang and the boat heels enough for the boom to go into the water, the opposing pressures of the boom vang and the lift of the sea can easily break a boom. Some famous ocean racing yachts have a vang pressure release on either side of the boat at the helmsman's position so that the helmsman can release that tension and so allow the boom to kick up rather than break.

As with almost all things on boats, if the proper pressures and counter-pressures and controls are applied to a mast it will have a good look about it. It will curve evenly and without deviations. The sail will set properly in it and look good in itself. And the whole rig will have a tight, powerful, efficient look about it.

The triple rig is just a matter of adding another little mast and that is rigged in exactly the way the intermediates are dealt with on a double spreader rig. The questions of diamonds and other masthead controls are really a matter for the expert. If you have a boat so big that it needs diamonds to control the top of the mast, you will without much doubt have on board the rigger and the sailmaker and the sailing master and all those other boat tuners and administrators who will do the job of setting up the mast for you.

H A R M O N I C S
I N   M A S T S

Some very recent research in Australia shows that many yachts which lose their masts do so because of sound waves. A company which has been in the forefront of research into the vibration of tall buildings constructed a computer model of the standing rigging of the ocean racer *Uptown Girl* which lost its rig during the 1988 Sydney to Hobart race. The mast had failed halfway through the race but not in the 'usual' way. After successfully negotiating a gale on the first night of the race, the boat was approaching Bass Strait in a 40 knot wind and in confused, although not very big, seas. It was first light, and the boat had fallen off several waves some minutes earlier. The mast was supported by rod rigging, rigged as in diagram 1.24 (which is taken from the computer model). The mast broke from the top in three places, each place being about 25 centimetres (10 inches) above a set of spreaders, and then fell over the side. The breaks above the spreaders did not crimp in the way that is usual when a tube fails, although the bottom break did. The other breaks were clean, as if the section had been cut through. There was no sign of any crimping.

The owner of the boat is an engineer involved in the management and development of very tall buildings. He suspected harmonic vibration and suggested so to a consultant company. One of their highly qualified staff constructed the computer model and confirmed that the mast had broken through harmonic vibration, and that many other masts must have done so earlier.

What happens is as follows. A mast supported by rigging is under compression through the tightening of the rigging. All structures, whether they be a mast, a tall building, an aeroplane or a hull, have their own natural frequency of vibration. In designing tall buildings, engineers take into account the vibration caused by wind on the structure, and by the vortices which are formed in the lee of the building. Wind tunnel tests on models have given the engineers a large bank of data from which they know which shapes are most effective in reducing the vibration. The force which sets up this vibration does not have to be large, but once the structure, for example a mast's natural frequency of vibration has been reached, the failure of the mast is inevitable, unless the vibration is cancelled out by easing the mainsheet, for instance, or by changing the amount of sail that is up. Unfortunately, while this might halt the vibration, it would probably return once the boat settled down again.

Diagram 1.24 *Continuous rod rigging (right)—in this rig, which is the one that collapsed, each spreader carries a separate shroud, allowing each 'diamond' to move independently. The side view clearly shows how each shroud is independent.*

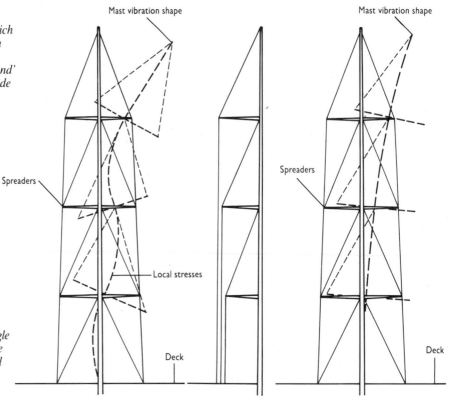

Diagram 1.25 *Fixed rigging single rod (far right)—with only one cap shroud, which touches all spreaders, and adjustable intermediates between each spreader tip and the mast above it, the rig moves as one.*

The difficulty is that the vibration cannot be seen. It is likely to be in the range of 10Hz (cycles per second), and so might be heard, but would not necessarily be. In the case of *Uptown Girl* losing her mast, her owner and I (we were both off watch) awoke feeling that something was wrong, but not knowing what it was. According to the engineers, this is because the body's own natural frequency is close to 10Hz (c/s), and so we would have been feeling distinctly uncomfortable from the vibration, which was probably triggered from falling off a wave.

According to the computer model, as the rigging of a vessel is tightened the frequency of the natural vibration is lowered until a natural frequency of zero is reached, and the mast buckles. So it follows that, if a boat falls off a wave, the natural frequency of vibration is first of all raised as the pressure comes off the rig, then enormously lowered as the boat hits the water and the load is sharply reintroduced. Again, the research shows that when the load is reintroduced in such a gross way, the rig is loaded with energy, which can set up the vibration. At the same time the mast becomes susceptible to what is called 'broad band exciting' which widens the range of frequencies which can start the destructive vibration. The mast becomes vulnerable to any harmonic of its natural frequency—half as fast, twice as fast etc. The trouble is that while the forces are understood because they are the forces that affect tall buildings, which have been thoroughly researched, there is no data on masts. Wind tunnel tests will need to be carried out on masts under load and unloaded.

Many people will have seen the famous film of the failure of the Tacoma Narrows Bridge in the US which failed in a wind of as little as 20 knots. The natural frequency of vibration of the bridge was reached and it began to undulate until the whole deck of the bridge waved and it eventually collapsed and was destroyed. It is precisely this sort of wave that travels through a mast when it is vibrating. If, for instance, the mast is vibrating at 10Hz (c/s), the vibration does not have to continue for long before hundreds of thousands of tiny bends have taken place in the rig. These minuscule bends represent fatigue damage, and fatigue damage is cumulative. So vibration during the life of a mast will determine how long the mast will function without failure.

In tall buildings, the movement through vibration can be damped down by the use of what are called 'tuned mass dampers' or TMDs. Sydney's 300 metre (900 feet) Sydney Tower, for instance, has a 196 tonne (200 ton) container of water which moves against the sway of the building, and so limits the movement to within international standards.

Similar TMDs, which need not weigh more than a kilo (couple of pounds), can be installed inside the rig of a mast to prevent vibration setting up and either causing the mast to fail, or storing up damage to cause later failure.

The computer model, which showed the rig swaying like a hula dancer under the great local stresses indicated in diagram 1.24, also showed that the rig in diagram 1.25, which spread the load in a more even manner, was far less likely to fail.

Diagram 1.24 is of rod rigging, with the cap shrouds (main shrouds) touching only the top spreaders before connecting to the chainplates. The intermediate shrouds touch only the next lowest spreaders, and the third set only the lowest spreaders. This system allows the three 'triangles' seen in the diagram to move independently when excited. The computer simulation is frightening, I can tell you. The rig in diagram 1.25 has the shrouds connecting with all the spreaders, and allows the adjustment of each set of shrouds in each of the 'triangles'. The mast cannot be bent as erratically with this system, but also, the loads are spread more evenly, and natural vibration would be harder to excite.

So, many top-flight racing skippers, who have deliberately rigged their boat as in diagram 1.24 to allow them more controllable mast bend, have been building failure into the rig.

The interesting argument now is whether tight rigging or loose rigging—the oldest subject for argument among yachtsmen—is best. The more computer information we have, the better our knowledge of masts and rigging will become.

If you wish to go further into the theory of mast rigging and tuning see Further References.

S A I L S

We now have an understanding of the basic construction, and stresses, of hulls and standing rigging. The next consideration is the sails that go on them.

The main aim of sailmakers—from the very first, centuries ago—to the ones working today—has been to get a material stable enough, and manufacturing techniques good enough, for the sail to retain its designed shape for as long as possible. With the introduction of synthetics and exotics over the past 20 years, this aim has been largely achieved. The next area of development will be in the glues used for binding the panels together. The aim is to reduce slippage at the seams, so making the sails even more stable. This will be done by using double-sided foam glues—an extension of the present method of attaching patches. A perfectly smooth, stable sail with no stitching in it, is the target of present day sailmaking research. The main cloths used by sailmakers are still Dacron, Mylar, Spectra and Kevlar for mainsails and headsails, and nylon for spinnakers. A third cloth, Genesis, is claimed to have less stretch than Mylar/Kevlar—and may well have—but it has not been in use long enough for the claims to be confirmed. Most sails are made from Dacron, cut to the tri-radial style, which gives a result as stable as some of the first Kevlars of about 10 years ago. Kevlar with a Mylar base is more stable still, having a shrinkage factor of about one per cent over six months. The Mylar section of Mylar/Kevlar sails, usually the front half, may have a greater stretch factor because it is not put under sufficient load to pull the sail back to its original, designed size. Kevlar alone is most stable, but it does not last long. Genesis uses a base of Tedlar, a different type of plastic film, instead of Mylar. Because Tedlar doesn't form stubborn creases the way Mylar does, it is claimed to reduce the shrinkage factor to almost nothing, and to give a sail that will keep its shape for longer.

Almost all sails now are designed by computers, and the panels are cut to take the strain along the lines disclosed by the computer. The tape drive sails that were popular a little while ago showed dramatically where those strain lines were. They are less evident in the latest sails because the tapes do not delineate them. But the fact that the new cloths are as strong in tensile strength as steel poses a new threat. The strength of these new materials is so great that rigging will sometimes carry away before the sails, so it becomes even more important to know when to reef so that the load on the mast and rigging is commensurate with the weight of wind the boat is experiencing.

The new sailcloths will put up with the most fantastic mistreatment. On a 960 kilometre (600 mile) race on a 12.6 metre (40 feet) boat which was running before a 30 knot front, the helmsman lost control and a standing jibe resulted. The spinnaker pole twisted and tore one metre (three feet) of track from the mast and a pad eye from the deck. It then speared straight through the mainsail, punching a hole about 50 centimetres (18 inches) across. Despite the strength of the wind, that hole did not expand or increase in any way in the hour that it took to clean up the resultant mess.

Suggested Sail Inventory

Whether cruising or racing, every boat, whatever size, will need a main and at least one large headsail, as this combination (as discussed in Chapter 2) is what makes a sailing boat work. The cruising boat will have a simple arrangement for changing the size of the sails as the wind increases, usually by winding the headsail around itself (furling) so that it is reduced to a size suitable for the weight of wind. The main will roll into the mast, or sometimes the boom, in a similar manner, or on older boats, around the boom. In most cases the controls will be in the cockpit, for safety and ease of operation.

From then on, the wardrobe of sails will be at the discretion of the owner, but common arrangements are to have a twin pole arrangement so that, when running, the cruiser can wear two headsails instead of a spinnaker. This is particularly effective in the steady, strong trade winds that occur in many of the great cruising grounds of the world, or can be used when crossing the oceans. The modern gennaker, a combination of spinnaker and headsail hoisted without a pole, is another good inclusion for the sailor who avoids sailing to windward.

A racing boat will have different considerations. Dinghies, because of size limitations and because they do not normally sail in very heavy winds, carry only one jib and the main, which usually cannot be reefed. There is normally also only one spinnaker, although some, like the Lightweight Sharpie, carry a flat spinnaker and a parachute. Smaller harbour racers will usually have two spinnakers.

It is only when a boat reaches about eight metres, although this is not an inflexible matter, that they will carry more than one jib. At first the combination will be a maximum size and the equivalent of a number three which will be about half the size of the maximum. As the boat increases in size, so the number of jibs increases. After a number three the next most likely is a spitfire or storm jib, very small and made of strong material to handle the worst that can happen. With the spitfire comes a storm trysail, which attaches to the mast in the usual way, but is loose footed (doesn't attach to the boom) so that waves cannot break into it and burst the material.

Once these four extra sails are in the locker, the limitation is only the rules of the class of yacht or the depth of purse of the owner.

A typical ocean racer of 12 to 16 metres or so will have a wardrobe of this sort:

- Main and spare (can only be used if the first is damaged)
- Lightweight maximum genoa
- Storm trysail
- No 1 regular
- No 2
- No 3 blade (very high aspect ratio sail, usually of Kevlar)
- No 4
- Storm jib
- Reacher

- ¼ oz (per sq metre) spinnaker
- ½ oz spinnaker
- ¾ oz spinnaker
- 1.2 oz spinnaker
- 1.8 oz spinnaker
- Brick wall (heavy cloth, small area storm spinnaker)
- Blooper
- Tall boy (high aspect ratio staysail)
- Spinnaker staysail

Both cruisers and racers will carry mizzen staysails to increase sail area off the wind. Large vessels with a mizzen mast will also carry mizzen spinnakers.

CARE OF SAILS

Before synthetics like Nylon, Dacron, Mylar, Kevlar, and Spectra sail care was a time consuming and important matter, but all that has changed. Where sails had to be washed free of salt after every exposure, and then dried and folded away, they now need washing only if they are thoroughly salty and can sustain much more rough treatment than before. It is still good practice to wash them each time if the climate is such that they can dry in time to be put away. If, however, this is not the case, they won't suffer too much if they are folded straight into their bag. In many smaller boats the mainsail is rolled and left attached to the boom and tied down. This has a lot to recommend it as the main does not then have kinks folded into it.

Whenever holes occur, particularly in the lighter material of spinnakers they should be covered immediately, on both sides, by some patch of sticky-backed sailcloth that can be bought in rolls. Rip Stop is a typical product. Cut a piece

Step 1

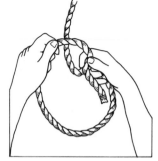

Step 2

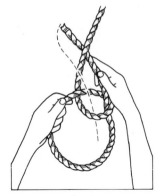

Step 3

Step 4

Diagram 1.26 *Bowline.*

the right size and be sure to round the corners of the patch. It is amazing how much longer they last if there is no flapping corner to catch and snag.

If the damage is greater, a sailmaker will have to make the repair. An ocean cruising boat, like a racer, will not have this luxury and will have to be able to carry out any repairs while at sea. This is usually easier for the racing boat because the crew is larger and often includes at least one sailmaker. The cruising skipper's sewing skills will probably have been honed by many hours of practice.

THE KNOTS
YOU'LL NEED

There is only a handful of knots that a sailor, to be considered skilful needs, but of all of them the most important is the bowline. The knot has two great virtues. The first is that it will not slip under load whilst the second is that it will undo easily whatever strain may have been on it. Diagram 1.27 shows you how to break a bowline's back.

Bowline. Almost no one ties a bowline correctly. There is only one way to do it, whatever anyone who has a method different from the following might tell you. The reason is that when tied this way, the knot can be tied in the dark, in the water, behind your back (or all at once) and it can save your life. It can also be tied whichever way you are facing, and with any size line. The reason most people do not tie it the proper way is because they have to practise. A week of solid practice, followed by continued use of the knot, will give you skill enough to last a lifetime.

First, learn on fairly strong line. Line which will collapse makes the job harder. Form a loop as shown in diagram 1.26, step 1, but make sure the right hand is held as in the diagram: the forefinger must be on top of the end of the loop and pointing along it. The rest of the fingers should hold the line.

Next, rotate the forefinger in the direction shown, so that the end of the line is forced down and round, and is guided by the forefinger into the loop formed by the rotating action. Practise this until you can form a loop and pass the end of the line through it every time. This is the secret of the knot. Do not go on to the next stage until you can form that loop.

When you have mastered the loop, the rest is easy. Supporting the joint of the loop with the left forefinger, draw the end of the line further through the loop and round behind the line as shown. The support of the joint is vital or the hand movements become too complicated for success. When the line has passed around the back or standing part of the line, curl it back down through the top loop. Now that the knot is formed, pull it tight by shifting the right hand to the standing part of the line and tightening the grip of the left hand on the bottom loop. Even if it takes hours of practice, please learn it this way. You can then convince the most hardened old salt that you know what you are doing.

Bowline in the bight. I have hardly ever used this knot, but it can be useful. It differs from the normal bowline only after you have formed the loop by rotating the right wrist. The looped double end is then put over the standing part of the line as shown.

Clove hitch. Useful for tying up, but remember that it tightens under load, and if used for, say, towing a dinghy, you may have to undo it with a knife. Practise around a rod. Pass the line around once, then to the left back over itself, round again and under the free part, as shown.

Slip knot. This knot needs strain, or at least friction, or it will not hold. The idea is that the weight of whatever it is holding, say a canopy or sailcover, will keep it tight, but it can be pulled undone in one movement. This is not a knot to use for something like tying up a dinghy, let alone a boat.

A **rolling hitch (timber hitch)**. Useful if you have to drag something along as it transfers strain in a straight line. More useful on the land really.

Two round turns and **two half hitches**. Two round turns are simply the line passed twice around a pole and finished with two half hitches. Half hitches are the knot, as shown, which most people use to tie a parcel.

Stopper hitch. This is invaluable on yachts. When passed around a line under strain, it can be put onto a separate winch and the strain transferred from the first line to the stopper hitch. It should be used when a line is jammed, as with an overriding turn on a winch, or when a headsail slide should be moved in position when under load. Take two turns round the line under load, then move the free end well to the right of the two turns, come around the line under strain and pass the end of the hitch under itself, as shown. You will have to keep this knot under strain as otherwise it is useless. The moment it comes under proper strain, as on a winch, it will tighten up and will not slip.

Reef knot (square knot). Remember the rule, right over left then left over right and you will always get it right. If you do it any other way you will get a granny knot.

Figure of eight knot. Probably the best knot for making a line too large to run through a block. Small boats use such knots, but ocean going boats do not. It is sometimes better for a line to run free than for the boat to be put at risk because pressure cannot be removed.

Sheet bend (becket hitch). This is useful for joining the ends of lines of different thickness, and is easy to manage from the illustration in diagram 1.36. However, for the same purpose I prefer the fisherman's knot.

Diagram 1.27 *How to break a bowline's back and so undo it.*

Diagram 1.28 *Bowline in the bight.*

Diagram 1.34 *Reef or square knot.*

Diagram 1.35 *Figure eight knot.*

Diagram 1.36 *Sheet bend (becket hitch).*

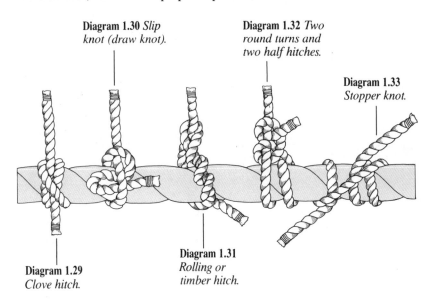

Diagram 1.30 *Slip knot (draw knot).*

Diagram 1.32 *Two round turns and two half hitches.*

Diagram 1.33 *Stopper knot.*

Diagram 1.29 *Clove hitch.*

Diagram 1.31 *Rolling or timber hitch.*

Fisherman's knot (sheet bend). As the name implies this has been developed by fishermen, and can be used on nylon lines as well as boat lines. Its beauty is that it is simple, you just tie an ordinary knot with the end of one line over the other's standing part, then do the same to the other line. The knot will slide together and not slip under load. When it comes to undoing, just slide the two halves of the knot apart and undo the separate knots. They might be tight, but they will undo.

Truckie's hitch. See diagram 1.38.

Now to complete your sea-going repertoire of line work you need to know how to do a **palm and needle whipping**, a **sailmaker's whipping**, a **long splice**, a **short splice**, and an **eye splice**. These are all explained in the captions to the diagrams that follow.

Diagram 1.37 *Fisherman's knot (sheet bend).*

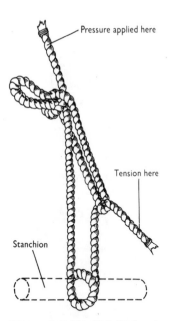

Diagram 1.38 *Truckie's hitch—tie one end of the line to something solid. Take the other end and loop it, doubled, over the object where you want to apply pressure. Pull the single part of the line through the just-made loop. Turn a small loop in the single part of the line and put the first loop through it. The single part of the line can now be used to pull down through the small loop, applying strain to the object being tied.*

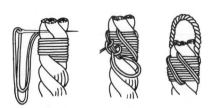

Diagram 1.39 *Palm and needle whipping—loop for attaching another line. Start a whipping, using a sailmaker's needle. Make a loop of smaller material and stitch it into the whipping. Finish with the lay as shown.*

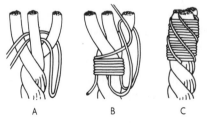

Diagram 1.40 *Sailmaker's whipping— whipping without needle. Loop line as shown in (a) make half the required turns (b) make balance of turns (c) and pull tight.*

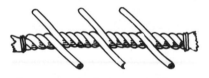

Diagram 1.41 *Long splice—as more turns are made in the 'vacated' strands each side of the join of the two lines, the fibres are reduced until only about a quarter of the strand is at each end. The result is a splice that will go through a block.*

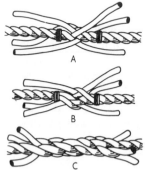

Diagram 1.42 *Short splice—unravel the lines to the distance wanted, usually about three 'tucks'. Tie light line around to prevent further unravelling. Lay one strand over matching strand of the other end of line (a) and continue doing the same with each in rotation (b) until condition (c) is reached. (You will have to cut the light line after the first three lines are overlaid—a tuck.) Shave the strands sticking out until they are smooth. Both long and short splices are finished off by rolling underfoot to smooth them out.*

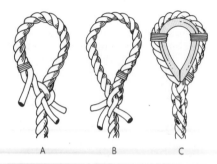

Diagram 1.43 *Eye splice—loop line as shown and tie to prevent unravelling. Make first tuck as shown (a) and continue as in short splice (b). Diagram (c) shows finished splice with a 'hard' eye.*

WIND AND SAIL

The explanation of how a yacht sails, how it is balanced, and how it is tuned applies to a sailing boat of any size. The principles do not change. What this chapter will do, however, is point out to the beginner, or the sailor with little experience, that there is no mystery to understanding why yachts behave as they do. Once that understanding is achieved, it can be put to use.

PARALLELOGRAM OF FORCES

Today, the understanding of the forces involved in producing forward motion in a sailing yacht, which took so many centuries to learn, can be summarised in the parallelogram of forces (see diagram 2.1), which we will discuss now. There are four forces involved, and these four forces allow the apparently simple yacht to be sailed as efficiently as the helmsman can make it.

To describe what happens we will presume the wind strikes the sails of a sailing yacht from the side—at 90 degrees to the direction the yacht is travelling. The sailing yacht will be forced to heel over—there is nothing more certain than that. It is the one feature that distinguishes a sailing yacht from other vessels. But this **heeling moment** is the beginning of the forward motion of the sailing yacht. A keel-less boat would be pushed flat onto the surface of the water, but the weight of the keel acts as a counter-balance. The counter-balancing effect of the keel is called the **righting moment**. If there are no waves and the wind is absolutely steady and the boat is held rock steady on its path, the angle will remain constant as the sailing yacht slides through the water.

There is, somewhere along the mast, a pivoting point, a fulcrum, where the two forces are exactly counter-balanced, but this balance is only in the vertical plane. To understand all the reasons a boat moves forward we have to understand the other two forces, the ones that work in the horizontal plane.

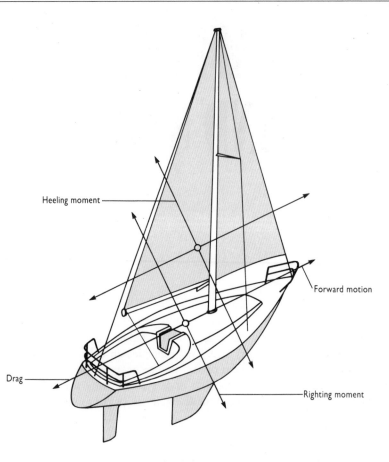

Diagram 2.1 *Parallelogram of forces.*

We know that with the wind blowing on the sails, the boat will move forward, but why? How is it that a wind blowing onto the side of a boat allows it to move forward? The answer is that the air hitting the leading edge of the headsail splits, some passing along the leeward side of the sail and some along the windward side. The air going along the leeward side, along the curve, has to travel further and so reduces in pressure. This reduction in pressure virtually sucks the boat forward. As well the air is being squeezed between the headsail and the leeward side of the mainsail. It is squeezed through what is called the slot. This accelerated air creates a Venturi effect, again sucking the boat forward.

We now have three of the four forces that make up the parallelogram, the heeling moment, the righting moment (which is the counter-balancing effect of the keel), and the forward motion of the yacht. So what is the fourth? It is **drag**, the effect of friction on the hull of the yacht as it moves through the water.

Have a look at the diagram again and you will see how each of these forces, if not countered, would have a gross effect on the yacht and either prevent it from sailing or cause it to sail inefficiently. If there were no sails, the boat would remain fully upright and stationary. If there were no keel the boat would be knocked flat on the water. Once those two effects are balanced the boat can move forward, but then the slowing effect of drag puts a limit on the boat's speed.

Once these basic forces are understood you will be able to sail because you will realise that only when these forces are balanced can the boat sail efficiently. In diagram 2.2 there is, in the middle of the mainsail, a circle with a line through it. This is the **centre of effort**, the point where the four forces are balanced. The difference between a good and a bad sailor is that the good sailor more often has the four forces in balance (hence a boat is balanced). If at any time, through mishandling of the boat, these forces become unbalanced, the boat loses efficiency. If you want a dramatic illustration of what I am saying, sail your boat with the mainsail up and no headsail. You'll find that it doesn't sail at a very good angle into the wind (it doesn't sail well to windward), it is sluggish, the helm has to be held firmly to hold the boat on track and prevent it rounding up into the wind, and it's generally quite unsatisfactory. Now hoist the headsail and trim it, and immediately the boat comes to life: it can be steered more accurately, it can be sailed closer to the wind, and it doesn't try to round up. The reason is that it's beginning to be balanced.

We discuss later in this chapter how if the centre of effort is too far back in the mainsail it applies too much turning moment to the boat, which will round up and become overpowered. If it is too far forward, the headsail will try to pull the boat away from its path and won't be counteracted properly by the main. But first we have to understand how the **true wind**, the wind that blows when nothing interferes with it, is modified by the forward motion of the boat and becomes the **apparent wind**. The true wind is the one we first described, which was blowing at right angles to the path of the yacht. If the yacht dropped all sail and sat upright in the water the wind then blowing would be the true wind. But as the sailing yacht takes up motion the wind will seem to draw forward, and this wind, when the boat is moving, is called the apparent wind. As long as the boat you are sailing on is moving, the wind you are dealing with is the apparent wind. If you can understand apparent wind, and turning moment, you can become a good sailor.

Now you have the theory, let's put it into practice.

Diagram 2.2 *Centre of effort.*

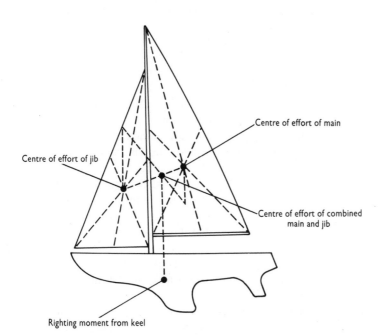

Centre of effort of main

Centre of effort of jib

Centre of effort of combined main and jib

Righting moment from keel

H O I S T I N G   S A I L S

To hoist sails you must point the boat into the wind, either by moving it physically on its trailer or in the water.

MAIN

Diagram 2.3 *Bowsing a halyard.*

Hoist the main first, and be sure that the mainsheet is uncleated and several feet of the sheet have been pulled clear through the block so that the boom can move about, as it will. Warn any newcomers to sailing to keep clear of the boom from this point on as it is dangerous. When you are pointing directly into the wind, detail a crew member or members if needed, to haul down on the halyard. The easiest way to do this is to pull the halyard out from the mast (see diagram 2.3) and have another crew member recover the hauled line at the winch (tailing). When the sail is almost hoisted, and therefore pulls at its heaviest on the halyard, the person at the winch can take over, cranking the last part of the halyard in with the handle. The sail will flap from side to side on its way up as the wind blows more strongly down one side than the other. But because the sheet is set loose, the sail is not full on either tack and the boat is not moving forward. Haul the halyard tight enough for there to be a very slight stretch mark parallel with the mast the length of the leading edge of the sail. Attach the outhaul and pull it tight enough for a similar, very slight, ridge to form. We'll adjust that tension more accurately later.

JIB

Next hoist the jib. We'll presume that the wind is perfect, about 12 knots and steady, and you will put up the biggest jib, if you have more than one. Attach the tack first, so that the sail is firmly attached to the boat if the wind should suddenly gust, then attach the halyard and the sheets. If the headsail has hanks, clip them on, and if they haven't had a spray of water-repellant recently, give each a little burst now. Make sure the sheets are free and hoist the sail. You will now have both sails up and flapping. Close-quarters boat handling is discussed on page 101, so for the moment we'll assume that you have no hazards and can simply sail free. From a trailer or beach, or under motor, this will be true; however, sailing off a mooring is usually a more difficult manoeuvre, but not for us, this time.

Decide which way you want to go off the mooring and ask a crew member to pull on the jib sheet on the opposite side. This will pull the sail back along the deck until it fills with wind from the outside of the sail and forces the boat's bow around to the direction you want to take. Do not let it fill with wind on the inside of the sail, or you will point away from where you want to go. Once the bow has fallen off sufficiently for you to point in the direction you want to take, turn helm in that direction, let the sail come across to the other side and haul the sheet on until the sail is full and straining. As that happens, detail the person in charge of the mainsheet to pull on the slack in the sheet until the main, too, fills and is held firmly. The boat will now heel and gather speed.

While the boat is being set on its course and the sails pulled on, another crew member will be detaching the mooring line and its buoy and, walking with it along the side of the boat away from the sails, dropping it over the stern as the boat gathers way.

If you were sailing away from a trailer, or a beach, or from somewhere free in a harbour, you do in essence the same thing. The bow of the boat is pushed away to the direction you want to take, the sails are pulled on, and the boat gathers speed and begins to sail. You don't have to worry about dropping a mooring.

C O N T R O L S

The sails transmit the power of the wind to the boat through the lines that control them, the sheets. Pulling on the sheet brings the boom, in the case of the mainsail, into the centre of the boat. The further the boom comes into the centre of the boat, the more the sail flattens and the less is the angle of attack of the sail to the direction of the apparent wind. Finally, when the boom has come as far inboard as it can and the sheet is on as hard as it can be pulled, the boat is ready to sail as close to the wind as it can.

If nothing has been done to the jib sheet in the meantime, it will now be flapping crazily and transmitting no power at all to the boat. Get the sheet hand (crew member) to pull on the sail (trim the jib) until it is sheeted almost as hard as it can be. Make sure there is not so much pressure applied with the winch, if it is being used, that it pulls the sail out of shape, or even tears it.

Now you are sailing, check the leading edge of both sails. They should be free of any ridges or creases. If there is a ridge, reduce the tension on the halyard until the luff of the sail is tight, but still smooth and unwrinkled. That will be just the right tension for the conditions in which you are sailing. Now do the same with the outhaul on the boom, reducing the tension until the foot is smooth. The sail will now have a uniform curve and will be free of any wrinkles or stretch marks. There will be a powerful look to the sails, and they will please the eye.

You now have control of the halyards, the outhaul and the sheets. As you gain experience, you will be able to adjust these basic sail controls with increasing skill and subtlety. Any other controls, such as barberhauls, snotters, foreguys etc., are refinements. The main transmission of power is through the basic controls and for power to be transmitted any control that is applied to a sail should be tight—not so tight as to distort it from its proper adjustment for the conditions of the day, but not so loose that energy is dissipated.

There is one control that ranks somewhere between the basic ones and the refinements, and that is the traveller. Travellers take many forms, but their prime function is to allow the mainsail to move away from the centreline of the boat, so reducing the turning motion and heel on the boat, without disturbing the shape of the sail itself. The mainsheet does not have to be released as the traveller usually has a track of its own, with its own controls (see diagram A2.58 page 302), which allows the whole sheeting mechanism to be released. This is not to say that the shape of the mainsail can't be changed at the same time, it is just that it needn't be. There are times when less twist is wanted in the sail and the sheet may then be released a little at the same time as the traveller is let down the track, but knowing when this should happen comes only with experience.

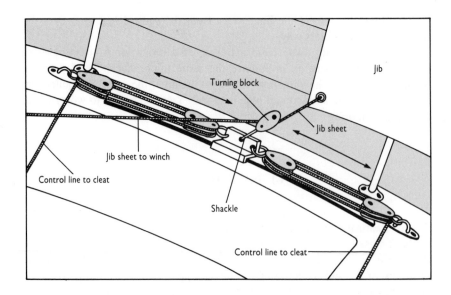

Diagram 2.4 *With this sliding car system the jib sheet can be adjusted in any conditions and under load.*

The type of jib control I believe in, very strongly, is the sliding car system (adjustable genoa leads system). With this method the car is not pinned in one position but is pulled along the track by a double purchase which can be cleated off wherever it's wanted (see diagram 2.4). This system allows the sheeting position to be changed at any time, particularly under load. I'm not sure many crews would want to go to the extent of one international racer which had a series of double purchases that could move fore and aft along the boat as well as in and out. It therefore had available an almost infinite number of settings for the clew of the headsail. I think it's too difficult to reproduce the optimum settings with this system so I prefer the simpler sliding car (adjustable genoa leads) system where the car does not have a pin holding it in position on the track. A line leads from the forward end of the car to a double purchase which leads back to the car then forward again and on to the control position in the cockpit. A similar arrangement runs from the back of the car so that at any time the car can be moved along the track to the optimum sheeting position. Very often, with no pressure on either tackle, the car will just go to the position where all the pressures equate. That position will be very close to the proper sheeting position. This allows the block to be moved by very small amounts to get exactly the position that's wanted. On other systems the pin holes for holding the block in position are anything up to 10 to 12 centimetres apart, which means the controls on the position of the clew are rough and ready to say the least.

Normally the sail would be sheeted to the outboard track. Just inboard of that, at the optimum sheeting angle for sailing in moderate winds and flat conditions, is another car which can be moved in the same way and through which a second sheet—usually with a clip-on for easy release—goes to the clew of the sail. With this arrangement it's possible to ease off on the main or primary jib sheet and haul in on the secondary one and to bring the sheeting angle closer inboard.

This system, to my mind, gives a wide variety of positions for control of the headsail. With an experienced crew it's very easy this way to get a fine adjustment to the conditions of the day. Obviously, as the boat bears away on to a reach, the sheeting angle needs to go further out, but it becomes too complicated to have a third track. The system then is to put a snatch block on to the rail and lead the sheet through there, easing off on the primary headsail sheet and taking up on the outboard one. There's quite a lot to be said for being able to barberhaul that sheet.

It's common for the head of the reacher, or the jib that's being used for reaching, to lose power because the clew of the sail isn't being pulled down enough. So a secondary sheet rigged temporarily to lower the clew is very handy. This is particularly true when running with poled out jib. Many crew believe that the spinnaker pole should be level because it extends the greatest area of sail. At first glance this will seem so, but if you look up at the head of the sail you'll see that it's falling off and therefore too much of the wind is being spilled. If the outboard end of the pole is dropped relative to the inboard end on the mast, that top part of the sail will be pulled tighter and more pressure of the wind will be used.

TELLTALES

Now that we have all our controls in place, we must learn how to take the best advantage of them by using telltales—probably the best single aid to the helmsman day or night, but particularly by day. Telltales are simple streamers made of wool or some light fabric which will respond to quite light winds. They are attached to sails to show the air flow over that sail. Telltales fly parallel when the boat is pointing optimally. It is usual to have at least two, but preferably three, rows of telltales. The first should be about 22 centimetres (nine inches) back from the leading edge of the sail, the second in the middle, and the third near the leech. On mainsails it is most common for the third row to be actually sewn to the leech, so indicating whether the sail is exhausting properly. The telltales in the rows should be about two metres (six feet) apart.

Properly interpreted they give the quickest indication of where the wind is moving and how the boat is sailing. Nevertheless telltales can be quite misleading and they need to be understood to prevent misinterpretation. There's a school of thought nowadays that says that telltales should break at the top of a sail first and the bottom last—even some sailmakers will tell you this. It's absolute garbage. If you allow the top part of a sail to stall before the bottom part stalls, the top part of your sail quite clearly isn't working properly, even with the different wind angle up there, and therefore some part of the area on which your boat has been rated is not being used properly. It cannot be sensible to have any trim on the boat other than that which so adjusts the sheet leads that the sail luffs along its full length evenly, taking advantage of the varying apparent wind angle at different heights. There is one proviso: the boat must be properly set up. If the position of the mast, the length of forestay and tension on the backstay are wrong then the sail probably won't break evenly—whatever you do to it. So if you can't make the sail break evenly, or performance falls off when it does, you have to look elsewhere for the problem.

Another trap for even quite experienced helmsmen is to be sailing hard on the wind in conditions where it's difficult to see the leeward telltale, but the inside telltale—the one the helmsman can see clearly—appears to be streaming beautifully. The interpretation of this may be that because boat speed is good the boat is pointing as high and travelling as fast as possible. That is simply not true. What's happening, is that the boat is head reaching slightly. This is a major fault in those boats that go for boat speed all the time at the expense of the compromise between pointing and speed, which gives the best velocity made good (VMG). The way to test whether the inside (windward) telltale is indicating that the boat is as close to the wind as it can properly be, is to nudge up every now and then and see whether the inside telltale starts to lift. A lot of helmsmen are frightened of that effect, but when sailing on the wind, particularly in hard winds, the inside telltale must lift. In moderate winds it should flick upwards every now and then so that the outside telltale streams steadily and does not flick upwards. Keep testing this and you'll soon get the idea and find that you're sailing almost as fast but very much closer to the wind.

In light winds the inside telltale is much more difficult to flick upwards because the draught in the sail is further forward and the angle of attack to the wind is much wider. By the time the helmsman has pushed the boat up into the wind sufficiently to make the sails stall and test the breeze, it will have stalled for perhaps a quarter of its leading edge rather than just a tiny bit. In light winds it is more important to keep the boat driving and heeled at the right angle and with both telltales streaming steadily and equally.

Lifting of the telltale is particularly important when sailing a masthead rig to windward because feathering the leading part of the jib does not have a significant effect on boat speed. Feathering is to sail higher than the optimum course in strong winds, and is indicated by the first foot or so of the leading edge luffing, that is, the leading section flaps and does not drive properly. The effect on a masthead is that the boat is not overpowered, and still maintains a good course and speed to windward. A fractional rig cannot be sailed this way, it loses speed and falls off to leeward. Perhaps the shallower angle of attack of the forestay on a masthead can stand breaking more than the angle of attack of the forestay on the fractional, which is steeper, making it more difficult to get an even feathering. Feathering a masthead is a good technique to understand because where a boat is balanced for the lulls, but slightly overpowered in quite heavy gusts, feathering will take care of that extra power and mean that the boat is rigged, as a racing boat should be, for the lulls.

S A I L I N G
B Y   T R I M   A L O N E

In some of the more comprehensive sailing courses there are sections on handling a boat by sail trim alone when the steering is broken. This is an admirable thing to teach people: first of all, it shows it's possible to do, although in many circumstances it can be very difficult; and secondly, it helps novice sailors understand the way a boat balances and how the forces work on a boat. We spoke earlier about the turning moment that comes from the mainsail and of the centre of effort, and we showed how the centre of effort can be moved backwards and forwards. It is precisely the control of where the centre of effort exists on a yacht which allows it to be sailed and steered in a general direction without the use of a rudder.

To illustrate, we will assume a moderate day, where there's a reasonable sailing breeze and little white caps and tiny waves, rather than extreme conditions. First, it will be impossible to sail anywhere near as close to the wind without a rudder as with a rudder. The whole technique of going to windward consists of judicious use of the rudder to push the boat up when it's trying to go down and down when it's trying to go up. Without a rudder, if the sails are clapped on hard to go to windward, the boat will round up head to wind or nearly head to wind and the sails will flap; the boat will start to go backwards and you'll lose control.

So let's see what happens if just the headsail goes off. If the headsail is let out considerably and the main is kept on, the main will be trying to turn the boat up into the wind, and the headsail being now at a broad angle, rather than a fine angle, the wind will flutter along the luff and be inefficient. If the headsail is considerably larger than the mainsail the boat might pay off enough for the headsail to fill and so overcome the turning moment of the main, but this is pretty unlikely. So if the main is then let off, what happens? The effect is that the turning moment up into the wind is reduced so that the boat can take a broader angle to the wind. As it makes that broader angle it will begin to move on a head reach—let's say—pick up a reasonable amount of way, and head off on a course at something like 70 degrees to the wind. Given no violent wave action or change in wind direction, you could then travel at that angle consistently until you reached a shore or you could go on the other tack at about the same angle and reach some other place.

Now that we've got the boat moving reasonably well, it may be possible to pull the headsail on a little bit as the apparent wind angle moves further ahead of the boat enabling the boat to point slightly higher into the wind. You have to be very careful here because as you bring the boat up closer to the wind, you have to bring the main on because it starts to flutter. As you do so, the boat will get back to its original condition of rounding up and stalling. So let's say 70 degrees is the best we can do. It's fairly easy from there on to fall away by letting the sails off and sailing just by sail trim at any number of angles to the wind on whichever tack you happen to be on.

Once you get the wind on your quarter, you start to have the same, or at least a similar problem, because the headsail is no longer working and the mainsail is turning the boat back up into the wind. There will be a limit to the angle you can make on say a quarter run. So far we've found that we can sail the boat reasonably accurately between about 70 degrees to the wind and 140 degrees to the wind. We know that we're not going to be able to deal with that section of the 360 degree compass which is between 70 degrees on port and 70 degrees on starboard—140 degrees of the arc. But we can deal with all the rest. To sail before the wind without a rudder it is simplest to drop the main entirely so that there is no tendency to turn up into the wind, then rig two headsails of approximately equal size. When running before the wind with those headsails the boat is able to run through the wind from side to side with no danger of a jibe. This method of controlling direction is fair up to moderate to fresh winds.

Practise sailing by sail trim alone, without a rudder. It will give you an unbeatable way of learning about the balance of a boat and getting the feel of what happens on a boat. Nothing could be more dramatic than knowing that you're steering a boat by controlling the sails, without any rudder to help you, and getting it to go where you want it to.

R E E F I N G

We have just learned what happens when there is too much turning moment on the mainsail and the boat becomes unmanageable. Exactly the same effect results when a boat has too much wind, and therefore too much turning moment. The only way then to restore the boat to a proper balance is to reduce that turning moment by reducing the amount of sail presented to the wind, that is, reefing the boat. This normally is done to the mainsail first. A boat needs to be reefed if the traveller is at the full extent of its travel, the helmsman is struggling with the wheel, and the leeward rail is well under water.

A good skipper will have polar performance curves of his boat's various sail configurations—and the relevant speeds, pointing angles and heeling angles. Of these the heeling angle is probably the critical one—particularly on anything built in the last 15 years—and there is nothing more important than that it should be on its right lines. If you don't have polar performance curves, the next best thing to do is to get a small inclinometer and put it in front of the mainsheet hand and tell him or her what angle of heel the boat should be on. Then it will soon become apparent when it's necessary to reef.

There's another factor involved here. There is an old rule of thumb that says that fractional rigs reef the headsail before they reef the main and that masthead rigs do the opposite, but you need to remember that the moment you've taken the one regular (No. 1 heavy) off a masthead, and certainly by the time you get down to the three, you've almost got a fractional rig.

It's always exciting when the gunwales are under and the water's washing along the deck but the boat is falling away to leeward too much. Another reefed down, better trimmed boat will be pointing up and still going as fast as you and will get to the weather mark before you.

Technique for Reefing

The technique for reefing is now pretty well universal. The days of roller reefing and hand-laced reefs tied in with reef knots are gone. The slab or jiffy reef is supreme.

Diagram 2.5 *Reefing lines as used in the slab, or jiffy, reefing system.*

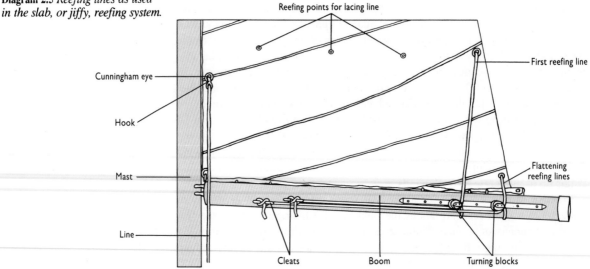

Reefing points for lacing line

First reefing line

Cunningham eye

Hook

Flattening reefing lines

Mast

Line

Cleats

Boom

Turning blocks

The best systems have a pulley arrangement at the mast, usually one each side with an attached hook which fits into the reefing cringle. When the command is given to reef, the hook is put into the cringle and one crew member stands by on the main halyard. At the same time another crew member, near the mast, takes hold of the required reefing line, which is always rigged, and puts it around one of the deck winches. With a properly executed reef the mainsheet need not be let off, although it may be prudent to do so. The halyard is eased at the same rate that the reefing line is taken on. The third crew member pulls down on the cunningham arrangement so that the slack in the main halyard is being taken up at the same rate as it's being let off. Properly executed the main simply appears to come down the main mast track and disappear as if into a slot in the boom. There need be no change in boat speed at all. When the reef has been effected the boat will point up higher and sit up higher: the turning moment will have been reduced and the traveller will come into the middle of its track again. The helmsman will be able to handle the boat with ease, and the boat will be standing up straighter, sailing on its lines. A glance at the compass will show that the boat is pointing better. The boat can now be trimmed for the new wind strength, and the navigator notified of the new course.

If the wind increases still further, and the signs indicating a reef is required recur, then a second reef will have to be taken, and so on.

But there is a question of judgement here, and of prudent crew management. If the first rule of reefing is that the moment you believe you ought to reef you should do it, the second rule is to avoid too many sail changes and so conserve the energy of the crew. This is particularly true if you are changing up (in a decreasing wind). Go one sail further than you first expect: if you're going from a four go to the two not the three, if you're going from a three go to the one regular (No. 1 heavy). If you're going from a two go to the one regular but have a long look at whether you can carry the one light (No. 1 light). If the wind is decreasing it's likely to continue doing so and you're better to be slightly overpowered with a new sail rather than slightly underpowered: at least if you are overpowered the boat will be going as fast as it possibly can. If you go for the intermediate sail, you almost certainly will be underpowered and your crew will be doing two sail changes instead of one. If the wind is increasing and you're changing down, it's usually still worthwhile to jump say from one regular (No. 1 heavy) to a three rather than to the two. The two usually has a very limited range from say 18 to 22 knots and if you're getting enough to overpower the one regular you're probably getting the 22 knots anyway. To go to a three will mean that the boat will stand up on its lines and point better and unless you find when you've made this change that boat speed has dropped because the wind hasn't increased as much as you'd expected, you will be better off than if you had gone to the two in the first place.

At the end of a long hard race crew morale, fitness and stamina are the most important factors on board a yacht. Morale on a cruising boat may be even more important, because there is not the same team desire to win, and there is more time to sit about and think. A cruising crew that has been exhausted will be an unhappy crew.

One important matter. Whether cruising or racing, the reefing lines must always be led. The last reefing line is never used unless conditions are extreme and that is just when a line will be most difficult to rig. If the skipper believes drag is a problem (which is nonsense) rig a mouse and make sure the reefing line has a strong loop stitched in the end so that it can be pulled through. But I still believe there will be conditions, particularly off the wind, where rigging a reefing line will be impossible without putting the boat into dangerous attitudes.

It's a common mistake that when a reef is tied in, the sail is quite baggy or shapeless. On good boats the reefing line will have been led in such a way that it's pulling back along the line of the boom almost as though it was also an outhaul. By changing the tension, the shape of the reefed sail can be varied. This is particularly important if you're reefing while running or reaching because while you may not want to have a great sail area up, you still want to have the most efficient shape—baggy if you're well in front of the wind, with more outhaul on if you're going across the wind, and, when on the wind, getting the sail as flat as you can. When you are fitting out your boat or if you're adjusting a new boat, make sure you treat each reefing line as a new outhaul, then you can get the sail shape you want.

We are now able to handle our boat going into the wind.

S P I N N A K E R   H O I S T

The spinnaker should be hoisted from the shadow to leeward of the headsail. Once it is decided which side of the boat the sail will be set (the opposite from the pole), the braces (guys) and sheets should be pulled around until they meet, on the rail, about halfway from the bow to the shrouds. The bag is clipped to the rail and the halyard, and sheet and brace (guy) are all attached. The forward hand (foredeck crew member) should take care that the sail does not pull out of the bag. He or she may even need somebody else to hold it in.

Meanwhile, the crew member on the brace (guy) should load the winch, but not before the foredeck crew have pulled the brace (guy) around far enough and not before they have set the spinnaker pole on the mast. Once the foredeck crew indicate that the pole is clipped in position, the cockpit crew member in charge of the topping lift can haul it up until the pole is horizontal (parallel) with the deck. At the same time the crew member tending the brace (guy) can begin winding the spinnaker out of the bag and back towards the beak of the pole. This must be done quickly because the sail will start coming out of the bag. The crew member tending the sheet should stand by.

At this stage the spinnaker pole should be firmly fixed by the brace (guy) (with the spinnaker pulled right up to the beak), the topping lift and the kicker. All that is loose is the sheet. One of the foredeck crew should go to the halyard at the mast and begin bowsing (raising) it as fast as possible, pulling the spinnaker up the mast. One of the cockpit crew will have been deputed to take in the slack as quickly as possible, wrapping the halyard around a winch as soon as it is clear there is too much pressure for the mast hand. The load can then be taken on the winch. The hoist should be completed as fast as possible.

The sheet crew member must not pull on the sheet until the spinnaker is at the top of the mast, but it must be done immediately it reaches the top. Once the halyard is locked off on a cleat the spinnaker cannot get away because everything is cleated and the sheet hand is applying the trim.

Many crews 'wool' spinnakers before hoisting. They slip elastic bands over the folded spinnaker, or tie wool around it, to prevent the sail from filling before it reaches the top of the mast. This is a good practice, particularly in heavy weather, but the skipper should watch carefully how much wool or stopping is done. Some put on so much that it behaves more like barbed wire—the sail is almost impossible to break out.

SPINNAKER DROP

Now let's talk about the manoeuvre that while it baffles most crews, is one of the easiest—the spinnaker drop. Spinnakers should almost never be dropped in the cockpit, the forward drop should be used instead. This is because no helmsman wants a cockpit full of billowing coloured sails, the sheet crew members don't want sheets or halyards and suchlike getting in the way when they're trying to trim for a new course, there is much more room on the foredeck than in the relatively crowded cockpit, and it's safer.

The sequence is straightforward but enough time must be allowed for the drop given the capacity of the crew. That means that if the crew is highly skilled and has practised together consistently, they will know, as if by instinct but in fact from experience, just how long any sort of drop is going to take in whatever conditions are prevailing. With a slow crew the prudent skipper will allow plenty of time because it is infinitely better to operate slowly than to rush and make mistakes. A slow manoeuvre properly executed will hardly affect the boat's speed, whereas a hurried one which ends in a wrapped spinnaker or a snarled halyard can lose minutes in a race.

It is important to remember that we are learning to cruise the ocean and to be self-sufficient while doing it. Nobody expects someone to run a marathon on their first run and so it is with serious ocean sailing. In all the manoeuvres we will discuss in this chapter, what we are really doing—apart from learning some relatively simple techniques—is developing the coordination and sense of timing, and above all, sense of control that comes from understanding one's own capabilities.

FORWARD DROP

Having chosen the time to begin the manoeuvre the instructions should be given loudly and clearly. The spinnaker drop normally precedes another leg to windward, otherwise you'd be jibing or simply hardening up. The jib should be hoisted first. Selection usually is left to the skipper or watch captain, but they have enough to do in such a hurried time and the navigator usually has the means to select much more accurately—either by drawing a vector diagram (see diagram 7.7) or—much better—by using a hand-held programmable calculator, which can do the job in seconds. What's more, the parameters can be changed slightly and the programme can be run several times and can come up with an accurate wind strength and direction on the new leg. There is no guessing. The calculator is unable to consider anything but the basic mathematical facts.

Once the jib has been selected, it should be hoisted without fuss and the sheet loosely cleated at one of two positions on what will be the leeward side of the boat on the new leg. The first, and the better, position to cleat the sheet is approximately where it will sheet on the wind. If that isn't possible, the next best position is where it will not flap and so interfere with the spinnaker drop. Otherwise compromise between the two positions.

The spinnaker is ready when the foredeck crew lets the cockpit know they are prepared. The three critical operations are: 1) to begin lowering the spinnaker halyard; 2) to let the spinnaker sheet forward sufficiently for the foredeck crew to be able to gather in the clew to which it is attached; and 3) for the person on the brace (guy) to let it run forward until the pole rests against the forestay—and I mean rest, not bang it forward so fast it dents the track. This person must be able to judge accurately how far the brace (guy) must run to allow the crew to gather in both the clew to which it is attached, and the other clew, which is attached to the spinnaker sheet. Basically, the forward crew members are trying to gather the two clews together so that they are pulling in a 'rope' of collapsed spinnaker, rather than pulling a fighting full sail.

It is a good idea to mark the distances on the brace (guy) and lazy brace (guy) and sheet and lazy sheet as well as on the halyard so that there's no guesswork involved about the amounts of slack which have to be let off. At night, in ocean racing, it would be imperative to do this. It might even be worth having something that glows so that as much room for error as possible is taken out of the operation.

The halyard should now be dropped, at the same rate at which the foredeck crew are able to pull in the spinnaker. The halyard crew has to watch the foredeck crew to make sure the rate of drop matches the rate of intake of the spinnaker. There should be as little friction on the halyard winch as possible, given that there may be still weight in the spinnaker.

Another crew member needs to be under the forward hatch pulling the spinnaker into the boat, and it is a good idea to send your smallest crew member as modern boats hate too much weight in the bow. There is a proviso here. The skipper will have to decide whether ocean conditions are sufficiently safe for the forward hatch to be opened at sea. If it is not safe, the sail will have to be dropped on deck, roughly gathered into its bag, and taken below to be repacked—immediately.

SMOKING THE HALYARD

After a drop has been done a few times in this fashion and the crew understands exactly what's involved, the really efficient way of dropping can take over— smoking the halyard.

When the foredeck crew have gathered in the foot of the sail and are ready to pull the spinnaker in, the halyard crew takes it off the drum completely and lets it run free, with absolutely no restraint. The halyard then runs out to a point where the spinnaker streams out parallel with the surface of the water. This is achieved by having a mark on the halyard. When the mark appears the halyard hand stamps his or her foot on to the halyard to stop it dead. This will be usually when the foredeck crew has recovered about half the sail. The sudden braking effect makes the head of the sail lift which prevents the spinnaker going into the water. The foredeck crew must work frantically to pull the sail in before it touches the water. A skilled crew can recover a spinnaker very quickly without it getting wet.

There are many advantages in doing the forward drop in this way—the forward crew does not have to stand on the pulpit to release the spinnaker;

there is no need to tie up the activities of two cockpit crew in lowering the topping lift and pulling down the spinnaker downhaul so that the pole is lowered within reach of the forward crew. This means that there is a stronger cockpit crew ready to set the boat for the next leg of the race. But of paramount importance, particularly in ocean work, is that weight is kept out of the bow.

When the crew has mastered this manoeuvre, which with deliberate practice may be after a couple of weekends, or after several weeks if the practice takes place in the ordinary run of competitive sailing, comes the time to learn the two most difficult manoeuvres possible with spinnakers. First is the float drop, where the boat jibes at a mark, drops the spinnaker without the pole attached, and comes on the wind. The second is the jibe set where the pole has to be hoisted and set as the boat jibes. The headsail must drop at the same moment. The crew that can handle these two evolutions without mishap is indeed a polished one.

Float Drop

In taking the float drop first we will assume that we are coming to a mark where it is necessary to jibe on to the next leg, which will be hard on the wind.

In plenty of time before the mark, the headsail chosen for the next leg is hoisted and cleated off somewhere near the hard-on-the-wind position so that it doesn't interfere with the spinnaker, which is still pulling. As in all cases where the helmsman is keeping as square as possible, the mainsheet hand must coincide the jibe with the movements of the helm.

From now on the manoeuvre is the same as a forward drop except that the pole is removed from the mast allowing the spinnaker to float. This system obviously can only be used in light to moderate winds. The pole is cleared from the end of the spinnaker and dropped onto the deck out of the way of the jib. The brace (guy) and the sheet crew members need to 'play' their lines to keep the spinnaker full, or at least with the clews widespread. The mainsheet hand brings the main in as the helmsman comes to the mark, and pins the traveller in the middle of the traveller track. He or she then takes in the rest of the sheet trimming as for on the wind. As the helmsman swings through the jibe and up into the wind, the spinnaker brace (guy) is allowed to run forward in the usual manner and for the marked distance. The boat will then be hard on the wind. The spinnaker is pulled in as the boat is travelling towards top windward speed.

A float drop isn't called for often, but it makes a huge difference in performance because the boat that can execute the manoeuvre when needed can, when racing, move inside other boats rounding a mark, and seal the windward position, taking command on the next windward leg.

J I B E   S E T

Perhaps the most difficult manoeuvre of all is the jibe set.

The boat is coming up to a windward mark and then going on to a run. The crew has to make gross adjustments to the position of the mainsheet and the jib to present them properly to the wind on the next leg. The manoeuvre lasts only a few seconds, so there is no margin for error.

The most common system is for the spinnaker pole to be attached to the mast and taken some way up the track. Each foredeck crew will know how far up that must be on their boat. The determining factor is that the mast end of the pole must not be high enough to interfere with the jib as it jibes across, but high enough to allow the outboard end to be tucked under the jib and so be free to hoist after the jib is jibed.

The order of execution is: the mainsheet hand makes certain that the main is pinned in the middle of the traveller track and that the sheet is in his or her hand ready for it to run out so that the boom goes to the correct position after the jibe. There is a lot of pressure on the cockpit in this manoeuvre. There will be a person needed for the halyard, one for the topping lift, and one for the spinnaker pole downhaul. The helmsman, the mainsheet and brace (guy) crew members will also be needed. The brace (guy) crew member has to pull the spinnaker pole back very rapidly into position after the main has jibed across.

Let's run through it. We are hard on the wind approaching the windward mark on starboard tack and we have to jibe on to port as we go around. The main is pulled into the centre of the boat with the traveller centred. The traveller will be let out only when the jibe has been completed. The pole is attached to the mast, as we described earlier, and has on all its attachments—except the topping lift. As the boat reaches the mark, the spinnaker goes up with one crew member at the mast bowsing (raising) the halyard and the other at the winch taking in the slack as fast as possible. The crew on the mainsheet and jib both ease their sheets as the boat starts to round the mark to allow the helmsman to make the turn. If they didn't release, there would be so much pressure the helmsman wouldn't be able to get round properly.

As the boat comes upright and onto its new course the main swings across and, after the boom has swung out to its new position, the car on the traveller is let down until it is at its full extreme on the starboard side of the boat. As this happens the spinnaker hoist is completed and the headsail jibed across. As the headsail clears the pole, the pole must be lifted rapidly by the crew member on the topping lift, and taken aft to its predetermined position as fast as possible by the crew members trimming the brace (guy). It is absolutely critical that there is no strain on the kicker as the pole moves up and back. But, as the spinnaker fills and puts pressure on the pole, the downhaul must be under control and pinned as near as possible to its final position for the new leg. Timing is essential to the proper completion of the manoeuvre. The pole literally moves up and back as the head of the spinnaker reaches the top of the mast. Everything is then firm and the boat takes off.

Practise this manoeuvre, not in light winds when it is very difficult to keep control, but in a moderate and steady wind. As the crew gets more and more practised and skilful, the same manoeuvre can be tried in harder winds.

Spinnaker Jibing

The simplest jibe is the one used on dinghies and smaller yachts—the end for end jibe. In this method, the spinnaker pole is taken off the mast and pushed towards the clew where the sheet is attached. As the end of the pole attached to the brace (guy) gets close enough, it is freed and the pole is attached to the opposite clew. The 'free' end is then attached to the mast and the sail trimmed. It is not a good technique to have the pole attached to both ends at once, as some people do—the spinnaker can take charge too easily. The timing is in the hands of the helmsman who, having seen that the foredeck crew member has the pole detached from the mast, begins, slowly, to take the boat into the jibe. When the spinnaker is free, the boat should be dead in front of the wind, and the mainsheet crew member should be jibing the main through the middle of its travel. Once the pole is attached to the mast on the new jibe, the boat can be brought to its proper course.

DIP POLE JIBE

A more difficult jibe, because it involves more people and takes place in heavier weather, is the dip pole jibe which is used on larger yachts and ocean racers. For this manoeuvre, the double sheet and brace (guy) system has to be used (see diagram 1.10). Once again, timing is the critical factor, and the only way to achieve it is to practise as often as possible. The jibe should take place only when the boat is dead proud (on a dead run), that is, directly in front of the wind. If the helmsman rushes, the boat will be at too sharp an angle for the foredeck crew to be able to handle the sail as it fills, and the job will be botched.

On the command, 'stand by to jibe', the helmsman brings the boat square and uses all possible skill to stay there without jibing. The crew take up their allotted positions. The mainsheet traveller is brought into the centre of its track and pinned into place. The crew on the brace (guy) winds the pole back so that the spinnaker is absolutely square to the wind, the crew member on the kicker eases it so that the sail can move, and the sheet crew eases enough sheet for the sail to sit up square. The crew member who will be changing over the old brace (guy) for the new will have pulled into the bow of the boat as much lazy brace (guy) (the one not being used) as is needed to carry it right into the bow. The crew member at the mast will hoist the inboard end of the pole up to a mark on the mast. This increases the angle of dip of the pole so that it will swing clear of the pulpit during the jibe.

When all this has been done, the order 'jibe ho' is given. The crew member at the mast fires the clew from the parrotbeak with a line which hangs from the pole for this purpose. The hand on the topping lift allows the pole to drop, but under control. The control is provided by the crew member on the kicker, who pulls the pole forward to the crew member sitting in the bow, facing aft, lazy brace in hand.

As this happens, the crew member on the brace (guy) takes the turns off his winch, but holds what will become the sheet under sufficient pressure to make sure the spinnaker does not collapse. The spinnaker is now free of the pole, so the helmsman must steer the boat under the spinnaker to keep it full. This should be done without any dramatic movements of the wheel or tiller. When the outboard end of the spinnaker reaches the bowman, he rolls his hand over and forms a half loop in the lazy brace (guy) (see diagram 2.6) and puts what is now the brace (guy) into the parrotbeak. He shouts 'right' or some other agreed word, loud enough to be heard by the cockpit crew. The main is now jibed and the traveller let out to its full extent. The crew member on the kicker takes all strain off it, without letting it go; the hand on the topping lift pulls like crazy to lift the pole up to the horizontal, and the person on the brace (guy), who is now the key, pulls the spinnaker around to the end of the pole. The mast crew lowers the inboard end of the

Diagram 2.6 *Side view of dip pole jibe, the for'ard hand rolls her or his wrist so as to put the new brace into the parrot beak correctly.*

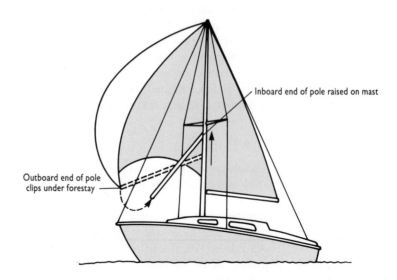

Inboard end of pole raised on mast

Outboard end of pole clips under forestay

pole on the mast. Once the spinnaker reaches the outboard end of the pole, the kicker can take on strain so that the pole doesn't sky, and the jibe is complete. The helmsman now comes to the proper course, and the pole, sheet and kicker are trimmed for the new course.

TWIN POLE JIBE

There is only one other jibe, which is performed only in the ocean on big yachts, and that is the twin pole jibe.

When a skipper believes a dip pole jibe will be too dangerous—mainly because weight needs to be in the bow—he may call for a twin pole jibe. This is very simple, but still involves the twin sheet and brace (guy) system.

The boat is brought dead square and the parrotbeak of the second pole is placed over the lazy brace (guy). The pole is then pushed outboard and the inboard end is snapped in place on the second bell on the mast. The pole is hoisted into position, so that the spinnaker is attached to both poles at once. Be very aware that under racing rules there is a limit to the amount of time it is permitted to have two poles attached.

Once the second pole is firmly in place, the original one can be detached. What will become the sheet is let forward and the parrotbeak is fired from the brace. The pole is pulled down by the kicker as the topping lift is let off, and the pole is then detached.

In all the jibes and manoeuvres described above, snotters if they are fitted, will have to be eased. They can be re-applied, if wanted, on the new leg.

SNOTTERS

In heavy weather, it is advisable to choke a spinnaker down by the use of snotters. They are simply a line with an open-sided block on one end. The block is placed over the spinnaker sheet and the end of the line is passed through a block on the rail. The line is then pulled down so that the spinnaker sheet, instead of going to the stern of the boat, comes to deck level at somewhere nearer the point at which the brace (guy) crosses the deck.

The effect of the snotter is to prevent the spinnaker rolling, as happens when the controls are led to the stern and the weather pipes up. Snotters prevent the death rolls, and make it easier for the helmsman to keep the boat under the spinnaker.

That simple phrase, keep the boat under the spinnaker, is the clue to good downwind sailing. Once the person at the wheel has learnt to keep the boat under the spinnaker—steer to the middle of the spinnaker as it moves slightly from side to side—he or she will soon reach the stage where it is possible to tell where the boat is going to move next and to correct it as it happens. By doing this the boat is kept on a straight track and makes a round-up or broach very much less likely.

Spinnaker Peel (Change)

We've now covered the major manoeuvres involving movement of the spinnaker pole and the spinnaker itself, but we have assumed a steady wind, and every sailor knows that the weight of the wind varies. And, when that happens, a racing skiff will have no other spinnaker aboard and will have to make do with the one that's up at the moment. However, some medium-sized harbour racers will have at least one other to choose from, and ocean racers will have as many as the international rule allows them to carry. So every competent crew needs to know how to change a spinnaker without losing speed.

The peel (change) is a manoeuvre which seems to worry a great many crews and yet it's much easier than some of the things we have described earlier in this chapter.

Whether you have to execute an inside or an outside peel (change) will depend on where the halyards are. This is where the owner finds out whether or not the forward crew member is any good. The crew must know where the halyards are, which are being used and be sure that none of them is crossed. The terms inside and outside should be clear, but they mean that the new spinnaker is hoisted either inside the one that is up, or outside it.

It is not possible, with a peel (change), not to have someone in the bow of the boat. However, that time should be kept as short as possible so that the boat is not slowed down for too long.

Most boats have a peeling strop, probably one metre (three feet) long with a clip on either end so that one end can be clipped to the rail or a fitting near the bow and the other end can be clipped on the new spinnaker. It takes the place of a spinnaker pole until the old spinnaker has been fired and replaced by the new. Let's say we are doing an inside peel (spinnaker change) first. The spinnaker pole has to be let forward and down so that it is within reach of the for'ard crew member. The new spinnaker clew, brace (guy) side, is clipped to the strop. The new halyard and the new sheet are then attached to the new spinnaker, which is hoisted and the sheet is then pulled on so that the peel sets into the old spinnaker.

Once that's neatly done and the sail is under control, the old spinnaker is fired from the parrotbeak at the end of the spinnaker pole and pulled in — on the fore deck and as close to the mast as possible. What is left is a spinnaker pole to which no sail is attached, and a spinnaker attached to the peeling strop.

The spinnaker pole is now let further down, so that the new spinnaker can be attached to it and released from the peeling strop. The spinnaker pole can

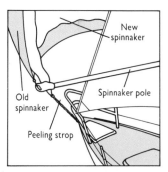

Diagram 2.7 *Spinnaker peeling strop.*

be winched back to the correct position for the wind angle and the sheet can be trimmed — hardly difficult at all.

There is not a great deal of difference between an outside and an inside peel (spinnaker change). The movements take place in exactly the same order, the difference being that the new spinnaker is hoisted outside the old one and the old spinnaker is pulled down inside the new one.

These quite simple manoeuvres are critical to the proper control of a boat downwind, particularly when peeling up (changing) to heavyweight spinnakers as the wind increases.

Heavy Weather Running

So far we have been talking about spinnakers and manoeuvring with them in moderate, steady conditions—in other words conditions that are ideal for practising and getting confidence. We have now reached a pretty high level of proficiency. We can handle every manoeuvre that is necessary on the boat, so let's talk about being in an angry ocean.

We are running. We've had to peel (change) progressively from the lightest spinnaker to the heaviest and the wind is still increasing. A little known trick for handling heavy weather at this stage is to let the spinnaker pole forward so that less of the spinnaker is presented to the heavy wind and more is spilled behind the main. This is actually an unbalanced way of sailing and quite tricky unless handled by an expert. But it is certainly a technique that can be used until the wind becomes too strong for even that to be sufficient and a reef becomes imperative. Then take one reef in the main and if that isn't enough take a second (see above page 30).

We have seen that the main acts as the principal turning moment on any boat. Going to windward it's trying to force the stern away from the wind and the bow into it. The headsail is there to counteract that force and give a forward motion that's as fast as possible and as close to the wind as possible. This effect doesn't stop whether the wind is coming across the beam of the boat or aft of the beam. The difference is that as the wind gets more and more aft, the main is pushing further and further forward. On an almost square run the pressure is much less likely to round the boat up while the wind is manageable than when you are reaching. But as the wind increases, the turning moment on the main becomes greater and greater. The spinnaker, which is shielded by the main and therefore not pulling directly forward as much as it would be if the pole were further back, has less effect in counteracting that turning moment. A good helmsman can overcome that turning moment for a long time but the area of movement off course that's available to him becomes less and less. Any deviation from course closer to the wind dramatically increases that turning moment.

It's at this stage that many less experienced skippers say the pressure is getting too much and they take the spinnaker off. This is not the right thing to do. Instead, to take the turning pressure off the boat, take one or even two reefs into the main. This will allow the spinnaker to take charge more and lift the bow, and it will increase the angle available to the helmsman so that he or she can go off course without rounding up and broaching. We're now talking about an apparent wind of 30 to 35 knots, which means the boat will be doing perhaps 12 to 15 knots on waves and 10 or 12 knots the rest of the time. Clearly everything is under great stress—not least of all the helmsman. But taking those two reefs will make a dramatic difference to the way the boat handles and to the ability of the helmsman to keep it on a straight course. This means the boat can maintain a better average speed, it will be steering straight more often, it will lift on to the crest of waves more easily and surf better and more often, and there will be a feeling of exhilaration among the crew. This will lead to better things. Morale will be so much better than it would be in a crew which is wondering whether it can handle the conditions and what's going to break next.

You can imagine the scene in the ocean now—running in a heavy, increasing wind. The seas are getting up because this progression will have taken place over an hour or so. More of them will be breaking. There will be white caps all round. Usually these conditions won't become more extreme but, of course, they can. When that happens there are two more stages a well-run boat can go through before it has to start seriously thinking about reducing rather than increasing speed.

The first stage is to put a small headsail inside the spinnaker. This may sound like madness but I will explain why it works. The ideal sail would be a three or a four blade. Probably a four is better because the area is slightly less, but more particularly it has a strop at the head and won't set so high. It will also be good if this can be tacked onto the weather rail rather than in the middle of the boat. This tactic works on the principle that the boat is still under pressure and if it rounds up, the spinnaker is likely to collapse as the boat points higher into the wind. However, as it rounds up the jib will fill and pull the bow away from the wind giving the helmsman a chance to recover before the whole of the hull becomes a rudder.

This combination of a small storm spinnaker carried high, with only that amount of the windward side of the spinnaker that can be managed presented to the wind, and a weather-tacked small headsail inside it, can probably be carried up to about 40 knots on most reasonable boats. This will only be possible as long as the seas remain relatively low. And it's not reasonable to expect that they will stay low if this progression of increasing wind and reefing of sail area has taken several hours. The helmsman will know when time is running out by the area of manoeuvre which will be down to perhaps as little as five or ten degrees. Only the very best will be able to handle this sort of sailing.

As the seas begin to build and more of them are breaking, the boat may well have to be manoeuvred through more than 10 degrees to present the proper angle to the seas and to ensure it doesn't broach through sea power rather than being overpressed by wind. But some prudent seamanship should come in at this time and even earlier. The washboards should be in and the boat locked up because the danger of a pooping, breaking wave increases with the length of the blow, the length of time of the run, and the fetch. Those on deck must be hooked on with their safety harnesses as there will be no warning if the boat either rolls or is pooped.

It's at this stage that the sensible helmsman will say: 'I can't hold it'; and the sensible skipper or sailing master will order the spinnaker taken off. A last resort is to wear two headsails, and, usually, this is just as effective as the rig we've just taken off—it is quite legal in racing, as long as one of the headsails is poled out and the other is held only at head and foot. They can't both be in a track. Don't forget we have two reefs in the main at this stage, so it is out square and taking much less of a dominant role in the forward motion of the boat. The two headsails being up means that the helmsman probably is able to manoeuvre through 60 degrees rather than 10 and can therefore handle the combination of wind and wave pattern better than he could with the spinnaker rig. The best choice of sails probably is for the two to be poled out to windward and the three to be loose to leeward, in other words, behind the main. The reason for this is that if the boat has to come on to the wind more, the smaller sail is already rigged. Certainly it's got to be dropped and fed into the track but this is much easier when it's held and under control than it would be otherwise.

This rig will be quite safe in very considerable winds, but if they should increase even beyond that, say up to full gale or storm force, there are still things to do.

The first is to drop the main entirely and secure it to the boom. This again allows the twin headsails to hold the bow up and takes away the turning moment of the stern of the boat. It also increases the area of manoeuvrability available to the helmsman, which of course means that the boat is safer. By now the seas will be very big and they will determine the course the helmsman must take. With the main removed there's no danger of sailing by the lee, which is one of the best reasons for taking it down. Even if the helmsman gets as much as 10 or 15 degrees off course, the headsail on the relevant side of the boat will be under extra pressure from the wind and tend to come back to course. One of the significant effects of moving the power more and more into the bow of the boat and away from the stern is that pressure is taken off the rudder which comes under very great strain in these conditions if too much weight is left in the main.

Remember, as long as we are travelling roughly in the direction we want to go, we are still racing this boat. The skipper has to think about whether it is still possible to race only when the seas become so big and so close together and so steep that the boat is being picked up by them rather than just lifting to them. It becomes dangerous when the boat is picked up like a surfboard: the bow hangs over a yawning chasm, a roar of white water comes behind and the boat takes off. The danger is that the bow will tip so far down that it might trip in the wave ahead and be pitchpoled by the breaking sea behind. Now it's necessary to make sure of two things: one, that the boat does not go so fast on the top of the wave that it can pitchpole; and two, that it doesn't go so slowly in the trough that it loses steerage way and so can be rolled in by the following wave. It is not easy to pick the middle way. As a wave comes behind and picks the boat up, the helmsman should set the boat at an angle of say 20 degrees to the wave to make it much more difficult for the boat to be forced to surf. In effect it's spilling part of the wind so that the boat doesn't get out of control and simply spear forward. If the helmsman goes too far on that angle the boat will tend to be broached and rolled down the front of the wave. So it's a pretty fine balance. But the beauty of this arrangement is that when the helmsman has successfully negotiated the wave and is down in the trough where the wind may have dropped from say 65 knots to 20 knots, there is enough sail up to be able to come up and present the stern of the boat at 90 degrees to the oncoming wave. And so the story repeats itself, probably once every 20 seconds for the next day or so.

Many people believe that at this stage the boat should lie ahull or stream warps. Obviously no one can have the experiences that others have had, but in the biggest wind and sea conditions that I've experienced—a certain 80 knots and seas between six and nine metres (20 and 30 feet)—either of these techniques would I believe have been quite wrong. In that instance, we took the main off the boat, a 13 metre (43 feet) long narrow boat, and had the storm jib up only. We were still doing eight knots on top of the considerable waves and four or so at the bottom. The point was that we had enough power at the top to be able to maintain steerage way at the bottom. If we had laid ahull I believe that we would have risked being smashed down a trough and suffering damage on the lee side of the boat; if we had streamed warps, I believe we would have had too little speed in the troughs to be able to present a proper attitude on the next wave. But of the two I'd prefer trying warps because one could wear a larger headsail and so be held back from too great a speed at the top of the waves but still have the power to get through the bottom. In this particular heavy blow, we would have preferred taking a third reef before dropping the main, but the third reefing line had not been led during the calmer conditions earlier in the race and it was quite impossible to try to lead it in the storm. I strongly recommend that, whatever skippers might think about the effect of drag from having heavy reefing lines up through the cringle and down again to the boom, when you really want that reef it should be there. In any case, if drag is a worry a mouse can be led and a little eye sewn into the end of the reefing line so that it can be pulled through when necessary. I really believe it's essential.

We learned one technique during this storm and that was because we had no alternative—but it's a nice enough technique to pass on. We were running back along a coastline and the wind made the coastline a lee shore, although at only a very slight angle. In other words we were closing the coast but very, very slowly. However, we still had to jibe. To jibe in a wind which was verified at 80 knots and where we believe some gusts were higher is not an easy matter. The watch on deck talked it out amongst themselves and decided that the only chance was to attempt the jibe in the bottom of the trough where the apparent wind was down to about 25 knots. It then became a mere matter of timing.

As we went down the wave at an angle, we started to pull the main in, which took considerable effort because the weight of wind in it was enormous. As the helmsman squared up in the trough, the boom was brought into the centre of the boat so that the wind was blowing on either side of the main. It was then let out on the traveller first and the mainsheet quickly after and the boat was then gradually brought back to present its square stern to the oncoming wave. We had to do this twice and on both occasions it was successful. And, if you think about it, to jibe with two reefs in the main in 25 knots of wind is not so bad. But it certainly got worse when we reached the top of the wave and were slammed over by the wind as soon as it could get at us.

Let's consider another situation. Many crews believe reaching is the easiest point of sailing, but power reaching on a big boat with a beam sea is certainly not easy. A good team can get a boat to sail at a remarkably fine angle to the wind with a spinnaker up.

Imagine there's a spanking breeze coming from the beam, the spinnaker is pulling the mast over, so is the main, and the keel is struggling to balance the heeling moment. A lumpy sea is picking the boat up and dumping it sideways, with even some waves breaking so that there is an occasional slap on the side of the boat from a metre or so (two or three feet) of white water. The spinnaker and main have to be balanced. We were talking before about the rounding up pressure that comes from the main. In power reaching this pressure is doing its utmost to turn the boat up into the wind. The spinnaker is pulling the bow away and the helmsman is trying to stay somewhere in between the course that rounds the boat up and the course that is below what it should be. As a gust comes, the main sheet crew member must ease the traveller so that the weather helm is reduced, otherwise the helmsman will finish up with a wheel that kicks against him and he loses the wind. While the power reaching is going well the boat will be doing 9 or 10 knots, its spinnaker's leading edge will be full and when it does fall in a little will be recovered by the sheet crew member. The main will be going up and down the traveller so as to maintain a steady weather helm on the wheel and the boat will be tracking beautifully on the desired course.

When it goes wrong, two things happen. The first is that the boat rounds up, the spinnaker falls in and the power is lost. The helmsman will have to fall away, perhaps as many as 30 to 35 degrees to fill the spinnaker again. Gradually, as the spinnaker fills and the boat's speed increases, the wind will draw forward and the boat will be allowed to come higher and higher onto that apparent wind until the same conditions of power reaching have been restored. To watch that angle and the boat coming up into it under a good helmsman is a delight.

The other problem that can occur is that if the wind goes further forward, the spinnaker will lose some of its pressure and if the main hasn't been eased, the boat will keep rounding up. If the spinnaker sheet crew member and the helmsman are able to recognise what's happened, the helmsman can flick the wheel down, taking the boat to leeward, and the sheet crew can ease the sheet off and snap it on again, making the spinnaker jump back into shape and thus allow the boat to come back onto course. But this will not last if the main sheet crew doesn't keep on with his or her responsibilities, continually moving the traveller up and down so that the weather helm remains constant.

If the wind should increase, the amount of pressure on the main will be too much. The traveller will be at the full extent of its travel all the time and the main sheet crew member will be easing the main sheet to take pressure off the helmsman. At this stage a reef must go into the main—not should, must. The reef is put in exactly the same way as if the boat is on the wind, although it's usually easier here to fix the mast end rather than the boom end of the mainsail first. When the reef is completed, the outboard end of the spinnaker pole should be dropped slightly to tighten the luff of the spinnaker, allowing the boat to point higher. If the wind seems likely to still increase when there is already a reef in the main, and if the crew is finding the boat hard to keep up to windward, then the handheld computer should be consulted to see which headsail should be put on in place of the spinnaker. However, this is one occasion where the experience of the skipper may override what is indicated by the computer. A series of polar performance curves, if the skipper has them, will indicate at what stage the spinnaker should come off and a headsail on. Whichever headsail is used, its sheet should be led through a reaching block which is set on the widest part of the vessel. This is usually a snatch block which is often left there permanently for just such an occasion.

The normal progression of sail reduction in the face of increasing winds then takes place. A second or if necessary a third reef can be taken in the main and the headsails can be made increasingly smaller if the wind remains in a reaching position relative to the course that's desired. The only consideration here is going to be breaking seas coming at the boat from beam on. The helmsman will avoid them as much as possible. The storm boards should be in and the boat snugged right down because nobody wants water down below. Any domestic activities below like cooking should stop and everything should be secured against being hurtled around inside the cabin.

While breaking seas aren't too much of a problem when reaching because the headsail is well out from the leeward side of the vessel, it can sometimes be a good idea to have a high cut headsail for reaching so that the waves can go under the headsail rather than breaking in it and tearing the sail. By now the helmsman will really have his hands full. With a beam wind and beam seas the boat will be leaping all over the place. The helmsman will be trying to sail a steady course but every now and then will be overpowered. The old rules hold: in the relative lulls push the boat up into the wind to increase the apparent wind and therefore maintain good speed. As soon as a gust comes, run away slightly. This will mean that while you're doing a sort of corkscrew course, the course made good will be in the direction you want and the boat will be maintaining good speed and will not be overpressed. If it becomes so strong a wind that the boat has to run away all the time, then the navigator should be consulted. It's hard to overstress how important the relationship is between the helmsman or watchcaptain and the navigator. The navigator makes plans on the basis of the available information, what he deduces and what he hopes for, usually in consultation with the skipper. If for some reason the helmsman is unable to meet these requirements it is imperative that he says so—not so that he can be abused as incompetent but so that new decisions can be made and new courses organised.

Another lesson that can be learnt from apparent wind and one which surprisingly few otherwise good sailors know, is how to build up an apparent speed which is greater than the actual wind. If that sounds like gobbledegook I'm sorry. But by following the method outlined below a boat can create its own apparent wind and that apparent wind can be of greater strength than the actual wind prevailing at the time. The method is not dissimilar to that described above in relation to a flat spinnaker.

The boat for the purposes of this exercise will be in conditions of near calm and will have lightweight sails on and, with a good crew, lightweight sheets as well. The main should be pinned in the middle of the boat as it will have little to do until some speed is attained. The headsail should be let out as far as it can go while still keeping some curve and shape in it. As much crew weight as possible should be on the leeward side of the boat to give some shape to the headsail. It may take several minutes of holding the boat in this position before some very slight forward motion begins. You can apply the preventer to hold the boom really still. Don't worry if the only way you can get the boat moving is to be going at 150 degrees away from your desired course. The choice you have now is whether you're going to be becalmed or keep the boat moving. And, as long as you're able to bring it up on to a course somewhere in the direction of where you want to go, it doesn't matter if at first you are apparently sailing away from your target. As the boat begins to pick up speed, the little amount of wind that there is will be drawn slightly ahead. This will allow the headsail to come on very slightly. This has to be the most gentle manoeuvre of any that you carry out on a boat. Soon the boat's speed will increase yet again allowing the helmsman to come higher on the wind and this technique will continue until the sail is on enough for the boat to be travelling at perhaps two to three knots, if the boat is fairly big, and at an angle of perhaps 50 to 60 degrees to the wind. This is nothing like the 30 degrees or so which can be achieved in a decent breeze, but it's still doing better than the boat that doesn't know this technique which will be doing 360 degree turns and going nowhere in a hurry.

If you're able to master this technique you can probably get up to an apparent wind speed of four or five knots and a boat speed of close to two. If you were in a race and were able to sail for an hour at this speed in the general direction of your mark and the other boats in the race were not moving, you would have a break of two nautical miles, which would be pretty valuable.

There's a corollary to this technique which is invaluable in ocean racing and in particular in ocean racing at night. In light conditions the boat can be travelling at, say, three knots with an apparent wind speed therefore of only a little more. To the inexperienced crew this can be seen as efficient sailing in light conditions. Actually the boat is in a critical situation. If the helmsman now makes the slightest of mistakes the boat will grind to an awful halt and unless the technique of wind creating is known it will be becalmed until a decent breeze comes up. It's worth telling your racing crew that if they do find themselves in conditions where boat speed and apparent wind speed are equal, they should get the best light weather helmsman on the wheel or tiller, get all the weight to leeward and keep the sails cracked off so that the apparent wind isn't lost. Drum this into them to make absolutely sure they do call the top light weather helmsman because this is where races are won or lost.

ELECTRICS

An electrical system is indispensable on a boat. Without it there are no lights, no electronic systems, not much in the way of refrigeration, and no starting. This is true even of diesels, but diesels, unless they are huge, can usually be started by hand.

If you are going offshore for extended periods into parts of the world where technology is limited and repairs may be difficult, it is vital to have someone among the crew who understands electrics; maintenance is more critical with the electrics of a boat than anything else. Every single wire, connection or link you put into a vessel is in a hostile environment. Nothing is worse for electrics than damp sea air, which just delights in shorting circuits, corroding fittings and finding weak spots. In fact, to talk about fault finding is to have failed: fault prevention is the secret. The prudent skipper is alert all the time, checking all the systems on board for anything that is out of the ordinary or functioning less well than it should. A combination of alertness and a regular maintenance schedule will minimise the chances of failure or even accident. It's an attitude of mind. If you see something that looks wrong—corrosion around a joint or a loose joint—then fix it straight away. Don't ignore it. When you fix it, look through the whole circuit so you're not just fixing one part and leaving the rest to fail later.

The table on page 48 is a suggested maintenance programme for a sailing yacht or motor boat, covering every aspect of what should be done. Some things are done annually, some monthly, some weekly, and some are done daily. However, the older a boat is and the more ancient its electrical system, the less likely it is to conform to new standards and the more problems there will undoubtedly be. Eventually you will reach a stage where if you are an enthusiastic amateur you will be unable to deal with the multitude of problems coming from cracked and corroded lines and from wiring hidden in dark, damp and inaccessible corners of the vessel. The boat will have to be rewired.

UNDERSTANDING ELECTRICITY

If you don't know anything about electricity, it is useful to learn some very basic facts and to be aware that you know only the minimum—just enough to find and correct minor faults. Remember that some modern appliances store very high and dangerous voltages—even on a 12 volt system—which can discharge in one great lethal burst.

BOAT MAINTENANCE PROGRAMME

ITEM	ACTION	FREQUENCY
AIR CONDITIONING	• Appliance generally for rust	At least monthly
	• Check strum box (sea strainer) on end of water inlet	Monthly
	• Check sea cock when checking as above	Monthly
	• Impellers in pumps	Twice yearly
BATTERIES	• Level of electrolyte	Weekly
	• Connections	Monthly
	• Corrosion	Monthly
	• Ventilator holes in caps	Monthly
DEPTH SOUNDER	• If digital	None
	• If with stylus, clean	Yearly
	• Replace bulbs	As needed
GAS DETECTOR/ EXHAUST FAN	• Run to ensure not faulty	Monthly
HI-FI SYSTEM	• System for corrosion	At least monthly
	• Speakers for heating	Twice yearly
RADIOS	• Clean with vacuum cleaner	Yearly
	• Check connections for tightness	Twice yearly

NOTE: Most other electrical and electronic equipment is not serviceable by non-qualified people, and it may be illegal to do so.

There are four terms you must know:

Volt, which describes the strength or pressure of the electricity.

Ampere, which describes the rate of flow, or current.

Ohm, which describes resistance, or friction, restricting the flow.

Watt, which measures the amount of power available.

The law you must learn is **Ohm's Law**, which states the relationship between voltage (E), resistance (R) and current (I). If you know any two of these elements you can find the third, so that:

$$I=E/R; \quad R=E/I; \quad E=IR$$

Once you know each of these elements, you can calculate the wattage of an appliance, that is the drain any appliance can make on your system (see also Assessing the Current Drain of Appliances below page 51). This is calculated either as volts multiplied by amperes, or as current squared multiplied by resistance.

The basic tools you need to enable you to troubleshoot are the voltmeter, the ammeter and the ohmmeter. With these you can measure any of the three elements above and so arrive at your calculation for wattage, as well as check whether or not individual circuits or appliances are faulty.

BATTERIES

The electrical system on most boats is 12 volt, although on some larger vessels, and particularly on boats manufactured in the US, 32 volt systems are used. When current is generated on board with a motorised generator, it is provided at the rate of either 110 or about 230 volts, depending on where the boat is operating and what sort of appliances it has on board. In many cases it's possible to switch between various voltage ratings, both to generate current and to use appliances or to store power. Some specially strengthened batteries are sold as marine batteries, but many so-called marine batteries are no different from other batteries.

The standard system for operating most boats nowadays is to have enough batteries to handle the house load for lights, small engines, refrigeration, and so on for 48 hours without recharging and to have a separate system which is used exclusively to start the engine. It is essential that the house batteries can operate normally for the full 48 hours. In other words they must be able to handle the demands of people who want to read in their berths, the daily work of the navigator, the refrigerator running for as long as necessary, and whichever other appliances are habitually used. The engine circuit must never be used to supply house electricity. It would be patently stupid to have flattened both batteries and so not be able to start the motor to recharge them. The modern switch which puts batteries on to one, or both, or none of the available circuits should be standard on all vessels, because in the case of a short circuit or problem with the engine starting, the whole of the ship's available batteries can be joined into one to give it enough of a belt to get it going and allow time for the fault to be found and the batteries to be recharged.

The batteries contain a series of cells, each of which produces approximately two volts and when enough of those cells are strung together—a 12 volt system requires six cells—a battery of cells is produced, which is where the name comes from. A 32 volt system requires four 8 volt batteries and they can be wired in such a way that 12 volts can be taken from them if required.

Electricity is generated by the action of acid on lead in the battery cells. Chemical changes take place during charging, and a reverse chemical change takes place during a discharge. Provided a battery isn't overloaded to the extent that it discharges too rapidly, it can recover from a loss of power by being charged up by a new current flowing through it. The state of the balance between the acid and the lead in the action taking place in the battery is measured by a hydrometer, which measures the specific gravity of the cell. About 1.260 is an average level for a fully charged battery. A fully discharged battery will show a specific gravity of about 1.135. This measurement, of course, depends on temperature and there are corrections which are made for the specific gravity for varying temperatures. A rough rule is a third of a point off for every degree above 25°C (77°F) and one third of a point off for each degree below 25°C (77°F). The corrections are normally given with the hydrometer when you buy it and you should follow them accurately.

RECHARGING THE BATTERIES

Everyone will have noticed that once batteries begin to fade they fade rapidly. There are some very complicated rules which govern the rate of recharge of a battery but luckily you don't have to worry about them too much, as they have been worked out for you. Whether you have a generator on board or are charging the battery from an alternator or a generator attached to the main engine, or whether you are trickle charging at a marina, the calculations have been done and the charging will take place at a satisfactory rate. It is a good idea to have a voltmeter on board because then the state of the batteries is displayed continuously and it can be seen whether charging is needed. An ammeter to show the rate of charge is also useful, particularly as it will also indicate if the battery is failing to hold its charge.

When batteries charge they very quickly get up to a voltage above 12— even close to 13—as the battery rapidly approaches the maximum charge that can be held by the cells and then the charging rate decreases until almost no current is going into the battery.

Assessing the Current Drain of Appliances

Batteries are rated at the amount of current they hold for a certain number of hours, that is, the amount of amperage they can supply for a fixed number of hours. The amount of power a battery can store normally is measured in ampere/hours, which abbreviates to amp hours. This is calculated from the number of hours for which the battery can sustain a discharge of a given rate. A typical rate for a ship's battery is five amps. If the battery could sustain that rate for 20 hours it would be a 100 amp-hour battery. A 60 amp-hour battery would be able to sustain the five amp outflow for 12 hours only. When you know the amp-hour storage of your battery, you can make up a list of the items in your ship's electric system, and calculate the drain on the battery with any combination of appliances operating. (See the equation given in Understanding Electricity above page 48.)

Maintenance of Batteries

It is sensible for the skipper or the navigator to be in charge of maintenance of the batteries since they will be in charge of most of the equipment on board which uses electricity.

First, it is important that the battery be mounted correctly. It's not good enough simply to think that they're going to be able to handle bad weather and rough water; they have to be mounted in such a way that if the boat turns completely upside down, those batteries will stay the way they are. They are very heavy and very dangerous and apart from the damage they can do to a boat they can do considerable damage to the people in it.

Next, some people consider that they maintain their ship's battery banks well because they have a hydrometer and check the level of the electrolyte regularly. They keep the level of fluid up if required, and they charge in such a way that the battery doesn't sulphate and lose power. But there is more to it than that. The top of the battery must be clean; the terminals need regular cleaning and scarifying (scraping) so that they make good contact and prevent leakage of the charge between the terminals. Everyone who drives a car has had an occasion when the starter motor simply won't turn over, even though the other circuits, like lights and radio, seem to be perfectly satisfactory. This

CURRENT DRAIN OF APPLIANCES

ITEM	AVERAGE DRAIN (WATTAGE)
Air conditioner	800
Autopilot	50
Battery charger	up to 1000
Coffee machine	550-700
Consol	3
Decca	up to 100
Depth sounder (small neon)	1-3
Depth sounder (paper recorder)	2-15
Direction finder	6-100
Electric blanket	50-200
Facsimile	100
Fan	25-75
Florescent light	low of 5, upper depends on fitting
Fry pan	1200
Heater	1000-1500
Horn	50
Instruments	1-6
Loran	10-50
Loudspeakers	25 (short use)
Microwave	1500 (short periods)
Oil heaters	75
Omega	50
Pumps	1000 per horsepower
Radar (3kW)	up to 50
Refrigerator	200-300
Compression	50
Absorption	30
Satnav (provide own battery)	1-10
Stove	550-1500 each element, 3000 average
Television	10
Toaster	800-1150
Vacuum cleaner	500
Water heater	1000
Water system pumps	10-15
12w cabin light	12 per hour

is because the very large currents needed to kick an engine over cannot get past any looseness or corrosion. So the terminal posts need to be cleaned and scraped with a knife or wire brush or any of the patent tools that can be bought for the purpose, and then smeared with a little petroleum jelly, or one of the special mixtures sold. Then the lead needs to be pushed well down to the base of the post and properly tightened. The clamps must be as tight as possible.

The effect of all this can be quite startling: you may not have put any extra charge into your battery, but you will find it will turn the motor over quite easily.

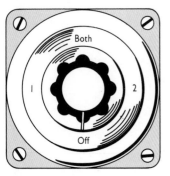

Diagram 3.1 *The battery switch is make–before–break, so that the generating system won't be damaged.*

BATTERY SWITCH

The battery switch of the type shown in diagram 3.1 is make-before-break to eliminate the danger of the generator or alternator suddenly pouring current into an open circuit, which will almost certainly damage the charging system.

DRY CELL BATTERIES

Small dry cell batteries are included in most of the electronic instruments fitted to racing and cruising yachts. Things such as logs, radio direction finders and depth sounders have ordinary dry cells in compartments in the back of them. Unless you are aware of these dry cells, the instruments they control can fail to give a reading, or, worse still give you all sorts of false readings, and therefore difficulty. It is remarkable how few people remember those little batteries when the instrument plays up and who immediately think it is the instrument itself which has failed.

At least once a year go through all the instruments that have batteries to maintain their accuracy or to preserve the memory of their computers, and remove the batteries. Check the battery with an ammeter to see that it is at or near full strength. If it is low, replace it so that you can be sure that the instrument will be right up to the mark. There's not a great deal that the average skipper can do with a highly complicated printed circuit of the kind used in a more modern Satnav or a loran, but later in the chapter we do talk about what little can be done (see Electronics below page 58).

It's better to use distilled water when topping up batteries, even though the water supply may be perfectly OK in most places that you are likely to visit. The trouble is that the chlorine in drinking water is not good for batteries, and so it is well worth the small amount of trouble involved in carrying a container of distilled water. To keep equipment dry and clean is the most essential function of a maintenance programme, and it's certainly so in the case of electronic equipment where some of the older Satnavs and similar mechanisms are not as well sealed as the more modern ones and where the installation site may not have been carefully selected and there is some chance that light spray or moisture has touched the instruments.

T H E   W I R I N G

The next most common problem is the wiring itself—the wiring that goes to pumps, lights, instruments and so on. The modern practice of using colours to indicate the purpose of the wire, or where it's leading, and of positioning wires so that they are always accessible and using a proper standard of wiring for special environments like the hot areas near the engine, is much to be commended. The following colour coding chart is in operation in North America and is recommended as a standard.

Using such a system is better than what is common practice on many boats: that is, wires tend to be bunched up into thick cables, which means that those in the centre of the bunch are hard to see and hard to maintain. The ideal method is to use the standard colours and have the wires run so that each

COLOUR CODING OF WIRES

COLOUR	ITEM	FUNCTION
GREEN (G)		• Earthing (Grounding) bond
WHITE (W) OR BLACK (B)		• Return, negative battery
RED (R)		• Positive battery
YELLOW / RED STRIPE (YR)	• Starting system	• Starter switch to solenoid
YELLOW (Y)	• Generator or alternator	• Generator or alternator to regulator field terminal
	• Bilge fans	• Fuse or switch
DARK GREY (Gy)	• Navigation lights	• Fuse or switch
	• Tachometer	• Sender to gauge
BROWN (Br)	• Generator armature	• Armature to regulator
	• Alternator	• Generator terminal to alternator
	• Charge light	• Auxiliary terminal to light to regulator
	• Pumps	• Fuse or switch
ORANGE (O)	• Accessory feed	• Ammeter to alternator or generator output and accessory fuses or switches
	• Accessory common feed	• Distribution panel to accessory switch
PURPLE (Pu)	• Ignition	• Ignition switch to coil and electrical instruments
	• Instrument feed	• Distribution panel to electrical instruments
DARK BLUE (Db)	• Cabin, instrument lights	• Fuse or switch
LIGHT BLUE (Lt Bl)	• Oil pressure	• Sender to gauge
TAN (T)	• Water temperature	• Sender to gauge
PINK (Pk)	• Fuel gauge	• Gauge

can be seen separately. These should be checked at least every six months to see that the wires aren't chafed or rubbing into each other, or kinked or in some other way damaged so that current can leak. They should also be checked for leaks if the batteries run low unexpectedly. If any fault is found during one of these inspections, or at any other time, the whole of that particular circuit should be checked.

T E S T I N G   F O R   L E A K S
(S H O R T   C I R C U I T S)

Turn off all the appliances on the vessel and use a test light as follows. Remove the positive terminal from the battery and then bridge the gap across the two battery terminals. If the test light doesn't glow, you should use an ammeter and, using increasingly sensitive settings, continue testing until you get a reading. If that reading is more than a few milliamps, you may have a leakage, and you should check to find out where. However, it is much more likely that you are getting a reading on the ammeter because some part of the circuit is still on. If there is a leak, it is not likely to be as serious as it would be if the test light had glowed, but it is rare to have a leakage of that magnitude.

If you use fuses rather than circuit breakers, they are often a neglected part of the electrical circuit. If they are not being held firmly, or if there is corrosion, they can easily cause problems and should then be cleaned or replaced.

E A R T H I N G   (G R O U N D I N G)   S Y S T E M

It is essential for all vessels, except those unusual ones that have a floating or non-earthed system, that all the circuits and all the major installations be taken to a common earth or ground. (See also Stray Current Corrosion below page 57.)

It is imperative that a good earthing (grounding) system or bonding system be used when a boat's electrics are being installed or modernised. Negative earthing (grounding) is used virtually everywhere in the world, so much so that if you have positive earthing (grounding) you're going to have difficulty in getting equipment that will work properly.

The common earth or ground should be as close to the batteries as possible. Some people recommend that it be located well above bilge water level, although others suggest that it should bond to the keel.

Diagram 3.2 *Earthing (grounding) circuit.*

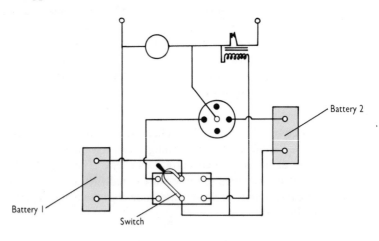

E L E C T R I C I T Y   A N D   T H E   C O M P A S S

Many books talk about the compass and the effect of electricity on it, and complicated experiments have been done to try to ascertain just what does make the compass needle deviate.

It is silly to put wires near the binnacle if you don't need to. Why take a risk? It's also important to keep any magnets, as in loudspeakers, away from the compass. I know many a navigational installation where the speakers from the hi-fi system are close to the fluxgate compass. This is highly undesirable. In the same way that metal and radios should be kept well clear, so should speakers and any other mechanism that may create an electro-magnetic field. If you absolutely must have some wires close to the compass, twist them in pairs to reduce the danger of deviation, but it is still far better to keep electric current away from the compass.

G E N E R A T O R S

Next we should consider generators. A generator needs a small amount of residual magnetism in its coils to be able to start creating electricity. This will only be a problem if the generator has not been used regularly. Without this residual electricity from regular use, the starting sequences of the generator can't take place.

If you feel confident, there's a way of dealing with this. Take a piece of heavy insulated wire, connect it to the unearthed (non-grounded) positive terminal of the battery and then put it straight onto the output terminal of the generator. You do this only for a second or two, because you can get quite a nasty burn and so can the machinery. It takes only that second or two for enough current to flow to cause the generator to operate properly again. If this doesn't make the generator start up, another method might work. Connect a similar piece of wire to the external connection of the field winding. Short this to the frame of the generator. If there's an increase in electrical output, the generator is in good order and your trouble must be somewhere else. But don't do this for longer than a few seconds either, because it isn't good for the generator.

Because there is a strong current in the generator, the brushes which press against the spinning commutator (see diagram 3.3) must engage it smoothly and must be clean. They are normally spring-loaded and so keep a good contact, but if there's been any arcing, the assemblies may have been eaten away.

Cooling fan   Field winding   Pole piece   Brush gears   Cable entry

Commutator

Diagram 3.3 *Generator.*

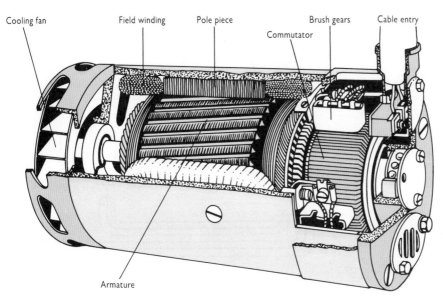

Armature

A L T E R N A T O R S

Alternators don't have the same problems of arcing and wear as do generators, and consequently they are easier to maintain. While maintaining an alternator is easier than maintaining a generator there are a couple of very important rules that must be observed.

They absolutely must, repeat must, be connected with the correct polarity to the battery. If not, the alternator will blow-out without fail. The other rule is that if your battery is absolutely flat the alternator cannot charge it. The only way you can overcome this is to use a good sized battery which is in good condition, or even half a dozen dry cells in a series, and connect this between earth (ground) and the terminal, which is the live brush of the alternator. You only do that long enough for a small amount of current to get into the main battery, which will then accept a charge from the alternator.

Motor cruisers can carry much larger generating plants than a sailing yacht, although a large yacht, of course, can have a fuel-driven generating plant which will produce 240 or 110 volts and so provide some electricity for some home comforts. Some on-board generators can give as much as 15,000 watts of output but can weigh anything up to half a ton. Obviously, if you are having a boat built you will get advice from an expert on what generating plant you'll need.

The generating engine needs exactly the same conditions for cooling, for maintenance and for ease of access as the main engine.

Many skippers quite rightly feel that to have too many through-hull openings is dangerous, and they therefore have inlet and outlet pipes going to a central cluster of pipes which then flow through only one skin fitting to the sea. These are generally controlled with their own cocks, and there is one main shut-off valve which can isolate all the pipes. This is what should happen with the generator inlet and outlet. There are so many cases of yachts sinking at their moorings because somebody has been ill-acquainted with the techniques of using a marine head or has helped with a chore with the generator and has left the inlet open. Because water has been able to flow into the hull the vessel has been, if not lost, at least badly damaged.

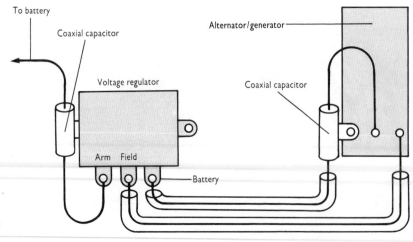

Diagram 3.4 *A typical charging system for a boat, motor or sailing, with a capacitor in series with the armature to provide noise suppression. A second capacitor is installed in series with the battery lead to the voltage regulator for the same reason.*

One of the great drawbacks of generators is that they're usually operating when the crew or neighbouring crews are trying to rest or are enjoying their happy hour. The last thing the crew wants is a raucous petrol (gasoline) engine juddering away near them. Unfortunately, the balance is a personal matter and isn't always resolved happily.

A detailed analysis of the various sections that make a reasonable power plant for motor boats or an auxiliary system for a sailing yacht is beyond the scope of this book. An excellent book on this subject is *Your Boat's Electrical System* by Conrad Miller and E.S. Malloney (see Further References, page 305).

G A L V A N I C   C O R R O S I O N

An unwanted part of a boat's electrics is electrolysis or galvanic corrosion. Galvanic corrosion or electrolysis should be a great worry to the boat owner, particularly if the boat is made of aluminium or steel. This is because any dissimilar metals in sea water will conduct freely and generate an electric current. The less 'noble' metal will corrode. The adjacent list roughly specifies the nobility of various metals; complete lists, containing specifications and alloys are to be found in books listed in Further References on page 305.

Galvanic corrosion can also occur within just one fitting, provided that fitting is made of an alloy. The current in this case will pass within the fitting itself without the need for any other metals sticking into the water further along the boat's hull. If you combine this with the fact that the wider the disparity in nobility between the two metals the greater the corrosion of the least noble, you'll understand why some alloys take only weeks to become useless in a severe marine environment. When you further consider that extra salty water, or chemicals, or pollution in general in the water, will accelerate the process of corrosion, you will almost despair.

But luckily there are ways of fighting it. The simplest method to prevent corrosion of the expensive fittings that you've bought for your boat, particularly if it's an aluminium boat, is to hang sacrificial anodes ('zincs') from wires over the side of the boat into the sea water. Provided those wires connect with a stanchion or safety rail and then hang freely into the sea, they will take all the corrosion: being made of a low nobility metal, they will corrode instead of the fittings. This is the best system of preventing corrosion. However, the other method is to be sure that your electrical circuit is properly bonded, and also to know that the ordinary rules of corrosion avoidance were followed when hardware was installed in your boat.

S T R A Y   C U R R E N T   C O R R O S I O N

The worst corrosion of all is stray current corrosion, which almost invariably exists either through a fault in the electrical system of the boat, or through improper bonding. If you do discover rapid deterioration of a fitting—usually a new fitting in an established boat—disconnect the battery and have an expert

---

LEAST NOBLE
ANODIC
ACTIVE

Magnesium and its alloys
Some aluminium anode alloys
Zinc
Galvanised steel, wrought iron
Aluminium and most alloys
Cadmium
Aluminium rivet alloy
Mild steel
Wrought iron
Cast iron
Stainless steels (if active),
Chromium
Lead-tin (50-50) solder, silver
solder
Lead
Tin
Muntz metal
Manganese bronze
Brass (60-40)
Gunmetal
Admiralty brass
Silicon
Copper-nickle
Yellow brass (65-35)
Aluminium bronze
Red brass (85-15)
Copper
Silicon bronze (various)
German silver
Nickel (various)
Monel
Titanium
Tin bronze
Silver
Silver plating
Graphite
Platinum

MOST NOBLE
CATHODIC
PASSIVE

check out the system for you. All devices on a yacht or motor cruiser should be joined to one earth (ground). This gives the best control of stray current corrosion, or galvanic corrosion, it is a straightforward and simple system, and it provides the greatest safety if lightning should strike.

ELECTRONICS

Electronics are probably the greatest advance in boat information services and therefore in safety that has occurred almost in the whole history of boating. Depth sounders can help us navigate with certainty to avoid hazards and to confirm our position. With radio we can talk to ports we want to enter, discuss with the Coastguard their requirements in terms of landing or customs or safety, and send an SOS halfway across the world. With Satnav and geostationary position equipment we can know where we are to an accuracy of a hundred metres. But when they fail, we are thrown back into old navigation systems which may seem archaic, but which are just as vital because our need for safety doesn't change (see Chapter 7). Unfortunately, when radar sets, satellite navigators, depth sounders and things of that kind do fail, there's not a great deal that can be done to fix them because they are usually in sealed units so that moist air is kept out of the equipment. At the very best they contain a number of printed circuit boards which, unless spares are carried, simply cannot be replaced. That doesn't mean no maintenance at all can be carried out. The standard care which ensures good, clean, dry, firm joints, leads from batteries which are clean and dry and tightly clamped, good grounding wherever it's required, a non-vibrating mounting so that connections cannot be loosened, should be automatic. Items should be mounted in a dry position so that the hazards of salt air don't become the disaster of salt water. It's a good idea to open electronic instruments every three months or so and just run a vacuum cleaner gently over them to remove what dust may have accumulated, although there's likely to be little. It is even possible, and I've done it, with a Satnav that has crashed, to open it and reset it by following the manufacturer's in-structions—pressing the switch or connection they specify.

There's very little you can do to maintain depth sounders apart from having spare bulbs for the flashing type and perhaps keeping the stylus clean on recording types. Most problems with depth sounders come shortly after a boat has been hauled out for painting or some other maintenance which has involved a number of jobs—including re-antifouling. It doesn't seem to matter how often you say to the enthusiastic people who are helping you that you don't want any paint to go over the depth sounder transducer, they always slap it on. There is metal in antifouling paint, and this metal may interact with the transducer itself or simply mask it so that its accuracy and range are reduced.

If a depth sounder does become erratic, it may be that the voltage is not correct, and if it stops entirely, it is most likely that the fuse has blown. If it's neither of these things it's unlikely to be the transducer and cable as they are straightforward items. You will then need to get specific help from a qualified person. This is why a vessel making a long voyage must still carry a lead line.

It is a good idea to carry plenty of spare fuses for each instrument, so that if one blows and is replaced and the set then works, that's fine. But if the new fuse blows, you know you've got a problem. You should turn the set off and wait until you can get an expert to look at it.

Another useful maintenance procedure for electronic equipment is to every now and then unscrew the coaxial connectors and see whether they are corroded. Clean them and, if you think it's necessary, spray on a little water inhibitor before reconnecting. The same can be done to antenna mountings, and it's also a good idea to screw down tight any of the equipment, such as the antenna, to reduce vibration.

The best maintenance for any of these highly sophisticated electronic mechanisms is to have the owner's manual aboard and, where feasible, to carry spares. On a racing boat, to carry all the spares recommended in this book would mean to carry weight that would reduce the chances of victory— no owner would like that. But a racing boat's effort is normally for a few days only, a week at the outside. The sort of competition that goes across whole oceans or round the world is limited to relatively few boats, and they're large boats which can afford to carry the sort of spares that we're talking about here.

However, as sailors can't rely on obtaining service for their boat's equipment at every port of call, it is advisable to be as self-reliant as possible and to carry, if not a spare satnav, at least a couple of boards, which even an amateur can install.

RADIO

Any boat which is planning to operate even 50 nautical miles offshore must carry a radio. Not to do so borders on the criminal, because a radio is required to both send and receive SOS signals, to receive weather information, without which the crew can get into serious trouble, and by not making this small financial outlay, the owner shows a serious lack of basic seamanship.

Ocean racing boats tend to carry single side band, medium frequency sets so that they can talk on the race frequency and on the international ship to shore and ship to ship frequencies. They have a wide range of channels or wavelengths available but usually will have a VHF set as well. They are in-expensive and offer a wider range of services with great ease. And in fact in many countries of the world, certainly in the US, UK and Australia, all marine VHF radios must be able to receive on Channel 16 (156.80 MHz) and Channel 6 (156.3 MHz) for distress and intership safety, plus another working channel for general communications. These are mandatory, but from then on you can choose whatever extra channels you want.

As holder of a ship's station licence, however limited, you are responsible for the quality and accuracy of frequency on your set. Maintenance of radios, however, is difficult because they are highly complicated and in many cases only licensed technicians are allowed to work on the transmitters. So you need to have a qualified technician check the set out every six months or at least every year. But there are certain precautions you can take. You should have on board the type of fuse needed for that particular set or sets. And it's sensible, particularly if you're on a yacht where the backstay or mast acts as the main aerial, to have an emergency aerial which can be rapidly clipped to its mounting and which is pre-tuned to the set so that you can continue sending if the mast is lost. The radio will, of course, then have less range than with the much taller mast aerials, but there are some tricks of the trade which can help you overcome this. For instance, I was skipper of a yacht which was dismasted 350 nautical miles from land in the Southern Ocean in winter and the mast broke only half a metre (two feet) above deck so there was little chance of rigging a very tall jury. We did manage a 9 metre (27 foot) mast but we didn't incorporate a radio aerial. The emergency aerial was three metres (nine feet) tall and screwed straight into a socket on the deck. The dismasting happened between sunset and dark and so as soon as we got the vessel snugged up for the night we set about trying to let people know where we were. Since we'd sighted only two ships in a week we knew that getting a message out about our predicament was important. At first we tried across four wavelengths and with three PAN messages on each, we got no response. We were unable to get any response from the aerial for 24 hours, although we did hear weather forecasts and other information from the coastal radio stations. In the end we discovered we could jump in on the coastal radio station at the end of transmission on a particular frequency after the operator had said: 'Any other messages on this frequency?' And so we were able to explain our plight. I think an operator on a particular frequency and listening just to that frequency, will be more likely to hear you than if the operator were on an all-frequencies watch.

There are now available on yachts and motor boats computers which will monitor just about everything that a skipper can ever want to know: engine revolutions for twin installations, fuel and water consumption rates, fuel and water levels in tanks, water temperature outside, air temperature, true and apparent wind direction, velocity made good (VMG), power supply polarity, ventilation and blower system capacity, automatic bilge level sensors—the list is endless. But the functions that are carried out are invaluable. Such computers are not terribly expensive and they enable you to run a series of checks and keep an eye on the basic operation of the yacht at any time. The sophistication of computerised monitoring plus the eagle eye of a good sailor make a very nice combination indeed.

F A U L T   F I N D I N G

A handy fault-finding device is the double-function, battery powered test light, which can take the place of a voltmeter and/or ohmmeter. If a circuit is working, but in poor order, the light will not shine with full brilliance. If the circuit is open, the light will not glow. The best attribute of the lamp is that it gives a clear signal, whatever test function it is operating, whereas

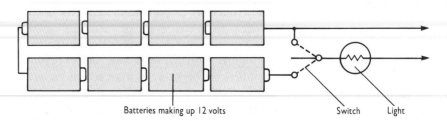

Diagram 3.5 *A double function, battery-powered test light which can be used to find faults in any electrical circuit.*

Batteries making up 12 volts   Switch   Light dial or gauge readings can mislead an amateur. The light should be made up as in diagram 3.5.

The batteries make up into a 12 volt total. The globe (bulb) should draw about a quarter of an amp. Use alligator clips on the test wires. When switched to IN the clips complete a circuit through the batteries and switch to the globe (bulb). On OUT the circuit is through the switch to the globe (bulb), and the globe (bulb) cannot shine without an external 12 volt source of power. The following is your check list for a 12 volt system.

Make sure all the switches in the system are turned on, but that fuses or contact breakers are in place. Leave the battery earthed (grounded), but detach the positive wire. If you have a master switch, make sure it is closed.

Ship's Circuits

When you put the test light—on OUT—between the positive terminal and the removed cable, the lamp should not light. If it does light, current is leaking, either to a circuit, or to earth (ground). If it is to earth (ground) your boat is in danger of suffering severe stray current corrosion. To locate the leak, disconnect one circuit after the other until the light goes out, then search for the fault in that circuit.

Appliances

Make sure the item being tested is turned off. Switch to IN. Clip one end to the housing and the other, one at a time, to the pins of the power point. The light should not come on, except when connected to the earth (ground) pin—the one with the green wire. If these tests fail, the implement is faulty, and dangerous, and must be repaired.

Motors

On IN, connect the leads to the terminals. It should glow. If not, turn the shaft, and if the light glows intermittently check the brushes or commutator, which may be worn.

To check whether there is leakage inside the motor, connect one alligator clip to the housing and test the motor terminals in turn. If the test lamp glows, there is leakage, which could drain the battery. The motor needs fixing. This test does not apply to the starter motor, or to induction motors.

Fuses

On IN, connect the clips to each end of the fuse, which should glow if it is in good order.

Circuit Breakers

On IN, connect to each end of the circuit. If it is open the globe (bulb) will not light.

Finding Breaks in Wire

On IN, connect to each end of the wire. If the light does not glow, there is a break in the line.

Engine Points

Switch to OUT. With the ignition turned on, clip one lead to the engine block and the other to the wire from the coil to the distributor. When you crank the engine, the light should be bright and should blink on and off as the points open and close.

If the light does not respond as it should, engine timing may need to be adjusted. Leave the test light connected as is. Turn the engine over slowly and check cylinder one as the timing marks start to line up. The light should glow as the marks align. If the light does not match the alignment, rotate the distributor body to adjust.

I have not suggested a test for generators or alternators as there are so many types that specific tests are needed to determine which each is. The books in Further References (page 305) contain relevant advice. You can use instruments, if you like, to test your equipment, but it is unnecessary unless you are qualified to do testing of a higher order than listed above.

Electrical Tools

- 12 volt soldering iron
- Two function trouble light and test leads
- Cutters
- Pliers (electrician's, longnose, diagonal)
- Wire stripper and crimper

- Ignition tool set
- Ammeter, voltmeter, ohmmeter (optional)
- Hydrometer
- Grease for battery terminals

Electrical Spares

- Drive belts for alternator/generator
- Several of each type of fuse aboard
- Several of each type of globe (bulb) on board
- Brushes for motors

- Solder (combined type with built-in flux)
- Electrical tape
- Moisture inhibitor
- Box of bits

WEATHER

Earlier in the book I talked about the growing awareness of sailors as they learn and become more confident. First of all their world is the size of the part of the boat they're in, and as their confidence grows, the world becomes the size of the boat, then it's the next wave, later it might extend five or six kilometres (three or four miles). Then, as experience develops it covers all the other boats in the fleet and eventually—certainly with navigators—there is a concept of the total voyage.

For instance, a sailor who has learned celestial navigation, even if not completely, would be a clod if he or she had no idea of how infinitesimal a boat is in the universal scale. Yet it's by the universal scale of stars that celestial navigation occurs.

The same sort of conception of scale should be applied to weather if it is to be thoroughly understood and forecast.

THE EARTH

So, there's a ball called Earth spinning in space on its axis and rotating completely once every day, even wobbling slightly when it does, and spinning so fast that none of us can grasp the fact of its motion. As the Earth spins, centrifugal force tries to throw everything off into space. Gravity counteracts this force, but there are other effects of the rotation of the Earth—one of which has a profound effect on how weather forms. The Coriolis effect, which is the result of the spinning of the Earth and air being dragged around by the Earth, causes the high and low pressure weather systems to rotate and the pressure in each to slowly equalise as the low pressure system decays. Without this effect, air from high pressure systems would flow directly into low pressure systems and fill them up. (See Pressure below page 64.)

Diagram 4.1 *Two thirds of the air enveloping the earth is below the height of Mt Everest.*

RADIATION AND MOISTURE

The fundamental ingredients of weather are the air, and the water that's in that air. The layer of air around our world is so thin that two-thirds of all of it is below the top of Mt Everest—that is a mere 14 kilometres (seven miles) or so.

The sun's radiation during the day massively increases the temperature of

Diagram 4.2 *Radiation from the sun heats the earth by day. The cycle reverses at night as the earth cools.*

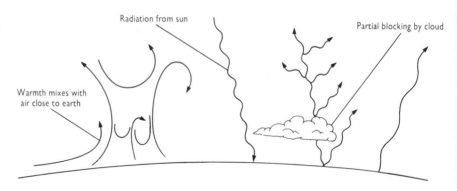

Radiation from sun

Partial blocking by cloud

Warmth mixes with air close to earth

the land and sea, although not uniformly. Some areas heat faster than others, and to a greater degree—a good example being a patch of bare rock on a summer's day compared with surrounding grassland. Most people on a picnic would rather sit on the grass and not just because it's softer.

As radiation from the sun warms the surface of the Earth, some is being reflected from the top layer of the clouds, some is absorbed by the clouds, yet more is absorbed by the little particles of dust and sand and water and pollution that are in the skies.

At night the cycle reverses and heat is radiated from the surface of the Earth and the seas. Some is trapped by the lower levels of the cloud layer and warms up the land beneath. By comparison, desert areas are clear of cloud and become very cold at night because so much of the radiation is lost. Because of these differences in heating and cooling there are shafts of air of different temperature moving up and down and across the Earth's surface.

To complicate matters even further the shafts of air contain varying amounts of moisture. And the amount of moisture a given volume of air can hold is a direct function of temperature. So the variables begin to mount up. If we were honest, we would have to admit the beginning of some feeling of compassion for the weather forecasters.

PRESSURE

So we now have a picture of air rising and falling and being dragged around attached to the surface of the Earth. But because of the disparity in the speed of rotation of the Earth between the poles (nil) and the equator (1000 mph (1610 km/h) east to west) and because centrifugal force tries to throw the air at the equator towards the poles, we get the last great variable: the movement of masses of air northwards and southwards—their movement depending upon the latitude.

It is interesting at this stage to have a look at any good chart of the world's major wind patterns. Perhaps the best one of all is the Roaring Forties of the southern hemisphere where tiny tips of land stick into winds that rotate almost endlessly from west to east. Those tips of land are Cape Horn, the South Island of New Zealand and the southern part of Tasmania—all interesting areas of water for the yachtsman. There is a similar belt of westerly winds in the northern hemisphere but because the Atlantic is a relatively small ocean,

and because great land masses interpose, they don't have the predominance
and simplicity of the Roaring Forties.

There is one more major variable that affects the bubbling, seething dance
of the weather. Hot air and cold air have different pressures and therefore
there are systems of cold low pressure and hot high pressure moving all over
the face of the Earth, interacting with each other. The high pressure is trying
to equalise the low pressure areas all the time, but, as we have seen, it is
not just a simple matter of the wind blowing from the high pressure directly
into the low.

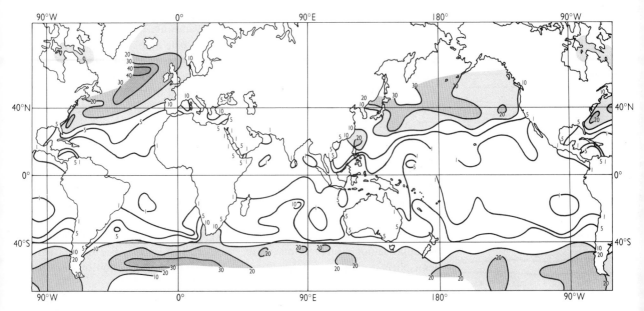

Diagram 4.3 *The diagram above, from* Meteorology for Mariners, *shows the
percentage frequency of winds of Force 7 (Beaufort scale) and higher in January. The
diagram below shows the percentage frequency of winds of Force 7 or higher in July,
also from* Meteorology for Mariners.

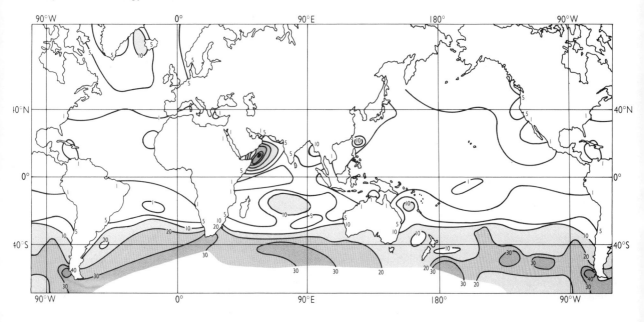

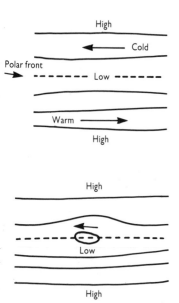

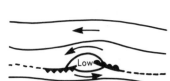

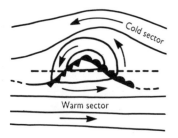

Diagram 4.4 *Four stages in the development of a depression.*

LOW PRESSURE CELLS

The rotation of the Earth peels blobs of cold dense air away from the polar caps towards the lower latitudes. As they peel away they move in a generally west to east direction. In the northern hemisphere they move from the north to the south and in the southern hemisphere from the south to the north. The Coriolis effect 'bends' their tracks, giving a generally south-easterly resultant in the northern hemisphere, and north-easterly in the southern hemisphere.

These 'blobs' or low pressure cells, are often associated with strong winds blowing along the 'front'—roughly at right angles to the track of the cell, as can be seen in diagram 4.4. High pressure cells are big and fat and lazy. They bring sunshine, warm weather and the winds are light. When the angry blob of cold air breaks away from the polar belt and starts squeezing the high, trying to push it out of the way, it meets resistance. But the inexorable laws governing the movement of the cold blob of air means that the winds around the high pressure system (clockwise in the northern hemisphere and anti-clockwise in the southern hemisphere) begin to increase, signalling the approach of a frontal system.

FRONTAL SYSTEM

The leading edge of a low pressure cell is usually called a **cold front**. As the front advances the winds in the high pressure system begin to strengthen from the north, then north-west in the southern hemisphere, and from the south, then south-east in the northern hemisphere. (From now on we will describe the approaching system as one in the southern hemisphere. For the northern hemisphere, simply interpolate the opposite winds and direction of travel of the system.)

As the front advances, the winds swing into the north and finally freshen considerably from the north-west. They may blow at greater than gale force, depending on the strength of the system, until the arrival of the front. The wind then backs into the south-west and begins to blow as hard, or harder, from the new direction. Diagrams 4.5–4.6, showing cross-sections of a cold front and a warm front, give a graphic indication of what happens.

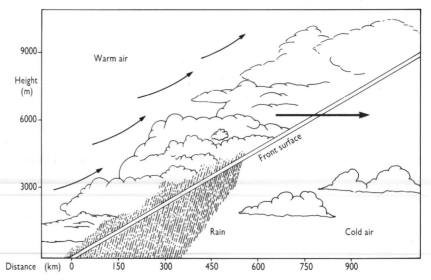

Diagram 4.5 *Vertical section through a warm front.*

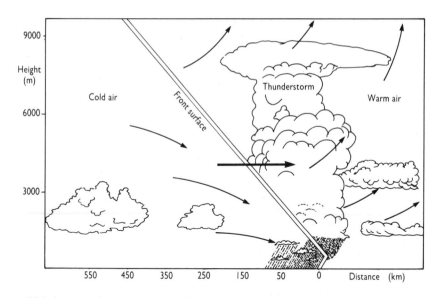

Diagram 4.6 *Vertical section through a cold front.*

This is a continuous process. The cold angry blobs are breaking away from the polar regions continually. As the cold air is forced towards the equator all the forces of nature try to make the pressure and the temperature equalise. It is the result of those forces that gives you the weather you experience. And it is these angry cold blobs which are the interest of the navigator. The person crossing an ocean will know that the closer to the polar areas he or she travels, the more of these 'lows' will be met and the stronger they'll get.

HIGH PRESSURE SYSTEMS

In the area of the highs, conditions generally will be a yachtsman's dream— steady winds, bright sunshine, ideal conditions. But as the high gets closer to the sailing yacht, so the wind drops, until there may be none. If it weren't for another low coming across and starting the whole sequence again, the yachtsman would enjoy the balmy conditions for days on end—and the yacht wouldn't be moving.

The high systems which bring us this lovely weather don't have any warning signs to say they are coming. They are really left over after the cold fronts have gone through. A stationary observer watching a vigorous depression over a number of days would have seen the weather go from good to less good, from hot, windy and oppressive, to cold and squally, and even with gale conditions as the front passes through. Then the winds swing around, following their circular path until they get into the good weather pattern again. The cycle goes on for ever.

But there are some consistent patterns in the position of high and low systems over the hemispheres, leading to the basic circulation.

BASIC CIRCULATION

The basic circulation in the southern hemisphere is that a belt of high pressure generally exists near 30 degrees south, and, to some extent it follows the sun as it meanders north and south of the equator. The strongest high pressure systems are over the South Atlantic, the South Indian Ocean and the eastern side of the South Pacific. Australia has a good high seasonally during winter and that high extends into the western area of the Pacific.

It's now suggested that at between 60 and 70 degrees south there's another area of low pressure and that the pressure increases again on getting to the Antarctic land mass.

North of the belt of high pressure that is at 30 degrees, the pressure gradually becomes lower and lower until it reaches the low pressure belt around the equator. A similar belt of low pressure, which in fact is part of the main equatorial low pressure belt, is in the northern hemisphere; then at about 30 degrees north is the equivalent of the high pressure that's seen in the southern hemisphere. However, because of the comparatively large amounts of land in the northern hemisphere, this high pressure belt doesn't behave with quite the same 'certainty' as does the southern belt. Over the large masses of the Atlantic and Pacific Oceans the belt remains fairly constant at around 30 degrees north, moving up and down only with the movement of the sun.

Over the continents there are quite different systems operating in summer and winter. During winter the belt is really two huge blobs, one over Asia and the other over North America. In the summer these high pressure blobs are mainly over the water—over the North Atlantic and the North Pacific. They are separated by the deep monsoon patterns which form over Asia. The northern polar regions seem to have higher pressure, as in the south.

These generalisations about the turbulence of weather patterns, it should be stressed, are simplistic and give only an outline of the sequence of events. The reality would hardly ever coincide with the theoretical. But given this model of the world and its moving masses of air—up and down, sideways and circular—we can make some more specific observations.

T H E   W E A T H E R   M A P

Now is the time to come to terms with the weather map as seen in newspapers and on television sets. The graphics on television weather maps are usually the work of people who understand very well how to capture your attention, but probably have no knowledge of the weather. They are reaching for an audience that wants to know what to wear tomorrow, not whether there will be a gale when they go sailing. When the forecaster starts trying to unravel the weather to prepare a synoptic chart for us he or she is dealing in three dimensions, with systems travelling at different heights and different speeds, and is trying to work out the interaction between them. For us it is easier.

Diagram 4.7 is of a typical synoptic chart. This will give you a graphic shorthand rendition of what's happening with the weather at one time. These graphics are another of our highly ingenious methods of portraying natural phenomena with symbols that can be generally understood and uniformly interpreted.

You'll need to know some terms. **Isobars** are lines joining points of equal barometric pressure. In areas which have not submitted a report, the lines are smoothed out to give an indication of the pressure. When all these observations have been put together and linked with information from weather satellites and other sources, a map is drawn which grossly indicates the areas of high and low pressure.

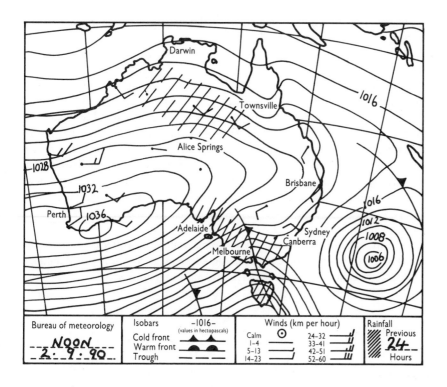

Diagram 4.7 *Typical synoptic chart. The arrows correspond to wind strength as shown in the table included in the chart.*

The **gradient** of the isobars in the various systems is what interests the navigator. The normal rule is that the closer together the isobars are, the stronger the wind will be. At a point where the high pressure system is touched by a low pressure system there is usually a **front**, which can be seen by a dramatic change in the direction of the isobars, usually of about 90 degrees, but sometimes of up to 120 degrees. Where those kinks appear in the isobars a line is drawn to indicate the advancing front of the depression system.

The front is normally indicated by a thick line, and on it there may be little 'pimples' which can be pointed or round. If pointed they indicate that a **cold front** is approaching. Rounded, conversely indicates a **warm front**. Sometimes there will be a double curve in the front, with a sort of cell of isobars tightly wrapped in the corner. This is called an **occluded front**.

Even though there may be warm fronts approaching, these warm fronts will be linked with a **depression**—a cyclonic system. The isobars give you your best indication of wind strength.

WIND STRENGTH

Normally, as we have said above, isobars which are close together indicate a steep gradient (difference) between areas of high and low pressure, and the steeper the gradient the stronger the wind will be. However, there is an exception in the tropics, where isobars are much wider apart than in higher latitudes, except during hurricanes. (If you ever have the misfortune to look at a synoptic chart depicting a hurricane, as I have, you cannot mistake what you are seeing. It is like looking into a funnel.) In the tropics, quite lazy-looking, far apart isobars can indicate strong winds.

A further aspect of the chart is that wind direction and strength are indicated by arrows. The direction is indicated by the way the arrows point and the strength by the number of feathers on the arrows. There is an explanatory scale with each chart to show what strength is indicated by the feathers. There is a sample scale in diagram 4.7.

Let's study the chart on page 69, which shows a front about 300 nautical miles away from your position in Sydney. You have heard on the radio that it is travelling at 30 mph (48 km/h), so you can forecast roughly when it is going to reach you. You can see what the wind directions will be: north-east until the front arrives and south-west after it. To the south-east is a severe depression. While you still might get some nasty weather even before that indicated by the chart (because local effects can create quite severe conditions for a short time) you now have a reasonable indication of what might be in store for you if you go for a sail. As a matter of course, you should keep in touch with the situation by listening to the radio news.

Normally you will be sailing in your home waters, so you'll understand the language. If you happen to be travelling in a foreign area, where your language is not the one being used, you can pick up long-range forecasts.

D E P R E S S I O N S

The weather patterns that most interest yachtsmen are the depressions and any associated fronts. We have seen how they are created, now we can discuss their effects, and then their anatomy.

In many areas of the world the arrival of a depression and a cold front is such a regular and well known phenomenon that there are terms for the winds. If you are interested to study *Meteorology for Mariners* (see Further References on page 305) you'll find that a great many of the world's winds are listed and described thoroughly there.

Perhaps the most famous areas for the sudden onset of dramatic wind changes are off eastern South America and south-eastern Australia. The pattern in these places will help the understanding of these weather frontal systems. In each case the sea in question is to the east of a large land mass, and one which gets very hot. In each case the high pressure system has heated the land to extreme temperatures and the last winds of the dying high pressure system have swung into the north-west. Coming off the land, as they do, they are hot and gusty. In the high latitudes south of the areas we are discussing are huge areas of ocean with almost unbroken fetch allowing the wind to roar in unobstructed for thousands of miles from Antarctica.

Pretend you are now an observer on a boat in one of those areas on a hot summer's day. The scene is of strong, gusty north-westerly winds, flat seas generally because the land wind hasn't had enough fetch to build them up; wonderful sailing conditions and very, very hot air. This can change, literally in seconds, and there may be little or no indication from the sky. Usually there is some indication—perhaps a long soft cigar-shaped roll of fluffy cloud, often with clear sky behind it, which looks quite innocent. You are a stranger in the area, but the people on the other boats are not: their crews are reefing.

Next, if you are lucky, you will see a line of white coming across the water towards you. When the front, for that's what it is, reaches your vessel, the wind will change from sub-gale force from the north-west to gale force or more from the south-west. It will happen in less time than it took you to read the last paragraph.

There is a classic videotape of *Windward Passage* and *Kialoa* sailing in the Sydney-Hobart race in 1977 when they were caught by just such a wind. Those giant boats, crewed by some of the best sailors in the world, were under spinnakers and staysails when they were hit. Within 30 seconds they were in a wind of 35 knots from an angle 90 degrees different from the one they were set for. Before they could bring their boats under control they had to square away before the raging sou'wester—which was still building—and run for 12 nautical miles, nearly an hour at the sort of speed they travel, and continue their race to Hobart into what was now a strong headwind. The wind is called a southerly buster. The same wind off South America is called a pampero. The world record for speed of increase in wind strength was claimed by an observer with a proper instrument at St Kilda pier in Melbourne in the early part of this century when the wind went from a calm to 92 mph (148 km/h) in 28 seconds.

While cloud may not indicate the approach of such a front, there may be other indications. An obvious indication, in the case of a very strong change, can be a line of foam across the water, particularly if, as is quite common, the wind has dropped just before the arrival of the front, and the sea is calm. This telltale line may be up to a foot high as it is pushed across the surface by the squall behind it.

A more common, although more subtle, indication of change is **sea smoke**. At long range sea smoke is a slight blurring of visibility when looking towards the front, particularly if there is land nearby. The land will seem hazy, as though seen through cigarette smoke, and slightly shaky. As the squall gets nearer the water will be seen to have a shimmering smoke above it (actually cold air beginning to condense above the warmer sea). As the front gets really close, whitecaps appear behind the smoke. By now you should have storm gear on the boat because a fierce storm is about to descend upon you.

ANATOMY OF A DEPRESSION

The prime condition for a depression to start is that warm air near the polar front must be moving east faster than cold air. As the two air masses move one against the other, the faster warm air begins to rotate through friction against the cold air. This begins a 'swelling'—a mixture of warm and cold air—which becomes turbulent and breaks away from the polar front (see diagram 4.8).

The depression reaches its lowest pressure at the cold front, where cold polar air cuts under the warmer, less dense air of the dying high pressure system (see diagram 4.9).

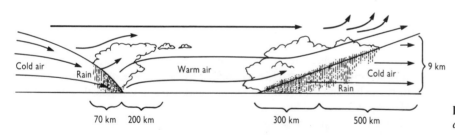

Diagram 4.8 *Formation of a depression.*

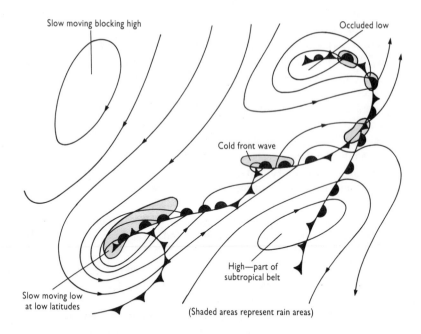

Diagram 4.9 *A family of depressions.*

TELLTALE SIGNS OF A DEPRESSION

The first indication of a depression is very, very high cirrus cloud—as high in the sky as jets like to travel. It may take the form of the classic mares' tails. It may show as a myriad little parachutes in the sky, little puffy clouds, or it may be the equally classic 'fingers' pointing from the direction of the depression and spreading out over the sky. This may happen as much as 48 hours before the front arrives.

As the relatively warm air is forced up over the denser cold air, the cloud will become thicker and lower, until quite heavy cloud with thundery conditions arises. In the meantime the wind will be increasing in strength, blowing harder and harder almost parallel with the axis of the approaching front. The temperature will increase steadily until it becomes quite hot and oppressive. The actual temperature reached will depend on the time of the year.

By the time the front is perhaps 300 nautical miles away the cloud will be much closer to the ground and there may be some rain. The barometric pressure will be falling. The closer to the centre of the depression an observer is, the more likely there is to be rain, which will sometimes be very heavy.

By the time the front is 150 to 100 nautical miles away there will be dense cloud overhead, heavy rain, and scud may be forming. If the rain has come before any strong increase in wind strength, get set for a long blow. The old rhyme 'Wind before rain, soon set sail again' doesn't apply in this case. When the rain comes first, the bad conditions last longest. The cold front is now very close.

The dense air of the front is acting like a chisel cutting wood, sliding under the warm air, forcing the warm air up into the sky. The pressure will drop sharply and the wind will back, becoming hard and squally. There will certainly be heavy cumulonimbus (thunder clouds) and if the associated thunderstorms break near you they are likely to be severe.

When the front arrives at the observer's position the pressure will rise quite sharply, then continue to rise steadily afterwards. The wind will back further and usually will blow harder from the new direction than it did from the old—sometimes dramatically harder.

Soon after the passage of the front, if the conditions behind it are stable, conditions will become quite good, although considerably colder. There may be a little cloud, bright sunshine, crystal clear air and a hard wind. Sailing in these conditions, just after the passage of a strong low or depression can be most exhilarating because of the freshness of the air, the sparkling quality of the scene, the far visibility, and the surge of adrenalin that comes from sailing in brisk conditions.

A further phenomenon of the depression that we should consider is the **occlusion**. The front has become occluded when the wedge-like cold air has lifted the entire warm air mass off the ground. Occlusion must occur before the lower pressure of the depression can be filled in by the surrounding air. The depression then ends its life and is replaced by warm and stable conditions.

Secondary Depression

Some understanding of **secondary depressions**, depressions which occur close to or within the system of a major depression, is necessary for safe ocean sailing. In many cases these smaller depressions do nothing more than confuse the issue, and create a slight difficulty in forecasting what the winds will do.

But sometimes a secondary depression will get close enough to the primary depression for them to merge and deepen, and very severe weather conditions can follow. Anybody who is at sea, or intends to go to sea, when there are two depressions near each other on the synoptic chart should be very wary indeed. There have been cases where almost dead depressions have been revived by a strong secondary and the resulting conditions have approached those of a hurricane. Keep an eye out if weather reports indicate that the central pressure is deepening, particularly if it is rapid. Remember that the lower the pressure at the centre of the depression, the worse the weather that is associated with it, because of the difference in pressure between it and the masses of air round it.

LOCAL EFFECT WINDS

When there isn't enough wind, the sailor has to try to find some, and so needs to know where it can be found. Winds at sea tend to be steadier in direction and strength than on the land, mainly because there are fewer obstructions. It stands to reason that the chopping up of air and water that occurs near mountains and estuaries, and the effect of heat discrepancy between land and sea, interfere with the steady flow of the wind. Most of the time the ocean cruising or racing person will take for granted that wind flow will be steady, and most of the time it is. But when sailing along a coast, or approaching one, more complicated effects begin to take place and the sailor needs to be aware of them.

The most common effects are **land** and **sea breezes**. As the boat steadily approaches land during the day, particularly in summer, and particularly in places that are in any case warm, there will be a sea breeze. Hot air over the land rises and cooler air from the sea comes in to replace it. These sea breezes can develop into quite strong winds when the heat disparity is at its greatest. Sea breezes of 25 to 30 knots are not uncommon. They normally arise a little before midday, when the sun has heated the land thoroughly, and they die out from sunset as the sun's radiation ceases. These sea breezes usually will not vary in direction and consequently one of the curses of listening to weather forecasts throughout the world is that the announcer will say 'afternoon sea breezes'. They and everybody who lives in the area know where the afternoon sea breezes come from, but the visitor doesn't. It would be better if the forecaster said there would be an afternoon southerly breeze or a north-easterly sea breeze.

After the sea breeze has died down there will be a lull for a couple of hours during which there will probably be light and variable winds of perhaps five knots or so. The land radiates the heat it received from the sun during the day, and the sea becomes warmer than the land. Then the colder land air will blow to the sea to replace the warm air rising above the sea. Land breezes are almost invariably less strong than sea breezes, and they tend to cross the shore at right angles, so that their direction is easier to pick than the sea breeze, which, being stronger, modifies the land effect.

Always remember, the wind, whenever possible, will cross the land at right angles, or as near as it can get to it. Even if a sea breeze is slanting in to a shore, when very close in it will tend to turn and cross the land at right angles. A classic example is along the great, curving, wonderful beach at Surfers' Paradise, on the Gold Coast of Queensland, Australia. In a winter race, several skippers who thoroughly understood the behaviour of sea breezes sailed inside the second line of breaking waves and lifted right along the curve of the coastline. Those boats which had sailed directly across the beach on what looked like the shortest course, were left several nautical miles behind.

Topography makes a difference, too. If there are high mountains the land breeze may skip the close inshore area and drop down further out to sea than normally expected. Close inshore it would be an absolute calm—one to frustrate the very best sailor. If the hills were not so high, and were set further back from the shore, they would create 'bullets' (puffs) (sudden short gusts) from air dropping down the front of the hills and adding their velocity to that of the already established land breeze. If the hills were regular, the breeze would also be more likely to be regular. If they were broken, the breeze itself would be broken. If there is cloud the heat loss on land would be less, and so the strength of the land breeze would be less. The variations are infinite.

This is where local knowledge and overall experience is important. Knowing the habits of the wind gives a sailor an enormous advantage and helps a really good sailor to understand what is happening locally.

F O G

While wind is our main concern, we can't ignore fog, or any weather effect like heavy rain storms, mist, sleet or snow, that greatly diminishes visibility. The method of dealing with fog is constant—try to avoid getting into it, and if you are caught, follow the rules about speed and sound signals listed in the International Regulations for Preventing Collisions at Sea.

Fog is much more common, and therefore important, in some parts of the world than others. On the eastern seaboards of almost any continent apart from North America and Asia, fog is unusual. On the other coasts, where fog is common, it is a worrying hazard. It could be argued that fog is more dangerous where sailors don't expect it and aren't used to it, but I believe fog can disorientate the experienced as well as the inexperienced. *Meteorology for Mariners* lists several kinds of fog, but what sort one is in is academic to yachtsmen. The sailor's only concern is that visibility is reduced and there is danger. But knowledge of how fog is formed can help in forecasting it, and makes avoidance easier.

ADVECTION FOG

This is the most common form of fog. Easily forecast, it consists of cool air flowing over the warm sea and reaching its dew point, so that the water vapour condenses and hangs suspended in a very fine cloud.

RADIATION FOG

Radiation fog forms almost invariably over land and normally affects the sailor only when the fog is in a harbour or a river, or drifts perhaps a few kilometres out to sea. Radiation fog is formed when a high level of water vapour in the air is in contact with the ground, there is limited cloud cover, the ground is comparatively cold and damp and there is a light breeze to blow the fog out to sea. Radiation fog is the more dangerous of the two, to my mind, because it occurs where sailors are making landfall, where they may ignore the rules of safety in fog because they are nearly home, and where they may be reluctant to do the seamanlike thing and keep away. How to behave in fog is discussed under Navigation below page 145.

TROPICAL REVOLVING STORMS

Before we talk about these storms we must note **Buys Ballot's Law**. It's a very strange name, but it's hard to forget. Buys Ballot was a meteorologist who formulated, in 1857, a law which gives an observer a good idea of the position of the centre of a depression without the use of any instruments. The law is:

IN NORTH LATITUDES, FACE THE WIND AND THE BAROMETER WILL
BE LOWEST TO YOUR RIGHT.

IN SOUTH LATITUDES, FACE THE WIND AND THE BAROMETER WILL
BE LOWEST TO YOUR LEFT.

This means that the wind circulation in an anti-cyclone must be clockwise in the north and anti-clockwise, in the south. But the law has significant further use in tracking the path of tropical revolving storms from a slow-moving sailing yacht. The method (northern hemisphere) is to raise your right arm to horizontal while facing the true wind, then move your arm backwards as far as it will comfortably go. You will be pointing at the centre of the storm. The opposite (left arm) is the method for the southern hemisphere.

Tropical revolving storms (TRS) are the most devastatingly terrifying manifestations of power on the face of the Earth. They unleash the force of thousands of hydrogen bombs. The average sailor is unlikely ever to see one, even if he or she sails every weekend and every holiday. This is because most pleasure sailing takes place in the temperate latitudes, or higher, where TRS rarely go. But the cruising sailor might, because although TRS are most prevalent at certain times of the year, they have also happened in most months of the year. They do sometimes reach the temperate latitudes. Caribbean hurricanes (the local name for a TRS) often reach New England in the US, and even further up to Labrador in Canada, and there are also cases of the storms of the Mexican coast reaching lower California. Cyclones from northern Australia have reached well south, even to the Roaring Forties. Revolving storms can have markedly varied lives: short, medium, long; sometimes they almost die out and then intensify; very often they travel slowly in one direction, losing their power as they go, and then recurve and travel in a new direction, picking up speed and power as they go.

The only sensible precaution is to reduce the risk of being caught by a hurricane, tornado, typhoon, cyclone or willy-willy (these are all names for revolving storms). Do not travel at the times they are most likely to occur. These times are listed in the Admiralty Sailing directions (Pilots) for the area, and in *Meteorology for Mariners*, for various parts of the world.

Unfortunately, this can be very difficult. Along the coast of China, for example, typhoons have been recorded in each month of the year. So if you followed the rule of avoidance to the extreme, there would be no traffic along that coast at all, and there is a very great deal of traffic. But no sensible person should cruise through storm areas unless they are certain they can get adequate warning and can reach shelter in time. (Still don't forget the basic rule of the sea, which is that, if caught in bad conditions, it can be more dangerous to try to achieve shelter than to stay at sea and fight the conditions —even a storm.)

THE WARNING SIGNS

The first sign, assuming you are in the 20 or so degrees of latitude north or south of the equator where these storms normally begin, may be a heavy rolling swell. The swell surges are the remains of huge decayed waves generated by the storm, but which travel faster than the storm. The day before the storm often is unusually clear and visibility is very great, much as happens in temperate latitudes before the arrival of a depression. Winds are warm and gusty.

The sky at sunset may be lurid and threatening, and the wind may change direction and strength markedly. The air will be oppressive and the cloud formations will point like an arrowhead towards the storm. If you have these signs and are beginning to suspect a storm is approaching, check the barometer which you must have for ocean cruising. Have on board the Tables for Diurnal Variation of Barometric Pressure. These tables, as the title suggest, list the twice daily variations that normally occur to air pressure throughout the world. If, after correcting the ship's barometer readings with information from the tables, the reading is 3Mb or more below the mean pressure for the time of the year there is a chance of a storm. If it is 5Mb or more below there's not much doubt there's a storm and it is about 200 nautical miles away. From then on the navigator must keep reading the barometer (every half hour) to see what the trend is.

THUNDERSTORMS

Thunderstorms cannot develop until the amount of vertical convection is so great that the typical, towering cumulonimbus clouds have formed, reaching as high as 30,000 feet into the sky. The rising air, rushing upward at about 1,600 feet a minute creates charges of electricity with enormous potential. This occurs when the typically large raindrops which precede a thunderstorm are torn apart by the violent updraught. Lightning occurs when the electrical charges are discharged either to earth or to another cloud. Thunder is the noise created when air expands because it is instantly made white hot.

A handy way to get a rough estimate of the distance away of a thunderstorm is to count the seconds between the lightning flash and the thunderclap. Very roughly speaking each second represents a mile.

From a yachtsman's point of view thunderstorms are a nuisance. A boat directly beneath such a storm will experience erratic winds from zephyrs to 50 knots with no warning and even the most expert crew will find it hard to reef and unreef fast enough to be neither over- or under-powered. The result is that damage is easily suffered.

One phenomenon of such storms that is handy, though, is that air rushes into the front of the storm as it is sucked in to create the violent upsurge of air that characterises them. If the storm is isolated (not part of a frontal system) the wind well away from it may be quite slight. It is worth sailing towards the storm to get stronger winds. But don't overdo it. At the back of the storm there is no wind at all, and there won't be any for quite a long time.

Remember, also, that you won't always be able to tell which is the front of the storm.

GENERAL BEHAVIOUR OF A TROPICAL REVOLVING STORM (TRS)

If you are caught by a TRS there are well-defined rules for getting away from it. These storms, as they rotate, are travelling around an anti-cyclone. It's quite common for the isobars in the quadrant of the storm next to the anti-cyclone to be squeezed tighter together than in the other three quadrants of the storm. This gives the quadrant the strongest winds and it is known as the **dangerous quadrant**. In there the wind and seas are absolutely chaotic. Every child who's played in a bath with toy boats knows that making waves with one hand results in waves that are long and regular—the little boats don't sink. But when both hands are used and the water is pushed towards one hand by the other, pointed, unpredictable, random waves occur and the tiny fleet is overwhelmed. That is precisely what happens in a TRS. At the centre of this very deep depression the wind drops, the sun shines and things appear quite normal again, although the seas are still mountainous. The 'eye' of the storm is passing. When the eye has passed over the observer the wind comes in again, just as hard or harder, from the opposite direction. That's when the chaotic seas occur.

There is some general uniformity in the movement of these storms, but it cannot be taken for granted that any one storm will follow the pattern of the average.

RECURVATURE

Most storms establish a fairly constant direction after they have formed, but after perhaps a few days, sometimes even less, they slow down and appear likely to decay. However, they do not. They begin moving in a different direction, often at greater speed, and they intensify as they move.

A sailor caught in such a storm must continually check for this **recurvature**. Not all storms do recurve, some have an irregular track, and some, particularly in the western Pacific, may loop so that they cross their own track. Usually these storms decay when they reach the temperate latitudes as they become absorbed in the larger systems of the depressions. But sometimes they do not and they travel further on until they 'die' in quite high latitudes.

However, the general movement of storms follows the same pattern in both hemispheres, although in opposite directions. A northern hemisphere storm goes to the west, bends more towards the north pole, then the north-west and finally north and north-east. In the south they go west, south-west, south and finally south-east.

Until they recurve these storms generally travel at relatively low speeds— as low as five knots and up to about 15 knots—but after recurvature they can double that speed, which is added to the wind speed in the dangerous quadrant. When plotting to avoid or run away from such a storm it is vital to keep the danger of recurvature in mind.

Although one quarter of the storm is the most dangerous, the other quadrant on the same side is considered little better, so for the sake of avoidance, that half of the storm is called the **dangerous semi-circle**. This is also because the dangerous semi-circle is on the side towards which the storm is likely to recurve. In the northern hemisphere the dangerous semi-circle is on the right hand of the path of the storm, and in the south, the left. It is imperative to head away from that path.

FIND OUT ALL YOU CAN

The smaller the vessel, the harder it is to know about a storm that may be a long way off, but is travelling fast relative to the small boat's speed. Larger vessels will probably have weather facsimile, and full time radio officers monitoring warnings and plotting the position and intensity of the storm. Smaller vessels will be reduced to finding out about the storm from weather forecasts, which shows the value of keeping a listening watch on the radio for appreciable parts of the day. Once a storm is identified, one crew member MUST keep listening for position updates. If the weather warning is complete it will indicate the position of the centre of the storm and will give a corrected barometer reading, a description of the weather conditions prevailing, and a course and speed of movement of the storm.

The skipper of any vessel finding itself in a storm area has obligations under the International Convention for the Safety of Life at Sea to tell other ships in the area, or any weather station or shore radio station of conditions and of where he or she is. The skipper can give a position by latitude and longitude, or if this is uncertain, can quote the Marsden square. This continues for as long as the ship is affected by the storm. Obviously, radio reception is likely to deteriorate as the storm gets closer.

If no specific radio message has been received, but a weather forecast has been given that indicates the possibility of a storm, and the mariner begins to suspect that he or she may be under the influence of one, the mariner must begin to use Buys Ballot's Law, as described earlier.

Where is the Storm Centre?

If the barometer continues to drop, the storm centre will be drawing forward of the vessel, rather than being on the vessel's quarter. The difficult matter will be to tell how far away it is, and in which direction it is travelling. A basic indicator is that, if the wind remains steady the yacht is in the path of the storm. If the wind strength is a steady 40 knots, the storm is about 100 nautical miles away. A steady 25 knots, indicates a distance off of about 200 nautical miles.

Even with the storm that far away, it is prudent to plot its position and direct your course away from it.

Getting Away From it All

Modern wind instruments have greatly improved the likelihood that a sailing yacht skipper can determine the path of a hurricane without outside information. The skipper needs to be able to observe whether the wind is backing, veering or remaining steady. Before efficient masthead wind direction instruments were generally available, the only way to do this effectively was to stop the boat and take two readings about three hours apart. Even then the chances of accurate observations from a small vessel were remote. Now the alert skipper can tell immediately there is a significant change in wind direction.

If the wind veers the boat is in the right hand semi-circle, if it backs the boat is in the left hand semi-circle, and if it remains steady the boat is in the path of the storm (see diagram 4.10).

Diagram 4.10 *The direction of the wind indicates which half of the storm's area the vessel is in.*

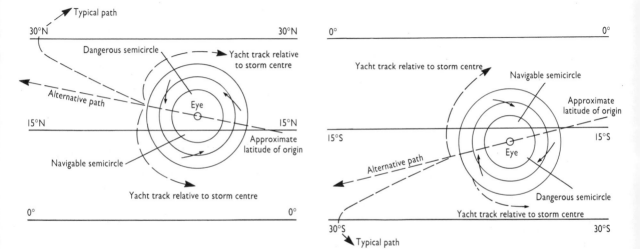

The main task now is to get the vessel as far away from the storm and its likely path as possible. A clearance of 200 nautical miles from the storm is the least that should be achieved. If the vessel has a barometer, the skipper should now depute someone to read it every quarter of an hour, and at the same time note the wind direction. A record should be kept of all these observations because, from them, any changes in the storm's path can be tracked.

We saw above that changes in the wind's direction can indicate which half of the storm's area the vessel is in (see diagram 4.10). Other information we can use this way is the fact that the barometer falls in front of the hurricane's trough and rises after it. Using the wind direction rules, and the barometric pressure rules, and applying them to the diagram, the skipper can plot which **quarter** of the storm the vessel is in.

Once the skipper has decided, with some certainty, where the vessel lies in relation to the storm, wind and barometric observations and, above all, radio information from other vessels or land stations, can be used to plot a course that will keep the vessel clear of the storm.

Diagram 4.11 shows a ship in position B1 steaming towards a storm south of it with its centre at position H1. The storm is travelling about 340 degrees at six knots. The ship is travelling at 15 knots. Allow for the differences in plotting caused by the difference in speed of the vessel. On deducing the position of the storm, sector 1 is drawn and the course is altered to avoid the storm. Six hours later, when the ship is at B2, the storm will be at H2, having altered course and speed. Sector 2 is drawn and the master surmises that the storm has recurved so the course is altered to pass well clear of it. Nine hours later, the ship is at B3, and the storm is reported at

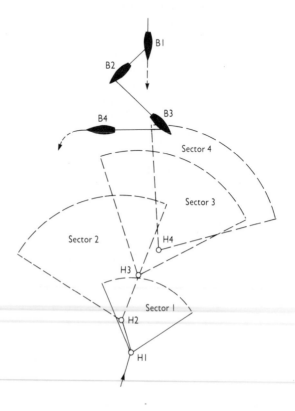

Diagram 4.11 *Manoeuvres used to run clear of a storm.*

H3, having resumed its original course. Sector 3 shows that the ship's course will take it into the new sector. The master makes a drastic alteration of course to get clear of the storm. When sector 4 is drawn six hours later, after the storm is reported at H4 and the ship at B4, it can be seen that the ship is running clear, but the master will still need to keep a close watch in case the storm behaves erratically.

It should be pointed out that for small vessels, even the navigable semi-circle is tremendously dangerous. If sufficient observations cannot be made, or there are no radio reports to guide the mariner, the following basic rules apply to keeping out of the path of hurricanes.

IN THE NORTHERN HEMISPHERE

If the wind is veering, vessel A must be in the dangerous semi-circle. A motor driven vessel should travel as fast as possible with the wind between 10 degrees and 45 degrees on the starboard bow and should steer round to starboard as the wind veers so that the wind stays in the same direction relative to the vessel. A sailing vessel should heave-to on the starboard tack and steer round to starboard as the wind veers.

If the wind remains steady in direction, or if it backs, so that vessel B seems to be nearly in the path of the storm, or in the navigable semi-circle, the vessel, motor or sail, should run with the wind on the starboard quarter, altering course to port as the wind backs (see diagram 4.12).

IN THE SOUTHERN HEMISPHERE

If the wind is backing, vessel A must be in the dangerous semi-circle. A motor driven vessel should travel as fast as possible with the wind between 10 degrees and 45 degrees on the port bow and should steer round to port as the wind veers so that the wind stays in the same direction relative to the vessel. A sailing vessel should heave-to on the port tack and steer round to port as the wind veers.

If the wind remains steady in direction, or if it backs, so that vessel B seems to be nearly in the path of the storm, or in the navigable semi-circle, the vessel, motor or sail, should run with the wind on the port quarter, altering course to starboard as the wind backs (see diagram 4.12).

Diagram 4.12 *Tropical revolving storm.*

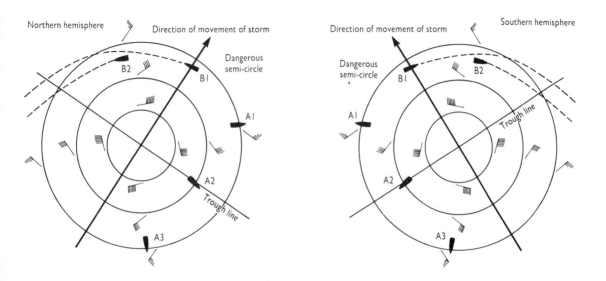

CHAPTER FIVE

CREW

When I was quite young and began doing overnight races my view of the universe was only as big as the area where I was working. I was only concerned with the task in hand. I was certainly unable to think in the sort of scope or range that the skipper of the boat would have been thinking.

I'm sure that limitation still applies to most crew in their early days of extended racing. But, as experience grows, so the 'universe' expands until it takes in, first of all, the watch one is keeping, and later the whole boat. Later still, it encompasses other boats in the fleet, and eventually weather patterns, current predictions, tidal patterns, where the boat stands in relation to others in the race, tactics and, eventually, strategy.

Although such experience can't be taught, acquiring it can be accelerated. While this book is trying to pass on nearly half a century of sailing experience, it's also trying to show what can be learned, so that this learning becomes easier and quicker.

For instance, if a skipper tells the crew what factors are being considered during a race, the skipper is helping them develop that larger view of the sailing world.

DINGHY SAILORS AS CREW

A lot is said, for instance, about getting young hotshot dinghy sailors to come on board ocean racers. I'm all for it. They have great basic skills in sail trim and boat handling, and are enthusiastic. They are also very often more aware of the forces working on a boat than people who have started their sailing on bigger vessels. Dinghy sailors often haven't learnt seamanship, and, because they have come from the explosive area of the sport which involves short distances and time spans, they don't understand stamina and the need to conserve energy. This is where the experienced skipper can take their undoubted sailing skills and mould them to the more demanding role of ocean racing.

A good ocean racing crew should know, for instance, that because weather patterns rotate in a certain way it's worthwhile sailing through the roughest seas with wind against current because when the storm abates, the new wind is going to come from a direction that will free the boat and allow it to sail the fastest possible course to its destination. But not all ex-dinghy crews are likely to have this sort of understanding. Sea conditions don't play a large part in the sailing of dinghies, which usually takes place in semi-protected waters.

Ocean racing and dinghy sailing are very different. The dinghy sailor does not have the slightest idea of what is involved in keeping a racing crew up to a high level of activity and keenness for four or five days and nights at a time. It can be hard to explain to the dinghy sailor that a lot of what he or she has learnt does not apply on the bigger boats.

WHERE TO FIND CREW

There are not many areas from which to recruit crew. Most skippers have a nucleus of people they work with, or friends, who start off sailing with them and gradually develop into crew—good crew, too, because they know the boat inside out through staying with it. The next best area of recruitment is those people which has been sailing for years but don't have their own boat and so form a pool of available, experienced talent. Most clubs have such a group. In fact, for ocean racing, there is often a local pool to which international crew attach themselves when a major event is due. Another productive area is the group of people which has been trained at one of the many good sailing schools which now exist throughout the world. They vary greatly in quality but there are some nuggets to be found.

The standard of training schools generally is good enough because people seem to learn well in small groups where questions can be asked and other people's reactions and learning capacity can be observed. But, ideally, the person who has completed a thorough course, and wants to go to sea, should then have at least a season sailing a small boat themselves. There is no better reinforcement of what has been learned, and, as well, the learner gains confidence from having to make his or her own decisions. A person learning alone is not afraid of making mistakes and will push rapidly through various sequences and become a competent boat handler.

Not everybody is able to become an ocean racer or cruiser—or wants to be—and so many decide to stay in the class of boat they learnt in or move to a class of harbour racing boats, or simply go straight into cruising. But we will assume that the intention right from the start is to become proficient on the ocean. Once proficient there, a sailor is proficient anywhere.

RACING IS THE BEST
TEACHER

Given this assumption, a sailor should spend at least one, perhaps two, seasons racing a solo or two-man boat. There's no better teacher than competition in a series of races against people who are of good calibre, so that you can take yourself up to the same level of skill that they have. If you've bought a production boat, brand new, to learn in, it will have come with a minimum of equipment and won't be set up for efficient sailing. Look for a similar boat or even sister ship in your area, one that has been sailing for a while, and get to know the owner. Most owners are flattered if a newcomer approaches them for help. If they've been sailing for a while they're going to know far more about it than you can as a beginner. Listen to what they say and set your boat up as near as possible to what they have been doing.

Racing is a very different matter from just jumping into your boat and practising manoeuvres. Just to start, you will have to have your boat in a certain position on a starting line at a precise time and in competition with perhaps 20 other boats. Nobody would suggest that the first time you go in a race you should try to get the windward position and beat all the hotshots, unless you are very confident. Rather you should try to start in a clear spot, on the line, with your boat going full speed and nobody interfering with you, as the gun goes or within a very few seconds of it. After you have tried that a few times you'll begin to judge your boat speed and the capacity you have for getting the boat into a particular position at a particular time. Then you can start trying to match the race starting techniques of the hotshots. You will have to look very critically at the way your sails have been set, and the way the sails on the top boats are set. Usually the beginner will pull the halyard on too tight, the foot will be out too hard, the sail will look flat and tight and the boat will be lifeless, whereas the faster moving boats will have a curved sail which seems powerful and smooth. The only way that the beginner is going to improve is by changing and following and copying. There is nothing wrong with copying because it's highly unlikely that your competitors are going to help you too much, unless you are very lucky, or are a member of a club which has a tradition of helping beginners.

There is a cardinal rule about starting a race—one that's broken by very experienced sailors and should not be. *You must have clear wind.* I am perfectly prepared to start a couple of seconds late in the right position, where I can get myself into clear air within a couple of boat lengths of the start rather than be at the mercy of the wind shadow of 10 or 20 boats. I'm going to be sailing in their shadow and at an angle perhaps 20 degrees further from the wind than they will. I can't stress how important it is. Start at the windward or favoured end, start a little bit late, flop off on to the other tack as soon as it's clear and then flop back again. You'll find you'll have absolutely clear wind and you'll be to windward of the fleet, even if a little behind. But you won't be behind for long.

At the end of these seasons in a small dinghy, you will have sufficient confidence to choose whether you want to be crew, or continue with your own boat, or move up to a larger boat with a larger crew. If you are not able to buy your own boat, get yourself a crew spot on the sort of dinghy we have been discussing. A skipper already sailing the ocean, if offered crew with the experience discussed above, would be delighted to give them a try.

CREW TRIALS

When you, as skipper, take somebody on trial as crew you should explain the terms of the trial. Explain that it isn't going to be only a matter of how well they sail, but will also involve a check on whether they get seasick, whether they can work when sick, and whether you feel they will fit in as a member of the crew.

The skipper has the final right of decision: it is his boat and he has to decide what sort of crew he wants to sail it. His selection will depend to a great extent on what sort of boat he has and what function on board he is trying to fill, or duplicate (remember there are watches). Whatever the size of the crew, the people involved must be clear about the specific duties they've been given and exactly what's expected of them. It's quite unfair to judge people unless they know why and how they are being judged.

Amongst young sailors experience is naturally likely to be limited. Somebody well versed in foredeck procedure is unlikely to have done much work on a mainsheet or as a spinnaker trimmer. The sensible young person who wants to get into ocean sailing would be wise to work in all positions in order to be able to offer a rounded bag of skills when first trying to get into a big boat crew.

When we start talking of crews of five or more we start talking about specialist sailors. A very experienced sailor friend once told me that he thought the ideal ocean crew of say eight people should have four helmsmen and 'four gorillas who will move the mast if you ask them to'. This isn't far from the truth. Of an ocean crew of nine, a minimum of four should be competent helmsmen. Some may even specialise in particular points of sailing.

In these days of Satnavs and positions by satellite being available every 20 seconds, it is wise to have a navigator who is also a helmsman. Because the navigator 'floats' between watches it makes great sense for him to be available as a relief helmsman to both watches, particularly in heavy conditions. If there can be more helmsmen on board that's fine, but they also will have to double up on skills, like the navigator.

Because oceangoing yachts work to a watch system, the aim of crew selection will be to achieve an equal division of skills, or as equal as possible between the two watches, covering all the functions necessary to work the boat. There will need to be people who can handle the foredeck, the pit, and the cockpit, as well as the helm in each watch. That's not so difficult because on most boats whenever a major manoeuvre is required, such as a spinnaker peel (change), a headsail change or a reef, those members of the off watch who are needed are brought up on deck.

O N E   H A N D   F O R   T H E   B O A T

As skipper, when you begin training your own crew, teach them something which every old sailor takes for granted, but which still needs to be passed on—the rule of 'one hand for yourself and one for the boat'. It's explicit and precise and invaluable. Once crew have learnt that they must first make sure of their own safety, and then do whatever work is necessary, they have made the first step from landlubber to sailor. Everybody has seen the willing crew who has hardly been to sea before, and really wants to help, but fouls everything up. He or she can't keep their balance, or gets thrown from one side of the boat to the other when there is the slightest lurch, whereas the experienced sailor has a handhold or has short-clipped his harness so that the work can be safely undertaken.

Keep that rule in mind until it becomes second nature. Major injuries that occur during heavy weather are usually caused by somebody having forgotten that adage. By climbing out of a berth without a good grip they are thrown across the cabin, or by coming up the companionway without having their safety line clipped on they are thrown into the cockpit, or even the sea. It is hard to make the inexperienced sailor understand that the most dangerous place in the boat is at the foot of the companionway stairs, inside the boat. Invariably conditions seem much calmer down below than they are on deck and the person about to climb the steps is going from a safe environment to a dangerous one. Crew members are not always fully alert to that so it should be standard practice that people coming up from below pass up their safety hook to someone on deck to be clipped on to the lifeline before they actually begin their ascent.

BUILDING THE TEAM

The ultimate skill of a good crewman is to be able to work efficiently with however many other people there are on the boat. This is learned through a combination of mutual respect and bonding. On many ocean racers you can see this bonding reinforced by crew uniforms or T-shirts with the name of the boat and the racing event on them. All this tends to make the crew think of itself as a unit which has its own territory which is the performance and reputation of the boat and the performance and reputation of the individuals that make up the crew. Mutual respect is so important that sometimes the bonding of a crew will overcome the limitations of any one member. It's this building of a team which the wise skipper, whether cruising or racing, will capitalise on and use to back his own authority. As skipper, it's hardly necessary to rant and rave and bellow to try to mould the team. It's much better to lead by example and train them. Really good sailors habitually train so that they tack and jibe almost without thinking and usually without fault. A jibe or tack when you sail alone becomes a simple manoeuvre because one person has no difficulty in developing a smooth technique. When one or more other people are needed to make the manoeuvre effective, cooperation and mutual timing are important. Only training can develop these attributes.

A great many people believe it is a good thing to slam a boat up as fast as possible when tacking and then hope that the headsail will come on. If it doesn't, they shout loud abuse at the grinder who hasn't been able to pull the sheet on properly in the time. It would be much more sensible to tack the boat a little more slowly, certainly if crew are beginners, so that the crew members involved in the manoeuvre can see what timing is necessary for letting off the old sheet, passing the bow of the boat through the wind, and bringing on the sail on the new side as the wind helps the sail round (rather than pulling against it). The good helmsman will make sure the bow is pointed high up into the wind long enough for the sail to be pulled almost to its final position without pressure on it. It's quite pointless for the helmsman to slam the boat across and then get almost on to a reach so that the poor crewman is pulling against the full pressure of wind in the sail. Eventually the coordination and timing of the crew will become so good that the boat will be able to tack fast, but no team will be able to reach that level of skill without a great deal of practice. It is difficult to keep a crew together, and the larger the crew the greater the problem.

BOAT ORGANISATION

Nothing builds up an effective team better than continuity. A boat may be entered for only four major events in a year, plus a regatta, yet it hampers the effectiveness of that boat if some crew are not available for all the events. If the whole crew hasn't sailed together for a considerable time, they won't have trained, and before each event they are going to have to rebuild old teamwork and skills. It's far better for the crew to be told at the beginning of the year what the boat's programme is, and to have them commit themselves to it. It's at this stage that the crew members should say if they are unable to come and the skipper can then decide whether that is acceptable or not.

Poor organisation is one of the major faults in many boats and one of the major barriers to good performance. Establish early in the season what the programme is and get a commitment from each crew member to be able to meet that programme.

BASIC TESTS

The first test by which crew should be judged is their capacity to be available. The second is their capacity and qualifications in terms of individual skills and individual personality traits. I've sailed on boats where a crew has been thrown together at the last minute. They had no chance to develop rivalries or dislikes, or closeness, but they were all highly experienced and so they became a very effective crew within a short period. But that's not the recommended way to choose a crew. It is best to have plenty of time to assess and put together a team that is not only efficient, but compatible.

COMPATIBILITY

Once the crew is assembled, we have all the mechanical functions we need, but none of the social or mental integration that goes towards the making of a great team (we don't know whether they are religious fanatics or dedicated communists, drunkards or teetotallers). Luckily, most of these extremes will make no difference to the crew. It's most unusual for any conversation of any depth to take place during an ocean race—such an event is hardly the time for deep philosophical discussions. On land, after the race, there may be time, when the crew is relaxing and the race 'rerun' takes place, but not necessarily. As a matter of policy, the crew should be encouraged to stay together for a little while so that the day's racing can be discussed and analysed and the bonding can extend even more deeply. From these discussions, each member comes to realise the value of the other members' contributions.

So how does the skipper make these much more difficult judgements of social compatibility, given that he is satisfied with the mechanical ability of each of the people selected? Within most crews there's a nucleus of people who are either friends or old shipmates of the owner—a nucleus of compatible experienced people. The new recruits have to fit in to this. There will be the usual reaction people have to somebody newly thrust into their own circle— in some cases there's instant like or dislike and in most cases there's a willingness to accept unless this is negated by some strong adverse reaction to the new arrival. It is quite rare, although I have seen it happen, for an entire crew to react so badly to a newcomer that the newcomer has no chance of fitting in. The skipper has to hope that the newcomer will then fit in by adapting to the existing crew, and through their accepting his or her effectiveness.

The selector must also bear in mind that the would-be crew member may have his or her own problems. In every case when people are getting on a boat, particularly when they're going on to the ocean for the first time, they have to come to terms with themselves and their own fear. There's nothing to be ashamed of in being frightened when taking on something new, particularly if it's something where there's a race memory of fear. A good sailing friend of mine has pointed out that there's a feeling of double isolation. The isolation of distance—the fact that you're a long way from help, that you're totally reliant on the people around you, some of whom you may hardly even know— and the emotional isolation that comes when one feels one's being tested. In reality the test is both subjective and objective—one is testing oneself, and the skipper and crew will also be judging. Fear of this judgement is a major hurdle in the mind of the beginner and one the wise skipper will take time to solve with the individual crew member. The potential crew member must be told that he or she will be assessed for his or her ability to fit in, as much as for his or her sailing ability.

Perhaps the major trap for the selector to avoid here is the creation of factions, a possibility if the crew is large enough for it to split into groups, which may work against the good organisation of the vessel. The need for rivalry is catered for in an oceangoing boat by the watch system, where it is quite usual for each watch to think less of the other than of itself. This competition leads to greater intensity and a better output from the boat overall. Factions that heighten serious divisions and dislikes are a danger to a boat and should be avoided if at all possible, even if it becomes necessary to put somebody off the boat who seems to be too divisive. It's never an easy job to put someone off, particularly since it is very often for reasons that are difficult to explain to the person involved but which are nevertheless important.

Once personality differences are sorted out, the skipper and the watch captain begin to think in terms of whether one watch is stronger than the other. As the crew training programme progresses, and the unity of the crew increases, they can start to select people for positions on the boat and for inclusion in one or the other watch. Selection now becomes more a matter of compatibility than anything else. Levels of mechanical skill can be raised, whereas social and mental capacities rarely can. If a person is considered to be skilful enough, then if he or she has a calm, equable character that can take the tension out of difficult situations it's an asset to consider. If somebody else has drive and forcefulness, which can increase tension but which is also useful in directing and improving the boat's performance, that's also worthwhile. If the equable character goes to the extent of being slothful and lazy, or the direct forceful person is abrasive and unpleasant this is likely to be counter-productive on a boat. It's all a matter of balance.

Luckily, people's ability to perform above what's expected of them is limitless, and it's one of the most satisfying things about sailing. I've twice been dismasted, in totally different circumstances, once cruising and once racing. What would have been called on paper a weak crew in numbers and experience behaved magnificently in the cruising situation. In the other, a team which had hardly sailed together, but which had greater numbers and at least the same level of skill, again performed without fault.

THE CRUISING CREW

I believe the cruising skipper, as much as the racing skipper, needs to select his crew along similar lines, although mechanical ability is less important for cruising than social acceptance. Crews on cruising boats are normally smaller than on racers so the level of skill and experience has to be high, though not as high as on top racing boats. However, cruising people are actually asking the crew to share their home, which is a difficult enough situation to make work on the land let alone at sea, so the selection process is different. Most cruisers are organised so that the work is not arduous—sails are smaller and they are not put up or taken down as often. Usually cruising voyages are planned for calm weather and so it's less important to have a highly honed crew.

Nevertheless, choosing crew for a cruise is probably the most difficult of all. The ideal is somebody who is a competent sailor, good cook, navigator, raconteur and jolly fellow or lass. Unfortunately, it's very rare that all the qualities you want come in one package. The overriding rule has to be the safety of the vessel. Compatibility and character, while terribly important, come second. It is so subjective a matter that there's really not much point here trying to suggest guidelines for crew selection. Everybody will have a different idea, but if there have to be three qualities that come first I would suggest that seamanship is first, compatibility second and lack of seasickness third.

There is now an itinerant population of young people throughout the world who are seeing the world by cruising in long or short hops, then staying a while in the port of arrival before hopping another ship and going further. It's wise to check out that they won't, or aren't likely to, jump ship in some strange port or form a clique against your own people, or simply turn out to be users who are prepared to accept any evident benefits of being on a yacht without making a financial or physical contribution. Unfortunately there are a lot of people like these, and they're hard to recognise.

The way to increase the odds of getting a compatible crew is to be completely open with applicants. Tell them precisely the aims of the voyage, where it's likely to go, how long it will last and what's expected of them. Then if they're honest it gives them a chance to refuse if it doesn't suit them and it gives you a chance of getting somebody who has exactly the same purpose as you. With that common interest comes a contented crew.

Once the crew has been selected, make them a part of the preparations. Let them know what responsibilities they have and then leave them to it. You will still have the final responsibility.

When you sail with a really good crew member you notice that, not only does he or she know what has to be done, but they watch the whole manoeuvre as it takes place. If they find that one of their team mates has a problem, they are able to wait until it is solved and then go ahead with the manoeuvre, rather than blindly continuing and so creating an even greater problem.

S E A S I C K N E S S

One of the responsibilities of the skipper is the health of the crew members during the voyage. The more extended the voyage the greater that responsibility becomes, because the greater is the risk of some serious accident or medical problem. So it's a very good practice to find out from crews before they join the vessel what allergies they have, if any, what special medications they might need, and whether they take some sort of anti-seasickness medication. Even the most seemingly innocuous thing may become important when at sea and when help is far less likely to be available easily.

Seasickness doesn't become a problem to crew unless the boat goes to sea. It is a matter of no concern at all to a dinghy or harbour sailor. But I believe very strongly that unless a potential crew member is taken sailing in rough conditions, conducive to seasickness, and can demonstrate that he or she doesn't get seasick, or that having done so they can recover sufficiently to work, they should not be in the crew of an oceangoing boat. I always ask people whether they get seasick. If they say no, I need some proof. If they say yes but they can work, I still need some proof. If they say yes and I'm unable to get proof they are able to work, then I won't take them. I learned the lesson the hard way in Port Phillip Bay in Victoria, which can get quite choppy, and which is quite remarkable for having a distinct demarcation between weather patterns. The weather north of a rough line of latitude was dramatically different from that south of it, the northern being controlled by the land mass and the southern by the sea. There was a 100 nautical mile race held inside the bay, which is almost totally enclosed, and it started in a flat calm. We had to motor to the starting line and were only just able to get enough way up to cross it when the gun went off. I was sailing my own 12 metre (40 foot) boat with a crew of ten. As we went further down the bay the wind increased until we reached this demarcation line, where we had 55 knots of wind and a short sharp nasty sea. Everybody on board was seasick except me as I'm one of the very lucky few that has never been sick. They were sick to varying degrees, but the effect was that there were insufficient crew members available to be able to handle the boat safely and to continue the balance of 70 nautical miles remaining in the race. So we withdrew. We turned and motored back to the marina and exactly the reverse pattern occurred. The wind abated as we went further north and when we got to the marina there was a flat calm. We motored into the pen and I vowed that never again would I pull out of a race because there was too much seasickness on board. To do so is an admission of failure by the skipper, and in this case the failure was completely mine. So don't take people to sea who will be unable to work and don't take their answer for granted.

Crew husbandry, or if you like man management, because they're the same thing, is an important factor in keeping crew together. If a crew knows that the boat they're sailing on can reach its destination whatever the conditions— including that of the people on board—they are likely to be able to work better and to last longer. If at the same time the skipper is able to conserve the energies of those crew members the boat is going to perform better in the race, or enjoy the cruising more, and that's the whole point.

BOAT HANDLING

Motor boats, because of their comparative unseaworthiness, don't go to sea as often or for such great distances as many sailing yachts do. Have you ever seen a cruising motor boat that's just crossed a great ocean? The answer is probably yes, but it'll be something the size of a small freighter with a paid skipper and crew. There isn't the same amount of motor boat journeying as there is of sailing yacht journeying or cruising.

The greatest difference between a power vessel making a coastal passage and a sailing yacht doing the same is the stowage of equipment. Motor cruisers are so much more like a mobile house in interior design than is a yacht that the sort of stowage available on a motor boat is less secure for cutlery, crockery, liquor bottles, and the like. If rough weather does begin, and the boat is tossed around, loose gear can fly about quite dangerously inside the boat. Anyone intending to make a passage of more than say 20 nautical miles should be certain that all the gear can be quickly secured if needed. I'm mindful that a powerful motor boat, in the event of trouble brewing, can quickly either return to base, proceed to its destination, or, if the final destination is too far away, to some intermediate place. That may solve most bad weather problems, but a cruiser that does a lot of coastal voyaging will, sooner or later, be caught out and it's then that considerable skill with the engine controls and the rudder is required to reach port.

Once the seas become so big that the cruiser cannot head straight into them, the boat must run with them. The speed of the cruiser is restricted, as it mustn't slow down so much that it is picked up and flung forward by the waves, risking broaching, or go so fast that it is zapping up the back and down the front of waves, still with the risk of broaching.

Until the storm and the wave pattern becomes so severe that it is no longer possible to head into it, the technique of approaching shore is to angle slightly into the waves with the motor on low power and so avoid being smashed by breaking waves. This also prevents the propellers coming clear of the water through travelling too fast and therefore over-revving (cavitating). Over-revving (cavitation) can be very dangerous because it can stress the engines and lead to failure. If they fail in these circumstances a motor boat is in serious difficulty.

The proper tactic is to try to adjust the speed of the boat to get on the back of one wave and to stay there as long as possible. When the boat can't stay there any longer it should be allowed to slide off the back of that wave, run forward as the next one comes under the boat, and then slide on to the back of it and stay there for as long as possible. Keep this technique going until the boat arrives in port.

There are many instances throughout the world of large motor boats surviving conditions which only a few decades ago would have overwhelmed them. Where most people come to grief is approaching the land. The deep sea doesn't hold as many fears as a twisting, difficult river estuary or a river entrance with a sand bar across it. These are very common in those areas where motor boaters like to go fishing or cruising.

The safest way to enter a river which is protected by a sandbank of any kind is to go through the bar on an incoming tide. The reason for this is a simple one, thoroughly understood by ocean yachtsmen but less so by coastal sailors and motor boaters. If you have wind and current opposing each other the waves will always stand up high and be more likely to break. At the change of a current, in this case the tide, the seas will become longer and will slope more and will break less. This is particularly noticeable in ocean areas such as the Gulf Stream in the Atlantic, the Agulhas current in the Indian Ocean and the east Australian coast current in the west Pacific.

Wait for an incoming tide, then when coming in, the technique is to sit on the shoulder of the incoming wave, matching the boat's speed to the wave and then waiting for a smooth patch. When that happens, accelerate and get through as fast as you possibly can. Even if you've been coming over a bar for 10 years, and you know it inside out, everybody on board must wear their lifejacket. When trouble develops in riding a wave over a bar it develops very fast indeed. There is no time to reach a lifejacket if you need one.

E N T E R I N G   A   B A R

Imagine running through a typical bar entrance with the tide coming in and with a sea lumpy but not curling and breaking. First stand off and have a good look at the prevailing conditions. It's very simple to see where the waves begin to feel the bottom and swell up out of the general level of the water. Stay back from there and to the side and just watch the waves for a while. See if there's any regular pattern to them or whether there are random waves coming in from the side which would be very dangerous if you didn't expect them (this happens quite often). Check whether they're running in threes or sevens, or whether every now and then there's a bigger one. While you're doing this you'll have to watch, making careful use of the throttle, that you aren't picked up by a wave and carried, before you are ready, into the maelstrom. It's quite common for a secondary bar to form further out to sea from the main one. If you should get in between the two without realising it a big wave could quite easily trip on the first bar and throw you into the second. That, if you weren't ready for it, would be disastrous. When you see a flat spot, if you do see a flat spot, is the time to hit the throttle and charge through into the calm water as fast as you can. You won't always be able to find such a break.

More commonly, you'll have to pick a particularly big wave so that you've got plenty of water and come in on the back of that. You will probably be following lead lights at the same time, or channel markers, so you keep to the deepest part of the approach. Keep in mind scend—the depth of the trough of the wave below sea level. The wave is above sea level and the trough is below. That trough will be equal to the height of the biggest wave, so you may well have a three metre (10 foot) trough if you have a three metre (10 foot) wave. You would need to look carefully at your chart to see that there was going to be enough water for you to get in, even if you could make it comfortably in smooth water. This leads to another rule. When you do get into the deep channel you must never run ahead of the wave that you're on until you can see that there is substantial water in front of you. It's better to keep on the back of the collapsing, breaking wave, at the same time keeping the bow out of the white water so that it doesn't drop into an air pocket and pitchpole you. Just sit in the white water as it foams and the wave collapses under you and keep ahead of the breaking water behind from the next wave. The problem of scend disappears once a wave collapses and smooths out. Once you're certain that you're through the bar and in the comparatively calm clear water ahead make sure you're in the channel proper, have a look at the markers around you and proceed, knowing you have performed one of the most dangerous manoeuvres in boating.

L E A V I N G   A   B A R

The only manoeuvre that's more dangerous is going out across a bar, particularly on a run out (ebbing or falling) tide. You should never go out on a run out tide. If you do you are risking your life. I've been caught quite often where I've had a look at a bar, particularly when there have been training walls (breakwaters) and even groins built out and the bar itself is dredged, where the conditions have seemed quite reasonable. When I've actually got there in the vessel I've found it's too dangerous to attempt to go out. The old adage of 'plenty of bold sailors and plenty of old sailors, but you don't see many old bold sailors' is true. It is hard to imagine circumstances so pressing as to make you cross a bar on a run out tide.

Despite all this, if you are insistent, then you have to do the same before you leave as you did before you came in. You must go down into the entrance and have a look at what's happening. Be very wary, because the strong current running out will try to take you with it. You'll have to apply throttle, and reverse, and helm to keep the boat nearly stationary while you use it as a platform to see what's happening with the waves. You must plan a track where you see the most broken water in the main channel. Broken water means that the waves have actually toppled and broken. They are not going to rear up under you and suddenly break, throwing you backwards, as can easily happen. If you give the boat one hell of a kick and get through that broken set of waves then you may well get safely across the bar. It is far more likely you will face another set of waves coming at you, and that they will mount and rear and be most threatening. In Europe you must plan a track which keeps you in the charted deeper water of the channel. If it is marked, identify the buoys. Broken water on European bars usually indicates shallows with insufficient depth to navigate. Once you have chosen your course and are happy that it's safe to go, do it quickly, checking constantly that you are in the deepest water of the marked channel. Consistently in this book I've stressed that seamanship is based to a great extent on foreseeing difficulties and avoiding them. The proper seamanlike thing to do in these circumstances is not to go out at all if conditions seem too bad. If it turns out that you have to leave the boat somewhere for a week or so until you can get back and bring it out, well then, so be it. You still have yourself and your crew and you still have the vessel itself. It is simply not worthwhile to take risks with the sea.

FOULED PROPELLERS

The next point of danger for a cruiser is unfortunately common, getting the propeller or propellers fouled. In most of the world's cruising grounds there are plenty of stray lobster pots, fish traps, commercial fishing lines, discarded floating line and all sorts of other hazards for which the only protection is a specialised rope-cutter mounted on the prop shaft. Some very well found boats put a guard over the propellers, or have a deep skeg running to them, but the majority don't. If you have any likelihood of suffering from jammed propellers you need equipment to clear the tangle. Sometimes it's possible to get hold of the end of the line that is the cause of the foul and pull hard and it will come undone. It is much more likely that the line will have jammed so hard that it can't be got off by any other method than by cutting. People with tilt drives or stern drives can get the propeller up near the surface of the water and work moderately comfortably on cutting through the tangled line. But if you have two big, deep propellers you need to be able to dive over the side, ideally with scuba gear, but otherwise with an ordinary mask and snorkel. You need to be able to keep yourself deep enough for long enough to be able to cut through so you should always rig a line under the stern of the boat to keep hold of. It will still be quite difficult to get yourself down, even the metre or so (two to three feet) that represents the depth of the propellers. A weighted belt will allow you to apply more of your time to clearing the jam rather than to struggling to get down to it. Some boats are fitted with tubes above the propeller, so that a cutting tool can be used from within the boat. When not in use the tubes are sealed with a watertight hatch.

STORM BOARDS

An area where motor boats fail in terms of safety compared with sailing yachts is in not having storm boards for the windows. The windows on motor cruisers are usually much larger than on yachts, in some cases very large indeed, and it's imperative to have shutters that can protect the glass from breaking seas. Another very useful thing for a motor vessel going to sea often is a rotating windshield, let into the ordinary plain glass. These are driven by a motor and by rotating at high speed they throw spray and rain off the screen and allow an area of good visibility for the helmsman. They look quite old-fashioned but they are very useful.

B O A T   T R I M

Two more matters which are important for all motor boats are boat trim and ground tackle. The smaller the boat the more important is proper trim. Everyone has seen the badly trimmed aluminium runabout with only one person on it, the bow sticking up at about 25 degrees to the water, simply asking to be flipped if a gust of head wind gets under the bow. Apart from that it's also very expensive because the extra fuel needed for driving a boat that way is considerable. It's easy enough to fix. You can either do it by putting weight up in the bow to bring it down or having an extension to the tiller so that you can sit in the middle. More sensibly, put the outboard tilt pin in the hole nearest the boat so that the stern of the boat is driven up by the propeller and consequently the bow comes down. Trim becomes less important as boats get larger, but larger boats usually have trim tabs fitted, either to the hull or to the outboard leg, or under the stern drive. By adjusting the trim tab the vessel can be kept on her proper lines so that she will come on to the plane easily and reach that ideal cruising speed where the engine isn't working too hard and the hull isn't dragging heaps of water with it.

A motor boat which has the wind behind it needs its bow lifted slightly so that it doesn't dig into the water in front, and so either broach or nose dive. The stern has to be pushed down by raising the thrust of the outboard. Otherwise trim can be used in a head sea to keep the bow down slightly so that the boat won't jump over the waves. But then this must be watched because the steering characteristics of a boat will change when the bow goes down, and a lot more spray will come on board.

A sight that invariably makes me shudder, and despite all the publicity people still do it, is a flat-out motor boat with four or five children in the bow having an absolutely wonderful time with their legs hanging over the side. It's murderous. If the speeding boat hits an obstacle of any kind, which suddenly reduces its speed, the children can be thrown off and into the water directly in the path of the propellers. It's an unfortunate fact that in drivers of some of the smaller motor boats, as well as some of the more phallic high powered boats there is something of the road hog element. People speeding through moorings, travelling at excessive speeds in congested areas and generally behaving dangerously and inconsiderately, and in many cases illegally, are all too often seen. It's an educational matter and one that the regulatory authorities in all countries try to address. Unfortunately many people who own boats do not necessarily possess much intelligence.

G R O U N D   T A C K L E

Suitable ground tackle for motor cruisers of various sizes is given in the following table, so we will assume that you've started off with the right gear on board.

When anchoring, because they have no keel and are much shallower in the water, motor boats have much less of a grip on the water than do yachts so they will tend to swing much more rapidly when there's a change of wind direction or strength.

In a crowded anchorage a motor boat has to be more careful than most sailing yachts to let out sufficient warp (scope) to make the anchor hold properly

RECOMMENDED ANCHOR GEAR

MAXIMUM HULL LENGTH		CQR		DANFORTH	CHAIN SIZE		CHAIN LENGTH		WARP BREAKING STRAIN		WARP SIZE			
											POLYETHYLENE		NYLON	
(m)	(ft)	(kg)	(lb)	(size)	(mm)	(in)	(m)	(ft)	(kN)	(lb)	(mm)*	(in)†	(mm)*	(in)†
Under 5	15	3.5	7½	4s	6	⁵⁄₁₆	2.5	8	4.5	—	8	1	8	1
Up to 6	20	4	8½	8s	6	⁵⁄₁₆	2.5	8	9	4400	10	1¼	10	1¼
Up to 8	25	7	15	13s	6	⁵⁄₁₆	4	13	9	4400	10	1¼	10	1¼
Up to 9	30	9	20	22s	8	³⁄₈	5	16	20	6600	16	2	12	1½
Up to 11	35	11	26	22s	8	³⁄₈	6	19	30	6600	20	2½	14	1¾
Up to 13	40	15	35	40s	10	½	8	25	39	8200	24	3	16	2
Up to 15	50	20	44	65s	10	½	10	31	39	10600	24	3	16	2
Up to 17	55	25	60	65s	13	½	12	37	45	12600	26	3½	18	2¼
Up to 19	65	34	75	80s	13	⁹⁄₁₆	14	43	45	15000	26	3½	18	2¼

*Diameter   †Circumference

Source: Australian Yachting Federation 1989-1993 Yacht Racing.

and yet not so much that the circle through which the anchored boat can swing will impinge on the swinging area of other vessels. There's very much an etiquette involved here. People who have already got their anchors down and who have sorted out their anchoring and the swing have an unwritten right over those who come later. If you know that your vessel yaws easily, or swings in rapid response to the wind, then you have to allow for that when you drop the anchor.

ANCHORING
(P O W E R   A N D   S A I L)

The inexperienced anchorer can be seen at a glance. He or she believes that the anchor has to be thrown to some wonderful spot just ahead of the boat so that it will immediately, through the speed of its dropping, stick into the ground and make everyone safe. If you throw an anchor the line tangles. The line often gets under the anchor and then falls in a heap on the bottom. Not surprisingly it won't grip and the vessel will drag.

The proper way to anchor is to approach head to wind or if the tide is stronger than the wind, head to tide, and have the anchor party standing or kneeling in the bow with the anchor in its roller and ready to drop. The person at the controls will bring the vessel almost to a stop and then call 'Let go'. When this order is given, the anchor party lowers the anchor over the bow and, under control, but not too slowly, lets it run to the bottom. The idea is to allow the anchor to go down and take the chain and warp with it, hanging like a plumb bob from the bow until the anchor itself reaches the bottom. At this stage the wind or tide or both will be pushing the vessel backwards and more line is veered so that the anchor can fall on its side and bite into the ground. The usual safe amount of line to let out is five times the depth of water, plus the range of tide. The range of tide is the difference between low tide and high tide for that day. So that if you're in six metres (20 feet) of water you'd want 30 metres (100 feet) of line, plus the tidal range. If that seems excessive, have a look at diagram 6.1. The anchor and chain will lie along the bottom and, being horizontal, there will be no upward pull to lift the anchor out of the ground. The curve of the anchor warp (rode) is like a spring that absorbs the extra pull when there's more wind or rides the boat forward when there is a lull. If you have 30 metres (100 feet) of line from the bow of the boat to the anchor you have a turning circle which is in the proportions as seen in diagram 6.2, where the radius of the circle is the distance from the anchor to the bow, less a little. If you are simply anchoring for lunch, and people are going to be on the boat all the time, and the wind doesn't change, you are not going to use up that whole circle. You'd need a considerable change of wind direction to use even half of it. But if you're staying in an anchorage for a reasonably long time you would have to allow that space— you certainly wouldn't be able to leave the boat unattended otherwise. If you intend to be away from the boat for quite a long time, or to sleep overnight, you must allow to have a clear swing of the order of that circle. You'll also have to watch out for anybody attempting to anchor within that circle.

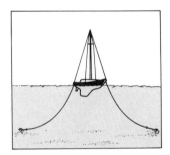

Diagram 6.1 *Anchored fore and aft.*

BAHAMIAN MOOR

In a particularly tight harbour where the normal amount of scope cannot be let out because of the swinging circle that will result, a technique known as the Bahamian moor is by far the best. In this case, an anchor is let out in the usual way from the bow and then another one, also from the bow, is dropped in the position where a stern anchor would normally be dropped. As diagram 6.3 shows, this means that if the tide reverses the boat will still be anchored and will have turned only through its own length. This is a highly recommended method of anchoring because it also prevents the boat from sailing around her anchor and means that she is less of a hazard both to herself and to other boats around her.

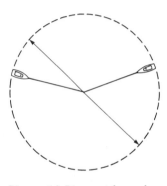

Diagram 6.2 *Diagram shows the area a relatively small vessel takes when anchored on a normal scope of, say, four to one. A wind or tide change can make a great difference.*

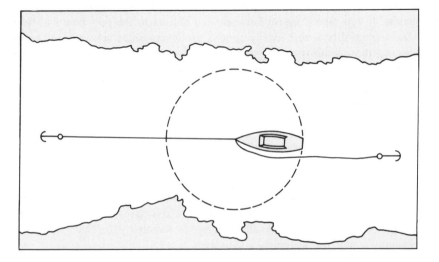

Diagram 6.3 *The Bahamian moor—a great change of wind direction will not affect the vessel so greatly: it will swing its own length.*

O C E A N   S W E L L   A N D   S U R G E

Another curse of the yachtsman who wishes to anchor, particularly if it's in the open sea near islands as in the Pacific or the Caribbean, is ocean swell. It's almost impossible to stop the rolling that occurs in these circumstances. In North America a device known as a flopper stopper has been developed, which is a type of paravane rigged to a boom and this can be adapted for a yachtsman to put on the end of a spinnaker pole. But it is rather elaborate and an extra weight in the boat. A more satisfactory method is to hoist a small flat sail, say a storm jib or trysail, on to the backstay in much the same manner as a motor boat uses a small sail to stop it rolling.

If you are able to take a line ashore, and the land is steep-to, a variation of the Mediterranean moor can be used. The boat is anchored a comfortable distance offshore and drops back on the anchor. A stern line is then taken ashore, either by a friendly local as in the Caribbean, or in the dinghy, and made fast on shore. The stern line can be tied around a palm, or rock, or can be the kedge which can be dug into the sand. The human body seems to prefer pitching to rolling, so this is quite a good solution. Obviously it can be applied anywhere in the world, whether it is ocean swell or local surge you are trying to overcome.

T W I N   A N C H O R S

I'm a very strong advocate of using two anchors, particularly in any area which is relatively unknown. They really can be tremendously effective. Once riding out a 70 knot gale to two anchors and only 300 metres (900 feet) from a weather shore, the vessel was quite comfortable on an anchor warp (rode) of about six times the depth of the water and although continually at the full pull of the anchors, she did not yaw. But in these circumstances even the smallest shift in the wind can be very dangerous so an anchor watch has to be kept and the skipper alerted the moment a change of wind direction occurs. As soon as the boat has taken up firmly on the anchor or anchors, bearings or transits should be taken of objects on the shore. Transits are probably the best because they will very rapidly indicate if the boat is dragging its anchors. If you take a transit between two objects to the port bow and two to the starboard bow with ideally about a 90 degree angle between, and keep checking those transits, you'll soon know if your anchor's dragging. There will be some variation in them as the boat comes up or falls back on the anchor but if the transits remain steady then the boat is not dragging. An anchor watch is necessary because a depth alarm that sounds if you get into shallower water isn't sufficient. You can sleep through such an alarm or simply not hear it, or it might not go off, and by the time you know you've got a problem you can't deal with it. If you set an anchor watch people can take it in turns to watch for an hour or two and then you'll know immediately if anything has changed. It can be difficult to check against dragging at night if you haven't got any lights or other objects on which to take a transit, but more times than not there's sufficient light to be able to make a transit through a couple of headlands or the shadow of a tree or something like that. Otherwise it's simply a matter of keeping a good watch.

B O A T   H A N D L I N G

Power boats are delightfully easy to handle, particularly when they have twin engines. Even the power boat with one propeller only, if it is well-placed so that the thrust of the propeller goes over the blade of the rudder, is a pleasure. Take a look at a medium-sized commercial vessel like a fishing boat or a smallish ferry, and you will see that they don't actually turn in the way a car does. When helm is applied they slide through the water looking as though the bow stays in one spot and the stern pivots on it. What is actually turning the hull is the extra water pressure on one side of the boat compared with the other. This is particularly true if the rudder has a strong flow of water from the propeller across it. It is also increased in one direction as against the other depending on the rotation of the propeller. Diesels nearly always are left-handed, the propeller turning anti-clockwise, and petrol (gasoline) engines are right-handed. Any vessel under power, even if it has a deep keel, can be made to turn quite fiercely by applying full helm and giving the engine great forward acceleration. This creates such a strong flow over the blade of the rudder that the vessel begins to turn before it starts moving forward. So when a boat has to back and fill to get out of a tight spot, this is the way to do it.

B E R T H I N G
(D O C K I N G   O R   L A N D I N G)
(P O W E R)

Nothing makes the competent boathandler stand out from the bumbler more clearly than berthing (docking) and unberthing (leaving a dock). Even if the audience is made up almost entirely of landlubbers, they can tell if the manoeuvre has been well done or botched.

If you don't want to be found wanting there are several things you can do. First, make sure everybody on board can coil a line properly. Everybody knows roughly how to coil a line, but they don't all know how to do it so that it will throw smoothly, uncoiling without snarling. The trick is to give the line—even modern synthetic lines—a half twist as each loop is formed in the hand. If you are doing it properly, the loops will lie in a slightly elongated circle. If you are not, they will twist into a figure of eight. If you are giving the half twist and the line still makes a figure of eight, you are twisting in the wrong direction. Start again.

Once all your crew have mastered coiling, let them practise line throwing. Nothing looks better than a line thrown properly, from the right distance, accurately to the catcher. It is seamanlike. Yet even people who are good sailors at sea make themselves look fools when berthing (docking), by throwing lines improperly coiled, too heavy, from too far away, which fall in a lump into the water. While it may raise a few laughs, if conditions are hard, and the vessel must be tied up first time to be safe, that scene is anything but funny.

Here is how to throw properly. If the vessel needs a heavy line to tie it up, it may be too heavy to throw. In that case, choose a lighter line (that is long enough) and tie it to the berthing (docking) line, which can lie in a coil at the thrower's feet on the deck. Take the throwing line, and pass the whole coil under the lowest rail of the pulpit, or pushpit. Bring it back so that a comfortable weight of throwing line is in the right hand, and about half a dozen coils in the left (the opposite if you are left handed).

When you are close enough to the catcher to be certain the line will reach, swing the line in the right hand a few times to pick up momentum. You will have to make sure you have enough room to swing. When ready, throw the line at the end of the swing towards the catcher, aiming high of the catcher's right shoulder. The line should be thrown as if to a position past the catcher, so that when it loses momentum it drops on him or her. The moment the line is caught, secure it to a cleat or bollard because the catcher can't pull you into the wharf until there is something to pull against. You can always tidy up, or transfer to the heavier line, when you are snug. If all your crew are equally competent, somebody will, at the same time, have thrown a stern line.

The lines you need are: **Bow** and **stern**, which, if long enough, can also extend to the **fore (bow) spring** and **aft (stern) spring** (although these can be separate lines) and **fore breast line** and **aft breast line** (see diagram 6.4).

The bow and stern lines prevent the boat floating away from the jetty, but do nothing to prevent fore and aft movement, which can be caused by wind, or current, or both. The fore spring prevents the boat moving forward and the aft spring prevents it moving aft. As you can see, once the bow and stern lines are tied off at the required distance they can be passed several times around their cleats and the remainder of the line used as the springs. If you are tying up in an area of great tidal range, make sure either that there is enough line to allow for the movement, or have someone adjust the lines as it becomes necessary. The breast lines are used to hold the boat firmly in position, particularly if the wind is offshore, but they do not invariably have to be rigged. By the same token, if there is a lot of surge, or heavy conditions, more lines may have to be rigged. The deciding factor is whether the boat is comfortable. If she is bumping in any way, or surging, lines must be deployed to control it. The most lines I have ever had to use to calm a boat down was 12, so don't be frightened to put them out if you think they are needed.

When approaching the berth (dock), but before getting ready to throw the mooring lines, put fenders over the side which will be alongside the wharf. You'll need at least three. If the wharf or jetty consists of unprotected piles, you should have on board a plank long enough to straddle two piles. Rig the three fenders over the side of your boat, then hang the plank so that it will rest between them and the piles. Let the plank take the wear, not your topsides.

As you approach the jetty, remember the first rule of berthing (docking or landing), which is to try not to have wind or current behind you, as this will force you to use more reverse to counteract the forward motion of the wind and/or current. But, as long as the reverse on your vessel is reliable, the matter is not critical. In the same way, you will need to approach a jetty faster if there is an offshore wind of some strength than if there is not, because the wind will push the boat away from its target. Conversely, with a strong onshore wind, the skipper has to imagine the jetty to be perhaps a metre (three feet) closer to him than it is, so that the way is off the vessel when it is parallel to the wharf, and the wind pushes it in the last little bit. Diagrams 6.5–6.12 illustrate most situations you are likely to encounter. But, wherever you are, and whatever the conditions, just look around you, be sure of where the wind and current are coming from, plan ahead what you will do, then make sure you tell the crew so that they can cooperate as a team.

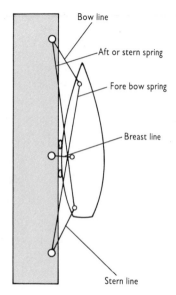

Diagram 6.4 *The basic mooring lines—bow, stern, breast, bow spring and stern spring.*

S T E R N - T O   B E R T H I N G   (M E D I T E R R A N E A N   D O C K I N G   O R   L A N D I N G)

When moorings are very crowded, they are often arranged parallel with the stern to the jetty or finger wharf, and the bow secured to a mooring buoy or the anchor. The method of approach is simple. Take a run past the spot you have selected to see whether any anchors are out, and if so which way they go from the bow of their boat. Then have a crew member in the bow with a long line. Approach the mooring buoy and attach the line to the buoy. When the crew member signals the line is attached, drop astern at a rate slow enough for the crew member to keep control of the bowline. When you are at the jetty attach the stern lines, then let them out and pull forward on the bowline until you are the distance off the jetty you desire.

If there is no buoy, go to a spot about three boat lengths out from the jetty, avoiding other anchors, and drop your own anchor, then proceed as before, but more slowly as the crew member in the bow will be busier.

B E R T H I N G   (D O C K I N G   O R   L A N D I N G)   (S A I L)

The same rules apply, except that you will have to know your boat well to undertake these berthings (landings), and you certainly will want to be sure your crew can handle lines, coil them, and throw them. Coming in against wind or tide, or both, you will have to approach at a speed of about two knots, which means the vessel has steerage way, but can be pulled up manually unless it is enormous. As well as the people handling lines at the bow and stern, you must have others standing by at the halyards to drop the sails. When on your final approach, and you are sure you can get in under the main only, drop the headsail, making sure it happens very fast and the sail is dropped out of the way of the bowman. When you see the bowman has got his line ashore, drop the main and swing the boat's bow away from the wharf, this will bring the stern in. The critical part of the manoeuvre is to get the bow line attached at both ends as quickly as possible, so that it can be used to hold the bow as the stern swings in.

If approaching on a run or reach, sail downwind of the berth (dock) and then sail up as if having approached from downwind in the first place. If there is too much wind, or you have to manoeuvre in a tight area of a marina or boat pool, drop the jib entirely and have somebody stand by the main halyard, reducing the amount of sail as less speed is required. If more speed is required, hoist more main. This method gives almost complete control of speed, but cannot be used unless there is enough wind, and is not efficient in going to windward. As in any other manoeuvre, think it out beforehand, then tell everybody what you plan to do. If you find you are going too fast, abort the final approach and sail in a circle to reduce speed before you approach.

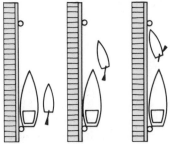

Diagram 6.5 *Berthing port side to.*

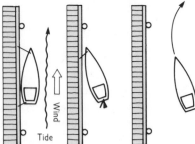

Diagram 6.9 *Unberthing with wind and tide behind.*

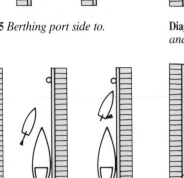

Diagram 6.6 *Berthing starboard side to.*

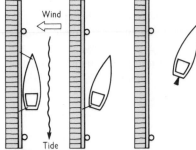

Diagram 6.10 *Unberthing with wind on to jetty and tide ahead.*

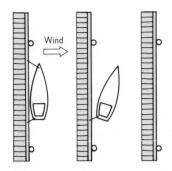

Diagram 6.7 *Unberthing with the wind coming off the jetty.*

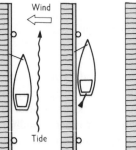

Diagram 6.11 *Unberthing with wind on to jetty and tide behind.*

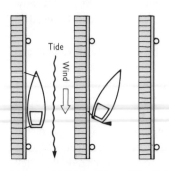

Diagram 6.8 *Unberthing with wind and tide dead ahead.*

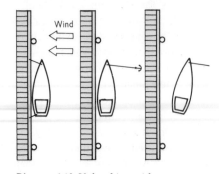

Diagram 6.12 *Unberthing with strong wind on to jetty.*

SWINGING MOORINGS

Millions of words have been written on this subject, but the only thing difficult about it is that there is always an audience and they are always knowledgeable. Only practice makes perfect, and the longer you have been sailing a particular boat, the better you will be. Basically, you are trying to bring the boat to a dead stop within boat hook's reach of the buoy so that your crew can pick up the buoy and pop its mooring line over the deck cleat, making you safe again. You don't want to extend the crew's arms by roaring past on a reach, and you don't want to fall short and have to sail round again, and again.

Always approach the buoy from downwind or downtide so that when you turn into the wind the speed will come off the boat and you will bring up at the buoy. If your approach speed is about two knots, whatever the conditions, you should have almost stopped by the time the boat has made its circle. The secret is to approach the buoy wide from whichever direction you come. Then you will always have about two boat lengths to stop. If the wind is so strong that the two boat lengths seem likely to be too much, and that you will stop before you reach the buoy, flop onto a tack and, the moment you fill on it, flop on to the other. That should see you make the extra boat length. But you will have to decide very quickly if you think you'll need to do that, because if you are too late you will drift sideways. A heartening thing about picking up a swinging mooring in a strong wind is that it stops you quickly, so don't be frightened to turn up into the wind quite close to the buoy.

UNBERTHING
(LEAVING A DOCK)
(POWER)

Any power boat owner should be as familiar as a sailing yachtsman with the proper method of heaving a line because very often the safety of the vessel can depend on it. If you have confidence that your crew can throw a line to somebody on the jetty and therefore secure at least the bow of the vessel, you will know that whatever the wind conditions you will be able to swing the stern in and have your boat snug. If the bow is held and pressure is applied with the propeller and properly angled rudder the forward motion is transformed into a sideways movement. The stern comes in to the jetty and the boat is alongside. Conversely, when leaving a jetty, if you need to swing the bow out you keep the stern line on, steering away from the jetty, and release the stern line only when the bow has swung out away from the jetty. The vessel then takes up its proper course and full steerage way and control. See above for other text on dockside manoeuvring.

Coming out of a pen (marina slip) into a congested area, the vessel may simply be put in reverse as in diagram 6.9 and swing comfortably out of the pen (marina slip) and into space, but then will need to make a sharp starboard turn to avoid another arm of the marina. As the vessel has almost reached the end of its reversing leg the helm is put across strongly to turn the boat to starboard and the engine accelerated hard. This happens while the boat is still moving astern. The boat will now swing fast, without going forward, until the desired heading is reached. The engine is then throttled back and the wheel centred.

If there are two propellers there is no need for such dramatics, the boat can be turned in its own length by opposing one propeller with the other, and by the proper use of the steering, as seen in diagram 6.12. The ability to move the stern of the vessel while the bow hardly moves can be taken advantage of in coming alongside or leaving.

M A N   O V E R B O A R D

The ultimate test of boat handling is rescuing a crew member who has fallen overboard. Here I am a heretic—most boating bureaucrats will fail an examinee who doesn't use their pet method of rescuing such an unfortunate. Their methods usually are suitable for heavy, clumsy boats of a past time, not the generally responsive lightweight modern vessel. I believe there are some rules which apply universally, but they concern crew behaviour and principles rather than inflexible responses to variable conditions.

Of course the whole crew must be alerted by the shout 'Man Overboard' as the floating line and the life rings are thrown over. Of course one of the crew should be detailed to keep watch on the person in the water, and nothing else. At night they must watch for the light of the dan (tall) buoy (also thrown to mark the spot) and listen for the emergency whistle attached to it. Noise must be kept to a minimum. But that's about the limit of standard procedure.

Almost every set piece of rescue consists of sailing further and further away from the victim while getting the boat organised. The situation seems more to be a test of the skill of the skipper and crew than the rescue of somebody who might drown. The proper tactics to use are the ones most likely to succeed. So, just stop the boat. In some cases the overboard crew member will be able to swim to the boat, or at least to the floating line attached to the boat, in which case the rescue is almost completed.

If under sail, round up, the sails will depower and lie to the wind in quite an orderly fashion, even a spinnaker. While the rest of the crew get all the sails down except the main and treble check that no lines will foul the propeller, another can start the engine. Many will say, 'but the propeller will be a danger when the man overboard is alongside being rescued'. Of course it will, but at least the person will **be** alongside. Then you simply take the boat out of gear. In the meantime, the boat hasn't sailed so far away from the swimmer that the one detailed to watch out can't even see him, as would happen with the other methods. The boat, and the man in the water, will both drift, but though they will drift at different rates, they will drift in the same direction, so maintaining contact.

Motor back to the person in the water and throw a line, or take in the floating line if they have hold of it, and bring the person alongside. If they are wearing a safety harness, pass them a strong halyard (remember, most boats have a topping lift, too) and get them to clip it to the harness. Then winch them aboard.

If they are in any way disabled, a man may have to go overboard to clip the halyard on, but that person should be attached to the boat with a strong line which is cleated off. The second person can be winched aboard after the rescue is completed. Many books speak of letting a sail over the side, slipping it under the victim, then hauling the sail aboard with the victim in it. It is ingenious, and there may be times when it is necessary, but boats have pulleys and purchases all over them, so it is unlikely the winching method won't work.

If you don't have a motor, you should have, you are in the ocean, remember. But if you don't, you should have rigged a Seattle Sling (see diagram 6.13). (I believe these will become a standard part of safety equipment in the near future.) After stopping the boat and getting it ready to sail again, sail back towards the one in the water and pass to windward with the sling trailing behind the boat. Sail in a circle around him so that the trailing line with the sling attached forms a loop around the victim. Once he grabs the line he can manoeuvre until the sling is right next to him, then he can get into it. Then the boat has to be stopped again, so that the crew can winch the man aboard. The harness acts as a strop and the person is lifted aboard, either directly, on a halyard, or by attaching a purchase to the end of the main halyard or topping lift. The end of the halyard will have to be raised far enough for the person overboard to be swung over the rail.

If you don't have a motor, or it has failed, and you haven't rigged a Seattle Sling, you will have to use whatever you have aboard. The immediate reaction of the helmsman will depend on what rig the boat has up. If on a run, with everything up, round up under control, as in the first example, and keep the swimmer under observation. You will know the course back to the swimmer even if he should drift out of sight, because the observer would have seen him earlier. The course back will be a beat so the boat must be rigged for that, and taken back towards the victim in a series of short tacks, so that the boat covers a fairly wide track back to the man. Once alongside, proceed as before.

If the man went overboard on a reach, simply reach back along the course on the other tack. If there is a spinnaker up, round up so that it can be handed,

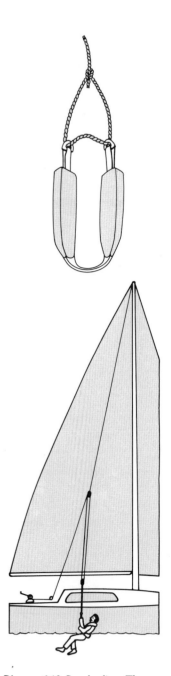

Diagram 6.13 *Seattle sling. The sling is thrown over on its long line and the boat is sailed around the person in the water. If they are unhurt they can swim to the sling and climb in to be winched aboard.*

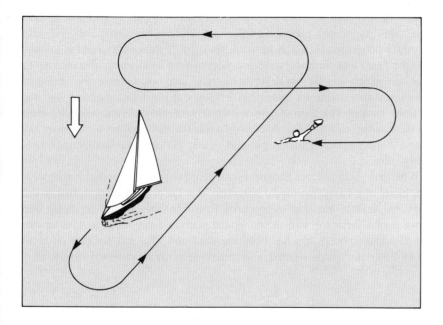

Diagram 6.14 *Searching for a man overboard from a reach.*

then sail back. If the accident happened on the wind, and there are sufficient crew on deck, then use one of the old methods—fall away on the present tack and jibe so as to make a circle, which should bring you back to within sight of the person.

The advantage of rounding up under control, apart from staying near the person in the water, is that the crew has time to get on deck and get the sail off in an orderly manner. Heavy weather will change the tactics slightly, as a depowered boat will be at risk in a big sea. But remember, in these conditions it is even more important than usual to stay as close as possible to the person in the water. Someone must keep their eyes glued on the victim. The best helmsman on board should take the helm and keep the boat under just enough way to have steerage, but not so much as to be sailing away from the man overboard. The motor should be started in the usual way, and as soon as it is going, it can be used to keep the yacht in a safe attitude while the boat is brought, not under control, which it already is, but under manageable sail.

SEARCH   PATTERN

If a person goes overboard at night, or is not immediately known to have gone overboard, a search pattern must be instituted. The first thing is to track back along the reciprocal (reverse) of the course you were sailing when the person went overboard. Bear off from course and make a large circle back to the track you were making. When the circle is complete, bring the boat on to the reciprocal and sail back along it. The navigator should note time and log and position, so that a plot can be kept. If there is no plot of the course from which the man was lost, it must be drawn on the chart as it is the most certain indicator of where he went over. While the exact position is not known, it must have been somewhere along that line. While the crew is keeping a look out and listening for the emergency whistle, try to establish a time for the man to have gone overboard, even if only from knowing that it couldn't have been earlier than the last time he was seen. This will help to establish an area in which he is likely to be. If the boat's speed is known, and the time since the man was seen, there will be a calculated distance along that line which will be where he went over. That will become the centre of the search area. If the navigator has a Satnav at his disposal he can use this to track back to the area of search—some even have a button which, when pressed at the call of 'man overboard', records the position as a waypoint, giving a course and distance back to it and plotting continually until it is deactivated.

When the yacht reaches the point considered nearest to where the man went overboard, the navigator should calculate how far he may have drifted in the time and search that side of the area first. The boat should reach up and down across the area, with the navigator plotting every move so that he can see at a glance what area has been searched and what has not (see diagram 6.14). When the man is sighted he is recovered in the way already described.

NAVIGATION

It's not an accident that navigators have a high standing in yachting and in flying. Navigation is, when properly executed, an art. Anybody can navigate along a coast, they have only to understand the elements of chart work and how to take simple bearings. But whether they can do it at night in a storm when a lot of the instruments on the console aren't working or in the middle of the ocean is another matter. To be able to navigate is more than to know where the boat is. Any navigator should be able to tell you where you've been and where you are now. But can he tell you which is the best course to take? Can he tell you where he thinks the next weather pattern will be? Can he tell you whether you're going to be lee-bowing a current and getting good effect from it or driven sideways by it and losing? All these and many, many other things. A good navigator knows that a Satnav, while a beautiful instrument, is only another aid to navigation. He knows that if it breaks down he's going to have to revert to what was the only form of navigation possible until recently—celestial. If the worst comes to the worst, he'll have to revert to dead reckoning and find out precisely where he is when he gets there.

I believe the true art of navigation is knowing where you should be going and using the conditions to get there as comfortably as possible. One navigator in a recent long race checked his log after the race and found that the boat had covered 30 nautical miles fewer than the recorded distance between the start and the finish. This meant that the boat had picked up 30 nautical miles through use of currents, 30 nautical miles the boat didn't have to sail. At an average of six knots, that's a five-hour edge on any opponent, and that's what it's all about.

Even the newest comer to navigation nowadays knows that there are vectors to work out in terms of wind and course, which those wonderful little hand held programmable calculators are able to produce for you at the drop of a hat. But there are vectors in the water, too, and they are far more important. Currents throughout the world can run at anything up to two-thirds the speed through the water of a yacht, in some places faster than a yacht can travel. If that movement can be harnessed for the yacht's benefit it is a great advantage, if it can't the competitors have that advantage. At worst, a three knot current can be pushing you three nautical miles away from your target every hour. In a race that lasts several days it's easy to see the effect. There are certainly other considerations than current—where the wind is likely to come from next and its strength, sea conditions, all sorts of other factors—but I believe none is more important than current and its proper use.

T O O L S
O F   T H E   T R A D E

We will start as though the reader knows nothing, then build up to be sophisticated enough to get out in the ocean safely. The books in Further References (page 305) contain additional advice.

You will need:

- Pencils
- Sharpener
- Erasers
- Tracing paper
- Dividers
- Portland or Breton Plotter (plotter with a rotating compass rose)
- Protractor (for vectors)
- Charts
- Hand bearing compass
- Sextant
- Hand held programmable calculator
- Accurate timepiece

For the small boat sailor an **HB pencil** is best, not the more usually prescribed 2B. The softer pencil smudges when wet and will leave marks when the chart is folded and put away. I know charts shouldn't be folded, but very few yachts have a drawer big enough for a half chart, let alone a whole one. The HB, used lightly, will leave a clear imprint on the chart, will rub out easily, and will not indent the chart. They do not have to be sharpened as often as softer pencils and do not break as easily.

The softer type of **eraser** sold in art shops is best. They are not as harsh as ink erasers and they last a long time. Never rub out when a chart is wet or several layers of the surface will be gone forever. Wait until the eraser can be used very lightly. Carry at least two.

Tracing paper is used for plotting horizontal sextant angles, three bearing fixes, course from bearing and soundings, jibe angles and vectors. These terms will be explained later, but it can be seen that tracing paper is a very handy item. Carry a book of paper, which is available from art stores.

Dividers are designed to be used with one hand only. I prefer the type with the rounded legs rather than the straight ones. The hinge at the top usually has a slot into which a screwdriver fits to increase or lessen the friction between the arms. The friction should be enough for the arms to hold their position when not under pressure, but to move when squeezed gently. They become very easy to use after only a little practice. Remember, when using dividers to measure distance, use only the latitude scale on the sides of the chart. The longitude scale is distorted because the meridians of longitude get closer together as they near the poles.

I don't believe there is any place for parallel rules on a yacht, yet almost every book I read recommends them. They are for ships only. On yachts the rolling type roll around on the chart table, they fall off the table, and they exasperate the navigator. The type with two sections joined by arms has to be 'walked' over the chart and invariably jolts out of line. The small boat navigator should use a **Portland plotter**, which is made of a plastic square with an arm which can rotate. Above the arm is a plastic compass rose which can rotate independently of the arm. The great advantage of the plotter is that the square can be lined up with any longitude or latitude and a course taken from the compass rose can be transferred anywhere on the chart without having to 'walk' or 'roll' parallel rules across the chart.

A virtue of the Portland plotter is that variation for the area being navigated can be built in. A variation scale is marked near the 0 degree heading, and on each side of it. The variation is read from the chart and the plastic compass rose is rotated until its north pointer (see diagram 7.1) indicates the variation. The plotter arm indicates which way to apply deviation. The courses indicated by the plotting arm are then magnetic and can be read straight from the plastic rose and passed to the helmsman. The **Breton plotter** comprises a rectangular plastic rule with a central rotating compass rose and grid.

Diagram 7.1 *The portland plotter.*

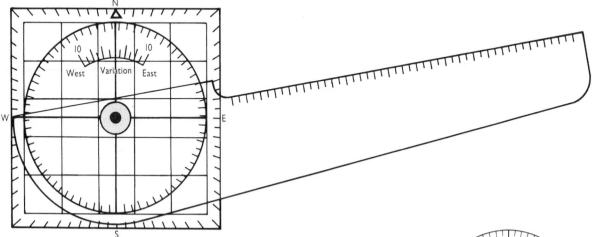

A **protractor** is useful for vectors. There is actually a protractor on the Portland plotter, but it is hard to use. Buy one of the circular types with parts of the centre cut out (see diagram 7.2) then mark a good big arrow with a black marker pen, so that north can be seen at night. Diagram 7.2 indicates how this should be done. It is a good idea to carry the black mark around most of the protractor to help the eye find north.

Charts are simply sailor's maps. On pages 130–134 some of the most common symbols used in charts are reproduced. You will have to become familiar with them, either through usage, or by learning them. Charts are so important they must be looked after with great care. Information on charts changes. Lights are given different characteristics, or are moved. New information becomes available about the depth of water, the position of dangerous wrecks etc. This information is given in Notices to Mariners, which authorised chart agents will transfer to your charts, for a fee. Charts should be updated in this fashion just before a voyage is undertaken.

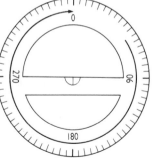

Diagram 7.2 *The protractor.*

The best **hand bearing compass** available is the Autohelm model with a built-in computer chip which gives it a memory. It will remember up to nine bearings. So you can take nine bearings of one object and average them to give you a very accurate bearing to use. You can do this for each of three bearings, so giving a very accurate fix in rough weather. If conditions are good you can take three and three and three, average them and still get a good position. The instrument has to be held level, both horizontally and longitudinally, but that's a relatively minor problem. You've still got to apply compass error to get the true bearing, but it's the only mechanism I've used in thirty years of navigation which has given me a three point bearing with no cocked hat, admittedly in smooth water. To have anything else, in my

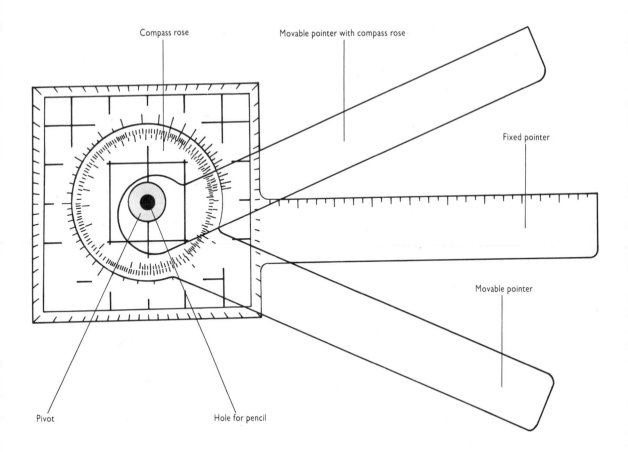

Diagram 7.3 *Three station pointer.*

mind, is crazy. It is so accurate that it will give you a good idea of what current the boat is in when sailing in short coastal races. I used to think the French hand bearing compass, with the rubber ring around it to protect the tiny compass inside, which was very well damped, was impossible to beat, but it has now been beaten. Another thing about the most modern hand bearing compass is that it has a little light in it for night time reading and it has rifle type sights on either side of it on top so that it can be lined up perfectly with the target. It is an absolutely super mechanism and no boat should be without one. Also incorporated in the Autohelm is a starting stopwatch. This performs well enough, but I find it more useful for timing lights at night. There is no guesswork involved.

The most invaluable instrument of the celestial navigator is a **sextant**, which you should cherish. Diagram 7.5 shows the sextant and the major parts of it, which are the arc, the vernier and the micrometer gauge. The index bar joins the micrometer to the main arc, and can be released usually by a pressure bar just behind it which allows free movement of the vernier along the arc. The eye piece is a small telescope bringing the stars closer, but a great many navigators prefer to take the telescope out, which is fine if you know precisely which star you're going for or if you've preset the sextant to the expected angle of a known star. The mirrors are the horizon glass, which is half silvered so that an image can be retained while another one is 'brought down', and the index mirror, which reflects the celestial object and of course moves as the index arc moves. There are shades for use in bright sunlight to reduce the glare both on the horizon glass and the index mirror. A sextant has errors which have to be allowed for. The major one a navigator needs to know about is index error, which can be checked very easily on land and at sea. If the index arm has been brought to zero and an object such as a bridge is viewed through the horizon glass the two images should have no apparent break in them (see diagram 7.4). An easy way to make this clear to yourself is to move the micrometer drum very slightly and you'll see that part of the image that you're viewing moves up or down. If there is a step when the arc is brought back to nought the error must be compensated for.

Sight the sextant on the object that you are testing for index error. If, when you turn the micrometer drum, it reads below zero you have to add that amount to the observed angle to correct it. If it shows above zero, in other words there is a small angle of altitude, then the error is subtracted to bring it to zero.

The basic observations needed for celestial navigation have to be corrected to make those observations accurate. First we need to know what exactly it is that we're taking a sight of. If you're taking a sextant shot of a star you must try to get the horizon to go through the middle of the star; the same applies to a planet. Because the sun and the moon are so much bigger there would be too much margin for error, so the reading is taken usually from the bottom of the object, which is known as the lower limb. The top is the upper limb. They are allowed to just kiss the horizon.

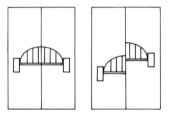

Diagram 7.4 *Index error—on the left there is no error; on the right index error is shown.*

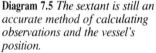

Diagram 7.5 *The sextant is still an accurate method of calculating observations and the vessel's position.*

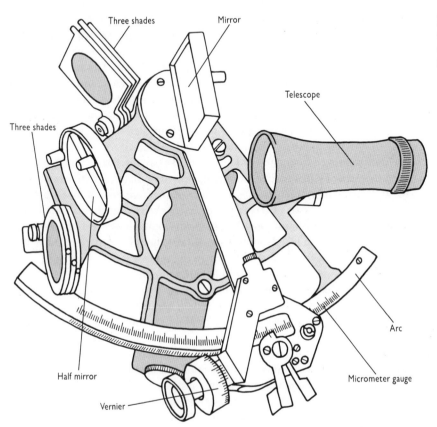

Three shades

Mirror

Telescope

Three shades

Arc

Half mirror

Micrometer gauge

Vernier

To make sure that the sextant is being held vertically, and so taking an accurate sight, it should be swung through an arc of about 20 degrees several times to make sure that the object is swung like a pendulum and goes properly into its position on the horizon.

Another possible error is refraction and a similar one is caused through wobbling in taking the observation. Refraction happens at low angles, where the light is bent as it comes through the Earth's atmosphere. Wobbling happens at high angles, where it's very difficult to bring a star down and get an accurate reading.

The simple way to overcome these problems is to take sights of heavenly objects only at an angle of between 15 degrees and 60 degrees. It would be possible to go above 60 degrees, but foolhardy to go below 15 degrees.

Now comes the most difficult thing to learn about a sextant—how to hold it and handle it. Practice is what you need. Let's start with a star, and we'll say that it's a wonderfully clear night and it's a star that you know absolutely without fail, and you have a smooth sea. Although we all know that this is an extremely unlikely combination, it means that your observation is going to be easy to make. Hold the sextant in your left hand, if you are right handed. With the other, grip the spring release on the index arm so that the arc will move freely.

Once you have sighted on the object, gently move the index arm until you've brought it down pretty close to the horizon, then release the spring grip, making sure the gear engages completely with the teeth on the bottom of the arc. From now on your adjustments are done on the micrometer drum. Rotate the drum in the way that brings the object to the horizon. It may well be that the star has been brought down below the horizon or it may be hovering above it. The direction in which you must turn the micrometer will soon become apparent to you, and you can then bring the object down to the horizon and do the little 20 degree swing that we described earlier. The normal routine now is that there is somebody with the navigator who has a torch (flashlight), an accurate watch and a notepad and pencil, who will take the reading. This assistant sits poised and waits until the person taking the sights calls 'ready' to indicate that he's about to take a reading and then 'mark' to show he has done so. At that moment the time is noted. There are navigators who say that one sighting is enough, and that may be so for those who have been doing so much of it that they're thoroughly practised. But many who are learning celestial navigation don't get a great deal of practice, so it's much better to take three or even five observations of each object and then average them to get the reading you're going to use in the reductions. The observation is taken in the first instance from the arc. Where the pointer is rested will show within an accuracy of 1 degree, perhaps in some cases half a degree. The micrometer will give readings to within half a minute.

A **hand held programmable calculator** is another must. It may well be that with the software they finish up costing you about twice your week's salary, but for what they can give you, they're amongst the best value of anything you can buy. Not only do they store the position of the stars for any time of the day and night for longer than a lot of us will stay alive, they can accurately turn your sextant observations into positions in a few moments. They're the next best thing to a Satnav, although obviously they're a great deal more work.

They can also tell you how you're going in terms of handicap if the other boat's handicap is known and the elapsed time is known. They will give you wind vectors, they will give you information that you can apply to polar performance curves, it's even possible now to get hand held computers which are so user friendly that they'll practically guide you through the steps that you require. One, the Casio, goes so far as to say 'oops' if you press a wrong button. What next!

Many sources recommend that yachts should carry a **radio direction finder**. I don't find them satisfactory for any more than two functions. One is to get a position in conditions of limited visibility and the other is to home in on a signal. The first I consider to be the least accurate of any method of obtaining a fix, unless the station, or stations, are right on the sea shore and there's no intervening land or islands. The radio beams bend and do all sorts of unpredictable things. I find it altogether too haphazard to be any more than an indication of position. However, a yacht can home in on a radio signal, even from a commercial station, if the position of that station is known, simply by following the null signal. That will bring you close enough to your objective for other more precise means of position finding to take over.

A **lead line** or **echo sounder** (electronic depth finder) is also a good thing to have, but it is virtually useless unless the display, or a repeater, is where the helmsman can see it. By the time one crew member can note a rapid decrease in depth, shout up to the helmsman and convince him that he's not joking, and get a reaction, the vessel is very likely aground. Echo sounders, like any other electronic device, can fail and so it's wise to have a lead line as a fallback. They don't take much room, in fact, for a yacht the line need not be more than 20 metres (60 feet) long.

Most people nowadays would be hard put to identify depth by the archaic method of putting pieces of cloth or leather at fixed distances along the line. A better method is to use plastic tags, which are impervious to sea water or rot, and mark off the depth in feet or metres with the marking painted on the plastic tag.

The old fashioned lead line, however, is still an internationally recognised system, so it is illustrated in diagram 7.6.

A yacht or motor boat must have some **speed** or **distance measuring instrument**, and they are usually combined into one. Of course, if you have a satellite navigator it is interfaced so that the computer continually interrogates the fluxgate compass and the speed impeller to find out the direction and speed of the vessel. This gives a highly accurate dead reckoning—much more accurate than any other navigator could possibly hope to get from observations made by crew.

If every conceivable instrument on board the vessel were to break down, except the compass, and the navigator had to rely on ancient methods, he would have to get answers to the questions: What is the boat's direction, what is its speed, is there a current? The direction comes from the compass, the current from observation, so all that is needed is an estimate of speed. In some cases experience will be a good enough guide. People who have sailed one boat for a long time can become remarkably accurate at estimating speed. But if there is no acceptable indication of boat speed, then use the Dutchman's log method. Get a crew member to go to the bow of the boat and drop something which will float in the water while at the same time calling out so that the time can be noted. The stopwatch is halted when the floating object reaches the stern of the vessel and the time taken to travel the known distance— the length of the boat—can be converted into a speed in knots. The formula

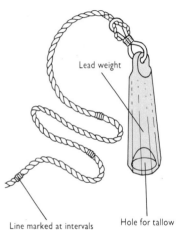

Lead weight

Line marked at intervals

Hole for tallow

Diagram 7.6 *A hand leadline. The tallow goes into the recess in the base and brings samples of the bottom to the surface to help identify the area by the sea bottom.*

is: If, say, the object takes 5 seconds to travel the length of a 42 foot boat, the boat speed will be 6080 feet (for this calculation near enough to a nautical mile) divided by 42 feet (length of boat) multiplied by 5 (time in seconds) divided by 60 (to convert to minutes). The resultant is that the object would cover one nautical mile in 12.06 minutes; sixty divided by 12.06 gives 4.98, which is the speed in knots.

Given the information above you will be able to dead reckon the boat. Even if you have a Satnav or a hand held programmable calculator you still should be able to navigate in the way that's been used since Captain Cook's time. You will need to carry books that contain the information you'll need to calculate your position, and to warn you of dangers en route, and to bring you information about tides, lights, radio aids, even your legal obligations.

These include:

- Pilot books
- *Nautical Almanac* (or Reed's)
- Nautical tables
- Tide tables or atlas
- Sight reduction tables

- Book of signals
- Notices to Mariners
- International Regulations for Preventing Collisions at Sea

There are several books that are absolute musts. They contain information that you're likely to need at any time and that might literally save your life. First and foremost are the *Admiralty Sailing Directions*, more usually called 'Pilots'. Pilots have been collated over many centuries and describe in great detail all the coastlines and major inland shipping routes of the world. Although they are written mainly for the large vessel they contain information from the days of sail, so they are of relevance to the yachtsman. They give descriptions of harbours and entrances, tell of hazards such as wrecks and shoals and contain the gathered wisdom of hundreds of sailors. They are updated regularly and are the first books to refer to, if in doubt.

You will also need *Notices to Mariners*, which are published weekly by most major mercantile countries and usually available free. There's a summary of those 'Notices' each year. Notices are used to correct information on charts and should be read in conjunction with your charts. You must also have the Admiralty Tide Tables or any other tide tables for the area in which you're sailing. They will give you knowledge of the tidal streams, directions and strengths you will need to take into account when deciding the course you want to take. Tidal information varies in importance in direct relation to the range and rate of flow for the area where you are sailing.

The other books mentioned above are for celestial navigation and their use will be described in that section (see page 154). We are gathering more and more information, and it is with information that we navigate.

THE LOG

A log contains information on the vessel's movement on its voyage. The table on page 115 shows the headings for a log as I use it. I have rather more headings than most navigators, but I have found through experience that they are all needed. They do not take very much longer to complete than fewer items, but if you don't have them when they are needed you cannot find them elsewhere.

Time	Magnetic Course	Speed	Log	Log Difference	Wind Speed	Wind Direction	Water	Barometer	Trend	Engine Hours	Sails	Comments

START TIME: 0900

START LOG: 1500

TIME

The first column in the log shows time. Some logs allow a 'from–to' for time, as from 0100 to 0200, but I prefer the simpler entry 0110, being the actual time of the entry. From this all calculations like average speed, rate of fall of the barometer, engine hours etc. can be calculated. The log should be written up at least every hour and in a major race, or severe conditions, every half hour. Then trends can be seen more quickly and corrective action taken sooner.

The most important function of a correctly kept log is to enable a dead reckoning record of the voyage to be recreated by another navigator if anything happens to the first.

COURSE

The second column in the log is for course. Here I enter the magnetic course, the one the helmsman is steering. This is because any alteration he might make will be written in the log. If every alteration is changed to the true course, every entry is a chance for error, whereas recording the compass (magnetic) course is straightforward.

SPEED

The next column shows speed. This is the first area where care needs to be taken. Mostly, when asked what speed the boat has done during the past half hour, the helmsman will give the speed that is on the instrument when you ask. You will need to stress that you want the average. Even the average will not be as accurate as one would wish, but it's better than something grossly wrong. Speed is important in racing where a slight change in course and resultant increase in average speed may improve VMG towards the finishing line.

LOG READING

The log reading, or distance travelled, is the next entry. Here you record the reading on the ship's log. The first entry that should go into the log is the log reading as the voyage started. This is not allowed for in most logs, so the place for it is at the top of the page, on its own. This is the prime bit of information from which all your dead reckoning will start. Don't write it in the first row under 'log', as the next column is called log difference.

LOG DIFFERENCE

This is where you take the last log reading away from the present reading, thus getting the distance travelled in the period between the last two readings. The entries will be opposite the wrong times if you fill in the first space with the reading before the voyage started. You can only have a log difference when you have travelled some distance. It is here that you will start getting discrepancies with the speed column. It won't matter, but it will indicate whether the people on deck are over or under-estimating speed.

WIND SPEED AND DIRECTION

In the direction column it is best to use the 360 degree notation. It is slower to get the direction this way, and can irritate a tired crew, but small shifts in the wind show up better, and in a race this can be critical in terms of strategy. Speed will be taken straight from the instruments, and again should be averaged. The helmsman feels really good telling you he's 'getting puffs of 50 knots' but that will only mislead you if that happened once in an hour and the rest of the time the wind has been blowing only at 25 knots.

WATER TEMPERATURE

The next column is for water temperature which is far more valuable in racing than cruising, although in the Pacific a rise in temperature, with very blue water, can indicate conditions where tuna fishing is good. In a race, a rise in temperature above that expected for the area (the Pilots have temperature distribution charts) indicates a current, and if the current is going the way you want, you are picking up speed for nothing.

BAROMETER READING

A column for the barometer reading is necessary. This is very straightforward, simply recording the pressure indicated by the barometer at the time of the entry. Be careful to get directly behind the indicator needle as parallax error can distort the reading.

BAROMETRIC TREND

It is a good idea to include a column showing the barometric trend which some would say would be obvious from the preceding column. It can be seen in the preceding column, certainly, but it is not obvious. I use arrows for up or down movement and a minus sign for 'steady'. If there is a clear succession of downward arrows, one soon looks at the figures to analyse the trend.

ENGINE HOURS

Note engine hours in the last of the narrow columns. This is very valuable as not only does it tell when the engine is due for servicing, it allows calculations of how much fuel is left (if consumption is known) and yachts do not often have fuel gauges. It allows conservation of engine fuel (don't forget fuel makes refrigeration and electricity possible) in circumstances where life would be difficult if the fuel ran out.

SAILS AND COMMENTS

The last column is very wide and is divided into two unequal sections. The first, smaller section, lists the sails the boat is using and the larger one consists of remarks, positions taken, unusual sightings or happenings, bearings, other ships seen and so on.

THE CHART

Combine the information in your log with the chart and you are getting close to starting to navigate. The beginner, or less experienced navigator, should bear in mind that charts and the symbols on them are really for big boats and ships. In harbours the major channels and therefore the entrance and leaving marks, the port and starboard marks and their lights, are geared for the channels where there is the deepest water so major commercial shipping can travel in safety. There are many areas outside those main channels in ports and harbours and estuaries which are navigable by smaller boats, but they are also less well marked. So the small boat navigator should keep in mind either to take the risk of travelling in a busy channel which is well marked and where the dangers are quite apparent, or avoid the crowd but maybe take a greater risk. In most cases the marking in more remote areas will still be adequate, but, for instance, there may be cardinal marks which are easy to see during the day, but not lit at night. One might well ask why they shouldn't be lit and why the less commercial waterways should be less well marked. It's part of the general problems the authorities have in trying to deal with things maritime. Of course it would be possible to put lights, particularly solar powered lights that don't cost a great deal on little hazards that are scattered around. But then you have to think in terms of the overall approach to harbours. Some harbours are very simple, particularly some of the better known harbours in the world, because the entrance is close to the sea, the lights at the entrance are not part of the general background of city lights and the wide expanse of waters leading to the protected harbour allow for easy identification of the navigation lights. But there are some places where just the opposite is true. There are ports which perhaps consist of only a breakwater or a mole or something of that kind, with lights on the end to identify the entrance. These lights very often are completely lost amongst a myriad non-navigation lights from the township behind. So to add to this confusion by marking hazards which are off the beaten track would not be sensible. The balance is somewhere in between, but clearly the main function of charts, chart symbols and lights and so on is to make navigation safe for commercial traffic.

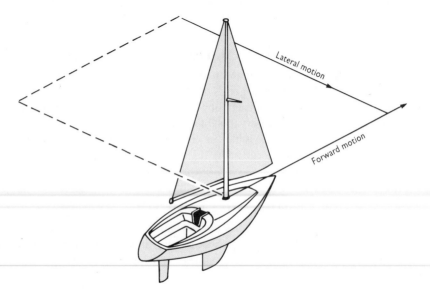

Diagram 7.7 *A basic tool of the navigator is the vector, which shows the effect of a sideways pressure such as wind or current on the forward motion of a boat. Apparent wind is the resultant of the boat's motion on the wind, 'bending' it forward and it can be shown as a vector.*

INTERNATIONAL CODE OF SIGNALS

 A
 B
C
D

 E
 F
G
H

I
J
K
L

 M
N
O
P

Q
R
S
T

 U
V
W
X

 Y
Z

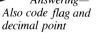 Answering—
Also code flag and decimal point

First substitute

 Second substitute

Third substitute

1

2

 3
4
5
6

 7
8
9
0

A *Diver down, keep clear*
B *Explosives*
C *Yes*
D *Keep clear*
E *I am directing my course to starboard*
F *Disabled*
G *Want a pilot*
H *A pilot is on board*
I *I am directing my course to port*
J *I am on fire, dangerous cargo, keep clear*
K *I wish to communicate*
L *Stop your vessel instantly*
M *Stopped and making no way through the water*
N *No*
O *Man overboard*
P *About to sail*
Q *Request pratique*
R
S *Going full speed astern*
T *Keep clear, engaged in pair trawling*
U *You are running into danger*
V *Require assistance*
W *Require medical assistance*
X *Stop carrying out your intentions and watch for my signals*
Y *I am dragging my anchor*
Z *I require a tug*

IALA MARITIME BUOYAGE SYSTEM

REGION A - BY DAY

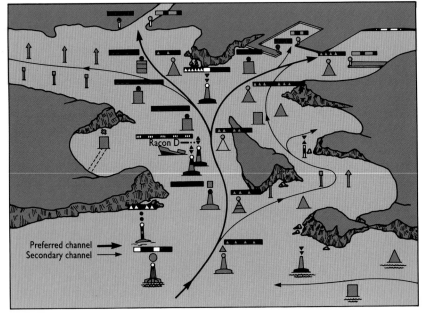

Preferred channel →
Secondary channel →

Racon D

REGION A - BY NIGHT

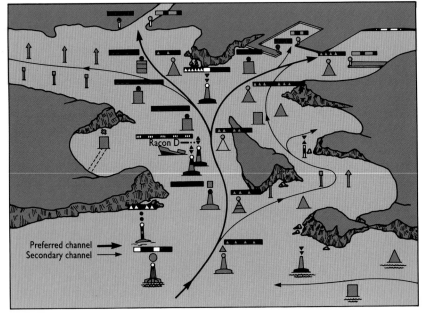

Preferred channel →
Secondary channel →

Racon D

REGION A
LATERAL MARKS

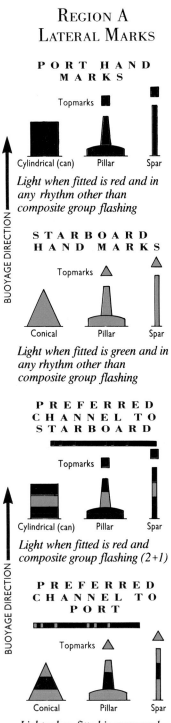

PORT HAND MARKS

Topmarks ■

Cylindrical (can)   Pillar   Spar

Light when fitted is red and in any rhythm other than composite group flashing

STARBOARD HAND MARKS

Topmarks ▲

Conical   Pillar   Spar

Light when fitted is green and in any rhythm other than composite group flashing

PREFERRED CHANNEL TO STARBOARD

Topmarks ■

Cylindrical (can)   Pillar   Spar

Light when fitted is red and composite group flashing (2+1)

PREFERRED CHANNEL TO PORT

Topmarks ▲

Conical   Pillar   Spar

Light when fitted is green and composite group flashing (2+1)

BUOYAGE DIRECTION

Topmarks should be carried, where practicable, when buoy is not can or conical.

R E G I O N   B   -   B Y   D A Y

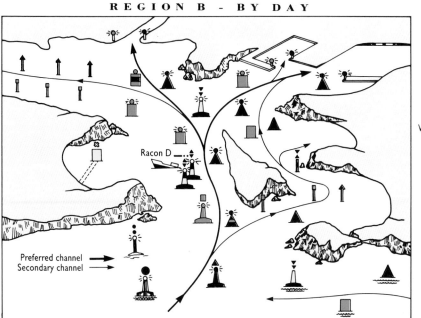

Racon D

Preferred channel ➡
Secondary channel ➡

CARDINAL MARKS

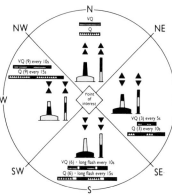

Buoy shapes are pillar or spar

Topmarks should always be carried.

Lights when fitted are white, very quick flashing (VQ) or quick flashing (Q)

R E G I O N   B   -   B Y   N I G H T

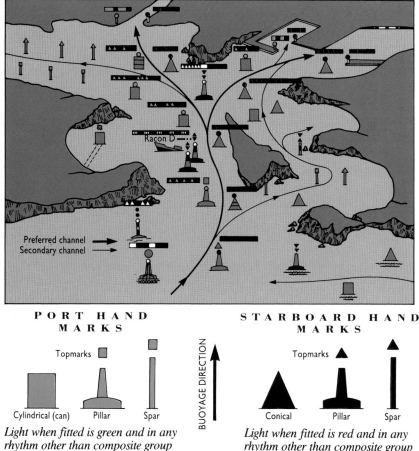

Racon D

Preferred channel ➡
Secondary channel ➡

REGION B LATERAL MARKS

P R E F E R R E D   C H A N N E L   T O   S T A R B O A R D

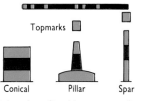

Topmarks

Conical   Pillar   Spar

Light when fitted is green and composite group flashing (2+1)

P R E F E R R E D   C H A N N E L   T O   P O R T

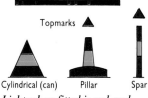

Topmarks ▲

Cylindrical (can)   Pillar   Spar

Light when fitted is red and composite group flashing (2+1)

BUOYAGE DIRECTION

Topmarks should be carried, where practicable, when buoy is not can or conical.

P O R T   H A N D   M A R K S

Topmarks

Cylindrical (can)   Pillar   Spar

BUOYAGE DIRECTION

Light when fitted is green and in any rhythm other than composite group flashing

S T A R B O A R D   H A N D   M A R K S

Topmarks ▲

Conical   Pillar   Spar

Light when fitted is red and in any rhythm other than composite group flashing

INTERNATIONAL LIGHT CONFIGURATIONS

Under the International Regulations for Preventing Collisions at Sea *the following lights are required to be exhibited:*

○ Masthead light over fore and aft centreline of vessel

◐ Sidelight on starboard side

● Sidelight on port side

○ Sternlight

○ Towing light

○ All round light

○ Manoeuvring light

A power-driven vessel underway.

A power-driven vessel underway less than 50 metres in length.

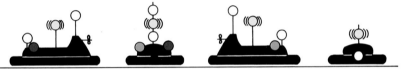

A hovercraft when operating in the non-displacement mode.

A hovercraft when operating in the non-displacement mode, less than 50 metres in length.

Sidelights if practicable

A power-driven vessel of less than seven metres in length whose maximum speed does not exceed seven knots.

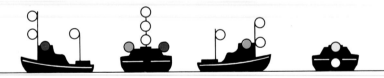

A power-driven vessel when towing.

A power-driven vessel when towing when the length of the tow exceeds 200 metres.

A power-driven vessel of less than 50 metres in length, when towing.

A power-driven vessel of less than 50 metres in length when towing when the length of the tow exceeds 200 metres.

A power-driven vessel of less than 50 metres in length, when pushing ahead or towing alongside, except in the case of a composite unit.

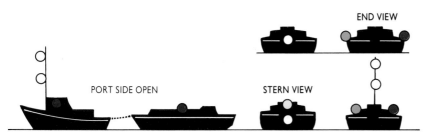

A power-driven vessel of less than 50 metres in length when towing.

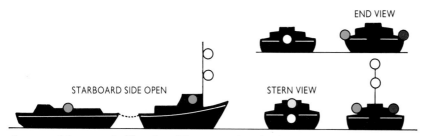

A power-driven vessel of less than 50 metres in length when towing.

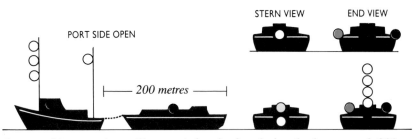

A power-driven vessel over 50 metres in length when the length of tow exceeds 200 metres.

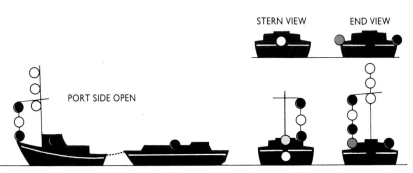

A power-driven vessel of less than 50 metres in length engaged in a towing operation such as severely restricts the towing vessel and its tow in their ability to deviate from their course.

A vessel or object being towed.

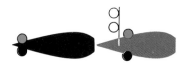

A vessel being pushed ahead not being part of a composite unit.

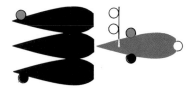

A group of vessels being pushed ahead.

A vessel being towed alongside.

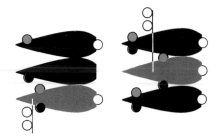

Two vessels towed alongside.

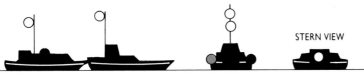

A pushing vessel and a vessel being pushed ahead rigidly connected in a composite unit and regarded as being a power-driven vessel.

A sailing vessel underway and a vessel under oars.

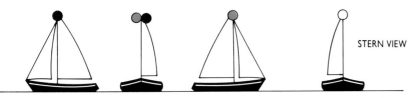

A sailing vessel underway of less than 20 metres in length and showing combined lantern.

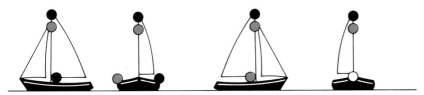

A sailing vessel underway and a vessel under oars.

A sailing vessel of less than seven metres in length and a vessel under oars in sufficient time to prevent collision.

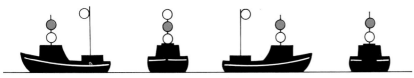

A vessel when engaged in trawling underway not making way through the water.

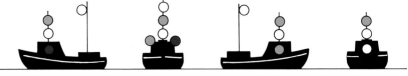

A vessel when engaged in trawling underway and making headway through the water.

A vessel of less than 50 metres in length when engaged in trawling underway not making way through the water.

A vessel of less than 50 metres in length when engaged in trawling underway and making way through the water.

A vessel engaged in fishing, other than trawling, underway or at anchor, not making way through the water, outlying gear extending 150 metres or less horizontally from the vessel.

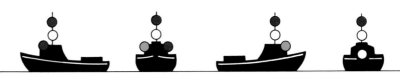

A vessel engaged in fishing, other than trawling, when making way through the water, outlying gear extending 150 metres or less horizontally from the vessel.

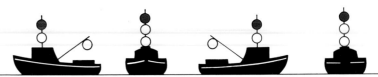

A vessel engaged in fishing, other than trawling, underway or at anchor, not making way through the water, when there is outlying gear extending more than 150 metres horizontally from the vessel.

A vessel engaged in fishing, other than trawling, when making way through the water, when there is outlying gear extending more than 150 metres horizontally from the vessel.

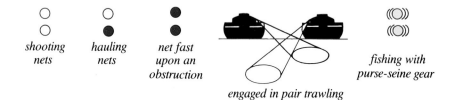

shooting
nets

hauling
nets

net fast
upon an
obstruction

engaged in pair trawling

*fishing with
purse-seine gear*

Additional signals for fishing vessels fishing in close proximity

A vessel not under command not making way through the water.

A vessel not under command making way through the water.

A vessel restricted in its ability to manoeuvre except a vessel engaged in minesweeping operations, not making way through the water.

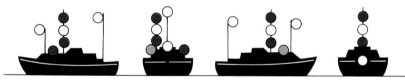

A vessel restricted in its ability to manoeuvre except a vessel engaged in minesweeping operations when making way through water.

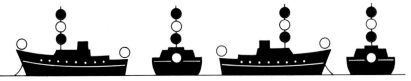

A vessel restricted in its ability to manoeuvre except a vessel engaged in minesweeping operations when at anchor.

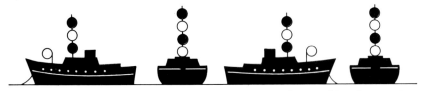

A vessel restricted in its ability to manoeuvre except a vessel engaged in minesweeping operations of less than 50 metres in length when at anchor.

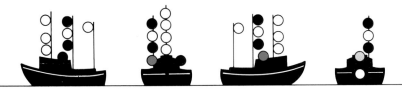

A vessel engaged in a towing operation such as renders it unable to deviate from its course when the length of the tow exceeds 200 metres.

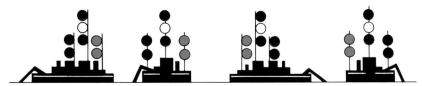

A vessel engaged in dredging or underwater operations when an obstruction exists when underway or at anchor but not making way through the water.

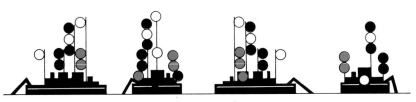

A vessel engaged in dredging or underwater operations when an obstruction exists when making way through the water.

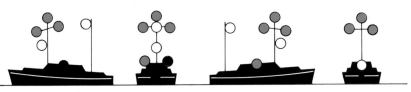

A vessel engaged in minesweeping operations.

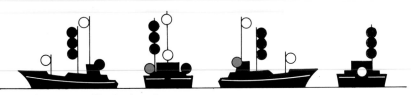

A vessel constrained by its draught.

A vessel engaged on pilotage duty moored alongside wharf.

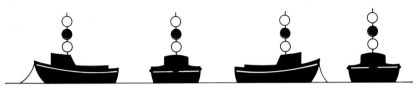

A vessel engaged on pilotage duty underway making way through the water or stopped.

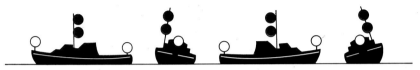

A vessel engaged on pilotage duty when at anchor.

A vessel at anchor.

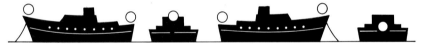

A vessel of less than 50 metres in length at anchor.

A vessel aground.

A vessel aground of less than 50 metres in length.

The Coastline

Ports and Harbours

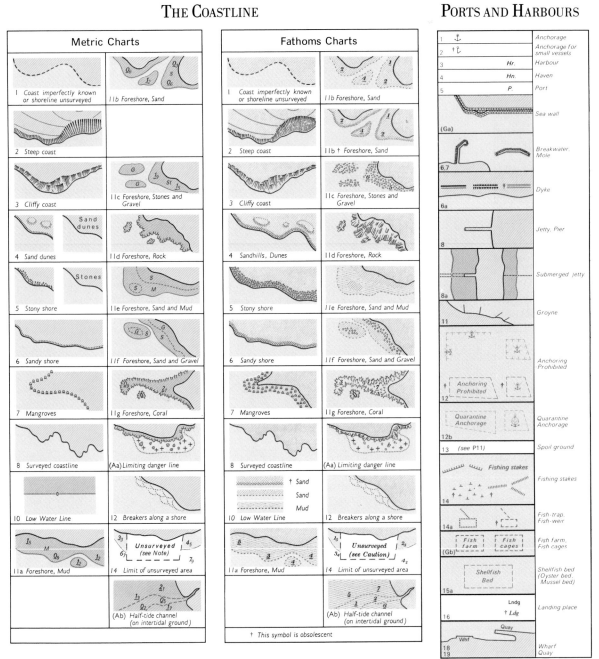

LIGHT CHARACTERS

Metric and Fathoms Charts			
CLASS OF LIGHT	International abbreviations	Older form (where different)	Illustration — Period shown
21 Fixed *(steady light)*	F		
22 Occulting *(total duration of light more than dark)*			
22 *Single-occulting*	Oc	Occ	
27 *Group-occulting* *e.g.*	Oc(2)	Gp Occ(2)	
(Ka) *Composite group-occulting* *e.g.*	Oc(2+3)	Gp Occ(2+3)	
23a Isophase *(light and dark equal)*	Iso		
23 Flashing *(total duration of light less than dark)*			
23 *Single-flashing*	Fl		
(Kb) *Long-flashing (flash 2s or longer)*	L Fl		
28 *Group-flashing* *e.g.*	Fl(3)	Gp Fl(3)	
(Kc) *Composite group-flashing* *e.g.*	Fl(2+1)	Gp Fl(2+1)	
24 Quick *(repetition rate of 50 to 79 - usually either 50 or 60 - flashes per minute)*			
24 *Continuous quick*	Q	Qk Fl	
(Kd) *Group quick* *e.g.*	Q(3)	Qk Fl(3)	
25 *Interrupted quick*	IQ	Int Qk Fl	
(Ke) Very Quick *(repetition rate of 80 to 159 - usually either 100 or 120 - flashes per min.)*			
(Ke) *Continuous very quick*	VQ	V Qk Fl	
(Kf) *Group very quick* *e.g.*	VQ(3)	V Qk Fl(3)	
(Kg) *Interrupted very quick*	IVQ	Int V Qk Fl	
(Kh) Ultra Quick *(repetition rate of 160 or more - usually 240 to 300 - flashes per min)*			
(Kh) *Continuous ultra quick*	UQ		
(Ki) *Interrupted ultra quick*	IUQ		
30a Morse Code *e.g.*	Mo(K)		
29 Fixed and Flashing	F Fl		
26 Alternating *e.g.*	Al.WR	Alt.WR	

COLOUR	International abbreviations	Older form (where different)	**RANGE** in sea miles	International abbreviations	Older form
67 White	W *(may be omitted)*		*Single range* *e.g.*	15M	
66 Red	R				
64 Green	G		*2 ranges* *e.g.*	14/12M	14,12M
(Kj) Yellow	Y		*3 or more ranges* *e.g.*	22-18M	22,20,18M
65 Orange	Y	Or			
63 Blue	Bu	Bl			
61 Violet	Vi				
ELEVATION is given in metres (m) or feet (ft)			**PERIOD** in seconds *e.g.*	5s	5sec

DANGERS

Metric Charts

1 Rock which does not cover (with elevation above MHWS or MHHW, or where there is no tide, above MSL)

2 Rock which covers and uncovers (with elevation above chart datum)

3 Rock awash at the level of chart datum

4 Underwater rock with 2 metres or less water over it at chart datum, or

rock ledge on which depths are known to be 2 metres or less, or

a rock or rock ledge over which the exact depth is unknown but which is considered to be dangerous to surface navigation

16_5
R $+ (16_5)$

5 Shoal sounding on isolated rock

$\frac{35}{R}$

6 Underwater rock not dangerous to surface navigation

6a Underwater danger with depth cleared by wire drag sweep

Historic Wreck (see Note)

† *Historic Wreck (see Note)*

(Oc) Restricted area round the site of a wreck of historical and archaeological importance.

(Covers and uncovers)   (Always covered)

10 Coral reef

Large scale charts

11 Wreck showing any portion of hull or super-structure at the level of chart datum

---

Masts

Mast (1·2)
Funnel
Mast (2)

Large scale charts

12 Wreck of which the masts only are visible

15 Wk

(Oa) Unsurveyed wreck over which the exact depth is unknown but which is considered to have a safe clearance at the depth shown

14 Wreck over which the exact depth of water is unknown but is thought to be 28 metres or less, and which is considered dangerous to surface navigation

7·3   *7·3*

Large scale charts

15 Wreck over which the depth has been obtained by sounding, but not by wire sweep

9·2 Wk

15a Wreck which has been swept by wire to the depth shown

16 Wreck over which the exact depth is unknown but thought to be more than 28 metres, or

a wreck over which the depth is thought to be 28 metres or less, but which is not considered dangerous to surface vessels capable of navigating in the vicinity.

♯   *Foul*   *Foul*

† *Foul*   *22 Foul*

Where depth known

17 The remains of a wreck, or other foul area, no longer dangerous to surface navigation, but to be avoided by vessels anchoring, trawling, etc.

18 Overfalls and tide-rips

19 Eddies

---

20 Kelp

21	*Bk.*	Bank
22	*Sh.*	Shoal
23	*Rf.*	Reef
24	*Le.*	Ledge

Br

25 Breakers

Well   *35 Well*

(Od) Submerged wellhead (with least depth where known)

Obstn

27 Obstruction or danger to navigation the exact nature of which is not specified or has not been determined.

24

(Oe) *Fish haven (with least depth where known)*

28	*Wk*	Wreck
29	*See 17*	Wreckage
29a	*See 17*	Wreck remains
30	*See 17*	Submerged piling
30a	*1 1 See also 17*	Snags, submerged stumps
32	*dr*	Dries
33	*cov*	Covers
34	*uncov*	Uncovers
35	*Rep* † *Repd*	Reported

Uncharted Dangers

38 *Danger line (see Note)*

(Ob) Areas of mobile bottom (including sand waves)

41	*PA* † *(PA)*	Position approximate
42	*PD* † *(PD)*	Position doubtful
43	*ED* † *(ED)*	Existence doubtful
	See Q1	Sounding of doubtful depth
44	*pos* † *posn*	Position
46	*unexam* † *unexamd*	Unexamined

Drying heights: See note in the Introduction.

Non-dangerous wrecks: Where the depth of a wreck exceeds 28 metres, or it is otherwise considered non-dangerous, the appropriate symbol is generally shown on the largest scale chart only.

Danger line: A danger line draws attention to a danger which would not stand out clearly enough if represented solely by its symbol (eg. isolated rock), or delimits an area containing numerous dangers, through which it is unsafe to navigate. A bold pecked line with explanatory legend may be used to delimit an area where there is inadequate information.

† *This symbol and/or abbreviation is obsolescent*

DANGERS

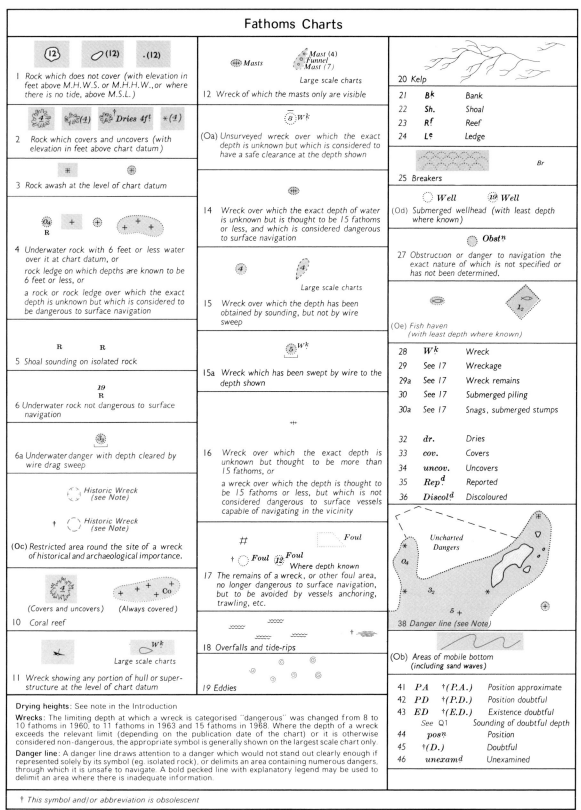

Fathoms Charts

1 Rock which does not cover (with elevation in feet above M.H.W.S. or M.H.H.W., or where there is no tide, above M.S.L.)

2 Rock which covers and uncovers (with elevation in feet above chart datum)

3 Rock awash at the level of chart datum

4 Underwater rock with 6 feet or less water over it at chart datum, or

rock ledge on which depths are known to be 6 feet or less, or

a rock or rock ledge over which the exact depth is unknown but which is considered to be dangerous to surface navigation

5 Shoal sounding on isolated rock

6 Underwater rock not dangerous to surface navigation

6a Underwater danger with depth cleared by wire drag sweep

Historic Wreck (see Note)

Historic Wreck (see Note)

(Oc) Restricted area round the site of a wreck of historical and archaeological importance.

(Covers and uncovers)   (Always covered)

10 Coral reef

Large scale charts

11 Wreck showing any portion of hull or super-structure at the level of chart datum

Masts

Mast (4)
Funnel
Mast (7)

Large scale charts

12 Wreck of which the masts only are visible

(Oa) Unsurveyed wreck over which the exact depth is unknown but which is considered to have a safe clearance at the depth shown

14 Wreck over which the exact depth of water is unknown but is thought to be 15 fathoms or less, and which is considered dangerous to surface navigation

Large scale charts

15 Wreck over which the depth has been obtained by sounding, but not by wire sweep

15a Wreck which has been swept by wire to the depth shown

16 Wreck over which the exact depth is unknown but thought to be more than 15 fathoms, or

a wreck over which the depth is thought to be 15 fathoms or less, but which is not considered dangerous to surface vessels capable of navigating in the vicinity

Foul

Foul   Foul   Where depth known

17 The remains of a wreck, or other foul area, no longer dangerous to surface navigation, but to be avoided by vessels anchoring, trawling, etc.

18 Overfalls and tide-rips

19 Eddies

20 Kelp

21	Bk	Bank
22	Sh.	Shoal
23	Rf	Reef
24	Le	Ledge

25 Breakers   Br

Well   Well

(Od) Submerged wellhead (with least depth where known)

Obstn

27 Obstruction or danger to navigation the exact nature of which is not specified or has not been determined.

(Oe) Fish haven (with least depth where known)

28	Wk	Wreck
29	See 17	Wreckage
29a	See 17	Wreck remains
30	See 17	Submerged piling
30a	See 17	Snags, submerged stumps
32	dr.	Dries
33	cov.	Covers
34	uncov.	Uncovers
35	Rep.d	Reported
36	Discold	Discoloured

Uncharted Dangers

38 Danger line (see Note)

(Ob) Areas of mobile bottom (including sand waves)

41	PA	†(P.A.)	Position approximate
42	PD	†(P.D.)	Position doubtful
43	ED	†(E.D.)	Existence doubtful
	See Q1		Sounding of doubtful depth
44	posn		Position
45	†(D.)		Doubtful
46	unexamd		Unexamined

Drying heights: See note in the Introduction

Wrecks: The limiting depth at which a wreck is categorised "dangerous" was changed from 8 to 10 fathoms in 1960, to 11 fathoms in 1963 and 15 fathoms in 1968. Where the depth of a wreck exceeds the relevant limit (depending on the publication date of the chart) or it is otherwise considered non-dangerous, the appropriate symbol is generally shown on the largest scale chart only.

Danger line: A danger line draws attention to a danger which would not stand out clearly enough if represented solely by its symbol (eg. isolated rock), or delimits an area containing numerous dangers, through which it is unsafe to navigate. A bold pecked line with explanatory legend may be used to delimit an area where there is inadequate information.

† This symbol and/or abbreviation is obsolescent

Lights

Metric and Fathoms Charts

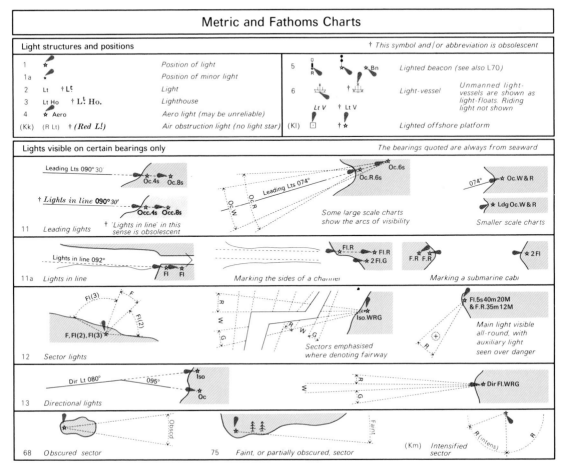

Light structures and positions † *This symbol and/or abbreviation is obsolescent*

1		Position of light
1a		Position of minor light
2	Lt †Lt	Light
3	Lt Ho †Lt Ho.	Lighthouse
4	Aero	Aero light (may be unreliable)
(Kk)	(R Lt) †(Red L!)	Air obstruction light (no light star)
5	Bn	Lighted beacon (see also L70)
6	Lt V †Lt V	Light-vessel — Unmanned light-vessels are shown as light-floats. Riding light not shown
(Kl)		Lighted offshore platform

Lights visible on certain bearings only   *The bearings quoted are always from seaward*

Leading Lts 090° 30'   Oc.4s Oc.8s

† *Lights in line* **090°** 30'   Occ.4s Occ.8s

11   *Leading lights*   † *'Lights in line' in this sense is obsolescent*

Leading Lts 074°   Oc.6s   Oc.R.6s   Oc.W   Oc.R

Some large scale charts show the arcs of visibility

074°   Oc.W & R   Ldg Oc.W & R

Smaller scale charts

Lights in line 092°

11a   *Lights in line*   Fl Fl   *Marking the sides of a channel*   Fl.R   Fl.R   2Fl.G   F.R F.R   *Marking a submarine cable*   2Fl

Fl(3)   F   Fl(2)   F, Fl(2), Fl(3)

Iso.WRG   *Sectors emphasised where denoting fairway*

Fl.5s40m20M & F.R.35m12M   *Main light visible all-round, with auxiliary light seen over danger*

12   *Sector lights*

Dir Lt 080°   095°   Iso   Oc

13   *Directional lights*   Dir Fl.WRG

68   *Obscured sector*   Obscd

75   *Faint, or partially obscured, sector*   Faint

(Km)   *Intensified sector*   R(intens)   R

Small Craft Facilities

Small craft facilities: special symbols

1		Visitors' mooring	a buoy reserved for visitors (may not be marked 'V' or 'Visitors')
2		Visitors' berth	part of a quay or pontoon reserved for visitors
3		Slipway	launching site, usually public (a charge may be made)
4		Public landing	usually steps or a ladder
5		Water tap	public access to drinking water
6		Fuel	diesel or petrol (may include car filling stations)
7		Public telephone	may not be shown if close to a charted post office
8		Post box	shown only in rural areas
9		Public house or inn	may represent more than one inn
10	×	Restaurant	shown only in rural areas
11		Yacht or sailing club	named on the larger scale charts
12	WC	Public toilets	
13	P	Public car park	
14		Parking for boats/trailers	shown where normally available to visitors
15		Launderette	
16		Caravan site	for touring caravans
17		Camping site	
18		Nature reserve	access may be restricted

C H A R T   S Y M B O L S

Most national hydrographic offices publish a chart or book of the symbols used on their particular charts. There isn't room in a book such as this to explain every symbol, but on pages 130–134 we have reproduced some of the most common symbols that appear on most international charts. If you get a grasp of these symbols, you'll be able to read a chart very soon. It really is worthwhile studying the chart for some time before going any further with this chapter. When you read further you will realise that I am being selective in the navigational techniques that I'm explaining to you. Many of the methods put forward in some of the more erudite navigational books are techniques that one would hardly ever use.

When you become familiar with the symbols on the chart learn in particular the ones that indicate safe anchorages, corners which are protected from prevailing winds, and so on. Always put your imagination to work. In an area where southerlies are the only winds that ever blow, you wouldn't look for an anchorage that is open to the south, you'd naturally look for somewhere protected. In other words, you may have to duck around the headland, travel east for a little while or west and then south and then anchor in a safe spot, so look for such places and learn to recognise the symbols. If you imagine yourself at sea and facing difficulties, you can see how the chart can give you much of the information you will need.

You can be selective. For instance, it won't very often be important to you to know what makes up the seabed, or exactly what kind of vegetation grows on a low headland that you're approaching, so for a start simply go for those symbols that will help you in pilotage. Become familiar with how to tell the depth of water you're in, whether there are any hazards such as rocky outcrops from the land or reefs or sandbanks or fierce currents. Are there submerged marine cables, are there overhead wires that perhaps the mast of your boat could touch? These are simple hazards that exist in harbours but as this is where you want to learn first to find your way about, you should familiarise yourself with chart symbols before you actually take off on a voyage, even if the voyage is only five or six nautical miles across fairly well known waters.

As you become familiar with the varying symbols and you plan your voyage beforehand you're developing good work practices for when you take up the more arduous and dangerous task of finding your way around the ocean. The

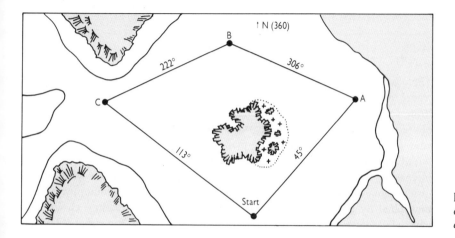

Diagram 7.8 *Setting a simple course around a rocky island in an enclosed harbour.*

next stage in learning about chartwork is measuring distance from the chart. It is not as straightforward as it might seem. When you measure a distance with your dividers or compasses you must take it from the latitude scale on either side of the chart directly opposite the area where you are plotting. The reason is that the longitude scale across the top and bottom of the chart is not consistent in various latitudes of the world. This becomes clear when you consider that the lines of longitude, the parallels of longitude as they are called, actually all join at the north pole and south pole because the Earth is a globe. Therefore the parallels become closer and closer together as they near the poles and cannot be taken for measurement in any way.

Now you can start piloting. As an exercise set yourself a simple little voyage around the harbour as shown in diagram 7.8. Plot the compass courses you will need for the boat to travel to the marks indicated, in the order indicated, and deal with hazards as marked on that chartlet. First of all, we're going to have to learn to do the very basic of navigation—to define and set a course.

DEFINING AND
SETTING A COURSE

We'll assume that everybody understands the 360 degree compass. To draw a course in its simplest way is to draw a line from your starting point to mark A (see diagram 7.8). So place a Portland plotter centre over the dot of your starting position and take the arm up through your destination. You then transfer the plotter to the compass rose on your chart, without moving the arm, and put the centre over the centre of the rose and read off the number of degrees around from 0 degrees and read 045 degrees off the chart. This is the first step towards defining a course. But unfortunately nothing is ever as easy or as simple as that. Your compass needle thinks that it's pointing at north when it is showing so, but in fact it is not. All over the world the needle is pulled out of line by the interaction of the differing magnetic fields from the north and south poles. Because the fields and their effect on each other vary from one part of the world to another, the pull away from true north varies all over the world. This effect is called variation.

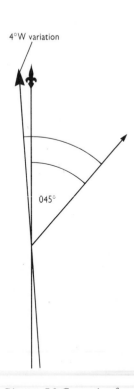

4°W variation

045°

Diagram 7.9 *Correcting for variation.*

VARIATION

There are parts of the world where there is no variation and there are parts where it can be up to 25 degrees or even more. Variation is not constant from year to year. However, sailors throughout the centuries very carefully plotted by observations what the variation is and what the difference is from year to year. This information is placed in the compass rose that's printed on all charts. You will see a printed statement that says 'Variation X degrees, increasing by x minutes annually'. The statement will give the year of the observation, so if you have a very old chart you may find the minutes increment, multiplied by the number of years, will bring the basic reading closer to a new whole degree than it was before. In plotting, allow for variation to the nearest whole degree. Nobody is able to allow variation to the accuracy of several minutes of a degree. Depending where we are in the world, the pull on the compass that we call variation may come from the east or the west and this adds another factor into what we have to allow in laying our course.

The simplest way of working out what happens to the basic course of 045 degrees that we got earlier with the Portland plotter, is that if the needle is pulled to the west it will move some degrees backwards along the compass circle and so to correct for it we have to add the same number of degrees to the circle. So when travelling 045 degrees with the needle being pulled 4 degrees to the west by variation, you would have to travel 049 degrees by your compass to achieve the true course that you wanted. It stands to reason therefore that if the needle is being pulled to the east—variation east—the compass course has to be corrected to a lower value. Therefore 4 degrees must be taken off the compass course so that you would be steering 041 degrees to make good a course of 045 degrees.

There are a great many memory tricks, or mnemonics, to help keep this rule in mind. The simplest states:

VARIATION EAST, COMPASS LEAST
VARIATION WEST, COMPASS BEST.

In other words, if the variation is east the compass course will be less than the true course, and with variation west, the compass course is greater than the true course.

We now have a method of setting a course in any part of the world provided we know the local variation.

DEVIATION

Another correction of the compass is called deviation which is easily found for any boat by observation. Deviation is the effect of those iron objects on boats such as engines, rigging, even the hull itself which can interfere with the magnetic field around the compass. Not only metal objects can cause this problem of deviation, having any sort of electronic or radio field can set up disturbances in the magnetic field which can make the compass quite inaccurate. So it's very important indeed to have good advice when putting a compass into a boat, if it hasn't already been sited somewhere sensible. What appears to be a great difficulty but is easy to overcome in terms of deviation (the magnetism of a vessel itself) is that the distorted field changes for every heading the ship travels on. It's therefore necessary to do one of two things. One is to work out a deviation chart, which we'll discuss presently, the other is to have a compass expert check out your compass and correct it by means of the small magnets that are provided with it. It's fairly expensive to do the latter, and it needs to be done quite often, so it really is better to learn how to construct a deviation chart yourself.

Diagram 7.10 *All the corrections needed to lay the first mark.*

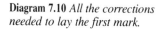

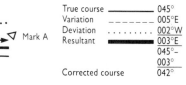

True course	————	045°
Variation	– – – – –	005°E
Deviation	. . . .	002°W
Resultant	▄▄▄▄▄	003°E
		045°–
		003°
Corrected course		042°

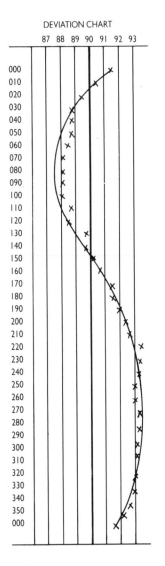

DEVIATION CHART

Diagram 7.10a *A typical smoothed out deviation curve.*

The ideal method is to have a friend tow your boat to a still area of harbour which allows a clear view of a known object some three or four nautical miles away that can be identified by an accurate position on a chart. The true bearing of this object can be taken from the chart and noted. Then take a series of bearings, first pointing the vessel directly at the object, then the port beam, then the stern, then the starboard beam. There will then be four readings 90 degrees apart taken of the object looking across the steering compass. When those four bearings have been taken, take four more, splitting the compass rose into 45, 135, 225 and 315 degrees. You will now have eight readings, which should vary by a few degrees if your compass hasn't been corrected. In most cases, eight bearings are enough, but if you want to be very thorough, then do the swing of the compass (as this is called) in a different way, taking a bearing every 10 degrees. Next, construct a chart similar to the one in diagram 7.10a. You will see that your readings have swung from side to side of the bearing which you know to be accurate—the first one you took. Lightly draw in a line that links each of these bearings and then smooth it out so that it makes a good looking curve. If you find that you have one or more bearings which are clearly outside the curve which represents the magnetic field, then you'll know you have a problem and you should take those bearings again. If that chart is then translated into a set of readings for each compass heading (see diagram 7.10a), the number of degrees of deviation for that heading can be taken either from the list next to the chart or by interpolation from the chart.

That, you'll be pleased to know, is the last correction that needs to be applied before we have an accurate compass course from A to B. As you can see from the chartlet that you produced, the deviation may be to the east or the west of the bearing that is known to be true. Deviation has to be conceived in precisely the same way as variation, and the same mnemonic applies. If you have like deviation and variation—in other words both go in the same direction—then add them together and correct by the total figures. If, however, you have 10 degrees east variation and 4 degrees west deviation, for example, they to some extent cancel each other, so you take the 4 degrees of west away from the 10 degrees of east, and you are left with 6 degrees of east variation. When you apply these compass corrections you have a compass, or magnetic, course to the object you're travelling to.

Now we come to a final and most important use of the mnemonic about variation east, compass least and variation west, compass best. If, after making your corrections you finished up with a correction that is east, then compass is least, which means that the course you give the helmsman from your position below at the chart table will be lower (fewer degrees) than the course you marked on the chart.

It's very important to remember this. A very good racing navigator and theoretician taught me that a simple way of remembering what to tell the helmsman and how to apply deck information on to a chart was that if you were calling up to the helmsman it was compass least for east variation, but when the helmsman called down to you the compass correction had to be added to arrive at the true course to be plotted. The reverse is true for variation west—compass best when calling up to the helmsman but take the correction away when plotting. Now that you have confidence in yourself you must learn not to have confidence in the helmsman unless you know for certain that the helmsman deserves your confidence.

H E L M E R R O R

This is not the person at the helm steering inaccurately. It is the same person reporting inaccurately. It is an unfortunate human failing to give a questioner the answer he expects. Unless a helmsman is experienced, or understands how important it is to give accurate information to a navigator, they will rarely admit to steering any course other than the one given them. They even get angry if you suggest they might not have done. If you have another compass down below, where you can check the course steered against the one given, try this as an exercise. Sit there for 20 minutes, no fewer, to check on the helmsman's course without letting him know you're doing it. See how the course varies and see whether you can get a good idea of the trend of that course. As you get more experienced, you can do the same with the 'course made good' function of a Satnav and you'll be able to get a highly accurate record of the course steered by that helmsman. Then go up and ask the helmsman what course he believes he's steered. Nearly all will say the course that you gave them. If you say: 'But I have been watching for 20 minutes and you have gone off 5 degrees to leeward,' they'll get angry and you'll lose a friend. Instead, store in your mind what difference there was between the desired course and the actual course made good with that helmsman. As you do more and more of this, you will be able to make allowances for different conditions and different helmsmen.

If you find that the amount of movement from the course that you want is significant, it's a simple matter to say to the helmsman: 'I think we can probably come up another 5 degrees without there being a problem' or 'Why not bear off 5 degrees, I think that'll give us a faster course,' or something of that kind. You then haven't had a confrontation, you've got the course correction you wanted, and the helmsman believes he's doing an absolutely top job.

In most cases they are—nobody deliberately goes off course. They may be underestimating the amount of wave slap that's pushing them sideways, the boat may be slightly overpressed and making more leeway than it should, or they may have a tendency to round up slightly high of a course which, in some circumstances, can be as bad as being low of it. So it's not worth having a fight every change of helmsman, but it is worth observing thoroughly what value or what quality of information you're getting from them.

Now that you've satisfactorily laid the course that you want, and decided how reliable you consider the steering to be, you have to take into consideration the fact that the water may be moving in such a way that the boat is actually being pushed away from or towards your target by a current.

C U R R E N T

A current is a tidal stream, or some such effect. Since our theoretical voyage is still within the confines of a harbour, it may be in a harbour that is sufficiently well administered that there is a chart that indicates to you the rate of flow of the tidal stream at various stages of the tide. In that case, it's a simple matter to lay off yet another correction to your course—the allowance for current. In a simple example (see diagram 7.11), if you're sailing five nautical

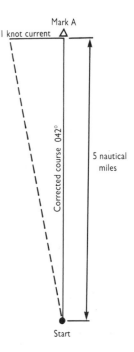

Diagram 7.11 *Correcting for a current.*

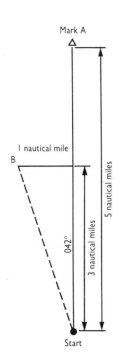

Diagram 7.12 *Course to steer to counteract a current.*

miles on a corrected course of 042 degrees from start to A, and there's a current running directly on your port beam at one knot, you know that in one hour the boat will be pushed one nautical mile from its course, to starboard. If the boat is travelling at five knots and the distance between A and B is five nautical miles, then the vector is easy. At the end of the hour's travel, draw a scale equivalent to one nautical mile in the direction of the current to port, which is where it's coming from. Draw a line from your starting point to the point where the one nautical mile has been marked in the direction of the current. Use the Portland plotter to read off the course linking your starting point and the end of the nautical mile. If you steer that course from your starting point all the way up that first leg, you will come out at the mark. You have steered into the current at an angle calculated to counteract it.

If the rate of travel isn't as nicely straightforward as this, the method to allow for it is simple (see diagram 7.12). If the boat's speed is three knots then you draw the one knot line of current towards its source in exactly the same way, but you do it at the three nautical mile point along the direct course from start to A. When the current line is extended one nautical mile you then join start to the position where the mile started (B), and that will give you the course. It can be seen from this simple explanation that known ocean currents can be counteracted in exactly the same way.

You now know enough about courses to be able to complete your journey around the harbour. You can apply the corrections for each compass heading and so arrive at a course that you can give the helmsman, and know that if he steers it you will get back safely to your anchorage.

L E E W A Y

This is the amount by which a boat, motor or sail, is pushed sideways by the strength of the wind. Many an owner, and some poor navigators, will tell you that their boat does not make leeway. This is arrant nonsense. There is no boat that does not make leeway, and the harder the wind blows the more leeway any boat will make. Certainly some boats will begin to make leeway later than others, because they are inherently stiffer, but all do it in the end. To judge leeway is very difficult but experience, both of a particular yacht and of yachts in general, and separately of motor boats, plays a large part.

A way to start gathering experience is to look at the wake of the yacht in relation to the course it is steering. The wake forms an angle with the direction of the boat (see diagram 7.13). In moderate weather this begins to give you a good idea of when the boat is beginning to make leeway. But once the seas get up a bit the wake disappears too quickly to give much help. All you can be sure of is that the angle will be greater when the seas get up than it was when the seas were relatively flat. If it gets rougher still, individual waves may push the boat several metres (feet) sideways—each. In very rough conditions a yacht may make only 60 degrees to the angle of the seas. I have seen a small yacht in a gale where the seas were big because the fetch was long, suffer such severe leeway that it was pushed sideways 80 nautical miles while sailing 180 nautical miles. It had lost almost one nautical mile sideways for every two nautical miles it sailed forward. So leeway becomes a prime concern in heavy weather. If, as a matter of practice, you always

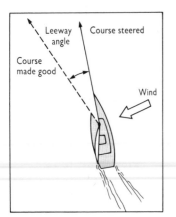

Diagram 7.13 *Leeway and how to correct for it.*

allow 5 degrees of leeway when giving a course to a helmsman, even in light weather, the worst that will happen is that you will come out high of a mark, and you will be putting away information that will help you make a decision another time. Leeway is deducted from the corrected course.

U N K N O W N   C U R R E N T

The skill you need to learn next is how to find out whether you are being affected by an unknown current and if you are, where it's coming from and how fast it is. A current not allowed for can put your boat in danger.

Your start is by obtaining accurate bearings of land objects. I mention again the Autohelm hand bearing compass, because you can believe implicitly in the results it gives you in flat water. For rough water, experience will still play a fairly vital part in judging the value of the bearings taken, even though you can take nine and average them. In my years of sailing I have never until now taken hand bearing compass readouts as being anything more than a rough position indicator. With this new device, I believe they can generally be accepted as accurate.

The method of finding current is as follows: Since we know where we started, the direction in which the boat is heading, and the speed at which it is travelling, we can work out where we ought to be a fixed time later, if there is no movement of the water around us. We would be x nautical miles along a course of 045 degrees. That is called **dead reckoning**. It is where you would be if you travelled at a known speed in a known direction and no other force had any effect on the boat whatsoever. Therefore, if we take an accurate position by observation, and it is different from our dead reckoning, there must have been some outside force which moved the boat to its observed position. The observed position would be taken by two or more bearings of at least two, preferably three, objects that are marked on the chart, so that those bearings, **when corrected for compass error** and plotted on the chart, would intersect and give us a position.

Even with the new compass it is likely that the three lines will not intersect at one point. Most probably they will leave a small triangle where they meet. This is known as a **cocked hat**. Put a dot in the centre and call that the observed position, unless there's a danger nearby, in which case the dot should be put as close to the danger inside the cocked hat as it can so that a safety margin is built into the new course (see diagram 7.14). We now have an **observed position** which is different from the dead reckoning position, so we can join a line between the two and read that angle off the compass rose. That will give us a direction in which the boat has been pushed. It is easy here to make a 180 degree error and therefore it helps to think in terms of the force that has pushed the boat from where you believed it would be to where you have found it is.

There is also a distance between the two marks. Again, taking the simple one hour's travel along the desired course at five knots, the scale distance shown on the chart compared with the five nautical miles of our course will give the distance the boat has been pushed off course in that hour. It follows, then, that if the boat has been pushed from a direction of 320 degrees and a distance of 0.75 of a nautical mile away from its desired course, it is sailing

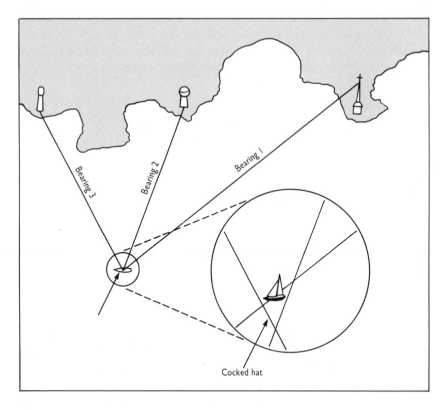

Diagram 7.14 *Position from three bearings.*

into a current that is setting 140 degrees at a rate of three-quarters of a knot. Note here that current is described in the opposite manner to wind. It is described as setting in its direction of travel. A current moving to the south is described as a southerly current, or set, even though it is coming from the north. A northerly wind comes from the north and blows to the south.

Now that this current is known it can be allowed for. But do not assume it will continue. It may well be that when you take your next observation one hour later the current is from a different direction, or there may have been none, or its rate may have doubled.

Now you have the major tricks needed in your locker as a navigator. From now on anything you learn is simply a different method of achieving the same result, a dead reckoning position and an observed position. So far you've only learned one method of deciding a yacht's observed position, which is by the three bearing fix. There are other ways of achieving good believable positions. When I say believable, I mean exactly that. As your experience as a navigator increases you will find that there are degrees of accuracy of fixes. You will attribute a level of quality to a fix. For instance, if you take a bearing of a mountain that has a sharp peak, you will know that bearing is highly accurate. If you take one of a rounded hill, the bearing is less accurate. A transit, where two charted objects line up, is perfect. Two headlands in line a long way off at dusk, is well short of perfect. Experience will tell you how far you can trust a fix, but the navigator of long standing has to be convinced that his observations are good. He doesn't believe he has arrived at a destination because that is where he is going, he believes it because observations demonstrate it to him.

VERTICAL SEXTANT ANGLE

A high quality fix is one by vertical sextant angle. Take a bearing of an object which is charted and which has a known height. Transfer the corrected bearing on to the chart. You must be somewhere along that line. To find out how far along the line, you take a sextant sighting of the object and read off the vernier scale the angle made between the horizon at the boat, and the top of the object (see diagram 7.15). That vertical angle, when corrected for height of eye (the height above sea level of the observer) and for the state of the tide, if that's relevant, can be checked against tables of vertical sextant angles and the angle equated to a distance off. When that distance off is marked out along the position line it gives a highly believable position.

A yacht navigator rarely wants his distance off to be so accurate that he will apply the correction for tidal level. The correction to his distance might be only metres (yards) in nautical miles, which will not affect him. But when a sextant angle is used to define a safe distance off a danger, accuracy can be important. This is the reverse use of the distance off technique. If the navigator decides he doesn't want to pass within, say, three nautical miles of a hazard, perhaps a rock with a lighthouse on it, he can look in the distance off tables (see diagram 7.15) and find out what the sextant angle is when three nautical miles off. While rounding the rock, or passing by it, he will know he is within the danger distance if the sextant angle increases.

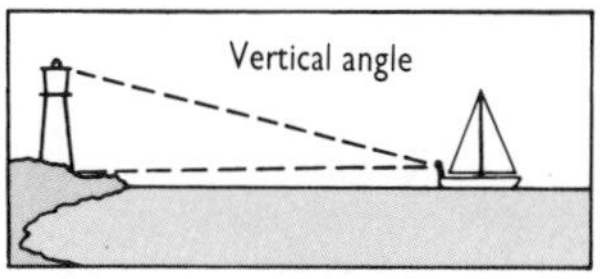

Diagram **7.15** *Distance off by vertical sextant angle.*

TWO TRANSIT FIX

Another good method of getting a fix, although it depends on several charted objects being in sight at once, and two pairs lining up, is the two transit fix. If there are two objects that line up perfectly it's clear that you must be somewhere along the line projected through them both. If at the same time another such transit can be observed, then where the two lines cross gives a very good position. You can also do a combination of a transit and a plain bearing to get nearly as good a fix.

DOUBLE THE ANGLE ON THE BOW

There are other methods which broadly involve known geometric principles. For instance, to double the angle on the bow (as in diagram A2.21 page 284), will show a position when you have only one object such as a headland, a tree on a headland, or something of that kind to use. The system is to take a bearing on the desired object when it reads a whole angle, say 40 degrees or 30 degrees or 20 degrees. You will be somewhere along that position line. As you take the bearing note the boat's speed and course and the log reading. When the angle doubles to 80 degrees or 60 degrees or 40 degrees, take another bearing and plot it on the chart, and at the same time or very quickly afterwards, read the log again. We now know the distance that's been travelled and the direction. That can be plotted off from any point along the first position line. The line should be drawn only as long as the distance travelled, and the second position line then transferred to the end of the line marking the vessel's position by dead reckoning.

Transferring simply means drawing a line parallel to the observed bearing through the dead reckoning position. If during the time between the first and second observation some observation has been made to establish whether the ship is being affected by current, that should be taken into account in plotting the dead reckoning position. So if a current of say one knot from dead ahead is established, then the amount of foul current suffered during the time between the two bearings must be calculated. Let's say this was 45 minutes and you're travelling at four knots, then the boat will have travelled three nautical miles between the two positions, but it will also have been hindered by the current, which in 45 minutes at a rate of one knot will have held the boat up by three-quarters of a nautical mile. So the actual position will be three-quarters of a nautical mile further back along the direction of travel. This is where the transferred position line must cut and this will be the ship's position at the time of the second bearing.

R U N N I N G   F I X

Another method of getting a fix is called a running fix. The method is the same as doubling the angle on the bow except that the angles do not bear any simple relationship to each other. The bearing is transferred exactly as in doubling the angle on the bow.

B E A R I N G   A N D   D E P T H

Yet another method of getting a ship's position is by a bearing and depth which means taking a bearing of one object and a sounding of the depth of water at the same time, but this is not particularly accurate and some rules need to be observed to achieve even a limited fix from this method. It is used mainly when shore objects are scarce, or there is limited visibility.

It can only be done satisfactorily close to shore, because the soundings need to be marked clearly on the chart and the contour lines should be distinct and, ideally, close together. The bearing also should cross the contour lines as closely as possible to right angles as this makes the fix more accurate. Also, and most importantly, you must allow for the tidal situation, particularly if in an area where the daily tidal range is great (see tidal section page 118).

L I N E   O F   S O U N D I N G S

A variation of this method is a line of soundings where the navigator plots a position line by taking several readings in succession of the depth of water. The timing of these observations should be related to the time it takes the vessel to cover the distance between the soundings on the chart. In other words, if you're doing one knot only and the soundings are scaled at a nautical mile apart on the chart, you'll have to take an observation every hour; at two knots, every half hour, etc. This won't be very satisfactory, so you'll need to be travelling faster, but that shows the relationship that's needed. When five or six observations have been taken, these can be plotted on tracing paper and put over the chart until the soundings match. This is more accurate than the sounding and bearing method as it gives a good position line and, when combined with a single corrected bearing will give a more believable position. While I would not make a practice of closing any but a thoroughly known coast in poor visibility—I'd much rather stay out to sea and keep out of trouble—if it's imperative to go in, this is a method to use. Perhaps its best use is to close the coast along the line of bearings and, when the soundings steepen sharply, to run along a fixed contour until the harbour that's wanted is found (see diagram 7.16). But as a general rule, unless there's some pressing need, it is highly dangerous to enter port in thick conditions. There certainly may be other vessels out there, but probably not many, and there'll be a lot of water between you and them.

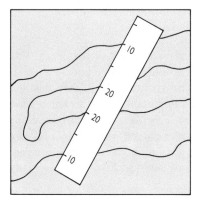
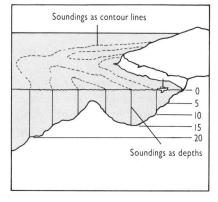

Diagram 7.16 *Running a line of soundings.*

N I G H T   B E A R I N G S

The same systems can be used to navigate at night except that, instead of taking bearings of a wide range of objects, one takes bearings of lights, each with distinctive characteristics which identify it (see pages 120–121). All the same methods can be used and, in particular, the bearing and loom (glare).

B E A R I N G   A N D   L O O M
(G L A R E)

This is a variation on the bearing and distance off. The bearing is taken in the usual way, but it's taken of a light at the moment it changes from a loom (glare) on the horizon to an actual light. Because yachts travel at a relatively low speed, this transition takes several minutes.

If you have a loom (glare) and you're standing in the cockpit and not sure how far off you are from the light, then go up somewhere higher in the boat to see whether that 'raises' the light itself. If not, you may need to go somewhere higher still, or you will have to wait. But at the moment the light breaks the surface of the sea, you can get the distance off from the tables by taking the height of the light from the chart, correcting for height of eye, and reading the distance from the table of vertical sextant angles. (These lights, as you will have seen when studying the chart symbols, always have their height above sea level marked on the chart.)

We've now covered the main techniques you need to know to be a competent pilot. You will still need to have a thorough knowledge of the buoyage system of the country that you're in, and remember that in large parts of the world including the US, the USSR, the Philippines and others, the buoyage system is the opposite to what it is in most of the rest of the world, and some parts of the world have no system. The buoyage systems of the world are covered in the illustrated section on pages 120–121.

P L A N N I N G

A   V O Y A G E

Now you are ready to step out into the great wide world of the ocean. You have the basic skills for travelling along a coastline from one port to another. People have been known to cross whole oceans with less skill than this, but that is neither desirable nor sensible. What's important now is to know what work you need to do before setting out on a voyage. You must have the appropriate charts and the plans for any ports between where you're leaving from and where you're arriving. (For some reason charts of ports are called plans.) It is good practice to have the plans of every such port, as you really do not know when you're likely to need them.

Diagram 7.17 A simple example of voyage planning. As the boat approaches a coastline, readings of depth are checked against the chart contours. Before the voyage started the danger circle was plotted on the relevant chart, where rocks are shown off a lighthouse. After clearing the danger circle, course is sailed to the next 'mark' of the course.

On a voyage recently, I was covering such a long distance that I felt perhaps I wouldn't take plans of some of the more remote ports, ones that we would pass by four or five hundred nautical miles. At the time of looking at one plan, of Esperance, in Western Australia, we'd all shuddered and said, 'Who'd ever want to go there?' because just outside this port is an ill-charted region 125 nautical miles wide by 40 nautical miles deep full of literally hundreds of islands, reefs, rocks and every hazard known to man and beast. I decided

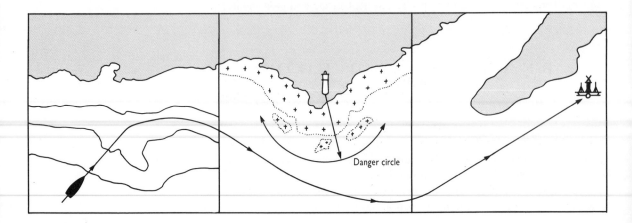

Danger circle

I would take all the plans and, as it happened, we were dismasted and had to sail more than 300 nautical miles under jury rig to get to Esperance, which was the nearest port to us after the loss of the mast. It was bad enough getting into Esperance in a gale with the chart and the plan, let alone without.

So it is essential to take with you all the required plans and charts. You'll need to spend some time going through them deciding what courses you're going to sail after taking into account the dangers. You need to decide, for instance, how far off a sandbank or rock or other hazard you wish to travel. If you decide you want to pass four nautical miles clear of it, use your dividers to measure four nautical miles from the scale on the side of the chart, level with the danger. Then put one point of the dividers on the hazard and with the other describe a clearing circle around the hazard. Then draw the new course from the edge of the clearing circle to the next point of the voyage. That will be a safe course. Diagram 7.17 shows a complete sample of a prepared voyage plan. Do the same to avoid each hazard.

L I G H T   R A N G E S

If you're going to be travelling at night I've found it a good idea to make a similar circle marking out the light ranges of each light. But don't forget that the range of lights as marked on the chart is for a height of eye of 10 metres (30 feet), the height of the average ship's bridge above sea level. Your height of eye is much less in a yacht, usually between 2–3 metres (6–10 feet)— look at your copy of the table of vertical sextant angles to adjust the range to your height of eye. By doing this, you will know where you will have dead spots where you cannot see any lights and where you've got easy navigation because more than one light is visible at once.

If you have more than one light available, you can get your bearings and fixes and get easy, accurate positions, but there's nothing to worry about if you're going through a blank spot. Just handle that part of the voyage by dead reckoning alone, a perfectly acceptable way of navigating. I've navigated several hundred miles by dead reckoning alone and been not too far out of the expected position when closing land and able to find out precisely where I was. It's quite likely that the longer the distance the better dead reckoning is likely to be, because the various currents and other effects tend to cancel out. But this won't always be so, and so it would be desirable to back up the piloting skills with skill in celestial navigation. But even then you aren't always able to get the fix you want when you want it, because of cloud or some other problem.

When you have finished plotting the courses, danger circles and light ranges, write the actual course that you are going to give the helmsman on the chart. The courses are corrected and written on the chart as they will be given. It is sensible, too, to mark the times that you hope to be going past various landmarks, navigational aids, dangers and so on, especially if tidal state is going to be important when you reach the position. It doesn't always work out that the courses or any of these other notations are what actually happens, but because they are done at your leisure and without any stress or other condition likely to affect accuracy, they give you more time to adjust to the conditions of the voyage and be alert to the developing situation.

T I D E S

Most textbooks cover tidal information in great detail, and most of the detail is hardly ever needed by the average yachtsman. Generally speaking, the larger the vessel and the deeper its draught, the more careful the navigator has to be of depth. The yachtsman can usually simply give dangerously shallow waters a wide berth. But the cruising yachtsman or motor boat owner will meet widely varying conditions—from almost no tides to tides of 12 metres (40 feet)—and they will need to understand the basic mechanics of tides. Diagram 7.18 gives all the definitions of chart depths and tidal heights that are used, and which are explained in the Glossary. However, only some of these definitions are of interest to the ordinary sailor. While we will give here a basic description of the forces that cause tides, we will not cover the detail that would be required by an expert.

Diagram 7.18 *Definitions of tidal terminology.*

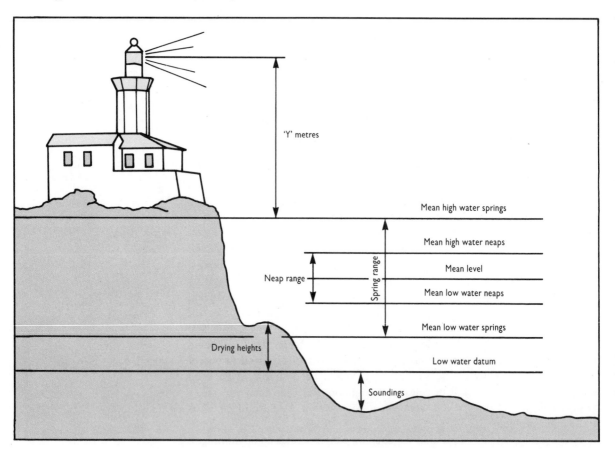

Probably everybody knows that tides are caused by the gravitational pull of the moon. It may not be recognised so widely that the sun also has an effect, and when the two pull together tides are larger than average. The moon's pull causes tides to be highest directly under the moon, and on the opposite side of the earth (see diagram 7.19). The highest tides are springs and the lowest are neaps, but this is only highest average and lowest average. Nevertheless, these are the tides of interest to the leisure boatman, so we will ignore the rest.

While tides, and their highs and lows, can be predicted for any time and any place because the orbit of the moon is thoroughly understood, there are local effects which make a great difference. A strong wind will pile water up against a weather shore, or delay a tide trying to run in against it. Local knowledge can play a great part in boating, but here we are concerned with calculations that will tell us, anywhere in the world where data is kept, the answer to the two most important questions about tides:

1. What will the depth of water be at a particular place at a particular time?
2. At what time will a particular depth of water be reached at a particular place?

To find the answers you will need tide tables.

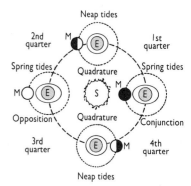

Diagram 7.19 *Effect of sun and moon on tides. Neap tides occur when the moon's effect is diminished by the sun. Spring tides occur when the sun and moon combine.*

TIDE TABLES

Many organisations publish tide tables, but they are not all the same value. The best are the ones that follow the style of the Admiralty Tide Tables, available from any chart agent.

Almanac information is given for standard ports—the major ports of the world. It comprises times and heights of high water and low water (springs and neaps). Springs occur, as we have seen, when the sun and moon are pulling together, and neaps occur when the sun and moon are counteracting each other to some extent. We saw that the phases of the moon indicate these times. In the bottom right hand corner of each daily page of the *Nautical Almanac* there is a symbol showing the moon's phases (see diagram 7.20). At full moon and new moon the tides will tend to be higher (springs) and at first and third quarter they will tend to be lower (neaps). Further information is given under the bold headings MHWS (mean high water springs), MHWN (mean high water neaps), MLWN (mean low water neaps) and MLWS (mean low water springs) in the almanac. The bold printed figures under these headings represent the average range at the tidal heights tabulated and whether a tide is spring or neap can be determined from the average range—if the range is higher it will be a spring tide and if it is lower it will be a neap tide.

Heights and times are not given for secondary ports but the difference in tide times between the standard and secondary port is listed as are corrections for the height.

The method for finding the height of tide for both standard and secondary ports follows. This method works for all ports anywhere in the world.

STANDARD PORTS

Times of high and low water are given in universal time (UT). When any other system of time is in operation (summertime or daylight saving time) these must be converted to universal time for all calculations. Heights are in metres and tenths above chart datum (CD).

Tide curves are given for each standard port enabling the navigator to use the predictions to determine the height of tide at a given time, or the time for a required height of tide.

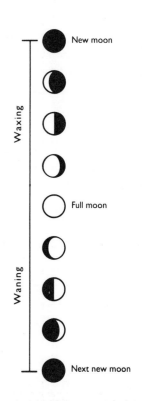

Diagram 7.20 *Phases of the moon.*

The standard port chosen as an example is Dover on Saturday 21 April 1990. The almanac information for Dover on that day is shown as:

21	0225	1.7
	0751	5.5
Sa	1475	1.7
	2012	5.7

The standard Admiralty curve for Dover shows the rise and fall of tides relative to low water, high water, and low water giving five hours of flood and seven hours of ebb.

The tidal curve and its depth matrix on the left hand side of diagram 7.21 enable us to find either the time of a required height of tide or the height at a given time. This is done by drawing, which is far safer than mental arithmetic!

When inserting information keep to a standardised procedure as follows:

1. Use tide tables for chosen port
2. Find appropriate tidal curve
3. Write in high water time (in universal time) in box directly below apex of curve
4. Enter times left (before high water) and right (after high water) in boxes
5. Use tidal information to mark in high water height (top of grid) and low water height (bottom of grid)
6. Join them with a pencilled line to give a reference diagonal

Diagram 7.21 *Tidal curve and depth matrix based on Dover because records have been kept there for longer than anywhere else in the world.*

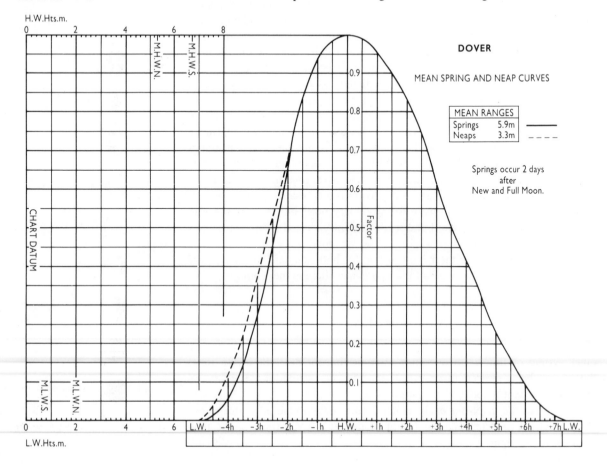

To find the time when a required height will occur, say 4.2 m in the morning of 21 April 1990:

A. Mark 4.2 metres on the top of the grid

B. Drop a line to intersect the reference diagonal

C. Draw horizontally until the line touches the appropriate curve (before or after high water, neaps or springs)

D. Drop a line to the base and read off the time (UT)

The time when the required height of 4.2 m of water will occur is 0541.

To find the height at a given time the process is reversed (shown as $- - - - \rightarrow$ on curve).

a) Choose the time and convert it to UT

b) Find the universal time (say 1115) on the time scale and draw a line up to touch the curve

c) Draw across to touch the reference diagonal

d) Draw down to height scale and read off value

The height of tide at 1115 will be 3.6 m.

Obviously once you are experienced you forget about the pencil and trace with your finger! The great advantage with curves is that you can use them all day once the information has been entered and the reference diagonal drawn.

Diagram 7.22 *How to apply the tidal information to the curve and matrix.*

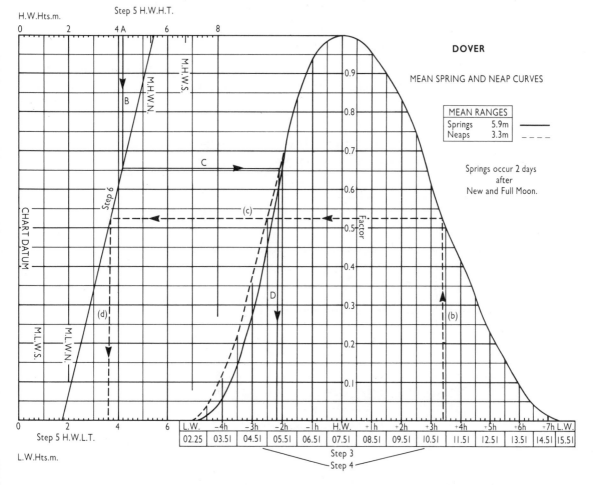

SECONDARY PORTS

Secondary ports are usually smaller yacht or fishing harbours. Almanac information is shown in a standardised format which gives the data to enable the navigator to calculate by interpolation the approximate times or heights of high and low water.

The secondary port chosen as an example is Folkestone, a small ferry port and yacht harbour to the west of Dover. The data given is:

Standard Port DOVER (——►)

Times				Height (metres)			
HW		LW		MHWS	MHWN	MLWN	MLWS
0000	0600	0100	0700	6.7	5.3	2.0	0.8
1200	1800	1300	1900				

Differences FOLKSTONE

-0020	-0005	-0010	-0010	+0.4	+0.4	0.0	-0.1

At first sight the entry is very confusing. Read the high water times at the standard port and the time differences at secondary ports vertically. So at 0000 and 1200 hours at Dover the difference at Folkestone is –0020 minutes, meaning high water at Folkestone is 20 minutes before Dover.

Height differences are read in a similar fashion from the table.

- MHWS Dover 6.7 m = +0.4 m at Folkestone
- MHWN Dover 5.3 m = +0.4 m at Folkestone
- MLWN Dover 2.0 m =   0.0 m at Folkestone
- MLWS Dover 0.8 m = –0.1 m at Folkestone

Diagram 7.23 *Grid to estimate times of high and low water at secondary ports.*

Using data for 21 April 1990 (see above page 150) high water at Dover is at 0751 hours with a height of 5.5 m. Low water is at 1457 hours with

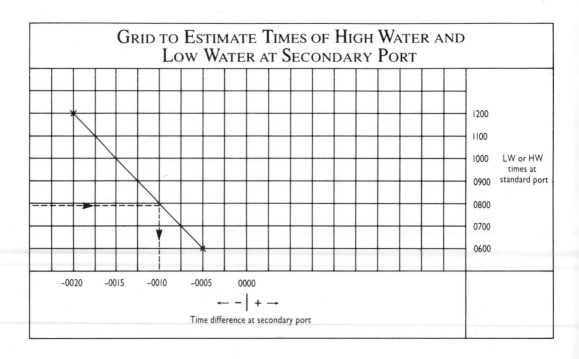

GRID TO ESTIMATE TIMES OF HIGH WATER AND
LOW WATER AT SECONDARY PORT

LW or HW
times at
standard port

1200
1100
1000
0900
0800
0700
0600

-0020   -0015   -0010   -0005   0000

← – | + →

Time difference at secondary port

a height of 1.7 m. Folkestone difference tables gives values at 0600 and 1300 for high water and low water so we have to estimate by drawing. Use an A4 sheet of squared paper to construct a time and height matrix graph (see diagram 7.23). Split the time graph into – and + values. To use the matrix:

i) Select secondary port and high water or low water as you require

ii) Refer to standard port information (Dover, 21 April 1990, see above page 150)

iii) Using high or low water times select the time difference scale and on the right hand side of the grid enter the values. (High water in this instance falls between 0600 and 1200 hours so these are entered.)

iv) Enter the 0600 and 1200 difference values (–0005 and –0020 minutes) on the horizontal column in the minus section

v) Draw a diagonal between 0600 and 1200 values

vi) High water for 21 April is 0751. Enter the time of high water (standard port) and intersect the diagonal

vii) Drop a line to give the time difference (–0010 mins in this example)

viii) Determine local time (0751 –10 minutes)

High water at Folkestone on 21 April 1990 is at 0741.

Height differences are worked out in a similar fashion (see diagram 7.24) and you can split the grid into minus and plus values if required.

It's a very good idea to use a folder of clear plastic dockets for the varied information and graphs needed by a navigator. Use a wax (chinagraph) pencil to avoid having to keep duplicated copies on board.

For a yachtsman, the Rule of Twelfths (see adjacent box) is usually quite sufficient to arrive at a depth that is safe for anchoring in areas where the range of tide is not high.

RULE OF TWELFTHS

The rule states that the movement of the tide either way is:

- **For the first hour, range** $\times$ $^1/_{12}$

- **For the second hour, range** $\times$ $^2/_{12}$

- **For the third and fourth hour, range** $\times$ $^3/_{12}$

- **For the fifth hour, range** $\times$ $^2/_{12}$

- **For the sixth hour, range** $\times$ $^1/_{12}$.

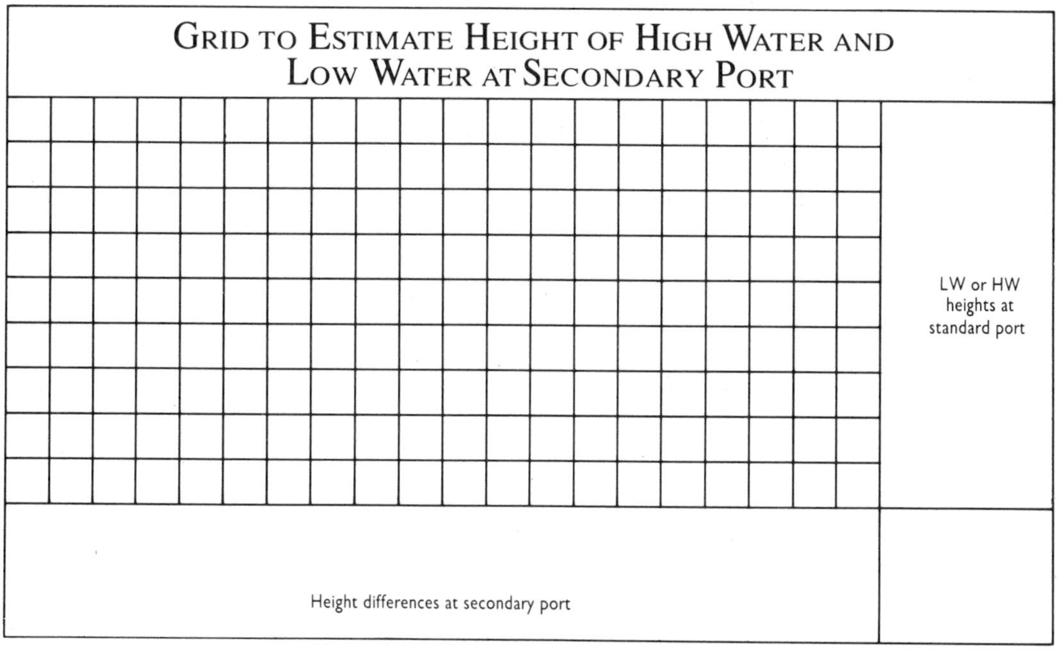

Diagram 7.24 *Grid to estimate height of high and low water at secondary port.*

GRID TO ESTIMATE HEIGHT OF HIGH WATER AND LOW WATER AT SECONDARY PORT

LW or HW heights at standard port

Height differences at secondary port

C E L E S T I A L   N A V I G A T I O N

In all societies, to have specialised knowledge that is kept to oneself is to have special status and special power. Knowing how to navigate has been such a special avenue to power and to preserve this power the knowledge has always been closely guarded. Amongst the Pacific Islanders their singular system was passed from father to son and jealously guarded. The Dutch and Portuguese in their early explorations of the then unknown world kept to themselves their records of navigational feats that resulted in the knowledge of new lands and therefore, critically, new and increased trade. This knowledge was the State secret of its day. Other countries took their own voyages, kept their own secrets. There was no central repository for all this information. Often those who held the skill of navigation deliberately spread misinformation so they could keep for themselves the benefits of their knowledge.

With the explosion of knowledge that's occurred in our society in the past hundred years, this is no longer true. Knowledge cannot be kept as the private property of a person or even a government, although many try.

Now anyone who wants to can learn to navigate by the stars and the following description shows that it is not hard. It's easy to do it, it's a little harder to understand, and true facility comes only with practice. So let's get down to it.

Diagrams 7.25–7.32 that follow explain each of the observations that are needed, and the corrections that must be made, in the calculations at the end of the chapter. They are repeated in the worked example we will do. They will show that you can find your position anywhere in the world's oceans at any time with only a sextant, an accurate timepiece, knowledge of the astronomical triangle, and of course good visibility.

The observations and corrections go towards providing accurate information about four observations. They are:

1) Time
2) Dead reckoning position
3) True altitude
4) Calculated altitude.

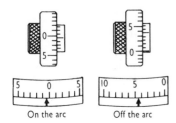

On the arc   Off the arc

Diagram 7.25 *In this example of an index error, the reading on the left is above the zero (on the arc) so must be subtracted from the observed angle of the object. The reading on the right is below the zero (off the arc) and must be added.*

T I M E

This is simple. You need a watch accurate to within a few seconds and the inaccuracy must be known.

D E A D   R E C K O N I N G   P O S I T I O N

If you are keeping a log you will know where you have travelled since your last observation. The dead reckoning at the time of your sightings of stars need not be accurate to the nautical mile, but it must be expressed as latitude and longitude. It provides a possible answer to a geometric problem as you will see.

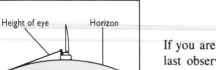

Diagram 7.26 *Height of eye.*

TRUE ALTITUDE

This is the angle you will read off your sextant, and then correct for three things: index error (see diagram 7.25), height of eye (see diagram 7.26) and altitude correction (see diagram 7.29).

CALCULATED ALTITUDE

This comprises the Greenwich Hour Angle (see diagram 7.28 and data from the *Nautical Almanac*), Local Hour Angle (see diagram 7.27 and data from the *Nautical Almanac*) and calculations from the Sight Reduction Tables. Once you have isolated these four elements, a position can be plotted. The reason we want this information is to establish a triangle on the surface of the Earth from which we can calculate our position.

The first corner of the triangle is the dead reckoning position of the observer. A competent navigator who has plotted each course that's been taken and the speed at which it was travelled and the direction in which it was travelled will be able to plot a dead reckoning position at whatever time of day he wants to call the end of his day. He won't know what currents have affected him, what leeway he's made or what else has happened to move the boat away from where he thinks it is. But for the purposes of celestial navigation the first step that's taken is the dead reckoning position.

The next point of the triangle is either the south or the north pole, depending on which hemisphere the observer is in. So already we have two of the three points which make up the triangle we want to establish, except that the dead reckoning position is an estimate only.

The third point is the geographical position (GP) of the sun or the moon, a star, or a planet. The GP is that point on the surface of the Earth where a light ray from the object, which went to the centre of the Earth, would pass. That point is moving all the time as the day passes, so every celestial object which can be used in navigation therefore has a GP where position can be related to time. If, therefore, we get a sextant angle (altitude) at a

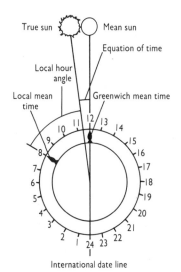

Diagram 7.27 *Local hour angle.*

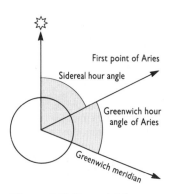

Diagram 7.28 *Greenwich hour angle.*

OCT.—MAR. SUN APR.—SEPT.						STARS AND PLANETS			DIP					
App. Alt.	Lower Limb	Upper Limb	App. Alt.	Lower Limb	Upper Limb	App. Alt.	Corrⁿ	App. Alt.	Additional Corrⁿ	Ht. of Eye	Corrⁿ	Ht. of Eye	Ht. of Eye	Corrⁿ
° ′ 9 34	+10·8	−21·5	° ′ 9 39	+10·6	−21·2	° ′ 9 56	−5·3	**1980** **VENUS**		m 2·4	−2·8	ft. 8·0	m 1·0− 1·8	
9 45	+10·9	−21·4	9 51	+10·7	−21·1	10 08	−5·2	Jan. 1-Feb. 26		2·6	−2·9	8·6	1·5− 2·2	
9 56	+11·0	−21·3	10 03	+10·8	−21·0	10 20	−5·1	°		2·8	−3·0	9·2	2·0− 2·5	
10 08	+11·1	−21·2	10 15	+10·9	−20·9	10 33	−5·0	42 + 0·1		3·0	−3·1	9·8	2·5− 2·8	
10 21	+11·2	−21·1	10 27	+11·0	−20·8	10 46	−4·9			3·2	−3·2	10·5	3·0− 3·0	
10 34	+11·3	−21·0	10 40	+11·1	−20·7	11 00	−4·8	Feb. 27-Apr. 13		3·4	−3·3	11·2	See table	
10 47	+11·4	−20·9	10 54	+11·2	−20·6	11 14	−4·7	°		3·6	−3·4	11·9	←	
11 01	+11·5	−20·8	11 08	+11·3	−20·5	11 29	−4·6	47 + 0·2		3·8	−3·5	12·6		
11 15	+11·6	−20·7	11 23	+11·4	−20·4	11 45	−4·5	Apr. 14-May 9		4·0	−3·6	13·3	m	
11 30	+11·7	−20·6	11 38	+11·5	−20·3	12 01	−4·4	°		4·3	−3·7	14·1	20− 7·9	
11 46	+11·8	−20·5	11 54	+11·6	−20·2	12 18	−4·3	46 + 0·3		4·5	−3·8	14·9	22− 8·3	
12 02	+11·9	−20·4	12 10	+11·7	−20·1	12 35	−4·2			4·7	−3·9	15·7	24− 8·6	
12 19	+12·0	−20·3	12 28	+11·8	−20·0	12 54	−4·1	May 10-May 25		5·0	−4·0	16·5	26− 9·0	
12 37	+12·1	−20·2	12 46	+11·9	−19·9	13 13	−4·0	°		5·2	−4·1	17·4	28− 9·3	
12 55	+12·2	−20·1	13 05	+12·0	−19·8	13 33	−3·9	11 + 0·4		5·5	−4·2	18·3		
13 14	+12·3	−20·0	13 24	+12·1	−19·7	13 54	−3·8	41 + 0·5		5·8	−4·3	19·1	30− 9·6	
13 35	+12·4	−19·9	13 45	+12·2	−19·6	14 16	−3·7	May 26-June 3		6·1	−4·4	20·1	32−10·0	
13 56	+12·5	−19·8	14 07	+12·3	−19·5	14 40	−3·6	° + 0·5		6·3	−4·5	21·0	34−10·3	
													36−10·6	

Diagram 7.29 *Example of Altitude Correction Tables for 10°-90° — Sun, Stars and Planets.*

fixed time, we can calculate a GP. The difference between the GP we observe with the sextant, and the GP we calculate is called an **intercept**. The intercept is either towards the object we observed, or away from it.

We need to bring this information into a form which is easy to manipulate or calculate so that we can find the position, so we will form a parallelogram to calculate our zenith.

ZENITH

The zenith is a point directly above our heads (see diagram 7.30). Forget about distance. As the diagram shows it's really quite immaterial how far away an object is for navigational purposes. We are only interested in the angle it makes in the skies and some of the geometry of parallelograms.

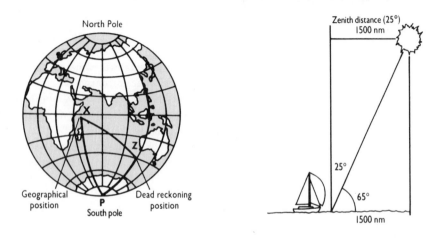

Diagram 7.30 *The three elements which make up the spherical triangle which allows calculation of position (left). P is the pole in whichever hemisphere you are travelling. X is the geographical position of the object being observed (the sun) which is obtainable from the almanac for any time of day, and Z is the ship's dead reckoning position.*

The sextant observation (right) shows the sun at an angle of 65 degrees. Zenith distance is the difference between the observed angle and 90 degrees, in this case 25 degrees. Each degree is 60 nm so the zenith distance in this case is 60 x 25, 1500 nm. This means the yacht is 1500 nm from the geographical position of the sun at the time of the sight.

ZENITH DISTANCE

We have one more thing to learn to give us all that we need to be able to navigate satisfactorily by the stars and that is zenith distance, which is the number of degrees which remain when the sextant angle has been deducted from 90 degrees. If the sextant angle is 60 degrees the zenith distance is 30 degrees. One degree equals 60 nautical miles, so a zenith distance of 30 degrees translated into nautical miles would be 1800. When you look at diagram 7.31 again, our parallelogram is now working. Because zenith distance can be expressed in nautical miles we are able to give an accurate position to the GP of the sun. We now have a triangle made up of points at the geographical position of the sun, the pole and our dead reckoning position.

The sextant observation is called HO—think of it as height observed. The calculated altitude is HC (height calculated). We have used the normal convention of calling the pole angle P, the angle at the geographical position X and our own Z. ZX is the zenith distance and now you will see why in the parallelogram in diagram 7.31 we used P, X and Z so the correlation could be seen. Because 90 degrees minus zenith distance is the observed altitude, therefore 90 degrees minus the calculated zenith distance gives the calculated altitude. The difference between these two angles once more is the intercept.

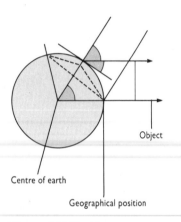

Diagram 7.31 *Zenith.*

POSITION LINE

We have taken an observation of the sun and produced from it an intercept which, to be useful, must be processed into a position line on a chart, exactly like a coastal navigation position line. When we plot the position line, we will know that we're somewhere along it. We need to be able to calculate just where. We need to find the intercept. To start we will express each point of the triangle as a latitude and longitude. With the dead reckoning position there is no problem because that is how it is expressed. The same is true of the poles whose positions are accurately known. So we'll concentrate on the GP of the sun as a latitude and longitude.

As the seasons progress in both hemispheres, the sun is first in the northern hemisphere and then later in the southern hemisphere, passing through a belt of approximately 45 degrees—half north of the equator and half south of it. This is called its **declination**. When the sun is north of the equator the declination is called north and, when it's south, it's south. This term, declination, corresponds exactly to latitude and can be translated as latitude, giving us the first position line for the geographical position.

Now for the second—the longitude. The lines (meridians) of longitude are vertical great circles (see diagram 7.32) through the poles which correspond to distances from Greenwich, and also times from Greenwich. When expressed as time they are called **Greenwich hour angles** (GHA). Because the hour angle of any celestial object can be calculated from the time of observation of the object the hour angle can be translated to a longitude. Luckily all the really hard work has been done for you. Assiduous navigators have over the centuries taken the observations of the astronomers and created tables showing the position of the sun relative to the Earth at any time in the Earth's passage around the sun. And we take Greenwich as the measuring point on the Earth's surface.

Taking the time of our sextant observation we can look in the *Nautical Almanac* for the Greenwich hour angle for the sun at that precise time on that precise day. Once the Greenwich hour angle has been established we have a longitudinal position for the GP of the sun, and now we have established the three corners of the astronomical triangle. To find the intercept we need to be able to compare the angle P in terms of our dead reckoning position and our real position. So we need to know what that angle is. It is called the **Local hour angle** (LHA), which is the Greenwich hour angle corrected for the dead reckoning position of the boat, making the angle relative to where the boat is rather than where Greenwich is.

Diagram 7.32 *Meridians.*

Here we get another complication. Greenwich hour angle is simple in that it is measured in a westerly direction from Greenwich through 360 degrees, or 24 hours of time, back to Greenwich. Local hour angle is measured east and west from **Greenwich**. In the eastern hemisphere LHA is 360 degrees plus the observer's longitude, and in the west it is 360 degrees minus longitude.

Now if that seems quite a lot, it is. You've actually learned about two-thirds of all the terms and concepts you'll need for navigation in the old style. If you have a programmable calculator you will already be able to get a good position, given that your sextant observation and notation of time are accurate.

If you are using Sight Reduction Tables, as we will in the example a little further on, there still needs to be a correction for the sun and the moon, which is called a semi-diameter. Sextant observations of the sun and the moon are taken of either the top (upper limb) or bottom (lower limb) of the object. The correction makes the reading the same as if the observation has been made in the centre of the object. Every observation of every celestial object has to be corrected for height of eye, which is the height of the observer's eye above sea level. If you are using a programmable calculator enter your boat's height of eye when asked. If you are using tables, there are corrections listed in the opening pages of the *Nautical Almanac*.

The next step is to convert the time from local zone time to Greenwich (zulu or universal coordinated time) by correcting for the time zone we are in. Be very careful when you apply zone time, which is the time where you are, that you allow for any summer time or other special local variation. If you do not, you will look up the wrong time for your observations and all your calculations will be wrong.

STEP BY STEP CELESTIAL SIGHT REDUCTIONS

RUNNING SUNS

Element	Action	Examples 1	2	3
ELEMENT 1				
Time	Check your watch against a known accurate watch	27-11-15-33	27-12-58-14	27-14-36-06
Correction for error (if any)	Deduct if fast, add if slow	–	–	–
Difference from universal time (11 hrs)	Plus or minus your local time (remember any local changes)	27-00-15-33	27-01-58-14	27-03-36-06
Corrected universal time	Look up *Nautical Almanac* at today's date. If universal time takes you back a day, look up that date. Look up time as corrected. All calculations will be based on this time	27-00-15-33	27-01-58-14	27-03-36-06
ELEMENT 2				
Dead reckoning position (DR)	As kept in ship's log	36°24'S-150°48'E	36°34'S-150°38'E	36°42'S-150°32'E
ELEMENT 3				
Sextant observations	Horizon must go through top or bottom of sun	64°08.2	76°20.0	64°51.2
Correct for index error	On the arc is minus; off the arc is plus	–	–	–
Correct for dip (Height above sea level)	Usually about two metres (eight feet). Table is on right hand side of opening pages of *Nautical Almanac*	- 2.7	-2.7	-2.7
Result is apparent altitude	–	64°05.5	76°17.3	64°48.5
Altitude correction (HP)	From altitude correction tables on opening pages of *Nautical Almanac*. Degrees and minutes on left hand page. Tenths of minutes on right hand page.	+15.7	+15.9	+15.8
Result is true altitude (HO)	–	64°21.2	76°33.2	65°04.3

STEP BY STEP CELESTIAL SIGHT REDUCTIONS (CONTINUED)

Element	Action	Examples 1	2	3
ELEMENT 4				
Calculated altitude	–	–	–	–
GHA (of sun)	From named column in *Nautical Almanac*, on day and hour of sight (universal time)	179°47.1	194°46.8	224°46.2
Add increments for minutes and seconds of time of sight	In grey pages of *Nautical Almanac*. Enter column with same number of minutes, enter row with same number of seconds	3°53.3	14°33.5	9°01.5
Result is corrected GHA	–	183°40.4	209°20.3	233°47.7
Chosen longitude	Choose a longitude which when added to (east long) or subtracted from (west long) GHA makes a round number	150°19.6	150°39.7	150°12.3
Result is LHA	If greater than 360 degrees take 360 degrees away	334°00.0	360°00.0	24°00.0
Chosen latitude	Nearest whole number to dead reckoning latitude	36°00.0	37°00.0	37°00.0
Declination	From object's column in *Nautical Almanac*. Note whether north or south	23°20.5	23°20.4	23°20.2
Declination correction	From sun column in *Nautical Almanac*	- 0.0	- 0.1	- 0.1
Correction for minutes of declination	From altitude correction tables of *Nautical Almanac*. Tables indicate whether + or -	- 0.0	- 0.1	- 0.1
Result is corrected declination	–	23°20.5	23°20.3	23°20.1
Enter sight reduction tables to obtain tabulated altitude	Take chosen latitude and LHA (top of page) entering page marked same if declination of object is same as latitude, or contrary if not	64°01.6	76°00.0	65°03.5
Extract correction for minutes of declination	From interpolation tables in end papers of sight reduction tables	+ 11.8	+ 20.3	+ 12.6
Result is calculated altitude	–	64°13.4	76°20.3	65°16.1
Tabulated azimuth (Z)	The figure Z extracted from the sight reduction tables	112°00.0	180°00.0	117°00.4
True bearing (Zn)	Either add or subtract Z from 180 degrees depending on whether LHA is greater or less than 180 degrees. Instructions are at top and bottom of each page of sight reduction tables	68°00.0	0°00.0	297°00.4
Take calculated altitude from true altitude to get intercept	–	7.8	12.9	11.8
If true altitude is greater intercept is towards	–	Towards	Towards	Away

For plotting, put each DR on chart as in example. Then put each chosen position on the latitude baseline – in this case 36°30', halfway between chosen latitudes of 36° and 37°. As these are running suns, DR 1 and DR 2 are incorrect at time of third sighting. They will have to be transferred for the distance and direction travelled. The new chosen position for DR 1 will move by the distance and direction travelled between DR 1 and DR 3. It is now called 1T (transfer). The new chosen position for DR 2 will be the distance and direction from DR 2 to DR 3 and will be called 2T. Chosen position 3 will still be used.

Draw true bearing from 1T, 2T and 3 and mark it. Mark intercept on bearing line in direction (away or toward) already calculated. Draw dotted line at right angles to bearing – this is position line.

The triangle where the dotted lines cross is the cocked hat inside which the yacht is positioned. Make the dotted line solid and put the yacht in the centre of the triangle.

This rough method will give a reasonable position to even the least experienced navigator.

It is a simple step from here to complete celestial navigation. Observations of the stars, moon and planets are done in the same way, but have different corrections applied to them.

STEP BY STEP CELESTIAL SIGHT REDUCTIONS
(CONTINUED)

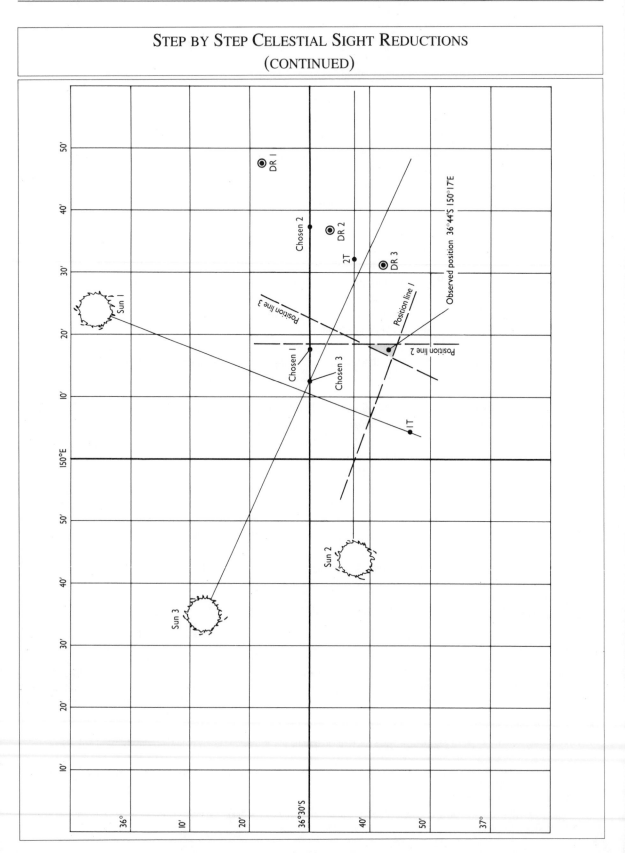

Take the lesser of the true altitude and the calculated altitude away from the other and the difference is the intercept. We now have all the information we need to plot this position line: the true bearing of the object, a dead reckoning position, and the intercept. If the true altitude is greater than the calculated altitude, the intercept is towards, otherwise it is away.

To plot the position line, take an appropriate plotting sheet. If you don't have such a sheet, use the following method: take a piece of graph paper and from the centre top draw a vertical line representing the longitude nearest to your chosen longitude. From the side of the chart, in the middle, draw a horizontal line representing your chosen latitude. Mark the chosen position of the object on the graph paper. Also plot the dead reckoning position on the paper. Through the chosen position, using a protractor, draw the angle of the azimuth, and put an arrow on the top of it. Measure the distance of the intercept away or towards the object and draw a line at right angles to the azimuth. This is the position line (see diagram 7.33). The convention is that the position line has two short lines dropped at right angles at each end and an arrow drawn on each. I find this very confusing when plotting more than one position, so I draw the position line as a dotted line. It is obvious where the dotted lines intersect and I then consolidate the lines where the cocked hat is formed, which happens with these position lines as it does with lines taken from bearings of land objects.

Three position lines give a very good position, but if you are using a hand held programmable calculator you can plot up to six objects, which gives a very accurate position indeed, taking less time than one position line by the method we have just followed. But, remember, this section has been included so that a person not versed in celestial navigation, but having the right equipment, can establish a position if the Satnav and the calculator both break down.

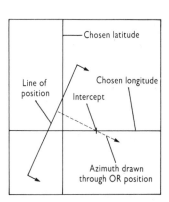

Diagram 7.33 *Plotting a single position line. With one more sighting, and therefore one more position line, a fix can be achieved. Ideally there should be three in all, which will provide a cocked hat. The yacht is somewhere within the cocked hat.*

CHAPTER EIGHT

SAFETY

Generally speaking, safety on boats involves willing acceptance of regulation by unregulated people. All sensible sailors willingly accept government regulations that are enforceable by law, and also accept the sometimes higher standards which are set by national and international bodies of yachting organisations that are not enforceable by law. Although there is no obligation to meet any of these higher standards once regulations governing the jurisdiction of the waters in which you are cruising have been met, you would be sensible, certainly if you want to be called a skipper, to accept the highest standards available in terms of the safety of your boat, yourself, and your crew.

I believe the highest standards are those of the major ocean racing countries of the world. The standards vary from country to country, even though there is an Offshore Racing Council standard which applies in most countries. The stringency with which the sailing fraternity applies the rules is the test of voluntary regulations—it is what makes them really bite. It is probable that in no country in the world are these standards more strict than in Australia— especially in radio position reporting. This does nothing to improve the standard of Australian yachting, but it means the sport has an enviable record of ocean racing safety, and an attitude towards safety among competitors which leads to the sport being as safe as it can be. Since the 1979 Fastnet disaster international regulations have come to include many of the Australian regulations relating to radio position reporting and improved liferaft design (especially for cold water regions). There is also a heightened awareness amongst owners that each yacht must be totally self-sufficient. As we deal with matters of safety, we will be going through the basic equipment an ocean-going sailing yacht needs, and describing many of the points a potential owner should look for in a boat.

Safety is an absolute. So the sensible harbour sailor will realise that, while all the equipment on an ocean-going yacht isn't essential for harbour sailing, most of it is necessary in order to cope with the unexpected. If, for instance, there is another pleasant sailing ground a day's sail away, the boat will have to function as an ocean-going yacht in order to pay a visit. It doesn't matter how careful the harbour sailor is in picking the weather and listening to the forecast, there will be times when extreme conditions will come without warning. The vessel must then be in sufficiently good condition to handle whatever comes. Those skippers who have done many nautical miles and visited many countries will know perfectly well that there are some areas that require more concern for safety than others, and different areas pose different threats to safety than others. For example, travel in shallow river estuaries requires equipment that can provide a good indication of depth, and the ability of the skipper to read a chart quickly; travelling long ocean distances needs a well-maintained, accurate satellite navigator, or celestial navigation equipment. If you are travelling in hot tropical regions between islands several days apart, you will need efficient refrigeration and a sure supply of water. The whole matter of safety is linked inextricably to seamanship, that rare mixture of prudence, daring, experience, caution, efficiency and knowledge.

There are regulations governing boat construction in most countries of the world. And this sort of regulation is spreading. The American Bureau of Shipping's (ABS) standard of boat construction has been adopted in most countries of the Western world. I was taking part in an international ocean race recently when, during the first radio schedule of what was to be a five day race, three boats were informed that because they had neglected to lodge their certificates of compliance with the ABS regulations, they were disqualified and would be racing to their destination in vain. This may seem harsh, but there were 175 entries in that race and if conditions had become severe (they did reach 50 knots, but could have been a great deal worse) it's feasible that those disqualified boats could have required the expenditure of a great deal of time, money and organisational hours to bring them to safety.

Anybody building or buying a boat, particularly if it is a second-hand boat, needs to be aware of these regulations. If you are looking to buy a boat, get in touch with the local authorities and find out exactly what is required. You will need to have a surveyor go over the boat, but you should still discover all you can about regulations. If, when investigating local regulations, you find they are not strict, don't take that as a bonus. You should set your standards at a certain level, which you will establish from research and convention, and meet that level even if you are not required to do so.

T H E   H U L L

Most countries have regulations governing the strength and form of the integral hull structure of boats. The hull of a sailing yacht or motor boat has to withstand enormous strains. The engines fitted to a power cruiser impart great twisting strain, particularly when a twin installation includes opposing propellers. Yachts absorb the stress of pressure on great areas of sail, which is then balanced by a huge lead weight. If all these pressures are transmitted to a sound hull, the boat as a unit can absorb it satisfactorily. Indeed, if the rig on a yacht is less powerful than the hull, there is an inbuilt safety factor. It means the rig will fail before the hull in the event of a knockdown, without affecting the integrity of the hull. This might not do for yacht racing, however, where tolerances are pushed to the limit. People can survive for a long time without a mast, but not long without a hull.

In motor boats the flexible mountings between the engine and the bed are of critical importance. They have to be enormously strong to take the power of the engine, and they have to disperse some of that power through vibration.

It is a great shame that once we achieve a boat that is sound, and safe, we start boring holes through the hull in all sorts of places, and so immediately reduce the level of safety. Holes for water cooling inlets, inlets to the lavatory, outlets from the lavatory, hot water outlets, bilge pump fittings, fittings for instruments sprout all over—every single one of them a threat to the hull's integrity. In themselves, they enable functions that add to the vessel's safety, but everybody should be aware that every time a skin fitting is designed into a boat a potential hazard has been designed in with it. Major openings into boats are essential, however. They are the entrance to the accommodation (the companionway) and, in yachts, hatches—either fore or aft, or both.

H A T C H E S

In power boats, engine hatches may be in the cockpit, and each of these hatches is a great hazard. They must be capable of being closed off properly. During an 8,000 nautical mile race which started in a 60 knot gale, with high seas and dangerous inshore conditions, a rescue craft foundered because it did not have adequate coverage for the cockpit hatches which were over the twin engines. A pooping sea broke into the cockpit, smashed the hatch covers away, and flooded the engines, stopping them. Because the vessel was then out of control, it sank. Storm covers, or a cover of some kind over the hatch covers, would have prevented this near tragedy, and it would have been just another slightly dangerous trip at sea.

There has to be some method of securing every single hole, whatever size, in the hull of a vessel. Some of the self-regulation on hatches that applies to sailing yachts applies equally well to power boats, although it must be remembered that power boats do not normally stay at sea in conditions as hazardous as does a well-found yacht.

Yachts have at least two escape hatches—the companionway and the forward hatch. The same should apply to power boats, particularly because the risk of fire is greater. Any forward hatch on a motor boat, as in a yacht, must be placed so that, if the boat is rolled 90 degrees, the hatch will be above water.

C O C K P I T S

Cockpits throughout the whole range of seagoing vessels vary enormously. Some are tiny and hold very little water. Some, particularly in modern yachts and power cruisers, are enormous and hold a great deal of water. That water, if it gets into the cockpit by breaking over the stern of the boat in heavy weather, can change the vessel's steering characteristics to such an extent that it gets out of control. Until the water is removed the characteristics are lost completely. If one wave breaks aboard and half a tonne of water cannot drain fast enough, the next wave will break in the cockpit, too. Eventually the vessel will swamp. Cockpit drainage must be adequate for any size of cockpit. Booklets published by the International Yacht Racing Union stipulate the size of the drain holes and the methods by which drainpipes can be crossed over so as to drain always to the side a yacht is heeling, or to that part of a motor boat where the flow of water in the tube will be gravity fed. The larger the cockpit, the larger the drain holes need to be, or the more drain holes there should be: it is better to have large holes, rather than more skin fittings.

Many racing boats, and now more and more cruising boats, arrange their drainage pipes, engine cooling pipes etc. to come together in a cluster and go through the hull at a single skin fitting. This is a very good system indeed, particularly if each pipe can be closed off separately from the rest if a problem develops in it. So, when you are looking for a boat, keep in mind the importance of adequate cockpit drainage. Some cockpits now are so efficient that, even in the heaviest conditions, water remains in them for only a few seconds.

It is a matter of seamanship to keep the drains clear. It doesn't matter how efficient the system is, if it is clogged with cigarette butts, matches, olive pits and wine bottle labels, the water can't go anywhere.

SKIN FITTINGS

Skin fittings are a problem if the fitting carries away or breaks and water comes in, or if an internal pipe bursts. However, there is another hazard in heavy conditions for both power boats and sailing yachts.

The engine has an exhaust system which, by its nature, is open to the sea. Unless it is properly fitted, the water from a big following sea or, in the case of a midships discharging system, a beam sea, can get into the vessel. This can be enormously dangerous to a motor vessel without other means of propulsion, because water in an engine may well stop it. A petrol driven engine will stop more easily than a diesel, and will be harder to restart, because it relies on electrics. In most cases a simple device overcomes this problem (see diagram 8.1). A part of the exhaust line loops up as high as possible within the hull so that it is well above sea level. This prevents water flowing back.

There are some skin fittings, such as the propeller shaft exit, which cannot be closed off in usual circumstances, but nevertheless each skin fitting should have near it, tied in place, an appropriately sized and tapered soft wood or rubber plug. If the fitting fails, the plug can be driven into place. There should be one near the engine shaft exit, because if for some reason the coupling breaks and the shaft drops out, it would be rather embarrassing if there were no plug for the resulting hole.

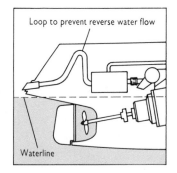

Diagram 8.1 *Exhaust pipe line, showing how line is looped above waterline to prevent water entering through the exhaust.*

SECURING
BELOW DECKS

A good exercise for a yacht skipper is to imagine a boat turned through 180 degrees—to imagine the mast sticking down and the keel sticking up and the boat staying that way. All the fittings and equipment below should be so secured that they stay in position. Now imagine what would happen if they did not—cupboards would fly open, and food cans, spare parts, heavy tools, batteries and other dangerous objects would fly haphazardly through the cabin, creating a shotgun hazard for the startled crew. A skipper walking through the vessel and looking at this chaos, will be amazed at how much there is to be strapped down.

M A I N
C O M P A N I O N W A Y

The main companionway must be capable of being blocked off with storm boards which can be removed from inside and out. After the Fastnet tragedy of 1979, when 17 yachtsmen died, it was found that the storm boards had fallen out of their slides when the yachts were rolled over. Now the boards are required to be held in place by a pin, which can be released by a lanyard, a simple piece of string which can save a yacht, and lives.

An added safety feature on some yachts is a bridge which goes across the cockpit at the companionway and so makes a permanent barrier at main deck level. It helps prevent a pooping sea going into the main cabin.

D E A D L I G H T S

Commercial vessels, liners, container ships and so on all have deadlights that fit over their portholes, so that hull strength isn't compromised in adverse conditions. This isn't always true of motor boats or sailing yachts which may have quite large window areas which are extremely vulnerable to breaking seas. The most danger is not where one would expect, on the weather side— the side on which the seas are breaking. It is more usually on the lee side, where a vessel is picked up and dumped into the trough. It is the windows on the trough side that are more usually crushed; so storm boards that can be fitted very quickly and firmly are essential. They don't take up much space, and their location should be known to all the crew. They must be used as soon as bad weather looks likely, not when it actually starts. The boards must have pre-drilled holes, and have their fixing screws attached, and the holes to take the screws must be pre-drilled into the boat.

L I F E L I N E S

These come in a myriad of shapes and sizes, but to be effective they need to come far enough above the deck so that someone falling against them won't be pivoted overboard. There needs to be a second rail or wire usually about halfway between the deck and the first rail to prevent anyone from slipping overboard. It is also sensible to have a toe rail of some kind round the gunwale both to provide a foothold, and to prevent anyone falling over the side.

Various authorities throughout the world have different regulations, but commonsense covers the whole subject. Lifelines should be tight, but not so tight that they act like a strung wire fence and cut, rather than give slightly. A small amount of give in the wires is much more likely to prevent a person from going overboard than something strung so taut they can pivot over it. It goes without saying that a pulpit and stern pulpit, or pushpit, need to be strong. If they are not strong enough to take weight, they are not strong enough to hold the safety lines against any sort of pressure. Stanchions have to be well secured to the deck—through-bolted, with a load-spreading plate underneath the deck. Combined with safety harnesses (discussed below page 172), lifelines are one of the most fundamental aspects of preventative safety on a yacht. As such they need to be kept intact by the skipper in heavy conditions. There have been many cases of headsails which have been reefed, and in doing so a dangerously flapping foot has been left to flog the lines to pieces near the bow. It is really very careless to allow this to happen. I can see no sense in reefing headsails. In any sort of wind, the de-powered section at the bottom of the headsail will flap so alarmingly that nobody would be game to go near it.

BILGE PUMPS

We talked at length about the integrity of a yacht's hull, so now we must discuss how to get water out if it does get in. Every yacht should be equipped with at least three bilge pumps, one of which should be in the cockpit. Bilge pump handles should be attached to the pump with a lanyard, and simple seamanship demands that the pumps, the bilges, and the limber holes leading through the floors, be kept clear of debris so that the water can flow freely. Remember, too, that by a switching of pipes (see diagram 10.11) a vessel's own engine can be used as a very efficient bilge pump, and one that won't tire the crew. Everyone knows the joke about the most efficient bilge pump— two frightened sailors with a bucket—but every vessel needs to have sufficient equipment on board to be able to pump out all but the most frightening inflow of water. Despite the joke, a yacht should carry at least two strong buckets, with strong lines attached, and large enough to remove a large amount of water. Buckets are always useful on a boat, so it is silly not to carry them. In any case, a bucket chain can remove a great deal of water. In the chapter on Emergencies (see page 180), we discuss in detail ways of stopping water coming into a vessel.

FIRE EXTINGUISHERS

Perhaps the worst hazard facing a boat at sea is fire, so nobody should put to sea without sufficient fire extinguishers of the right type, in a readily accessible position. It is very important to select the right type of extinguisher for boats. There is not a great deal of merit in filling a boat full of poisonous gases or foam that cannot be removed and may be toxic. Extinguishers recommended for boats should be of the dry chemical type that are dispersed by stored pressure, or the BCF type. C type extinguishers should not be used.

An important point about the siting of fire-fighting appliances is that they should not be placed where a fire is likely to be—the galley, or the engine, for instance. It is better to have them where the fire fighter can get at them without being burned. The extinguisher can always be carried to the seat of the fire. Having gone to the expense of installing extinguishers in the right places in a vessel, they should be serviced regularly so they will work when wanted.

A N C H O R   G E A R

One way to keep a yacht safe in dangerous circumstances is by the use of anchor gear, yet many yachts put to sea with inadequate ground tackle. No vessel should have fewer than two anchors with an appropriate chain and warp (rode) to match. The table on page 96 indicates a starting point to help you identify anchor characteristics, but it is a good idea to get some expert advice.

The two anchor styles mentioned—Danforth and CQR—are the best all round designs, but two other types—the fisherman (kedge) and the Bruce—are useful in special conditions. The fisherman (kedge) is good in rock, but can be hard to release and needs to be much heavier than other designs to be as effective. Once they hold, with sufficient scope, they are perhaps the best anchor for heavy conditions. The Bruce was designed for anchoring oil rigs and has tremendous holding power when well dug in, but to my mind doesn't match the CQR or the Danforth. I recommend these two, with the CQR as the main or bower anchor. If you want a third anchor, take a fisherman (kedge), but find somewhere secure to stow it below.

You must have at least 12 metres (40 feet) of suitable chain for the bower anchor and three metres (10 feet) for the kedge, and you should have a spare anchor warp (rode) the same as that for the kedge in case it is needed. (They can double as tow lines if necessary.)

M E D I C A L   K I T

There are all sorts of damage-producing surfaces and mechanisms on board yachts, and the bigger the yacht the more dangerous these can be. Even the power of some of the purchases on board is enough to break arms. A line can burn appallingly when dragged through a hand with a whole spinnaker full of a strong wind pulling it. As well as an accident, there can be a sudden onset of illness, which can occur not only on a long voyage, but also in the middle of an afternoon trip. The medical kit set out below lists what is considered adequate for any length of voyage. The individual skipper will have to decide how much should be carried.

A skipper making a voyage of any length with people he or she doesn't know has not only the right, but the obligation, to ask whether anybody is taking specific medication or has any specific medical problems. The skipper is ultimately responsible for what happens to the crew and it is too late after some tragedy to explain that this responsibility wasn't taken seriously enough to find out whether any of the crew had a problem.

Most of the items mentioned in the table below will have their own instructions within the packaging. Read these instructions carefully before using the item and, when compiling the kit, ask a chemist for advice. Remember, if you are faced with a serious medical emergency, use the radio to get advice.

In addition you should carry the latest edition of *Ship Captain's Medical Guide*. Carry also a good first aid guide obtained from either the St John Ambulance or the Red Cross.

BASIC OCEAN-GOING MEDICAL KIT

USUAL NAME	AMOUNT	REMARKS
Aspirin, Panadol or Panadeine	100 tablets	For relief of moderate pain
Veganin	50 tablets	For relief of greater pain
UV filter cream (+15)	50 gm tube	To prevent sunburn
Iodine, Metaphen or Betadine	25 ml bottle	Skin antiseptic for minor wounds
Antiseptic cream	1 tube	Skin antiseptic for minor wounds
Crepe bandages 75 mm	6	
Crepe bandage 150 mm	1	
Bandages (woven on woven) 75 mm x 6 mm	6	
Triangular bandage	1	
Cottonwool	2 rolls	Use for padding only, it will stick to open wounds, burns
Non-stick dressings—Jellonet, Unitulle, Telfa, Melolan, Bactigras	10	For burns, similar wounds
Sticking plasters	1 packet	
Stainless steel scissors, medium	1 pair	
Stainless steel splinter forceps, pointed	1 pair	
Assorted safety pins	24	Thread on largest pin
Clinical thermometer in protective container	1	
Self-adhesive sutures	24	Use to close wounds
Eye patches or similar	4	
Dericain eye drops $1/2\%$	25 ml	For eye injuries; cover eye
Sulphacetamide eye ointment or other antibiotic -- Neosporin Chloromycetin, Ophth 1%	1 gm tube	For eye infections
Lomotil, 5 mg, or Kaomagma	20 tablets	2 every 4 hours for diarrhoea
Septrin or Bactrin 80/400 mg	20 tablets	2 every 4 hours for infection
Gramycin cream or a neomycin compound ointment	1 tube	For infected wounds or burns
Doloxene Co	25 tablets	2 every 6 hours for moderate pain
Xylocaine ointment	1 tube	For burns, skin irritation
Tetracycline 250 gm	25 capsules	Two at first, then one every 6 hours. Watch expiry date
Codral Forte	100 tablets	For relief of strong pain
SCOP anti-seasick patches	4 boxes	These patches can have side effects. Try them on a short journey first. When effective they are the best treatment
Other anti-seasick potions	4 boxes	May help people who cannot wear patches
Stemetil suppositories 25 mg	20	For severely seasick people
Coloxyl tablets, or other strong laxative	1 packet	Constipation is common in the first few days of a voyage
Fortral 25 mg	100 tablets	For severe pain. Two tablets every 3 hours
Fortral injections 2 ml	20	1 ampoule (2 ml), with another half ampoule 4 hours later if needed

(The actual strong pain killer stocked here will depend on local regulations. In any case, a doctor will have to prescribe them and will need to be satisfied as to the bona fides of the applicant.)

Disposable syringes, 2 ml, with hypodermic needle	20	One use only

N A V I G A T I O N   L I G H T S

At night a yacht needs to identify itself. During the day one expects to be seen, or in bad visibility, to be heard, but at night international regulations demand that all vessels carry navigation lights that will identify them. More importantly they will indicate, to those people who have experience of lights, in which direction the vessel is travelling, and whether it is sail or motor powered.

These lighting regulations are standard throughout the world, but unfortunately there are large areas of the world where commercial traffic ignores them. Off the coast of China, where there are enormous fishing fleets, it is not usual for vessels to display lights. This situation is changing, but it can be very frightening to discover oneself in the middle of a fishing fleet of hundreds of boats, and see only a few of them, and then only dimly.

There are also many people on the commercial highways of the world's oceans with illegal, even criminal, intent, and I don't mean just pirates, although there are plenty of them about. There are, for example, fishing fleets which are poaching in waters where they have no right—they don't carry lights for obvious reasons. There are stealthy craft that are illegally in sovereign waters to gather intelligence. There are drug runners, and then there are the plain stupid. It's because of this widespread misuse or flouting of the international regulations that one has to keep an exceptionally good look out at all times.

On pages 122–129 are colour plates which show the configuration of lights vessels are required to carry to indicate their condition and their course. Apart from the mandatory lights it is good sense for any yacht to carry a good number of hand-held lights that are water resistant and have spare batteries and bulbs. Their use conserves the ship's own battery supply, and in the event of failure of the ship's batteries, the radio may no longer work and any signalling device may be lost, so a battery-powered flashlight can be used to signal for help.

Emergency Navigation Lights

The regulations of the International Yacht Racing Union require that battery-powered emergency navigation lights, which can be quickly clamped into place, be available on board to replace the standard lights if they fail. While that is mandatory for ocean racers, it is also good sense when cruising.

S T O R M   S A I L S

Sailing yachts which race in the ocean under international rules are also required to have storm sails and there are a great many regulations about the strength of the sail's cloth, how the sails should be rigged, how they can be used on stays or wire strops and in the conventional luff grooves. Remember the strength of Kevlar. If it is used as a strop at the head or tack of the sail it is much easier to use than wire and at least as strong. The storm trysail should be sheeted free of the boom so that heavy breaking waves will roll over the boat rather than take the mast out of it. Make sure that the storm gear is rigged every now and then so that the people aboard are familiar with it, and so that any faults in the sail are seen. When these sails are required is not the time to be wondering what goes where.

SPARE PARTS
AND REPAIR KIT

All cruising boats should carry a prefabricated emergency rudder—not an emergency tiller, but a replacement if the rudder breaks. Racing yachts carry U-bolts and their associated nuts, with a board—usually one of the removable boards which cover water tanks or lockers in the main cabin—which can be quickly made up into a quite effective steering device (see diagram 8.2).

It is also mandatory to carry adequate repair kits for the standing rigging, gear, engines, and sails. Every vessel should have on board at least the spares that are required to perform any service task on the engine or other machinery on board.

Each yacht certainly should have boltcutters so that rigging can be quickly cut clear if necessary, as well as a hacksaw and several high speed blades. Having been dismasted in mid-ocean, I firmly believe in having on board a swaging iron and the relevant swages to make a jury rig that can stand considerable pressure.

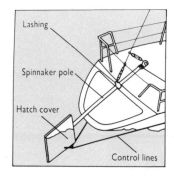

Diagram 8.2 *An emergency rudder made of prepared parts carried for the purpose.*

STORAGE TANKS

Loss of water can cause serious danger at sea, so the storage tanks are critically important especially on boats which are used for long distance cruising. Water should be in at least two separate containers, which, ideally, are capable of interconnecting. The best method is to have plastic pipes running between each tank with a single T-joint taking water to the 'main' pipe. Each tank should have its own tap so that it can be sealed off if it is holed, or if water in one section is contaminated. With this arrangement the rest of the water will not be lost. Very often yachts have tanks on each side. I like to carry at least one further container quite separately as a precaution.

The air temperature where a yacht is cruising or racing dictates the amount of water each crew member needs each day. The absolute minimum is two and a half litres per 100 nautical miles per person, but that in itself can be misleading as a yacht can often travel 200 nautical miles in a day, meaning each person would need five litres of water. In fact, the five litres is more likely to be needed on a day when the boat is becalmed, especially if it is a hot day. If when on a race or a cruise which you think will last six days, you become becalmed for one day or more, your water supply might be inadequate. A skipper on a racing yacht that cannot use its engine except to charge batteries or to pump water, would accept the inherent risk and take only the legally required amount of water. A skipper on a cruising yacht should not in any circumstances do this. Usually a cruising yacht can be motored through a flat patch, but this is not always possible and so it would be better to estimate the time the voyage might take at the boat's average speed (which will allow time should the boat be becalmed), and then calculate the amount of water needed on the basis of five litres a day per person. For instance, a yacht with an average speed of five knots, travelling 400 nautical miles, would take 80 hours to complete the voyage (say four days including a safety margin)—with five people on board 4 x 5 x 5 = 100 litres of water would be needed for the voyage. Even so, the water would have to be monitored carefully, and washing up done in salt water etc.

There have been examples of shipwrecked people living very long periods, indeed months, with only a minimal amount of food. The life expectancy of crew, even in moderate temperatures, without water is five days.

L O S S   O F   F U E L

Loss of fuel or contaminated fuel can certainly be highly inconvenient, and can even become dangerous, although it is much more likely to become dangerous to a motor cruiser than to a yacht which can travel under sail. Fuel storage tanks need to be both well-constructed and well-fixed in place, and made of materials of which engine manufacturers approve. They must be vented to the open air, and it is preferable that they be earthed (grounded) electrically as well. For both diesel and petrol (gasoline) tanks there should be a shut-off valve or cock as close to the outlet from the tank as possible so fuel cannot escape if the fuel line fails. With a petrol (gasoline) engine the valve should be operable on the main deck, or in the cockpit. Otherwise there must be an extra valve in the cockpit to cut off the fuel if there is fire. At least two large fuel filters (water separators) should be fitted to diesel lines.

L I F E J A C K E T

There must be a lifejacket for each person on board, including small lifejackets for children. Each person must know where they are stored and be able to reach them easily if they are needed. A fairly recent addition to the regulations is that lifejackets must be fitted with retro-reflective tape, to enable them to pick up light at night. Inflatable lifejackets must carry an annual certificate saying the jacket has been inspected and found serviceable. These jackets should have whistles attached to them (not pea whistles which don't work with water in them).

S A F E T Y
H A R N E S S

There must be a safety harness for every person on board. Early model harnesses had only one clip, at the outer end of the strop. These caused some deaths because, when yachts foundered very fast, crew members were pulled down with them and couldn't swim against the pressure of suction to release the clip. Harnesses now have a clip at each end of the strop. I would still recommend each person to carry a knife. Harnesses need to be clipped to strong points on the boat and there should be one near the companionway so crew can be clipped on, or unclipped, while below. All ocean-racing yachts carry safety lines (jack stays) which run from bow to stern down both sides of the vessel. These allow crew members to clip on and move comparatively freely almost anywhere around the boat. But there also need to be strong points of the U-bolt or pad eye type to which crew can clip. There should be a strong point on either side of the helmsman, who, in severe conditions, may need to be clipped on both sides.

LIFEBUOY

Many cruising boats still carry a ring-shaped lifebuoy and often they are painted white and red, white or pale blue, or some other light colour which matches the deck of the yacht. The only effective colour for safety equipment at sea is bright orange, it is the only colour that can be seen clearly in the water. The horseshoe-shaped lifebuoy is best because it is possible for the person in the water to unclip the little retaining lanyards, slide into the buoy, and be supported. These lifebuoys should also have retro-reflective tape on them and should have attached to them a package of dye marker, a drogue, and a whistle. Each yacht should carry two such lifebuoys, and to one of them should be attached a flag marker or Dan (tall) buoy—a tall pole weighted at the bottom which flies a flag upright well above the surface of the water. This flag is visible from a considerable distance. Attached to the buoy should be a high intensity electric light with an automatic switch which starts the light flashing immediately it becomes upright in the water. The light must flash for at least 12 hours, or one session of darkness.

It is usually specified that the marker flag and lifebuoys be positioned close to the helmsman, which is sensible as very often the helmsman is the only person on deck when they are needed.

FLOATING
LINE

A highly recommended piece of equipment is a buoy and a floating line which can be stowed within arm's reach of the helmsman, and which is permanently attached to the boat. The helmsman can, almost with a backhand flick, throw the line into the water while at the same time taking the way off the boat. If this is done quickly enough, it's very likely the crew member, if not hurt, could swim to the line and tie it on, making rescue so much easier.

These markers do not only give buoyancy to the jeopardised crew member, with judicious use they can also help establish a path back to the person who has gone overboard (see chapter on Boat Handling above page 104). The order of events is to first throw over the floating line, then the lifebuoy with the marker attached, then the other buoy. Follow this up with any debris you believe will float. The rate of drift of these objects will vary, but the average direction of all the objects will show a reasonably accurate path to the person in the water. The longer the path the less accurate it becomes.

F L A R E S

If you need outside help, you must be able to attract it. The best way to do this, if you believe there is a vessel nearby, is to use flares. Ocean racing yachts are required to carry 22 flares, made up of 12 red parachute flares, four red hand flares, two white hand flares, and four orange smoke signals for use during the day. An alternative is to use a Very pistol, although this will not fire as far or as high as a rocket flare. Nevertheless, a Very pistol is compact, as are the shells it uses, and I think they are a useful extra although they may require a firearms certificate.

Remember when using flares to follow the instructions about lighting them and have in the flare container a heavy industrial plastic glove to use to prevent a misfire from burning you. The chemicals in rocket flares stick to the skin and cause horrible wounds. When you fire the flares, if there is considerable wind, fire straight upward. Rockets turn to the wind, which will push the flare high into the sky where it will burn for longer and so be more likely to be seen. Also, the wind will blow the flare back to you, and its light will appear in the sky nearer to your position. In light to medium cloud, even with low cloud, aim lower so that the flare stays visible—fire at a slight angle from the vertical. Aim in the general direction of the vessel approaching you, if you can see it.

Keep your flares in a lockable waterproof container, preferably with a screw top, and when in port or celebrating, keep them locked up. This precaution is required in many ports as a flare fired in fun is a frightful hazard to oil tankers and other vessels with explosive cargoes.

Flares have a 'shelf-life' of three years only, and while they may last longer than that, they should be replaced at the end of the expiry date. The moral is to keep them up to date all the time, and when you use them, make sure they will be seen. There is no point in a one-man firework display.

I N T E R N A T I O N A L
D I S T R E S S   S I G N A L S

If you run out of flares, or if they do not work, there are other signals which are recognised as international distress signals. These are:

- Code flag N above code flag C
- Any explosive noise (such as a gun) repeated regularly about a minute apart
- Any continuous sound from a foghorn
- A square flag with a ball above or below it (in Australia a lanyard-held sheet with the letter V on it)
- In daytime, orange smoke
- At any time, flames and/or black smoke on board (usually a fire set in a container, held outboard in some way or left floating behind the boat)
- Slowly and repeatedly raising and lowering both arms stretched out.

These are signals that are accepted, but obviously a successful signal is one that attracts attention, so anything that will do that without endangering the vessel could be used.

R A D I O

Use your radio to call for outside help. If you are going to sea you must have a single sideband radio with, at least, the following frequencies: 2182, 4125, 6215.5 kHz, each of which is a distress channel, and 2284, 2524 and 4483 as communication channels. If you are going to be a long way from shore it is advisable to have higher frequency channels, for instance, in the Pacific Ocean the frequency 4143.6 kHz is used as a supplementary channel.

To pass your Restricted Radio Operator's Licence you will need to know how to operate a UHF radio, how to give your vessel's position relative to a charted point, how to send a mayday message, the phonetic alphabet, general operating procedures especially in heavy traffic areas, which channels to use, and which have the greater range in varying conditions. Always try 2182 first— even if you are in enclosed waters, or blocked by high land—it is the channel on which most people expect to hear emergency calls. But if you don't receive an acknowledgment on that frequency, try 4125 or 6215.5, which have greater range during the day, and which are more likely to be heard. At night, the range of radio signals increases because they are bounced back to Earth by a layer of ionised air about 350 kilometres above the Earth. During the day the layer is lower, and so the signals are bounced back earlier and do not travel as far from the transmitting station.

The major radio installation should use the backstay as an aerial to increase the range, but elsewhere there must be a socket to take an emergency whip aerial. This aerial should be pre-tuned to the frequencies the yacht has in the main radio, and must be earthed (grounded) or it will transmit only in line of sight.

Vessels in more sheltered or coastal waters should be equipped with a 55 channel VHF set. The principal use is for ship to ship, ship to shore and ship to landline.

SILENT PERIODS

DO NOT

Transmit on 2182 or VHF Channel 16 in the three minutes after every hour and every half hour. These are the silent periods when only distress calls may be made on these channels, and when every ship should listen to find out whether another vessel is in distress. Ship's wall clocks are available with the silent periods marked on the dial, which provide a very good reminder.

DO NOT

Even outside the silent periods, transmit on the emergency channels (2182, 4125, 6215.5 and VHF Channel 16) except to call up a working station (usually on land). These channels are not to be used for communications between vessels, but can be used to make an initial contact. If you do use these channels to call up a shore station, you will hear the operator tell you to go to a working channel such as 2284, 2524, or several in the higher frequency range. If you don't have the channel nominated you will have to tell the operator, but be quick because they move pretty fast. If you know which countries your travel will take you to, find out which frequencies are commonly used in each country, as only the emergency frequencies are standard between countries.

Transmit any messages without including the ship's name and call sign (which will have been assigned to you when you took out a licence for the radio). Do not use obscene or profane language or transmit unnecessary messages—you could lose your licence.

Radio Emergency Card

Prepare a radio emergency card and keep it in a prominent position near the radio. On it list the vessel's call sign and the following pro-forma emergency message. The card should be followed slavishly, because anybody on board can use it, although not without the permission of the skipper, or the person charged with responsibility for the radio. The prudent skipper will show every person on board how to change the radio to the emergency frequency.

Select the emergency channel or frequency and use high power.

MAYDAY MAYDAY MAYDAY

THIS IS (Name of vessel, followed by call sign). Say this three times

POSITION OF VESSEL (Give bearing and distance from a charted feature or a latitude and longitude)

NATURE OF DISTRESS (Sinking, on fire, other emergency)

WHAT HELP IS REQUIRED (Rescue, tow, medical emergency)

OTHER USEFUL INFORMATION (This will vary according to the emergency, but shore stations usually want to know how many people are on board)

There is another urgency call which takes a lower priority than a MAYDAY. This is a PAN call, which follows exactly the same form, but begins PAN PAN PAN PAN PAN PAN. This is used when there is no immediate danger, but the vessel needs help to avoid a danger to itself or someone on board. Remember, if you hear a MAYDAY or PAN message you MUST help, you are legally required to do so. However, if it is clear that the shore stations or some nearer vessel than yourself have all in hand, you can stand by unless of course you have some capacity to offer better or more specialised help than is otherwise available.

Phonetic Alphabet

Next to the emergency radio card, you should have a copy of the phonetic alphabet. The emphasis is on the bold section of the word:

PHONETIC ALPHABET LIST

ALFA	HOTEL	OSCAR	VICTOR
BRAVO	INDIA	PAPA	WHISKEY
CHARLIE	JULIET	QUEBEC	X-RAY
DELTA	KILO	ROMEO	YANKEE
ECHO	LIMA	SIERRA	ZULU
FOXTROT	MIKE	TANGO	
GOLF	NOVEMBER	UNIFORM	

Most publications which publish the phonetic alphabet do not present the associated phonetic numeral list. It is vital that this information be on the emergency card. After all, if radio transmission or receiving conditions are bad, the most important information to pass on is your position, and that is given in numbers. Here it is, with the pronunciation in the third column.

PHONETIC NUMERAL LIST		
NUMBER	**CODE**	**PRONUNCIATION**
0	NADAZERO	NAH-DAH-ZAY-ROH
1	UNAONE	OO-NAH-WUN
2	BISSOTWO	BEES-SOH-TOO
3	TERRATHREE	TAY-RAH-TREE
4	KARTEFOUR	KAR-TAY-FOWER
5	PANTAFIVE	PAN-TAH-FIFE
6	SOXISIX	SOK-SEE-SIX
7	SETTESEVEN	SAY-TAY-SEVEN
8	OKTOEIGHT	OOK-TOH-AIT
9	NOVENINE	NO-VAY-NINER
Decimal point	DECIMAL	DAY-SEE-MAL
Full stop	STOP	STOP

In any conditions whether bad enough to use the phonetic numbers or not, it is conventional practice to pronounce five as 'fife' and nine as 'niner'.

EMERGENCY POSITION INDICATING RADIO BEACON

These are radio beacons, with their own battery packs, which when triggered by someone in distress will transmit signals by satellite and on the emergency wavelengths received by commercial and military aircraft. In particular, the signals can be received on the COSPASS/SARSAT system which is a joint exercise of the US, USSR, France, Canada and Australia. Four low orbiting satellites, which travel an almost fixed pole to pole orbit, scan the Earth continuously as it rotates within the orbits. Every spot on Earth is seen by satellite at least once every three hours. The information which locates a vessel in distress to within a few nautical miles is passed to the ground station nearest the vessel, and local rescue authorities then take over. The signal will continue for up to 48 hours. If once a radio position has been reported to the authorities, a continuous emergency tone is transmitted from the EPIRB, so the search area will be reduced. It is important to note that the EPIRB is designed to float in the sea and must be allowed to do so: the aerial of an EPIRB tends upright and so the signal is 'strengthened' by the plane of the sea. It can be seen that the EPIRB is a vital piece of equipment—it is not infallible, but it can greatly reduce the worry and cost involved in a sea search.

A B A N D O N   S H I P

If the worst comes to the worst you will have to abandon ship but you must be most reluctant to do so. The boat is your best liferaft and you should not abandon it until you are certain it will not stay afloat. Even when you have boarded the liferaft, stay near the 'mother' ship in case it does not sink.

Racing boats are obliged to carry a liferaft big enough to take all the crew—naturally enough—but their crew size has a stipulated maximum so it is easy to know what size raft is required. The cruising skipper often does not know how many crew will be on board and so needs to carry a raft which will accommodate whatever he considers will be the maximum crew he will have aboard. The crew members will then have to be policed. Racing skippers have to have their liferafts checked once a year, and show the resultant certificate of survey to a safety officer at their club. There is no such pressure on cruising skippers. Because it is expensive to have liferafts checked, there is a temptation to not carry out this vital function. But if the raft doesn't work when you want it you will regret the false economy—you won't get a second chance.

Even people who have sailed for years often don't have the faintest idea what is in a liferaft, so below is a list of the essentials:

- One sea anchor
- Knife
- Bellows
- Signalling torch
- Signalling mirror
- Baler
- Sponge for each person
- Repair kit
- Rescue quoit and line
- Four red hand flares
- Two smoke signals
- Two red parachute flares
- Signalling whistle (there should be whistles on the lifejackets too)
- Enough water to provide five litres per person
- Two tin openers (be careful where you stow them, they can abrade the raft)
- One tin emergency rations per person
- Two tubes sunburn cream
- At least two packets of dye marker
- Five plastic bags per person
- A 'How to . . .' card, waterproof or stencilled inside the raft
- Recommended: Solar still, radar reflector.

This list is a minimum of what can be taken; if there is room to pack more there is no reason not to do so. If there is no room for more, pack a special emergency wallet of extra food, water (most important), flares, charts, radio etc. and keep it next to the raft so it can be taken when the raft is boarded. The raft has quite a lot of room available when it has been inflated.

To board the liferaft, remove the liferaft from its secured position and gently lower it into the sea alongside the stern of the boat, making sure you have hold of the line which goes into the raft's casing. When the raft is in the water, pull on the line until the easily extracted part of the line is out. When some resistance is felt, yank hard on the line. This should release the gas bottle(s) inside the raft and inflate it. The pressure of the expanding raft will pop the light casing which surrounds it. When the raft is fully inflated it sometimes has to be turned over as it can inflate upside down. This is still easier to do from the yacht, rather than having someone go into the water— particularly if the water is cold. If there is an emergency pack, stow it in the raft. Unless the yacht has sunk, stay near it and stay tied on. Only cut the line if there is a threat to the raft. A yacht is much easier to see from the air than a raft.

I've been on liferaft exercises in 30 knot winds and fairly lumpy seas and know they tip easily. Of the nine rafts that took part in our exercise six tipped over, spilling to the ocean floor radios, balers, cans of water and other equipment which would have extended the time the occupants of those rafts could have stayed alive. We found that the larger rafts were the ones that tipped most easily. We were three in a four person raft, with one of our members very seasick. We discovered that the raft was far more stable when the drogue was not used. We experimented many times to see whether or not this was imagination. In the end we surmised that, because the waves were so steep and narrow (it was wind against current) the drogue was breaking out of the top of the wave, then catching again, and so spinning the raft and sometimes tipping it alarmingly (see diagram 8.3). Don't take this to mean I consider drogues to be unsatisfactory. If you are ever unfortunate enough to be in a liferaft in an angry sea, experiment to see what you consider best. If a drogue can be used to slow the rate of drift before the wind, it will be wise to use it. Any rescue operation is virtually certain to take into account the effect of a drogue on drift patterns. If you don't use a drogue, and you drift faster, you may well find yourself outside the area being searched.

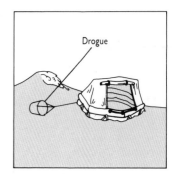

Diagram 8.3 *How a drogue can affect the stability of a liferaft in steep seas.*

EMERGENCIES

NAUTICAL

The greatest single emergency any yacht can face is loss of hull integrity—more simply known as a hole. This can come from collision, increasingly from striking containers discarded by ships at sea, one of the most murderous acts that takes place on the water nowadays, or else from large sea life. To anybody who spends much time on the ocean, it's apparent that the attempts to preserve whale species that were being hunted have been successful. Whale sightings in their common grounds are increasing dramatically, and whales are a hazard.

Consider the dangers from a hole big enough to threaten sinking. A hole is a threat to life, whereas a leak allows you time to deal with it. Even a quite small hole will let in 300 litres (80 gallons) of water per minute. A fist-sized hole well below the waterline will let in water under pressure at a rate most ship's bilge pumps will not be able to handle. An engine driven pump handles between 450 and 2000 litres (100 to 450 gallons) a minute, so that is the only way to stem the flow from even a reasonably small hole. In some cases damage to the hull will be so great that the only option left to a crew is to take to the liferaft, and take with them as much emergency equipment as it is possible to do (see suggested list page 178).

For the moment we assume we have some chance of beating the water. First cut down the inflow by placing a cabin cushion or pillow over it, then wedge a piece of timber against the cushion, even if the timber has to go right across the hull. That should bring the flow down to the level of a leak and provide time to deal with the problem permanently. If the hole is not easy to reach, you may have to remove some of the yacht's fittings to get at it. Having stemmed the flow, you can start cutting down the amount of water entering the hull even further. If the hole is deep in the hull, you probably need to start fothering it immediately, but if not, there are a few steps you can take before fothering. The first is to calculate whether the boat can be made to heel enough to bring the hole above water level, or to make it intermittently above water level. This has two benefits: first, much less water will get in, and, second, the hole will be in an area where it can be worked on directly from outside as well as inside.

Heeling to get a hole higher is useful even if the hole is quite deep. Going on the tack that raises the hole, even if it doesn't raise it above sea level, will reduce pressure and the rate of flow into the boat will be less. It is worth forcing an abnormal amount of heel on to the vessel by moving the anchors to one side and shifting all the sails and other heavy equipment that can be moved, as long as this doesn't affect stability.

With **timber** vessels, the method of repair, if the hole can be reached, is to tack some pliable, thinnish plywood over the hole, with a sealant between the ply and the outside of the hull. The flow of water will have almost stopped. Then, inside the hull the hole can be filled with epoxy and a tingle nailed to the hull from the inside. This tingle can be either another piece of ply, a cut-open tin or piece of flat metal, or anything that can be held firm and that will hold the sealing compound in place while it sets.

If the hole is further down the hull, depending on conditions, quick sealing epoxy can be put into the hole in the same way, but it's more likely that the conditions will be difficult and the problems of the vessel might be compounded if someone were put over the side to handle the repair.

F O T H E R I N G   (P A T C H I N G)

This will allow a reasonable repair to be done from inside the boat, and when conditions are better the fother can be removed and a more permanent repair done to the outside of the hull. Fothering is a small boat version of what happens with collision mats on large vessels. On those vessels the collision mat is permanently rigged with chains attached to its corners. The mat can be moved to the area with the hole, dropped until it sits over it, and it can then be pulled in and held in position.

It's unusual for a small vessel to have a ready-made collision mat. There are some commercial umbrella-like contraptions which can be pushed through the hole and then expanded and pulled back against the hull. There may be a good argument for carrying one of those on a long voyage—they are not very big or heavy (see diagram 9.1). Generally, though, the yacht's crew will have to put something together to act as a fother after the event. The simplest thing to use is a heavy duty sail, and the best of the heavy duty sails is the trysail, which has lines attached to the clew and, usually, the foot. There will need to be a weight attached to the head, as well as another line. The weight will carry the sail down under the boat so that it can be pulled into position. Once in the right spot, it can be tied off. Water pressure will force the sail against the hull, to which it will cling, and the flow of water through the hole will drop dramatically. Ideally, the sail should stay as a gasket even when

Diagram 9.1 *A commercially available 'collision mat' for small vessels.*

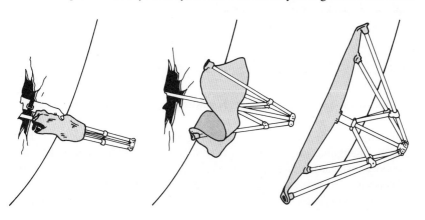

a tingle has been put in place. It would be better to rig a large piece of cloth, something say two metres by two metres (six feet by six feet), and then nail the tingle through it, rather than to destroy the storm trysail, which might still be needed if there is a long way to go to port. If needs must, the quickest way to fother is to use the trysail. Don't worry about whether it looks pretty or not, that's something that can be fixed on the land. At this stage, all that matters is that the hole be repaired and the water kept out.

ALUMINIUM

Mending aluminium boats is rather more difficult, but they can be patched just as effectively as can other materials. It takes a bit longer, and you will need bedding compound because the rivets that will bring the repair plate to the hull will not seal sufficiently well without it. If you have nothing else, cut a piece of rubber the same shape as the metal plate, or make a gasket out of greasy rags which will do just as well. The most important thing about repairing a hole in aluminium is to smooth down the edges of the hole so that any plate being fixed over the outside or inside will sit as close as possible.

First, if the hull is split, drill holes at each end of the split so that it cannot spread. Some books recommend that only aluminium should be put on to aluminium because of the dangers of electrolysis, or galvanic corrosion. Since nobody is going to stay at sea longer than necessary with a hole in the hull, it seems immaterial what metal is put next to the hole for a few days. That sort of corrosion is what to look out for when making the permanent repair.

FIBREGLASS

Flexible metal or timber can be used to repair fibreglass boats. The difference is that the patch should be a good deal larger than the hole. Again, if the hole involves any splitting or tearing, the ends should be drilled out to relieve the stress at those points. Any putty, or gasket or epoxy jointing or filling compound should be used, and if the hole is large enough make sure the patch is considerably larger so spreading the load widely on the hull. The inside and outside plates can be bolted to each other. Most chandlers have emergency packs for fibreglass repair.

STEEL

At first sight steel seems to pose more problems than any other material for a quick repair, although, of course, it is less likely than other materials to suffer the sort of damage we are talking about. But if it does, welding is clearly impossible, so the same sort of repair as for aluminium is called for. Provided two large plates can be held in position, with a jointing compound in between, the amount of water getting into the boat will have reduced to the easily manageable which is our intention. Longer-term repairs come later.

FERRO CEMENT

This is one of the easiest materials to fix, especially if you have on board one of the ready-mixed, fast setting compounds which have only to be exposed to air to set hard. As with all holes or cuts, the area should be clean if putty is going in. If you don't have a commercial ready-mix repair pack on board, you can make one up out of a two-pot epoxy. If there are difficulties with the epoxies jointing to the cement, you will need a tingle over either side.

EXOTIC MATERIALS

Exotics such as Kevlar, carbon fibre, and various sandwich materials should be dealt with as for fibreglass. Extra large tingles, at least externally, are vital because the strength of these ultra-light materials depends to a large extent on the hull remaining in one piece. They can lose structural strength when one section is holed.

OTHER HULL DANGERS

The hull can be threatened by dangers other than collision or accident, but good management can reduce the risk. For instance, if your boat has large areas of window, and in a storm these are broken, you have only yourself to blame if you didn't have on board wooden covers as suggested in the chapter on safety (page 161). It is very difficult to save a boat if you have large areas open to the weather, and when you don't have pre-designed and pre-manufactured blanks ready to stop the water coming in. In the same way, to have been sailing in rough conditions and not to have closed the vessel off in case of being rolled or pooped is poor seamanship. Such accidents can be foreseen and should be avoided. Other dangers are not so easy to detect.

Seam Opening

This danger in old wooden hulls is very hard to foresee—the boat needs to be in a seaway for the condition to be apparent. A boat that is leaking through a number of places is a serious problem because almost nothing can be done to stop the leaks. About all that is possible is to keep the water at bay. The flow of water in these conditions usually is less than through a hole, though not always. If you have the slightest suspicion the hull of a boat you are planning to sail in is likely to leak badly in a seaway, then you shouldn't go to sea. But if you are at sea and you find to your horror that this is happening to you, you have to make a very quick assessment of whether you can handle the flow of water. In desperate cases it will soon become apparent—by the level inside the boat while everybody is pumping furiously on every available pump—whether the problem is insoluble. If it is, reluctantly, the vessel will have to be abandoned.

If you seem to have a chance of winning, don't forget the engine. In most engine installations there is a pumping system for taking the cooling water from the sea, through the engine, and back out to sea again. If the water inlet is closed off at the sea cock, then disconnected and placed in the bilge, the engine will then pump the bilge water through itself and then out through the normal outlet. There are some hazards, because if there is debris floating in the water it can easily block the engine water cooling ways and cause further problems.

There should be time to attach a strum box (strainer), or some other filter, over the end of the hose. In the meantime, detail someone to watch the intake and remove any gross impediments as they float towards it. Diesel engines can operate when they are completely under water, provided the air intake is above water level. It is not too difficult to take a pipe up, even into the cockpit, so that the diesel can gulp the air on which it depends while gulping the water that is threatening your safety. Engines won't tire as a crew will, they can pump much faster and more efficiently, and they can buy you the time needed to radio for help or find a way to stop the water coming in.

LESSER THREATS

Threats such as a burst hose, or failure of an anti-syphon pipe are considered less hazardous because the problem, once seen, can be solved, even though considerable amounts of water can be pumped into a vessel very quickly, with the resultant inconvenience. The situation isn't really life threatening.

A greater risk, although not as serious as a hole or large leak, is posed by loose ballast. We discussed in the safety section how anchors and batteries should be clamped down, doors should have catches to prevent them flying open, scattering goods about, and all heavy items should be well secured. A vessel caught in a 90 knot storm in the Tasman Sea, very well found with experienced people on board, was almost lost because the stove broke free and careered around inside the hull—and you can imagine what the movement of a hull must be like in a 90 knot storm. Not only was it a hazard to the integrity of the hull, it was a distinct hazard to the people on board. While they were trying to keep clear and work out how they could tame the beast, it snapped one of the diesel feed pipes. The inevitable water inside the boat during a gale carried diesel fuel over almost every surface of the interior of the yacht. This made doubly difficult their efforts to bring the rampant stove under control, as they slipped and slid everywhere. Eventually they managed to lash the stove down, but they then had to face the prospect of riding out the gale and getting to safety in a vessel that had been so thoroughly coated with diesel you would have thought it was painted on.

FIRE

Nothing is more frightening than fire at sea, whether it comes after lightning or explosion, or from a seemingly innocent flame in the galley. It counts as a threat to hull integrity because it may burn the vessel entirely, or make it uninhabitable. Naturally every boat will have well-charged extinguishers on board, but there are some techniques for giving the extinguishers a better chance.

A boat which is going fast can be slowed down. If the wind is strong, put the boat into an attitude where the wind blows the flames away from the people, or reduces the intensity of the fire by reducing the amount of oxygen it is getting from the wind.

In the case of electrical fires, first disconnect the battery, and then try to find the source and put it out with the equipment you have on board. Anything on fire that can be thrown overboard should be. If people have their clothing on fire, they must be wrapped in a fire mat or blanket, or they should attach a line to themselves and jump into the water, providing the boat is moving slowly or stopped. On no account point a CO_2-based fire extinguisher at exposed parts of a crew member's body, as the CO_2 freeze burn that will result will be as bad as the fire burn.

Think very hard before you open a hatch or doorway. The only possible reason for wanting to do so would be to get at the fire and put it out. If you aren't able to put it out, or control it, opening a door or hatchway will make an extra through draught which will increase the intensity of the fire. If this emergency is taking place where help cannot possibly reach you in time, make the liferaft and/or a dinghy ready, filling it with the ready-prepared emergency kit and anything else (food and particularly water) which you may think useful. Let out a line to keep the raft some distance from the burning boat. When those fighting the fire realise the risk of the fuel tanks exploding is too great, or that they have no hope of beating the flames, they can pull the raft towards them and get on board.

After Fire Routine

If the firefighting is successful, it is very important that the areas that have been burning should be cooled down by dousing with water; otherwise, those areas that have been subjected to a high temperature might reignite. Go throughout the boat and make sure everything is damped down to a safe temperature.

L I G H T N I N G

A great fear at sea is lightning although sailors fear it more than might be justified. Relatively few instances of lightning strikes on boats have been recorded, although it might be that some of the yachts that just disappear each year have been struck. To my mind, they are much more likely to have been struck by a whale or a container or something of the kind. The preventative measure that can be taken to avoid lightning strike is to install a VHF aerial at the masthead, and to bond all the electrics to earth (ground), so putting a cone of protection over the whole boat. When lightning does cause damage, the worst kind seems to be that the bolt blasts through the hull on its way around the chainplates. Providing this hole is at deck level it is unpleasant, but easily dealt with. If the chainplates go further down, then there could be a nasty hole of considerable size, and the only way to deal with that is to heel the boat quickly on to the opposite side of the hull so as to get the hole clear of the water, and then make whatever temporary repairs are possible.

The other danger from lightning strike is that it may start a fire, and the dangers from the fire are considerably greater than they are from the lightning strike itself. On some racing boats and on increasing numbers of recently designed commercial yachts, the rigging and chainplates are bonded to the keel, which, combined with the cone from the VHF aerial, is probably the safest combination.

R I G G I N G   O R   S P A R S

The next set of circumstances which can leave the boat damaged, but able to continue is loss of rigging which sometimes might also entail loss of sails. Often a boat that has suffered dismasting will be harder to get to safety than one that has overcome a collision or fire, but is otherwise intact.

The paramount rule when any part of the standing rigging carries away is to reduce the strain on the mast on the side where the damage has been done. If the forestay parts, the boat should be put on a run, and if the backstay parts, the boat should be turned into the wind. If the weather shroud parts the boat must be tacked.

The next rule is that the boat should never be jibed, largely because this is likely to take the stick right out, and also because there is more likely to be some other damage caused. If the forestay has parted and there is a headsail up, it should be left up. The headsail itself will support the mast. Once the boat has been put on a reach on the tack that reduces the strain, a proper repair can be done. If you are on a racing boat, your rigging is more likely to be in good shape than that of a cruising boat because you probably will have running backstays. If the main backstay goes, you can immediately support the mast by taking them both on. If the starboard shroud goes, the starboard runner can be taken on to provide some support laterally.

Most yachts have a topping lift which can carry some of the strain. The most useful devices on board at this time are wire-rope clips otherwise known as bulldog clamps (see diagram A2.12 page 278). In all cases a loop must be made to join the end of the rigging that has broken to whatever is going to replace the other part of it. So you need at least two clamps for each loop. I believe that, if standing rigging has carried away, what replaces it should be capable of tensioning the new support, so that the rig can be brought to something like its old strength. This is relatively easy if the break is at the top or the bottom of the stay, or even if it is the turnbuckle itself that has gone. It is more difficult if the break is somewhere in the centre and a filling piece is needed to support the mast. Diagrams 9.2 and 9.3 show the ways that stays can be repaired. Most advice that is given on cutting rigging so that repairs can be made talks about using cold chisels and wire cutters—use bolt cutters instead.

When I was dismasted in the Southern Ocean I was delighted to find that the huge bolt cutters on the boat went through every piece of rigging as if it were cheese. And that's exactly how it should be. Every edge was clean as a whistle and ready to be used, if it could be, in the jury rig. If you don't have bolt cutters you will be forced to use wire cutters and cold chisels. To prevent sprung wires or flying small pieces that can injure crew, wrap some electrical tape around the spot you are going to cut and for about three

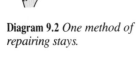

Bulldog clips

Section of anchor chain

Turnbuckle

Diagram 9.2 *One method of repairing stays.*

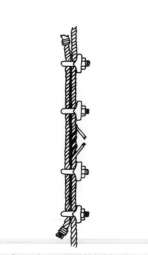

Parts of wire joined by bulldog clips

Diagram 9.3 *Another way of making repairs to stays. Almost any break can be repaired with these materials on board.*

centimetres (an inch or so) either side. When the cut is made, the wires are held in their original shape, and if they have to be led through some rigging, they won't be sprayed out like an old toothbrush. You'll have no difficulty in reeving them. Another reason for having big bolt cutters is that if you want to use part of the anchor chain to replace a section of a shroud, there'll be no difficulty cutting off the amount you want. It will take seconds, not agonising minutes with a hack saw. Bear in mind that all the methods of repairing standing rigging shown in the diagrams can be used in putting up a jury rig if the mast breaks.

L I G H T E R   R I G G I N G   B R E A K S

These are a much less serious threat, and so there is more time to consider what to do with them. If the mast is not threatened simply swage an eye into a loop at the broken end (see diagram 9.4) and shackle another line or wire to the end. The repaired line can be rerigged to fulfil its old function. Swages are so strong they rate almost as well as the original wire, so it is well worthwhile to carry a range of swages and an iron in the tool kit.

B O O M   B R E A K S

The best method of repairing a broken boom is to have a sleeve already on board. You then cut the two broken ends so that they are smooth, insert the sleeve, butt the outboard end of the boom to the inboard and rivet it in place. If it's not possible to do that, and you're on a cruising boat which has twin running booms, lash those on either side of the break and so strengthen the boom. A difficulty here is that, if you have the sort of mainsail that has a footrope which goes into a groove, you'll have to cut a hole in the mainsail to allow the lashings to go right around the boom. Many boats sail very efficiently with loose-footed mains, and so it might be that you leave the foot of the main out and so avoid damage to the mainsail. In many cases on racing yachts, the spinnaker pole would be nearly long enough, particularly with high aspect ratio mains, to take the place of the boom, or it may sit inside the remainder of the boom still connected to the gooseneck. If the boom is completely useless, it's possible to arrange a couple of purchases from the main clew out to the weather toe rail and so arrange a barberhaul which will get shape into the mainsail. You will have to experiment as to where the tackle should go on the toe rail, but you can get a surprisingly efficient sail that way.

J U R Y   R I G S

Any repair that is done to a boat and replaces the damaged part with something made up on board is known as a jury rig. So you can jury rig a boom, a mast or the rudder. Anybody crossing an ocean should have an emergency tiller, and the materials to make an emergency rudder in a few moments.

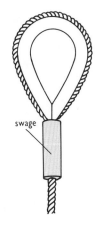

Varied sized holes for crimping swages around wire

Swaging iron

Diagram 9.4 *A simple swage. Quite heavy wires can be repaired with a swaging iron carried on board.*

swage

These rigs will sail a boat very efficiently if the sails are well trimmed at the same time. The normal jury rudder consists of the spinnaker pole, two U-bolts, and a board or locker top or door which has holes drilled in it (see diagram 8.2) so that the parts can be assembled very quickly. In an emergency the board is attached to the pole with the two U-bolts, which bolt up tight. Then the new rudder is lashed over the pushpit. Once the jury rig is in place there is a tendency to think, 'O.K., that's well done, now we'll press on,' and no more permanent repair is attempted. Don't neglect the basic fault. Very often, a competent crew in flippers, weights and goggles, can go over the side and effect repairs.

More usually, with wheel steering, it is the system of wires and pulleys that fails. Whether you are cruising or racing, it doesn't take much room to have ready, cut to the right length, and swaged, a complete replacement. Usually when the steering has gone it is because the boat has been under some pressure and conditions were bad. Having a complete replacement gives you plenty of time to make up or repair the broken part, which can then act as the spare for the future.

It is a good idea to organise an inventory of all the blocks, tackles, lines, winches, small sails and so on that are on board (or have such an inventory prepared before you leave) in case a jury rig will be needed. I learnt the value of this when I was dismasted in the Southern Ocean. One of the crew was a young engineering student who had insisted, quite properly, that the first thing we should do was to make such a list. The count took more than half a day, but we knew exactly what we had available to build our jury rig. We were able to make a design which worked. The result was a mast of eight metres (27 feet) with a designed amount of overlap between the two spinnaker poles which made it up, which was two metres (six feet). We knew that the storm trysail, on edge, would act as a main, even though it hugged the deck and didn't have a boom. We also knew that we would be able to carry the storm jib and sheet it in such a way that it would set to its proper shape. This rig served us for more than 300 nautical miles, survived a 50 knot gale, and worked to windward quite effectively in winds up to 30 knots.

Diagram 9.5 shows a possible jury rig with a method of leverage to raise the new mast, because no crew is strong enough to lift one without mechanical advantage. Most yachts are equipped with winches sufficiently powerful to lift a jury mast, but even the most powerful can't work unless the angles are right. If the angle of the pull is as slight as shown in diagram 9.5, it is quite

Diagram 9.5 *A jury rig made of two spinnaker poles.*

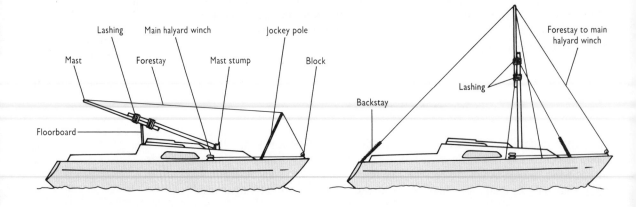

obvious that the spar is not going to lift. If the jockey pole is used as a cantilever, and the angle at the mast head is widened, then it will be possible. Once you start raising the mast, it must be under control at all times. One person must be detailed for steering, one should go on each new cap shroud, and a fourth should haul on the new forestay. It is difficult to see how fewer than four people could raise even a small jury mast. As the caps release, so the forestay must be taken up. This coordination must continue bit by bit until the new mast is upright and can be locked down. There is no one way of saying how a jury rig should be arranged. The most common is where the mast is broken about a third of the way up, and a headsail with the foot as luff is arranged so that the boat can travel on a broad reach. However, if you want to be free to travel wherever you wish, you need a mast tall enough to set a jib that will take you to windward. It may well be that to go on a broad reach will land you in a country for which you don't have the right papers, or where the customs or military authorities may be hostile— somewhere you don't really want to go. So it's worth every effort to get a windward-going jury rig. Your own experience and ingenuity will decide what sort of jury rig you'll put up. Naturally, if you have a couple of thousand nautical miles to travel, rather than a couple of score, you'll have to put up a rig that's going to handle a larger range of weather. But there's a great satisfaction in getting to port under your own power in trying circumstances. You and your crew will be euphoric if, after a period of stress, you're able to limp into port with the boat and most of its gear saved, and your pride not only intact, but bursting.

SURVIVAL CONDITIONS

If you are travelling close to shore on a trip of two days and your mast goes, it is unlikely you would be more than 50 nautical miles from shore. Getting to a port would not normally be difficult. If you are doing a trans-Atlantic crossing or a long voyage involving a great circle, you may well be hundreds of nautical miles from the land. In the first case, you probably will have packed stores for three to four days, at least double the expected length of the trip. On the longer voyage, you will have worked out, carefully, what you believe you will need, and then added a prudent amount of extra food and water in case of such an emergency. But if the circumstances are really bad—you've lost your mast and engine, and you are unable to make more than two or three knots, with the danger of being blown back again by a contrary wind— then your supplies become a matter of very great importance indeed.

WATER

This is vital. You must measure it and control its distribution as soon as possible. Without water, it is exceptional for a human to last more than five days. With water, but no food, survival for a month or even more is possible although illness and weakness would be suffered by that time. There are two schools of thought about whether water should be rationed, some people saying the body can store water, so it doesn't need to be rationed. If the body can survive only five days without water, how can it store it for longer than 5 days? If there is no prospect of being able to replenish the water, it would seem to me to be reasonable to have an equal, small amount each and hope that more will fall from the sky. Other liquid is available in the blood of birds, if you can catch any. Don't drink the blood of fish—it is too salty. There is another point about rationing—if everybody knows each is sharing the same danger and the same water there is less likely to be trouble.

Everybody knows that rain water should be collected from the sails, any awning, or other receptacle if rain falls. But if rain does not fall, there is a very different problem. There have been some very long voyages made, experimental ones, where the only water drunk was salt, but the people who took part in these experiments had trained themselves to drink increasing amounts of salt water before they started the voyage. It is a very different matter getting somebody who has been drinking nothing but potable water all his or her life, and to suddenly expect them to adjust to salt water. They cannot.

In one of the most astonishing records of survival in recent years, a family survived for 154 days in a raft in the Pacific Ocean and when they were found they were quite capable of continuing until they reached land and safety. The major technique that saved them was that they were prepared to have salt water enemas when there wasn't sufficient fresh water. The wife and mother of the family, a nurse, knew that the body could absorb significant amounts of water through the intestines, which can filter salt, something the stomach cannot do. The family was able to avoid dehydration when there was no fresh water, and to collect fresh water when it finally came to them because they were fit enough to do so.

S O L A R   S T I L L S

It is possible to obtain fresh water from salt by using a still working on the stove, or from one using the sun. The stove method is more efficient than the sun, but the sun's energy is limitless. You would use a considerable amount of gas to obtain the water. But water is more important than gas so here is how to go about it using the stove. Use a metal pot with a funnel over it (see diagram 9.6), or a reasonably large teapot with a spout, and take a length of pipe and force it over the tapering spout. Then lead the pipe to a receptacle for water. You will need a supply of sea water to pour over rags you have lagged around the pipe between the spout and the receptacle. The principle is that steam rising from the boiling sea water will pass through the tubing, but will condense where it is cooled. The water that drips out at the end is not salty—at worst, it might be slightly brackish. Beggars can't be choosers, but if there's time and the need isn't urgent, there is no reason why the brackish water can't be distilled again.

The solar still is simpler, but makes less water (see diagram 9.7). You will need two containers, one about four times the capacity of the other. The larger one is half filled with rags and salt water put in with them to about a third the capacity of the container. The smaller container is placed in the centre of the larger one, clearing the rags away from the spot. Put a black plastic

Diagram 9.6 *A still for obtaining water using the ship's stove.*

garbage bag over the top of the two containers and put a weight in the centre of it. The inverted cone of the plastic bag should now be poised over the smaller container. Put the still into the sun. As the heat evaporates water in the rags it condenses on the underside of the plastic, runs down the cone and drops into the smaller container. This is a relatively clumsy, slow method of producing only a little water, but has the merit of using everyday materials. If there is no other method, this could save your life.

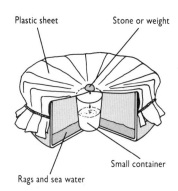

Diagram 9.7 *A solar still of the kind used to obtain water in deserts. They work just as well at sea.*

S H O R T A G E   O F   F O O D

This is less serious than shortage of water, but can still become a great problem if either or both of two conditions occurs. The first is that a large crew is faced with a greatly extended voyage, so that the supplies per day become very little. The second is that, through spoilage or refrigeration breakdown, or some other such disaster, considerable amounts of food are ruined, leaving limited supplies either in the actual or a dietary sense. Rationing may be necessary, and, while everybody should be given basically the same, there may have to be some consideration given to people who are unable to eat certain foods, or are allergic to them. This would have to be worked out by open and frank negotiation, so that everybody knows and accepts the arrangements.

In case of spoilage, make sure that whatever has gone off is disposed of immediately. It must be thrown out, in case in later hunger something dangerous is eaten. If there is refrigeration failure there may be some time—with frozen foods—before they will become contaminated. Eat the perishables first. The rate at which they are eaten should be calculated as close as possible to the rate at which they will decay. If there are some fresh supplies on board that will last only a day or two without refrigeration, set to and cook as many meals as possible from them. It doesn't hurt if meat gets a little gamey, it can be put into stews and be perfectly acceptable. Cooked food will keep longer than raw materials so extending its life by a few days at least.

It would be intelligent to get the views of the most experienced cook on board to ascertain in what order the food should be eaten and how it could best be turned into a product that would keep longer. Dry biscuits and such will keep for a very long time and should be kept to do just that. Onions last a very long time if there is plenty of air around them, so keep them until later. Try to work out how many days you believe the food can last when it is managed in this way, and set out your rationing on that basis. Make sure at least part of the crew is given the responsibility of trying to get food from the ocean. If you are fairly close to shore, it is likely there will be fish about. Often they are simply sculling about in the shade under the boat. While these fish may be frightened and nervous, very often a long gaff can be made out of the boathook, with a large fish hook lashed to it. Seeing one of their number hoisted struggling into a boat doesn't seem to put off the other fish, so several can be caught this way. Fish can be dried for later use, but remember, dried fish takes a lot of water to digest. Fish kept this way can be tacked on to the end of your resources, so extending the time for you to get to shore or be rescued.

It is unusual for any crew not to contain at least one sailor who is also a good fisherman. As with any other expert, take his advice as to which fish can be eaten and which cannot. As a rule of thumb, the uglier a fish, the less likely it is that you can eat it. Anything that has spines, or puffs up, that has a wart-like skin, or seems in any way repulsive is almost sure to be poisonous. If in the slightest doubt, leave a fish alone.

Also be aware that, in tropical waters, large fish, well along the food chain, can also be dangerous. They feed on smaller fish which feed on smaller ones still, and these smallest may be of a kind that crunch coral between their massive teeth and extract sustenance that way. Very often that sustenance can be poisoned, and it is passed on through the food chain. It causes a severe food poisoning in humans called ciguatera which can be fatal. So a good rule for the tropics is if there's no one who can advise you in particular, eat the smaller rather than the larger fish.

A prolific source of food at sea is birds, and all birds are edible, although they may not taste wonderful. I've been in large areas of the ocean which seem to have no fish population, but I have rarely travelled a day without seeing a bird of some kind. Some are quite wary and hard to catch, so ingenuity is the name of the game. I'm sure most sailors have had days when birds have dived at fishing lures being towed behind their boat. Well, adapt that line to attract birds even more, allow them to settle near it by not trolling too fast, and let it catch it. If you can catch a bird you have a supply of good protein, as well as some liquid from its blood.

P R O B L E M S   O F   A R R I V A L

Let us assume now that, despite the horrendous succession of problems that have befallen you and your crew, you have got close to shore in your crippled boat. Your very arrival close to shore poses a new series of hazards, amongst them running aground, being on a lee shore with a jury rig and not being able to get off, anchoring at sea, or closing the coast in bad visibility.

The best way to avoid a lee shore is to recognise its capacity to become one. If the port you are heading for has a prevailing wind, but you are not sailing in that prevailing wind, recognise that it can develop at any time, transforming the shore into a dangerous one. Plan your approach on the basis that it will be dangerous and set your course so that the danger is minimised or eliminated. If you don't go into a bay you can't become embayed. If you don't go close to a lee shore, you can't finish up on it. You may have to delay your arrival by staying out to sea and so avoiding the effects of bad weather. The delay is worthwhile if it means survival.

A G R O U N D

One of the worst situations is running aground. Let's assume conditions are bad but not so bad that you are in danger of being smashed to pieces. First, ascertain whether the tide is rising or falling. If it is falling and you don't get off quickly, you won't get off for a long time. You may as well prepare to stay where you are until you have at least the amount of water under you on the next rising tide that you have now, on a falling tide.

The most dangerous case would be if you went aground at the highest point of the highest tide of the cycle. You would then not have enough depth to get off until that great height of tide occurs again. You will be well above water level while you wait, but your boat would be in danger all the time.

The next most dangerous situation when stranded is if you have gone aground near the top of a normal tide. You'll have a good chance of getting off if the next high tide is going to be as high or higher than the last one. If you've gone aground on a rising tide, you may have to wait only a relatively short time to be able to float and be on your way. Whichever, the first thing to do is to try to lower the depth of the boat, and the easiest way to do that is to heel it. Get all the weight on to one side. Let the boom right out, with people on it. If you have hit a shelf that is sloping toward the land, try to heel away from the land, but be careful the wavelets don't bounce the boat further ashore all the time. If your engine is working, use it and try to back off exactly where you ran on.

Wind direction is important. If it is blowing onshore, your task of getting free is going to be much more difficult. If blowing offshore, the wind will help you. With an offshore wind you may even be able to back the sails, heel to leeward and bounce off.

Sometimes using a kedge to haul off will work, but, usually, if you have got to this stage you are well stuck. Your chances are better if the tide is rising, but don't be daunted if it is dropping. Don't let your attempts to refloat blind you to the penalties of failure. If the tide is dropping fast, there may be the possibility that you are going to dry out where you are. You'll need to form a plan of action, such as using the spinnaker poles as legs which, when lashed to the side the boat is heeling, will prevent it going right on its side. Damage isn't necessarily great from the boat heeling over completely, but the danger is when the tide rises again. If the water gets inside the boat— in other words, if it doesn't rise properly to the tide—you may lose it.

MEDICAL

T H E   R U L E S

There are five rules which must be applied by every skipper putting to sea where the vessel will be further than 12 hours from land, whether cruising or racing.

Rule 1: If faced with a problem that is beyond the skill of anyone on board, the skipper must get on the radio and get advice.

Rule 2: Don't guess. Unless you are absolutely certain the treatment you are applying to a patient is correct, get back to Rule 1 and get advice.

Rule 3: Reassure the patient, who, while considering you a good fellow to sail with, may not want to accept you in the role of doctor.

Rule 4: Before leaving port, if you are going to be more than a few hours from help, find out the allergies each crew member might have, and any medication they are taking for short-term or chronic disease. Make sure they have enough with them. This ties in with Rule 1 as you will not be able to answer the first questions of the land-based doctor without this information. It may be that the patient won't be able to answer you in the emergency.

Rule 5: Unless you have a doctor on board, you will need reference books which will be a guide to any sort of emergency you are likely to encounter. The best of all is the latest edition of the *Ship Captain's Medical Guide*. Also you will need a comprehensive book on first aid.

If you follow the five rules above, you will be surprised how serious and potentially life-threatening problems can be dealt with using a combination of the rules, good sense, and, if necessary, the radio. Talking of radio, keep in mind that there are thousands of volunteer organisations all round the world which give an almost continual watch on even the most remote coasts. Nothing makes these volunteers happier than being able to help a boat that's in distress.

The best idea of all is to have someone on board who is thoroughly trained in advanced first aid, but if that is not possible, carry a first aid manual such as one the major airlines provide to their cabin crews, or a Red Cross or St John Ambulance manual.

In all cases of medical trauma it is wise not to give the patient alcohol. It does not help. It is a fallacy that it will warm the body, at least on deck, as it actually expands the small blood vessels in the skin, so releasing heat more easily.

For the sake of clarity, I've divided the kinds of medical emergency on board into three categories: life threatening, serious and minor. But some of the cases listed as minor can become serious, and some of the serious can become life-threatening. As with accidents, it is the progression from minor to serious to dangerous that has to be halted by taking firm and appropriate action.

While the most serious of the life-threatening conditions is collapse of any kind—heart attack, stroke, internal haemorrhaging, choking, etc.—a condition which is part of any accident or illness is shock, and it can turn the serious into the dangerous very quickly. We will now cover the most common medical problems encountered at sea.

APPENDICITIS

This is greatly feared on small vessels at sea where the erratic movement of the boat is thought by some doctors to aggravate the appendix of those who are unused to the sea and susceptible to appendicitis attacks. Appendicitis is the inflammation of a sac at the top of the large intestine. Medical science still has no real explanation of why the sac is there. Unfortunately it can become inflamed if it becomes strangulated (twisted), if it ulcerates, or if decaying food catches in it. If the attack is acute, it can develop into a deadly infection in six to twelve hours, an infection which is beyond the capacity of most sailors to treat, as the only effective treatment is to surgically remove the sac.

THE SYMPTOMS

There will be dull, nagging pain in the abdomen, perhaps with vomiting. The pain will become more severe and move, usually to the lower right hand area of the abdomen, although the site of the pain can change. One symptom that distinguishes appendicitis from other abdominal pain is that the breath will be foul and very strongly so. When the attack has continued for several hours the abdomen is hard to the touch and the patient has some level of fever. The pain will be more severe and the muscles may go into spasm.

These symptoms in a woman must be treated with caution, as they could indicate different internal complaints, including ovarian cysts. However they should always be taken seriously.

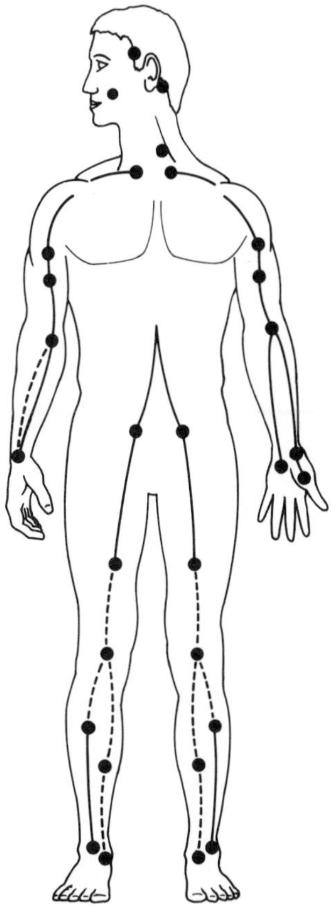

TREATMENT

Pain killers should be supplied and antibiotics used to control the onset of the infection, which is known as peritonitis. If there is the slightest suspicion that appendicitis is occurring, make contact through a shore radio station, with a doctor, who will 'talk' you through the treatment. If you are unable to make contact, the usual treatment is 500ml of ampycillin four times a day for eight days. Ampycillin is related to penicillin, so if the patient is allergic to penicillin— and it is important to check this—administer aurethromycin instead, at the same dosage but only twice a day. One assumes that before the eight days have passed some outside help will have arrived.

The patient must be treated for shock by being put to bed and kept warm and comfortable. On no account offer food—only occasional small drinks of water.

Use a middle-level pain killer such as Veganin or Doloxene at the rate of two every four hours, maximum dose eight per day, or as directed. Heavy duty pain killers, such as morphine, may cause complications and should be used only on medical advice, or in the middle of an ocean where it will be days before the vessel can reach help. If pain is severe use Fortral tablets (25 mgm) at the rate of two every three hours. In extreme circumstances inject 2 ml of Fortral, following up with another half ampoule, 1ml, four hours later.

Diagram 9.8 *Pressure points to control bleeding.*

BLEEDING

Bleeding can be controlled by applying direct pressure to the wound. If this is ineffective, pressing on the pressure point between the wound and the heart may be necessary (see diagram 9.8). If pressing the point restricts the flow of blood, the coagulating mechanisms of the bloodstream get a chance to come into action. Once the bleeding has stopped, direct pressure should be reapplied. If this pressure is inadequate, and the flow of blood is still too much, a constrictive bandage must be used. Roll a handkerchief, or tea towel or similar small area of cloth to make a 'rope'. Put it firmly around the limb just above the wound until no pulse can be felt below the bandage and the bleeding is stopped (see diagram 9.9). This treatment must be used only as a last resort and the bandage must be released after 15 minutes at most. Apply direct pressure if bleeding restarts after bandage is removed. Seek outside help if the blood loss does not slow down.

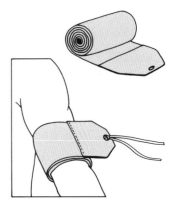

Diagram 9.9 *A constricting bandage used to halt bleeding.*

B U R N S

These occur quite frequently on boats, mainly from rope burns but sometimes from fire. They are treated in basically the same way, whatever the cause, although there is controversy over what treatment is best. The argument is over whether burns should be covered. Some doctors have thought water should be poured over the area for a considerable time, and the wound left open to the air. Others had felt this was a way to infection. Consensus now seems to be that at sea burns should be covered with petroleum impregnated pads (there are many proprietary lines, some listed on page 169) and the patient given salty drinks. One of the best drinks is orange juice diluted in warm salty water.

The Symptoms

There is never any doubt that a burn is anything but a burn, the seriousness being decided by the amount of the body which is burnt, and whether the burns are first degree (surface skin only), second degree (through many of the 24 layers that make up the skin) or third degree (through all the layers).

Treatment

For a large area of third degree burns, most likely the result of an engine room fire, there are unlikely to be enough burn pads. The only thing possible is to clean the area thoroughly by gently washing it in tepid soapy water. Then treat the victim for shock, not the burn. Do not cover the wound, keep the victim warm and give liquids, as described above, as often as possible. It will be difficult for the patient to be comfortable, but be very careful, as any movement will be agonising and may result in loss of flesh. Administer pain killers and seek medical advice because the patient will be suffering moderate to severe shock and will be in a serious condition.

For a smaller area, apply burn pads so that the area is completely covered. Even though the wound may not seem nearly as severe as a larger one, the patient will still be suffering shock and must be treated for it with rest, warmth, and salty drinks. Give Fortral tablets at the rate of two every three hours if the pain is severe, otherwise give Veganin, two every four hours.

For the most common burn, the rope or wire burn, treat as for the medium wound, even to the treatment for shock. Give pain killers only if the patient wants them, and offer salty drinks. There is quite an element of shock in rope burns, because it is usually associated with a struggle with a sail getting out of hand, or a halyard running too fast. If the burn is caused by wire rather than rope, it can be very painful because the wire digs deep into the flesh and melts it. Infection is less likely because the skin usually is not broken.

C H O K I N G

This is a nasty problem since the person whose air supply is blocked will not survive very long and because it takes time for anyone except the choking victim to realise what the problem is. At first it just seems that someone is coughing, so valuable time is lost before the realisation gradually dawns that this is indeed an emergency.

TREATMENT

Try to dislodge whatever is causing the choking. Lie the victim down so that the head is lower than the chest and see whether you can push your finger down the victim's throat and hook the object, but don't spend long doing this. Hit the back of the victim firmly with a clenched fist between the shoulder blades, and alternate that with clasping the hands together around the victim, putting the hands on the upper part of the stomach, between the navel and the sternum, and squeezing sharply by clenching the muscles of the forearm. In the case of children, it often helps to get them to lean well forward so that their torso is virtually upside down, thus helping to dislodge the article. If there is time, this procedure may be helpful with an adult as well. If breathing stops, begin artificial resuscitation.

ARTIFICIAL RESUSCITATION

If you were unable to hook out the object before, it is vital you do so now as time is of the essence. There should be somebody on board trained in artificial resuscitation but if not, follow these steps. Put the victim on his back on a hard surface and tilt the head backwards, with the neck lifted so that the airway is open. Commence mouth-to-mouth resuscitation by blocking the victim's nostrils and breathing into the victim's mouth. If the victim is not breathing and has no pulse after you have breathed half a dozen times into the open mouth, then, and only then, commence cardiopulmonary resuscitation: put the heel of the hand over the top part of the stomach close to the breastplate and, putting the other hand at right angles on top of the first, press down firmly so as to depress the breastplate at least three centimetres (an inch). Follow the sequence of pressure, release, pause; pressure, release, pause. Fifteen depressions of the sternum should be followed by two breaths into the victim's mouth. Repeat this sequence four times per minute then check for breathing and pulse. Continue mouth-to-mouth resuscitation if the pulse returns. When breathing becomes normal, cease the treatment, put the patient to bed and treat for shock.

C O N S T I P A T I O N

This is unpleasant and can be quite painful, but it is not usually dangerous. The first aid kit should contain Coloxyl tablets, or some other laxative, but don't be too quick to take it. Constipation on the first day or so of a voyage is quite normal, because the body is moving in different muscular ways, the diet has changed, even the times of eating will have changed. The whole system is thrown out of kilter as the body adjusts to new tasks. So, normally speaking, on the second or third day the condition remedies itself. One of the standard jokes of ocean racing is that the queue forms at the loo (head) on the beginning of the third day.

If the condition doesn't resolve itself, you should drink plenty of fluids and eat fresh fruit and vegetables like potato, beans, etc. that contain considerable amounts of roughage. Sailors commonly eat packs of mixed dried fruit and nuts for energy, and these will help relieve constipation, as will breakfast cereals such as muesli, or some of the bran-based foods. If the constipation persists, take Coloxyl, as directed on the label.

C U T S , B R U I S E S , A B R A S I O N S , S P R A I N S

These are the most common problems on board. If the skin is broken the area should be cleaned and an antiseptic applied. Antiseptics are what the name implies, substances which inhibit the chance of infection. Dab iodine or betadine on the wound and cover it with a suitable dressing, taking care not to put a dry dressing on a wet wound. The wound will stick to the dressing and have to be soaked off with hot water—very unpleasant. For very small wounds Elastoplast or Bandaids will do, for larger ones you will need to carry rolls of the same material. Many boats have a 'ready drawer' which contains standard dressings, bandages, eye drops and other medications which are needed quickly for minor wounds. It is a good plan.

Be aware that some wounds are more likely to become infected than others. Coral cuts and oyster shell cuts will almost certainly become infected unless every piece of the crumbled coral or splintered oyster shell is removed. This can best be done by pouring a little hydrogen peroxide into the cut. The fizziness will kill anything that is likely to cause infection. If, after a day or so, the cut does become infected, take Septrin or Bactrin 80/400 mg, two tablets every four hours or as directed on the packet.

For larger cuts, once cleaned, pull the flesh together with plastic sutures, such as Leukostrip, made for the purpose. Once the wound has been pulled closed, bandage it so that the flesh stays together and begins to knit, and bleeding stops. Check the wound twice a day for infection.

If the wound is larger still, or won't pull close together with plastic sutures, traditional stitching will be needed. For long voyages the first aid kit should contain several stitching needles. Spray or wipe the skin with an anaesthetic, such as those used by sporting first aid personnel. Check that the sterile pack has not been torn or damaged. If not, the needle is sterile. If the pack has been breached, sterilise the needle in disinfectant. If there is no disinfectant,

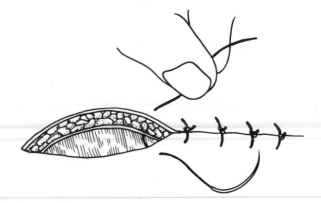

Diagram 9.10 *Closing a wound by suture. Note the small stitch which holds the closing stitch.*

make the needle red hot over one of the top burners on the stove. Use it when it cools.

Thread the needle while the anaesthetic takes effect, allowing about 15 centimetres (six inches) of thread loose on one side, and three times that on the other. Push the needle firmly through the flesh with the bottom of the U in the air, as in diagram 9.10. Use a circular motion so the needle makes a curve and comes out opposite where it went in, but on the other side of the wound. Use about one stitch for every centimetre (third of an inch). Bring the thread back along the wound when it has been stitched closed, so that the knot can be tied. Tie it gently, so as not to pull the stitches near it. Disinfect the wound.

Bruises largely have to be left to nature. They can be quite deep-seated and take days for the typical colours of bruising to flare and then fade. The bruising contusion is caused by crushed blood vessels. It is not until they heal and flush away the damaged cells that the bruise disappears. The best treatment is packing the bruised area with ice for 10 minutes in each hour, but this is unlikely to be possible on most yachts. If the yacht has a cool brick, that should be applied to the bruise, even though it won't contact the contours as well as blocks of ice. Anything that can make the bruise cooler will do. If there is no ice, cold compresses are effective. On a hot day, sea water will be relatively cold. Replace the compress as soon as it has reached ambient temperature.

Sprains have to be treated as a bruise would be, except that the patient should also lie down and take the weight off the injured limb. A sports medicine doctor once told me that he could always tell if somebody had a broken bone by the way they held the rest of their body. The victim automatically favours the limb or joint which is having to take the extra load because of the break. So, if somebody has a really bad sprain, they are going to favour that part of the body which is taking the extra strain. Make sure, when they rest, that they rest the part they are favouring, as well as the injured part.

If the leg is sprained, raise it above the level of the patient's body. If it's an arm, use a sling to take the weight off the shoulder. If the shoulder itself is injured, the weight of the arm will be reduced by a sling, so aiding the healing process. The patient probably will have to remain immobilised until the vessel reaches port, particularly if the sprain is bad.

D I A R R H O E A

This is not to be taken lightly. The condition can cause rapid dehydration, particularly in children and people without great body weight. Diarrhoea may be caused simply by improperly stored or impure foods, in which case it will not last long, but it may be a symptom of a far more serious disease, and if it persists medical help must be sought. The main treatment is to prevent the patient eating until it's clear that the bowel has settled down. But while food should not be ingested, drinks should, such as clear broth, milkless tea and mildly saline solutions. If the body manages these without further symptoms, and that means after several hours, some light food, such as unbuttered toast, can be tried. The no food, plain drinks regimen should be continued for long enough for the bowel to purge itself of whatever is causing the problem. If the diarrhoea continues, then medication should be taken such as Lomotil (5 mg), two tablets every four hours, or a Kaomagma mixture as directed on the label. If, after two or more treatments, the diarrhoea continues, there may be a more serious cause. This is when outside help should be sought. If there is blood in what is passed, an antibiotic should be taken, for instance Tetracycline capsules (25 mg) two, then one every six hours or as directed.

EXPOSURE
(HYPOTHERMIA)

This condition exists when the body has been exposed to cold long enough for the core temperature, the temperature of the organs which control life and life's functions, to drop below a safe operating temperature. Exposure is a very serious problem and it is insidious. It can happen even in quite temperate climates without any but the most seasoned sailors being aware of it. It often occurs during rough weather when people suffering from seasickness do not want to go into the cabin because it makes them feel worse. They will stay on deck for many hours if allowed to, during which time their core temperature gradually lowers, to a possibly dangerous degree, without them being aware of it. Bad weather, which is usually colder than good weather, accelerates the process. The sufferer becomes sluggish, loses willpower, and may become quite obstructive. Whether the person wishes to go below or not, and whether the people below like the idea of someone being sick in their home or not, the person must go below and must keep warm to avoid exposure. Do not brook any argument.

Anybody who has been in the water for a long time (through accident, or doing a repair etc.) must be treated afterwards as having suffered exposure. Even somebody who has been on deck for a long time on a particular job in cold weather should be treated the same way.

In higher latitudes frostbite can occur. This again is a serious matter, as tissue can be badly damaged. The symptoms are mottled legs and limbs that appear to have gone to sleep. The only treatment is gradual warming by body heat only. Trying to warm the victim too fast is very dangerous. This treatment applies to exposure.

TREATMENT

First get the victim out of any wet clothing and into warm, dry clothing and wrapped in a blanket. Be sure that the top of the head is covered to retain heat, as this is an area which loses heat quickly. A very effective method of restoring the temperature of somebody who has suffered a loss of core temperature is to have him or her lie between two people, whose radiant heat will gradually warm up the cold body. Do not rub the skin to dry or warm it, pat it gently.

After the sufferer has attained normal temperature again, as shown by the thermometer, keep them quiet and warm. A notable feature of hypothermia is that the body temperature takes a great deal longer to restore to normal than it took to drop in the first place. Somebody who may have suffered a severe drop in core temperature over two hours may take 12 hours of gradual warming to get back to a reasonable condition. Anybody who has suffered from hypothermia is going to be unable to act as an efficient crew member for at least 24 hours—and should not be asked to work.

E Y E   I N J U R Y

The eye, as everyone knows, is a most delicate and vital organ. The slightest injury must be treated as serious when a long way from help. If there is an object in the eye, try to flush it out with a mild saline solution, say one part salt water to 10 of fresh. Do not try to get it out with a rolled up handkerchief, or something even harder. If the object is successfully removed, bathe the eye in disinfectant eye drops such as Dericain ½ per cent. Don't allow the patient to rub the eye, and if they can't be stopped, cover the eye with a sterile dressing to prevent them. If the object isn't located, bathe the eye with Dericain, cover it, and make the patient rest. The eye is very good at evicting things it does not want. Seek medical assistance to remove the object.

For eye infections, use an antibiotic ointment such as Neosporin or Chloromycetin, or a sulphacetamide ointment as directed.

In the case of serious eye damage, get expert help immediately. Don't waste any time. You can only make the damage worse unless you know what you are doing.

F A T I G U E

This condition is difficult to diagnose on boats. It shows up in mistakes in well-understood operations, lack of concentration and general unwillingness to tackle even the simplest of tasks. It is a condition only the person affected can diagnose, and not always then. Often it is not discovered until it is well advanced. It is really a function of management of the crew to prevent fatigue taking hold. One of the main dangers of the breakdown of the watch system in a small boat is that the workload falls on too few people, who then become susceptible to fatigue. As might be expected, the cure is rest, at the same time keeping warm. The treatment can also include eating and drinking sweet things—heavily sugared cocoa (a naval special) or tea, even sweets and lollies. It is no accident that very popular foods on racing boats are mixtures of nuts and dried fruits or chocolate, which give a very quick release of energy.

F E V E R

This is one of the body's ways of indicating that it is fighting off infection or some internal damage. Above 37.8 degrees C (100 degrees F) is a moderate fever, above 39.4 degrees C (103 degrees F) is a high fever and above 41.1

degrees C (106 degrees F) is a dangerous fever. Above 42.2 degrees C (108 degrees F) is usually fatal. While dangerous is obviously worse than high, and high worse than moderate, any fever must be brought under control as quickly as possible.

The patient should be kept cool and treated with aspirin, which will reduce fever most effectively. The dose should be regular, no more than two tablets four times a day. It is very important that this dose should not be increased but should maintain a steady level of aspirin in the system. For patients who are sensitive to aspirin, offer Codral Forte tablets at the same rate.

If there is shivering or chill, and the fever gets worse, guard against dehydration by mopping the body with cool towels and trying to get the patient to take slightly salty drinks.

If there are no symptoms apart from the fever, medical help should be sought urgently—there are too many possibilities for the cause of the fever to select a treatment. The cause most likely will be an infection, but do not give antibiotics without medical approval.

F R A C T U R E S

These are fairly common on shipboard, particularly in rough weather. Luckily, the really serious fractures, those of the spine and the skull, are not common, although they can happen. But in those cases, apart from immobilising the patient and giving pain relief, the best thing is to get urgent advice and call for help to have the patient taken ashore. For what might be called ordinary fractures, those of fingers or toes or limbs, immobilise the patient and apply a splint to hold the broken limb rigid. Follow the instructions in the medical book you should have on board. If a limb is broken, use one of the pneumatic splints. If it is a broken toe or finger, place a pencil, or thicker piece of wood as a splint, alongside the break and bandage around the splint and the toe or finger to hold it still.

It is important that a broken bone is immobilised as described, but no attempt should be made to set it. In any case where the back has been severely injured, even if it's apparently only bruised, it should be treated as a fracture and the patient not moved at all. In the case of serious fractures, do not give narcotics. Use codeine and aspirin instead. Seek outside help urgently.

There will certainly be shock in the case of a break of any kind, so keeping the patient warm and quiet and, above all else, reassured, is important. In the case of any blow to the head, whether a fracture is suspected or not, the patient should be kept under close observation for the night and for 24 hours after the blow occurred for symptoms such as loss of consciousness (apart from sleep), drowsiness, vomiting or even unfocussed eyes. If any of these symptoms is evident or, when the patient is sleeping, the eyes are rolled back, there is a chance of concussion. The patient must be awakened and treated as for shock. He must not be allowed to return to sleep until it is certain he has returned to normal. Keep him as quiet as possible. Do not give him anything to eat or drink until he has recovered.

HEART FAILURE

The only symptom of heart failure the layman is likely to understand is that sometimes the victim will be in extreme and obvious pain, very likely clutching his chest, and his face will rapidly become blue. There is little anyone can do except try to make the patient lie down, however, don't lie the patient down if he is breathless. If the attack passes, treat the patient for extreme shock and radio for him to be taken ashore. If the patient collapses, follow the treatment for artificial resuscitation given on page 197.

INFECTIONS

Infections of cuts or abrasions should not occur if they are treated as discussed on page 198, but if they do occur, it is important to remove any areas of pus, either by gently squeezing, or wiping with a sterile gauze. If the symptoms are of some more serious infection, there will be other indications, such as general malaise, perhaps a headache, and even fever. In that case give antibiotics, Septrin or Bactrin 80/400 mg, two tablets every four hours or as directed, and keep the patient rested and warm.

JAMMED FINGERS

This and other injuries to the hand are common, particularly on larger boats. This is because the Kevlar sheets and braces on spinnaker gear are stronger than steel, or else they are wire. Because the loads on big boats are bigger than on small ones, the injuries suffered when these controls break, or run free, are more severe. In the case of seriously jammed fingers, immobilise the whole hand, apply ice if that's possible, and give pain killers. If the skin has burst, treat it as you would an open wound by washing it clean with an antiseptic and then covering it. If infection develops, treat with Septrin or Bactrin, two tablets every four hours. If bones are broken as well, the patient's condition is serious and outside help should be sought. The possibility that the patient might lose the hand, or some of its functions, should be kept in mind. Immobilise the hand, and treat the sufferer for severe shock.

SEASICKNESS

Everybody should try to find out whether they become seasick by going on to the ocean for the first time without taking any treatment. This might mean they have a miserable afternoon, but if they find out they don't need treatment they know they can sail without being debilitated. If they find they do get sick, the most recent proprietary treatment is by far the best, although some people do have bad reactions. The treatment is the scopolamine patch, a small round patch like a Bandaid which is impregnated with scopolamine. It is adhesive and is attached to the skin on the mound behind the ear. Pull all the hair out of the way and simply rub the patch until it is firmly attached.

The only way you can find out whether you have a serious reaction to the patch—and some people do—is by experience. If you are not reactive, they provide the most reliable method of control with the fewest side effects. The main advantage the patches have over any of the tablet or liquid motion sickness cures is that, because they release the medication steadily into the bloodstream, they cannot be vomited out of the system and so be useless. The fault of most treatments is that they aren't effective when they are most needed.

An interesting fact about the patches is that the person wearing them often can't tell when the effects are wearing off, up to the time when they become ill again. The patches seem to be effective for a different amount of time from person to person, and even from use to use with the same person. One person I know uses the patches with great success, but I can tell when they are wearing off because the friend becomes irritable, which is unusual. If the patch is changed immediately, good humour is restored. The time when this becomes necessary varies from 12 hours to two or three days.

If you find you cannot use the patches, there is still hope. Most over the counter cures are a mixture of a soporific to reduce the body's reaction to the abnormal environment, and an 'upper' to counter the soporific. No two people react the same way to these mixtures. A well-respected navigator told me what I believe to be a good solution. The individual should go to a chemist and explain that they are trying to discover which mixture is right for them, and ask the chemist to mix varied balances between the upper and the downer. By trial and error over a couple of months you will be able to find out which mixture is the right one for you.

For those who still suffer from seasickness, the only cure is to lie under a tree. While I admire people who suffer seasickness and still go to sea, having too many in one's crew is a mistake, particularly in a racing boat where it's necessary to have the use of all people at all times so that the boat can be at its full strength.

Seasickness, if it is allowed to continue, can be life-threatening in that it causes rapid dehydration and severe mental depression leading to a complete lack of will, even the will to improve one's condition. It can lead to shock, in which case follow the instructions on page 196. The body's resources are rapidly depleted, and the core temperature can lower very quickly because there is no food fuelling the system. Even the physical effort of vomiting or dry retching can rapidly weaken the victim. They will be unable to keep down food or drink. It's really up to the skipper of every boat to make sure that if someone is unable to function because of seasickness, they are put into their berth and treated as a hospitalised patient. Somebody must be deputed to check them every hour or so to see how they are progressing. If somebody consistently suffers seasickness to this level, they should not be included in the crew of a racing yacht.

SUNSTROKE

This can be life-threatening. If, through not wearing a shady hat, or by neglecting to put on sunscreens and then staying too many hours in the sun, a crew member becomes ill with sunstroke, they must be treated as a medical emergency immediately. In the lower latitudes, sunstroke occurs on perfect sailing days when the sun is hot and shining, there's a light breeze, the sea is sparkling and the victim has no idea as he works hard at his job of sailing that he is exhausting his supplies of fluid and is becoming quite ill.

The symptoms are a dryness of mouth and a dry, flushed, hot-looking face and skin, then loss of concentration and dizziness, and in severe cases, loss of consciousness. If this occurs, the body's system of temperature control has failed and goes into a sort of overdrive. If something isn't done to prevent it, the body temperature will continue to rise and there can be the sort of appalling result that occurs to runners who get heat exhaustion, where whole muscles and areas of tissue literally melt.

At the first sign that anyone is suffering from sunstroke they must be put into the shade and every effort made to cool them. Put their feet in buckets of cold sea water, and their hands, too, if possible. Throw water over their body and fan them with towels. Remove excess clothing so the body can get rid of excess heat as fast as possible. If the system is not brought back to normal temperature, death is possible. So too is brain damage, as well as muscular damage, as mentioned.

When the victim recovers consciousness, cool drinks should immediately be given—either just water or water with a flavouring of juice. It will be as much as two to three days before the body's system will recover sufficiently for normal activity to take place.

The best thing to do about sunstroke is to avoid it. A very good way of doing that is to encourage the practice of wearing towelling hats which are dipped into the water every now and then. As well as feeling good, the air passing over the damp hat has a cooling effect, through evaporation. It is invigorating and helps keep the core temperature at an appropriate level.

S U N B U R N

This doesn't always accompany sunstroke, but it can, in which case it complicates an already dangerous situation. Sunburn, like sunstroke, is something that should be avoided rather than treated. With blockout creams available, and zincs in fashion colours, there is no excuse for getting seriously sunburnt in normal circumstances. If it does happen, treat it like any other burn. The sufferer should take plenty of liquid, warm and slightly salty. Sunburn sufferers should also be given vitamin C, either as tablets or liquid.

T O O T H A C H E

I have a great fear of toothache at sea. I am worried at the thought of some clodhopper pulling one of my teeth using a pair of boltcutters! I believe the best treatment is to do nothing except relieve the pain, with the exception of a tooth that has been dislodged by a swinging boom or a clumsy crew member. In that case, most often it can be pushed back into its proper position and the gum will grow back around it to hold it firm. Any other condition is likely to hold for long enough for outside help to be reached. If not, this is a case where I believe my grandmother's remedy is best. Oil of cloves is extremely effective in relieving the pain of toothache. Every medical cabinet should have some.

While we are talking about grandmothers' remedies, another very good one, for sore or ulcerated throats, is to mix together one teaspoon each of butter, sugar, and vinegar. It is difficult to get them to mix thoroughly, but just put the mixture a little at a time into the mouth and let the butter melt. It runs down the throat and eases it wonderfully. The sugar makes it cling to the throat and carries the vinegar, which cuts some of the stickiness. The butter then soothes.

The medical advice and procedures outlined in this book should not be taken without first consulting a doctor or a trained paramedic.

READY FOR SEA

PASSAGE PLANNING

No matter how short or long your cruise the first decision you will have to make will be to decide which places you will treat as staging posts or refit bases. Not just stops but full scale ports where you can make use of any facilities you might need. It is an unrealistic dream to cruise the Pacific islands for months on end without ever touching what we call civilisation. Eventually the boat—a sophisticated piece of modern design and technology—will need the sort of back up that technology demands. Even the best equipped boat runs out of parts, or some of the electronics don't work properly, or there may be some structural fear with the mast or rigging. So even if you plan to be cruising for a year you need to know that there'll be, say every three months, a well-equipped port where you'll be able to refit.

RESEARCH

For any short cruise it's really a matter of working out how much time you have and therefore how far you can go. You may have a boat which you know averages five knots, taking in being becalmed or running hard in heavy winds or just sailing along beautifully. The longer the voyage is going to be, the more accurately that judgement will apply. But over a short voyage you may be becalmed for 24 hours and therefore have a big disparity between your estimated time of arrival and your actual arrival time, so allow for the possibility by leaving a healthy balance of time up your sleeve. Finding refit bases is relatively easy if you're cruising the well-sailed grounds. There'll be enough information passed between cruising skippers for you to be able to find the most reliable, the cheapest, or the quickest marine specialist. But in the more remote areas of the world you'll have to be self-sufficient and it will become important that you know you can easily get to a modern port. If you've planned this in advance you won't have a last minute scramble in case of an urgent need. It doesn't take long on land to do a bit of research, and then to keep the results with the ship's papers in case you need it. Bear in mind when you're planning and selecting your staging posts that in a foreign country you will have to enter through one of its prescribed ports—a port of entry. Luckily most well-equipped ports are ports of entry, partly because of the facilities and partly because they are on main shipping routes. But you'll also need to be able to arrange for money, mail and other information to come to you in these ports. To do so means you're able to cruise with complete freedom and yet not be so out of touch that some disaster can happen without your knowing about it.

The research you do before you leave really will decide whether you'll have a comfortable and successful cruise or not. Only the very rare cruising boat isn't going to some destination and doesn't have a time limit. Even people cruising around the world for three or five years have to have some sort of itinerary, however loose. So working back from the amount of time you have available and how much time you want to spend in various ports, you'll know how much sailing time you have and that will decide how much fuel, water and food you'll have to carry, and what number and kind of crew you'll want.

CRITICAL PATH

It's a good idea to set out a critical path and if you have already decided who some of the crew are going to be, to start allocating responsibilities. If another member of the crew is doing the navigation, they should be told precisely what their responsibilities are in terms of arranging for charts, celestial navigation equipment, electronic navigational aids, required reference books and so on. Starting on page 266 there is a series of checklists that should be completed before a vessel starts a cruise. A very important item for instance is packing for the stern gland. It's a constant source of leaks in boats and therefore there should be ample material on board so that the box can be repacked several times.

If there will be someone on board who has medical skill, it's a very simple matter to ask them to look after all that's required. If not, look at the checklist on page 169 and depute somebody to take that responsibility. A cruising vessel is a highly sophisticated series of interrelated functions and the relaxed comfortable cruiser is the one that has been well organised beforehand. If nothing else in your cruise is precisely defined be sure of the departure date. Given a particular date on which to leave all the organisation can be geared towards that day. If you're a member of a yacht club that membership will now become valuable to you. For a start, the club, particularly if it's a cruising club or a member of a cruising association, will have a lot of information about the places you're likely to go which has been gathered by other club members and pooled. This is usually available on request. But you'll also find that club membership will give you reciprocal rights in large areas of the world and that can be of great use, particularly when it comes to non-English speaking countries.

SHIP'S PAPERS

Keep the ship's papers in a file, or on a larger boat on computer, making sure they include all the information that is likely to be wanted. This means dimensions of standing rigging, dimensions and lengths of halyards, make and model of engine, make and model of all electronic or mechanical equipment, the weight and design and cable for the anchors, details of the ship's electrical system, and the kind of fuses—all the sort of information that you may need if you're in a foreign port and trying to get replacements or repairs done. It means going through every department of the vessel so that everything is recorded. It should be more a matter of filing than of research because all that information should already be on board, either in manufacturer's handbooks, in your own checklists, or from your own knowledge. Anything you don't know you have to make it your business to find out and to fill in.

If there hasn't been a recent survey you should certainly have one done before you leave on an extended cruise because that will tell you of any defects that should be corrected before the cruise starts. A properly conducted survey will collate a great deal of the information that you require.

You also need to list all the safety equipment that you carry, covering the life raft, harnesses, life jackets, bilge pumps, flares, fire extinguishers, and so on.

PLANS OF THE VESSEL

Carry numerous copies of the plans of the vessel, not accurate in the sense of following the design, but in the sense that the ship's systems can be marked on them. All the through hull fittings can be marked on one, all the safety equipment on another, all the food on another, the electrical system on another and so on. If everybody knows that there is one place on the boat where all the information is kept then panic stricken searches in case of emergency aren't necessary. It's important to record the types of lubricant used on the various mechanical fittings, particularly for instance if there are bearings, as is often the case, which shouldn't be lubricated with anything but water. It would be disastrous if a nylon bearing started to squeak and oil was put on it instead of water, causing the bearing to seize.

The medical kit, which should be on the safety equipment plan, should have a list of its contents in a waterproof cover on top of the container. Very often medical kits are in more than one container and it saves a lot of time if you can read on top what's in the container you're searching. As well, if something is used up it can be crossed off the list, so providing an easy form of stock control to keep the kit up to the mark.

Many vessels nowadays, particularly larger power vessels, have computers which monitor oil levels, water levels, fuel tank levels, engine revolutions, engine hours and so on. If you're able to put the information onto disks that can be used with this system then make sure that you have a back up disk in case of loss of information through power failure.

All information about the engine and its associated systems such as generators, gear boxes, alternators, compressors, etc. should be marked on a plan of the vessel, but should also be contained in the manufacturer's own manual. The electrical system should be detailed so that the capacity of the batteries is known. It's a good idea to work out a maximum drainage rate for any electrical equipment that you have on board so that power consumption can be controlled (see Current Drain of Appliances, page 51). Certainly the size and position of all fuses should be known in case of any failure in the systems.

Radio and navigation gear are closely linked and should therefore be listed together and any manuals that came with the log, echo sounder, fluxgate compass, Satnav or other equipment of that kind should be kept in this repository of information. The radio call sign details should be kept but should also be displayed somewhere close to the radio itself.

An important item to have completely catalogued is insurance and it would be wise before leaving to contact your insurance company to find out where they have foreign offices, if they do, because that may have some bearing on which staging posts you choose.

It's normal on most boats to have complete details of the sail inventory. Important information here is when the sail was new, the date of its manufacture and the manufacturer, because memory can play strange tricks and if you need to replace a sail which has worn out but with which you are otherwise satisfied it's very simple to get back to the original maker.

The standing and running rigging is quite a big job on its own, but it's well worth detailing down to the last piece of line on board, because a boat by its very nature settles down over time, and equipment that works efficiently is kept and that which is not efficient is discarded. To be able to replace like with like means that efficiency will continue, whereas if you take a stab at the material and diameter you want to replace and it turns out to be marginally different it may well change the level of efficiency quite dramatically.

Once you have all the required information about your vessel filed, copy everything and leave that copy on shore with somebody you can trust so that if anything happens to your information you can at least replace it. Once that task has been completed and the route and refit points decided the actual mechanics of the voyage planning can begin.

Navigational Pre-departure Work

When planning the voyage it's advisable to check with *Ocean Passages of the World* and the *Sailing Directions* for the countries that you're planning to visit so that you do not go there at a time which may put you at risk from the weather. Obviously, it's foolhardy to plan to visit a country in the hurricane belt during the season of greatest frequency of those storms. It would be just as silly to sail against prevailing winds.

By now you will have got the voyage planned enough to be able to do some broad chartwork. You almost certainly won't be able to plot every part of the proposed voyage because that takes away some of the freedom on which the whole cruise is based. Half the fun is simply deciding to go to a certain place and then just going there.

THE RULES OF
VISITING

Perhaps the first thing should be to get in touch with the marine and health authorities of the countries you're going to visit and have them send to you, as they will, brochures which outline their requirements for your smooth entry to their country. You can't just turn up and hope that everything will be all right. Not every country requires that your ship be registered, that you should have proof of ownership, or that you should have a certificate of competence, but some do and so it's prudent to have amongst the ship's papers all those documents. The advantage in being a registered ship, usually registered in the country of your nationality, is that in case you need help your country's representatives abroad can give it to you because you are legally a part of that country, with all the protection that entails.

When you receive from the relevant authorities their information about conditions of entry, make sure that the information is kept with the ship's papers and that you can find it easily when approaching that country. The first impression you want to make on customs and health services is that of a competent well-prepared skipper. News travels fast. If the authorities know they're not going to have to deal with a haphazard, careless person who's going to cause them trouble and give them headaches, they will make things very much easier for you. They're ordinary human beings with a job to do and they react well if they know that you've done your best to make their job easy.

C U S T O M S
A N D   I M M I G R A T I O N

It's often said that sailing is one of the last great freedoms—in some ways it is. Drive a motor boat and you have to get a registered number, which doesn't always apply to yachts. Motor boaters have to pass an admittedly undemanding test and show they have the rudiments of boat handling ability. There are some limits on speed but these regulations vary from country to country and in many cases from State to State. In most places four or five knots is considered reasonable in a crowded mooring. However, speed ultimately comes down to good boat handling and consideration towards other people. I've touched often in this book on the fact that seamanship is not simply the ability to handle a boat but the ability to understand the circumstances and react properly to them. If seamanship is to understand storm and react properly to that, it's equally to understand manoeuvring in tight spots and to have thought for other people. As one gets further from land there are fewer and fewer regulations, but it's quite wrong to think there are none. For instance, while the whole weight of society will be used in a genuine emergency at sea, if someone calls out the resources of a society in a flippant or even a negligent manner, then they can find themselves having to pay the full cost. The skipper has responsibilities. The closer you are to land the more restrictions you have to observe. Nobody will stop you setting sail from port if you wish to do so, but if you turn up in a foreign country with no evidence of where you came from the least the customs in the new country will think is that you may be a smuggler, or worse, a drug runner. They may worry that you are bringing in some disease which they don't want imported to their country. They may wonder whether you stole the vessel and they may confiscate it while they investigate. If you cause them trouble by not having the proper immigration papers, visas and so on you may find that you are conducting your negotiations from a cell. If there had been a calamity during the voyage and one crew member was lost overboard and another is seriously ill, you may find yourself being chased by the relatives of one claiming damages, and of the other wanting you to pay hospital bills and even air fares for repatriation. Some of your obligations are becoming clear. Your first is to the vessel, because in that vessel you will live and travel and so will your crew. It is merely good management to let the relevant boating authorities know when you are planning to arrive in their country and when you are planning to leave it. You will need to have the proper ship's papers which show that you own it, and that it meets the requirements in terms of safety and seaworthiness, that it is insured, and that you and your crew are covered

TABLE OF CRUISING LICENCE RECIPROCAL ARRANGEMENTS

Argentina
Australia
Bahama Islands
Bermuda
Canada
Germany
Greece
Honduras
Great Britain (including Turks and Caicos Islands, St Vincent (including the territorial waters of the Northern Grenadine Islands), the Cayman Islands, the British Virgin Islands and the St Christopher-Nevis-Anguilla Islands)
Ireland
Jamaica
Liberia
Netherlands
New Zealand
Norway
Sweden
United States of America

against accident or death. As in any other human undertaking the basic responsibility is to be both prudent and efficient. A court of marine law investigating the loss of the vessel, or even worse some of its crew, will not be impressed if those basic conditions have not been met. The law of the sea is highly complicated and varies quite considerably around the world.

This section covers the regulations as they will affect boating travellers in those countries where leisure boating is most common. Not the least of the obligations you have is the medical one. You must check not only people who are crewing with you, but also the casual people you pick up in some remote and exotic port. You must know if they are suffering from some chronic or severe illness or if they are taking medication and you must satisfy yourself that they have enough supplies on board. In the same way that water and food should be sufficient to last longer than the voyage so should medication. While it's not likely a skipper could be held responsible for the illness of somebody who failed to bring their own medication—the negligence would basically belong to that person—it's not impossible an action could be brought and it's best avoided, as are any legal difficulties.

Most countries will allow yachts to enter with the intention of cruising and will allow temporary residence to the skipper and other people on board, usually up to a year. America has a further requirement covering yachts turning up for a short term visit in order to compete in races. If the boat is not re-exported in 90 days then it must be covered by a bond. If neither of these actions takes place within 90 days the boat is subject to forfeiture. Forfeiture is a constant of customs regulations throughout the world if any breach of regulations occurs.

B O N D S

Those owners that present their yachts properly to customs, and who wish to stay for less than a year may be subject to a bond. It's best to assume that you will be subject to a bond and have the necessary financial backing available. In Australia you have to pay as a bond the same amount of customs duty and sales tax that you would if you were to bring the vessel in permanently. **Australian** customs will accept only a bank security or a carnet valid for Australia. This amount is refundable on leaving Australia, but the customs department requires early notice so that it can pay you when you leave. The **United Kingdom** does not usually require a bond although it remains open to a customs officer to impose one if he or she wishes. In any case the vessel has to be exported when it has been in the United Kingdom for a total of six months. In the **United States of America** the bond is an amount equal to twice the estimated duty. This again is refunded if the boat is exported within the time specified and with the knowledge of customs.

Many countries provide cruising licences for vessels which wish to holiday in their waters and this reciprocal arrangement exists between countries listed on the left.

A cruising licence allows vessels to use harbours without paying harbour taxes and dues at every port they visit, but only if the first port is a port of entry. This is a fundamental point. Cruising yachts are not entitled to turn up at whichever port they like and then expect to be cleared through customs.

PORTS OF ENTRY

UNITED STATES

ALABAMA
Mobile

ALASKA
Ketchican
Wrangell
Sitka
Juneau
Skagway
Valdez
Anchorage

CALIFORNIA
San Diego
Los Angeles
Port Hueneme
San Luis Obispo
San Francisco

CONNECTICUT
Bridgeport

FLORIDA
Jacksonville
Port Canavaral
West Palm Beach
Miami
Key West
Ft. Myers
St. Petersburg
Tampa

GEORGIA
Savannah
Brunswick

HAWAII
Hilo
Maui
Honolulu
Kauai

ILLINOIS
Chicago

LOUISIANA
New Orleans

MAINE
Portland

MASSACHUSETTS
Boston

MICHIGAN
Muskegon
Sault Ste. Marie
Port Huron
Detroit

MINNESOTA
Lake of the Woods
   (Call Pembina, N.D.)
International Falls
Grand Portage
Crane Lake

Ely
Duluth

MISSISSIPI
Pascagoula
Gulfport

MONTANA
Great Falls

NEW JERSEY
Newark
Perth Amboy
*(If you arrive in New
Jersey south of the
Manasquan Inlet
contact Customs'
Philadelphia, Pa.
office.)*

NEW YORK
New York City
Albany
Buffalo
Ogdensburg

NORTH CAROLINA
Wilmington
Morehead City

NORTH DAKOTA
Pembina

OHIO
Cleveland

OREGON
Coos Bay
Newport
Astoria
Longview
Portland

PENNSYLVANIA
Philadelphia

MARYLAND
Baltimore

SOUTH CAROLINA
Charleston

TEXAS
Port Arthur
Galveston
Houston
Freeport
Port Lavaca
Corpus Christi
Brownsville

VERMONT
St. Albans

VIRGINIA
Alexandria
Norfolk
Newport News

WASHINGTON
Vancouver
Aberdeen
Neah Bay
Port Angeles
Port Townsend
Seattle
Tacoma
Olympia
Everett
Bellingham
Friday/Roche Harbors
Anacortes
Blaine
Point Roberts

WISCONSIN
Green Bay
Milwaukee
Racine

PUERTO RICO
San Juan
Mayaguez
Fajardo
Ponce

U.S. VIRGIN ISLANDS
St. Croix
St. John
St. Thomas
Yatch Haven Marina

UNITED KINGDOM

Aberdeen
Aberystwyth
   (see Fishguard)
Ardglass
Ardrossan
Avonmouth
Ayr
Barnstaple
Barrow
Barry
   (see Cardiff)
Beaulieu

(see Lymington)
Belfast
Berwick
Blyth
Boston
Bradwell
Bridgwater
Brightlingsea
Brighton
Bristol
   (see Avonmouth)
Brixham

Buckie
Burnham-on-Crouch
Burnham-on-Sea
and
Highbridge
   (see Bridgwater)
Campbeltown
Cardiff
Chatham
Christchurch
   (see Lymington)
Clevedon

(see Avonmouth)
Colchester
Coleraine
Combwich
   *(see Bridgwater or
   Watchet)*
Corpach
   (see Fort William)
Cowes I.O.W.
Dartmouth
Douglas I.O.M.
Dover (West)

Dundee
Edinburgh
Elgin
Ellesmere Port
Exmouth
Falmouth
Faversham
Felixstowe
Fishguard
Fleetwood
Folkestone
Fort William

PORTS OF ENTRY (CONTINUED)

UNITED KINGDOM (CONTINUED)

Fowey	Kirkudbright	Maldon	Royal Docks	*(London Port)*
Fraserburgh	*(see Stranraer)*	Milford Haven	*(London Port)*	Tilbury Docks
Glasgow	Kirkwall	Minehead	*Includes*	*(London Port)*
Glasson Dock	Lancaster	*(see Watchet)*	*St. Katherines Yacht*	Torquay
(see Heysham)	*(see Heysham)*	Montrose	*Haven*	Trent
Goole	Larne	Mostyn	Rye	*(see Scunthorpe)*
Gravesend	Lerwick	Newhaven	Salcombe	Walton-on-the-Naze
(London Port)	Littlehampton	North Shields	Scarborough	Warrenpoint
Great Yarmouth	*(see Shoreham)*	Oban	Scunthorpe	Watchet
Greenock	Liverpool	Padstow	Sharpness	Wells
Grimsby	*(Hoylake/Southport)*	Par	Sheerness	West Mersea
Hamble	Londonderry	*(see Fowey)*	Shoreham	*(see Colchester)*
Hartlepool	London Port	Penzance	Silloth	Weston-Super Mare and
Harwich	*See also:*	Peterhead	*(see Workington)*	Uphill
Heysham	*Gravesend*	Plymouth	Southampton	*(see Avonmouth)*
Holyhead	*Royals*	Poole	Southend-on-Sea	Weymouth
Hoylake	*Southend-on-Sea*	Porlock	*(London Port)*	Whitby
(see Liverpool)	*Tilbury*	*(see Watchet)*	Southport	Whitehaven
Hull	Lossiemouth	Portavogie	*(see Liverpool)*	*(see Workington)*
Immingham	*(see Elgin)*	Port Edgar	St Marys (I.O.S.)	Whitstable
Invergordon	Lowestoft	Portpatrick	Stornoway	Wick
Inverness	*(see Great Yarmouth)*	*(see Stranraer)*	Stranraer	Wisbech
Ipswich	Lydney	Portsmouth	Sunderland	Woodbridge
Itchenor	*(see Sharpness)*	Preston	Swansea	Workington
Kilkeel	Lymington	*(see Fleetwood)*	Teignmouth	Yarmouth I.O.W.
King's Lynn	Macduff	Ramsgate	Thames Haven	*(see Cowes)*

AUSTRALIA

NEW SOUTH WALES			WESTERN AUSTRALIA	SOUTH AUSTRALIA
Botany Bay	Melbourne	Maryborough	Albany	Cape Thevenard
Coffs Harbour	Portland	Rockhampton	Broome	Port Adelaide
Lord Howe Island	Westernport	*(including Port Alma)*	Bunbury	Port Lincoln
Newcastle		Thursday Island	Carnarvon	Port Pirie
Port Kembla	QUEENSLAND	Townsville	Dampier	Port Wallaroo
Sydney	Bowen		Esperance	Whyalla
Twofold Bay	Brisbane	TASMANIA	Exmouth	
(including Eden)	Bundaberg	Burnie	Fremantle	NORTHERN TERRITORY
	Cairns	Devonport	Geraldton	Darwin
VICTORIA	Gladstone	Hobart	Port Hedland	Melville Bay
Geelong	Mackay	Launceston	Port Walcott	*(Gove)*

NEW ZEALAND

Auckland	Hamilton	New Plymouth	Tauranga	Wellington
Bluff	Invercargill	Opua	Timaru	Whangarei
Christchurch	Lyttelton	Palmerston North	Waitangi (Chatham	
Dunedin	Napier	Picton	Islands)	
Gisborne	Nelson	Rotorua	Wanganui	

Each country designates its ports of entry and you must go to one of those first. It is only at these ports that the regional customs chief or customs staff can issue the cruising licence. Having a cruising licence doesn't mean you don't have to pay a bond, it just means your costs of travelling are reduced. The ports listed above as ports of entry double as ports of departure.

The master of any yacht leaving through one of these ports must ensure that customs knows the details of the departure. Apart from anything else clearance from one port helps establish your credibility when you arrive seeking clearance at a new port. Detailed regulations by area follow.

UNITED STATES
OF AMERICA

American regulations don't specify the use of code flag Q, the yellow flag which indicates that you are seeking pratique or customs or health clearance. Nevertheless, it is an international sign, and it should be flown when entering any port of entry where you are seeking customs clearance. The minimum ship's papers you'll need when you arrive at a designated customs port in America are the original bill of lading if the boat has been shipped or carried and the bill of sale and foreign registration if there is one. If you are master of what is termed a foreign flag vessel you must report to customs within 24 hours of your arrival and make your formal entry within 48 hours. It's much more sensible, and a courtesy, to radio ahead. If customs wish to direct you to a special berth they can do so. They have more time to deal with your application and since you have cooperated with them it is unlikely they won't cooperate with you. If you have a cruising licence you will need a permit before you can go to any subsequent US port, and you will have to clear customs. You will have to pay for navigation fees, for the formal entry, for the permit to proceed, and for the clearance of your vessel. When you arrive only one person will be allowed to go ashore, usually the skipper. He should make sure that the vessel is tied up or securely anchored. He may then proceed ashore but immediately after reporting must return to his boat and remain on board. Nobody may leave until customs give permission. To do so may result in a severe penalty, even forfeiture of the boat.

Customs and Immigration Clearance

At a formal entry you'll need the following documents which customs will give you. You will have to fill in the original register, the original customs form 1300, the master's oath on the entry of the vessel, the general declaration of customs on form 1301, a declaration of the ship's stores (customs form 1303) and the declaration of the crew's belongings (customs form 1304). You'll need the clearance from the last foreign port, the original crew list and original passenger and cargo declaration. It is only after all these have been completed and, if required, the bond paid and medical clearance granted that you'll be free to travel around. You will reduce charges from customs if you turn up at a designated port during ordinary working hours. If you turn up after hours or on a Sunday or a holiday, you'll have to pay a fee not exceeding US$25. Boat harbour dues will vary according to where you arrive. You may in some circumstances have to pay a processing fee of another US$25 but you should ask the customs people about that when you get there.

You must have a passport for yourself and every member of the crew or any passengers. It will have to be valid and have the appropriate visas, which should have been obtained before you left your home port.

There is one major restriction in America and the Coastguard will see that it is observed. While you may trade between your home port and America you may not engage in trade along the coast of America while you are cruising. You can't take anybody on board as a passenger, nor take fishing parties for hire. If customs decide your boat is dutiable and a bond is required, it will be at 1.6% for pleasure boats valued at more than US$15,000 and 1.9% for those valued over US$15,000 which means most boats. The dutiable value with a new boat is normally equal to the cost of that boat and if you have an old boat then an allowance will be made for depreciation and the dutiable value will be proportionately lower.

In some circumstances in America you may not have to pay duty at all. That would be if customs assessed you as being a non-resident importing a pleasure boat for personal use and the transportation of family or guests, that you own the boat, or that you ordered it before your departure. If you are given a duty free exemption and then sell the boat or offer it for sale or for charter within a year of importation, duty will be payable.

The people on board the vessel will be subject to the same customs regulations as any other visitor to the US and will be allowed duty free entry of only those tobacco, alcohol and other products which are allowed from time to time. Be careful of spare parts. Any you carry may well be subject to duty as well. If you had sufficient engine parts to practically rebuild the engine at sea you may find you'd be charged duty at the rate of a new engine. You also have to meet the requirements of the Coastguard in terms of sailing and documentation. It's a good idea before leaving for the US to write and get those documents because the pamphlets given out by the consulate, while useful as a guide, may not be complete.

If you are involved in an emergency which is threatening to either life or property on the US coast you may go to a non-designated port, but the restrictions are more severe. You must report as soon as possible to either a customs, immigration, agricultural or public health officer. Nobody may leave the vessel except in extreme emergency, nor may any merchandise or baggage be removed from the boat.

One last thing to remember is that all countries are very wary of the importation of fruits and plants, meats and animal products, and birds and pets because they do not want to import diseases which may affect people, crops or livestock.

UNITED KINGDOM

The UK, being an island close to heavily populated areas, has had centuries of need to control its waterways. Its government publishes a comprehensive pamphlet called Notice 8A which it will send to anybody wishing to sail the coasts of the British Isles. The pamphlet starts with definitions of a vessel. The definitions ensure that anybody cruising a yacht or motor cruiser in UK waters will be covered by the regulations. An important definition is of the 'person responsible'. It means that the person on board a pleasure craft under whose command, or subject to whose personal direction, it has arrived can include a master other than the owner. Because person responsible is defined so clearly the responsibilities are easier to follow. Next comes a list of warnings including the warning that pleasure craft are liable to be searched by customs officers at any time. This is known in the UK as being rumbled and it can happen without warning even after you have cleared customs. It can happen weeks after you first entered the UK and anywhere customs like.

CUSTOMS AND IMMIGRATION CLEARANCE

Customs in the UK have powers of entry and search which far exceed those of the police and they are not afraid to use their full power. The penalties for smuggling are severe and can include not just forfeiture of the craft but fines and imprisonment and once again customs officers are strict in their enforcement. It would be most unwise to land any goods or transfer them to another vessel or leave your vessel until clearance has been given.

Not wearing flag Q in the UK is an offence, as is failure to notify intending departure. Either can lead to prosecution. The fine for failure to fly Q can be as high as $1,000. If you arrive at night the flag should still fly and should be illuminated.

The documentation required in the UK is rather less than in other countries. Form C1329 is in three parts covering: first, the report of the person responsible on arrival from a foreign port; second, the declaration seeking temporary importation, made either by the importer or the person responsible; and third, the declaration of goods, which has to be filled out by all persons on board. Nobody may leave the vessel, nor any goods, until the authorisation of the customs officer is received. If you don't get form C1329 before you leave for the UK the customs officer will normally be able to provide you with one. He'll give you back the second and third parts, which you keep because you will need them when you clear your last port.

If you are not entitled to live in the UK you will require permission from the immigration officer—this will apply to crew and passengers alike. In most cases the customs officer can double as immigration officer and fulfil both functions.

It is mandatory to declare any animals or birds which will be kept on the pleasure craft and customs will advise of the regulations governing such pets. The UK is particularly sensitive about animals and birds, including pets which have to be restrained. They have to be securely confined within a totally enclosed part of the vessel on the lower deck from which they cannot escape. They are not permitted to land under any circumstances, nor to come in contact with any animal. This is because of a major fear of rabies.

All people on the yacht must declare any goods they have which are dutiable such as tobacco or alcohol. It is wise, if there are any doubts about some of the effects, to declare them anyway, so that your relationship with customs is clear and honest. There is a substantial number of prohibited or restricted goods such as drugs, firearms, indecent or obscene items, knives, and so on. As far as stores are concerned customs duty and VAT (value added tax) are payable, but the officers most usually allow stores to remain on board, under customs seal, without any duty being paid. If for any reason the customs seal is broken or removed before the vessel has left UK territorial waters there are severe penalties. Otherwise the officers may allow the goods to be taken to a bonded store on land and kept there, at some expense, until they are reshipped as stores.

If your vessel is less than 12 metres (40 feet) it is liable to customs duty in the UK. If it is less than 15 tonnes gross, and designed for recreational pleasure, it is also liable to VAT. Therefore all pleasure craft, motor or sail, are liable to both duty and VAT but they may be temporarily imported free of customs charges if the visitor meets the following conditions.

- He usually lives outside the United Kingdom for at least 185 days in every 12 months

- If the vessel is exported when the importer next leaves the country, or on the date when, in any one 12 month period, the vessel has been in the UK for six months

- That the vessel is used only by the importer or some other similarly entitled person

- The vessel can be neither lent nor hired out nor otherwise disposed of in the UK.

However, it is difficult for a yacht to remain in the UK for more than six months. These conditions are not exhaustive but are a good guide. Customs can, if they want, impose additional conditions. It would be wise to check on spare parts and accessories to make sure they are not dutiable. It's a simple enough matter to write a letter before you leave.

When you are leaving the UK the person responsible must obtain clearance by giving part two of form C1329 to the customs officer after having completed the notice of intention to depart on the back. It can be posted or delivered personally but it is better to do it personally. Duty free stores are available to pleasure yachts leaving the UK, although strictly speaking they are only allowed to vessels over 40 tonnes net register. If you have been in UK waters for some time and you have obeyed all other regulations the usual thing is for customs to allow you to ship out a reasonable quantity of food and other stores. If bonded stores are still on board or have been put back on board from a bonded store they will be put under customs seal. The same regulations apply as before—the stores must not be used until the vessel is out of the UK territorial waters.

Health and Medical Clearance

The UK has also simplified its regulations covering public health and ships. It doesn't, as it once did, require every vessel to get a health clearance, but it does require code flag Q to be flown. Some ships will be boarded and checked at random. A vessel needn't seek health clearance if there has been no item to report. Clearance must be sought:

- If there has been a death other than by accident

- If there has been an illness with a temperature of 38°C (100°F) or greater accompanied by a rash, swelling or jaundice

- If there has been an illness that lasted for more than 48 hours or the patient had diarrhoea so severely as to interfere with work or normal activities

- If anybody on board suffered from an infectious disease or symptoms that seemed like an infectious disease

- If there was mortality among any animals, captive birds, rodents or poultry.

If none of these things occurred the master need not obtain a health clearance although customs may direct him to do so. In these circumstances the master can proceed under customs direction and may not need to do any more about health clearance. If, however, there is something to report the master has obligations. If he has radio he should send a message to the port health authorities or phone the harbour master who may be able to direct him as to what to do. This message should be sent not more than 12 hours and preferably not fewer than four hours before arrival. If there is no radio the person responsible must report if possible before arrival but otherwise immediately on arrival.

There are special question and answer codes for health clearance and these are listed below.

INTERNATIONAL CODE OF SIGNALS

HEALTH CLEARANCE MESSAGES

ZS	My vessel is 'healthy' and I request free practique	Q
*	I require health clearance	QQ
ZU	My Maritime Declaration of Health has a positive answer to question(s) (indicated by appropriate number(s))	
ZW	I require Port Medical Officer	
	ZW1 Port Medical Officer will be available at (time indicated)	
ZY	You have health clearance	
ZZ	You should proceed to anchorage for health clearance (at place indicated)	
	ZZ1 Where in the anchorage for health clearance?	
	I have a doctor on board	AL
	Have you a doctor?	AM

* By night, a red light over a white light may be shown, where it can best be seen, by ships requiring health clearance. These lights should only be about 2 metres (6 feet) apart, should be exhibited within the precincts of a port, and should be visible all round the horizon as nearly as possible.

Health clearance may be given in three ways:

(a) Wholly in plain language.

(b) Partly in the above signal code; remainder in plain language.

(c) Wholly in the above signal code.

A vessel entering a port at night and seeking health clearance must show a red light over a white which should be no more than two metres apart and be seen all round. Until the vessel has been given free pratique nobody may leave it and only a pilot, customs officer, immigration officer or some authorised officer may come aboard without permission of the medical officer. Next the person responsible must complete a maritime declaration of health and arrange for this to be given to the authorised officer. If free pratique is needed the master or person responsible should have ready for the authorised officer a list of passengers and crew who will be leaving the ship, together with their addresses in the UK. This is in case any follow up is needed.

A U S T R A L I A

A radio report is required at least three hours before arrival by calling up on 2182MHz and giving customs and quarantine officers warning of arrival through the Overseas Telecommunications Corporation of Australia (OTC). They will want the name of the craft, estimated time of arrival and the number of people who are on board. OTC will pass on the port instructions to you. As in the UK you must display the yellow Q flag and then nobody may come on your craft other than a customs or quarantine officer and nobody may leave the craft until you have been given customs, quarantine and immigration clearances. If you fail to arrive at a listed port and fail to obtain clearance from these authorities you can be fined up to A$50,000.

Australia requires a significant amount of information and documentation when a vessel arrives. You will be asked to fill in on arrival a primary health report listing any illness of any person on board, quarantine will have to give clearance, a cargo manifest will have to list any cargo you may be carrying and a ship's store list will be required. The Australian customs information booklet also lists any articles which are restricted or dutiable, or on which sales tax must be paid. There must be a declaration of animals on board, a crew list listing the master and the crew, passenger cards for each person on board who is neither the master nor crew. Each person must also have a passport with any visas that are required, plus a clearance from the last overseas port.

Australia, by its remoteness, is free from many serious diseases, including yellow fever, rabies, foot and mouth disease, anthrax, and others which are scourges throughout the world. Consequently, Australian government departments are among the strictest in the world in policing the quarantine laws. If you have travelled through an area, or landed in a place, where yellow fever is prevalent each person over 12 months of age on board the vessel will need a valid vaccination certificate even if there was no outbreak when you were at the infected place. This is the only health certificate you'll need to enter Australia.

Don't bring any form of animal life to Australia, as the quarantine officials will allow the boat to mid-water only. The animal will not be let off the vessel, and you will have to enter into a bond saying that it won't come ashore or into contact with Australian animals. Any violation of that bond could lead to the animal being destroyed, the bond being forfeited, and yourself being prosecuted. Any foodstuffs and any articles from animal products may be prohibited and will certainly have to undergo quarantine examination on arrival, so be sure that you report everything to the collector of customs if you believe it may be prohibited or restricted. The same is true of plants, their seeds, and products from plants, vegetables or wood.

Tourist craft may come to Australia for up to a year without paying customs duty and sales tax, but customs have the right to ask you to pay a security equal to the amount of duty and sales tax that would normally apply if you imported the boat into Australia. This security may take the form of a carnet valid for Australia, or a special bank security. To get the money back when you leave you have to give advance notice to the collector of customs at your port of departure. The collector of customs at your arrival port will have to be satisfied that you are a tourist and not intending to use the boat commercially in which case you'll be given permission to visit places around Australia not controlled by customs. Customs will ask you for an itinerary and will give you pre-addressed postcards which you have to complete and mail regularly so that customs can see that you are following the itinerary. If you want to change it you will have to tell the collector of customs at the nearest port, but you may not necessarily be given an amended tourist licence. It is wise to be certain of your itinerary and to ask permission to visit as many places as possible so that later additions aren't needed.

If your vessel, as a foreign vessel, is not registered under the law of the foreign country then when you leave Australia you have to make a declaration about the nationality of the craft to satisfy Australian customs. Your vessel may only leave Australia from one of the listed ports of departure and you cannot leave without a clearance from the collector of customs at that port. When you wish to clear customs you have to provide the following documentation:

- Passports for each person on board
- Crew list of the master and crew
- Passenger manifest for those who are not the master or crew
- Passenger cards filled out by each person on board except the master
- A cargo manifest
- Ship's store list
- Certificate of registration or a declaration about the nationality of the craft
- An application for export.

All these forms are available from the collectors of customs.

Australia has a law which says that any person on board over 12 years old must pay departure tax to the collector of customs, currently A\$10. For some unknown reason the master is exempt. In the unlikely event you'd want to take more than \$5,000 dollars in Australian currency out of Australia you'll have to get prior approval from the Reserve Bank of Australia.

INSURANCE

Only the foolhardy boat owner doesn't have insurance, particularly some third party cover in case of personal injury or property damage through accident or collision. The standard insurance form varies little from one company to the other. You'll be asked questions about the design, registered number if there is one, construction, type of motor, the rig, what equipment and accessories are on board, the sails, mast, standing and running rigging and so on. With motor boats you'll be asked details of the engine, whether it is turbo charged, what fuel it uses, and very importantly, what sort of extinguishers are on board and when they were last serviced. The insurer naturally wants to be certain its risk is as little as it can possibly be. When it comes to accessories it pays to be very careful indeed to list all that you have on board. List the serial number and sums insured on as many of the items as can be insured—items such as personal effects, fishing gear, cameras, binoculars and transistor radios are not insurable. The equipment and accessories cover actually applies mainly to safety equipment required by statute and other equipment intended for safety use on the boat. The sort of items you can insure are liferafts, radios, radars, radio direction finders, autopilots, depth sounders, compasses, and even the dinghy, the propeller, and auxiliaries if you have them. But if you intend to go more than 200 km (124 miles) off the coast you'll have to fill out a blue water cruising or racing extension. This normally adds about 20 per cent to the premium. In the case of races it is straightforward. You say where you are going, how long the race is and when you expect to finish. If you are going on an extended cruise the insuring company or broker will want to know much more about the vessel in terms of its internal and external ballast, whether it has a centreboard or lifting keel, what sort of self-steering it has, the type of construction, and particularly the thicknesses of the topsides, deck, and cabin top. There will be a number of items covering radio call signs, the colour of various parts, the sort of radio sets and the frequencies on board, what radio watch schedule is proposed and more details about the engines. These items are needed in case a search has to be initiated. The insurer will want you to list the navigational and emergency equipment on board, the country of registration if the boat is registered and its registered number. It will also want to know when the vessel was last surveyed and have a copy of that survey attached to the questionnaire. Very importantly, for extended cruising you will have to advise your itinerary. If you don't have one you'll need to define by latitude and longitude the area in which you plan to sail and advise the departure date and the date of completing the voyage. The insurers will want some idea of the history of the vessel and the ability and experience of the person in charge. This has a bearing on the premium. Insurance is a competitive game, but it is best to deal with a company which specialises in marine insurance and so has experience. Evidence of insurance helps satisfy customs that the vessel is yours and that you won't be a burden in their country. A document proving insurance is very good prima facie evidence of ownership.

S A L V A G E

Salvage is a very complicated and highly technical branch of the law. If by some miracle you come across a boat floating in the middle of the ocean and you tow it to safety, don't believe it is then yours or that you will receive money to the value of the vessel, or some other such wonderful stroke of luck. I know of exactly such a case where a yacht had been abandoned during a major race and was found floating days later. It was taken under tow in hazardous circumstances and in heavy conditions to a port more than 160 km (100 miles) away. There followed many days of time-consuming argument and negotiation with representatives of the owner and the insurance company, and of complicated meetings with lawyers and officials. At settlement the people concerned were paid an hourly rate for their trouble and that was all.

S A F E T Y

A benefit of being a member of a yacht club is that racing a boat of any size is not permitted unless certain basic standards of safety are matched and boats are inspected regularly so that they are kept in tiptop condition from a safety point of view. It's easier for racers than for a cruising man who must remind himself and motivate himself to keep the boat up to scratch but the obligation is as strong with the cruising man as it is with the racer—perhaps even stronger because cruising men tend to be loners and are further from help in an emergency. The cruising sailor has more difficulties, for instance to service his liferaft every year when he may not be in a place where such service is possible.

It is important for him to have a schedule of maintenance to which he adheres. If a cruising man should be in an accident a long way from home he must at least keep an accurate record of the incident and the circumstances leading up to it—of the positions of the two vessels and of the damage caused, and details of any injuries caused. An insurance company will demand such evidence in exactly the same way as with a car accident. You have to be careful though if there has been an accident, particularly if you are in a foreign country, to advise the relevant civil officials as there may be regulations of which you are unaware. While this may involve you in some waste of time, it's much better to have wasted some time than to find oneself in a weak position through having failed to observe the laws of the land.

CHAPTER ELEVEN

NOW YOU'RE ON YOUR OWN

If you are already an experienced sailor, or if you have read this book assiduously, you are now ready to put to sea, where you will be as responsible for your own fate as any person can be. Certainly you will have the means to call for help if something serious happens and you need outside help. But you are hardly likely to call out the Coastguard for fresh ice, or because the head is blocked. You have to be self-sufficient in the real sense of the term. Long term cruising people are essentially good improvisers. Anything that can go wrong at sea will, and most things have happened to them, so they have a pretty good idea what to do. But nobody is expert at everything, so this chapter gives you some tricks of the trade.

First and foremost, whatever machinery, appliances, pumps, electronics, engines and so on that **can** have a manual **should** have a manual. If you bought the boat from somebody who is not completely organised and who didn't get the manuals, write to the manufacturers who are mostly obliging people who will be glad to provide the document, or a photocopy, if it is still available. Get hold of every single one, and if you simply cannot get some of them, get manuals for machines like them. Very often something near the mark, intelligently interpreted, helps you get the job done. This chapter covers general principles and includes exploded drawings of basic appliances. If you combine the brains of the people on board with the information here, you should be able to solve all but the most recalcitrant of problems.

The following description of engines is split into two sections—diesel engines and petrol (gasoline) engines. Refer to the applicable section.

DIESEL ENGINES

The principle of the diesel engine is that fuel is compressed to such an extent that it becomes superheated and explodes. It is tremendously efficient as unexploded fuel can be returned to the supply, and it relies on electricity only for starting. When we discuss petrol (gasoline) engines we will see what an advantage this is in a sea-going boat. The disadvantages with diesel used to be that they were very heavy, thus having a poor power to weight ratio, and very expensive. Over years of development, these disadvantages have been overcome, so that almost invariably new installations, or replacement engines, are diesel. This is less true with motor cruisers, but even there the petrol (gasoline) engine is being phased out.

Perhaps the very best and safest system for the cruiser that wishes to make offshore passages (usually coastal) is the twin diesel. The great merit, of course, is that if one engine should fail the other can bring the vessel safely to port. Diesel engines have another great plus—they are utterly reliable and simply love to work. The more you run a diesel, the better it is. Generally speaking, the troubleshooting you do on a diesel will be confined to seeing whether air is getting into the fuel supply, whether there is any fuel supply, and whether the electrics of the starting system are playing up.

Tools You Will Need

This will depend on the job you have to undertake, so check with the master list on page 271. At the least you will need:

- Full set of spanners (wrenches) for the engine
- Adjustable (shifting) spanners (wrenches)
- Vice grips
- Set of screwdrivers
- Electrical tools (screwdrivers, pliers, strippers)
- Allen keys
- WD-40 or similar product

Spares You Will Need

- Fuel pump
- Gaskets
- Gasket sealant
- Impellers for pumps
- Injector(s)
- Fuel filters
- Oil filters
- Solenoid
- Plug for thermostat socket
- Can of ether
- Grease for water pump
- Hose clips (clamps) (various)
- Drive belts
- High pressure fuel line
- Engine oil

Engine Failure

The first problem to deal with is the engine failing to start after it has been running for a while. This sort of failure usually happens in the middle of a voyage or part way through a holiday or some equally frustrating time. When the engine fails to start, at the worst, an outing might have to be postponed, whereas if it stops at sea it could even be dangerous.

The Fuel System

When a diesel engine stops, it will be caused by a fuel problem so check to make sure there is fuel in the tank and it is getting through. If the fuel tank is empty, the whole system will have to be bled to get rid of air that will have entered the pipes. This technique is described on page 227. The same will be true if some part of the fuel system has been jarred or damaged which let air into the pipes, even if there is fuel in the tank.

Since you now know that you will have to bleed the system, it is a good opportunity to check it for other faults, especially for clogged or dirty filters. Turn off the fuel isolation tap (shut off valve), which should be at the base of the fuel tank. Have a look at the first filter, placing a receptacle under it to take any fuel that may spill, and see whether it is clogged. If it is, replace it. If it is the type that catches water at the bottom of a bowl, and at least one filter in the fuel line should do this, and it is clean, drain the water and leave the filter. If it is dirty, it too needs replacing. If you do not have a second filter in the system, now is the time to install one. Even though much of the diesel oil which is bought nowadays is of very high quality, if you are cruising you will be visiting places where the fuel will be, to say the least, suspect. Your on-board system must be sufficiently good to filter out water and other impurities.

If fuel is getting past both filters it will be getting as far as the entrance to the fuel pump. All engines have a small tickler valve or hand operated pump (see diagram 11.1). Manipulate the pump and see whether fuel floods out from around it. If fuel does not pump out around the small pump, the blockage is here. The pump itself may have to be dismantled. The most that can be done on board probably is to take the pump apart and see whether anything internal is broken, bent, or clogged. If the fault is obvious it may be possible to fix, but it is more likely that it cannot.

The same problem of space recurs. Is the boat able to carry a complete spare pump, which is the ideal solution? If you have made a repair yourself you will have to reassemble the pump, put it back into the fuel system, then bleed the system from there on. You will need a new gasket and its sealant. If you don't have one, look for a compound on the boat that is like the material in the old gasket and cut one to shape. But be wary. Rubber seems ideal, but sometimes dissolves, depending on the fuel going through the pump. If you install a homemade gasket, keep an eye on it until you are sure it is functioning well and replace it with the proper thing as soon as possible.

Diagram 11.1 *A typical tickler valve on a diesel engine.*

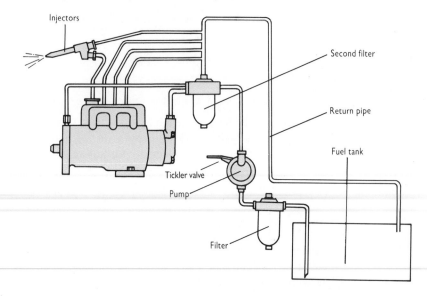

If fuel flowed when you tickled the hand-pump, the system is OK to here, and the next stage to check is at the injectors. If there are several injectors it is unlikely that they will all be faulty. It is more likely that you will have found your fault at the pump, especially if one pump feeds all the injectors.

If there is a suspect injector (the one not flooding when the securing nut is loosened) the simplest thing to do is to take it out and replace it with a spare, and trace the faulty one's problem at your leisure. But you will have to be highly skilled to do so, and even so could not carry on board the large complex machinery needed. So injectors are on the must list for spares.

If, after you have made the checks listed above, you still have not found any problem, you have only one more option, to check the air supply.

Air Supply

Although air in the fuel system will kill a diesel engine, it needs great quantities of air, through the air supply filter, to operate properly. If the air filter is restricting the supply of air, the motor will stop. Simply cleaning the filter usually allows the engine to start again. If not, you may have to remove the air breather. However, if you do this, control very strictly the hours you run the engine and have an expert check it when you get to port.

Bleeding

This is simple although messy. First you will have to put fuel in the tank if it does not already have some in, and then open the fuel isolation switch (shut off valve) near the base of the tank. As a general rule it is more important to keep a diesel tank topped up than a petrol (gasoline) tank. The reason is that the contents of a nearly empty diesel tank, when they slosh around at sea, will allow air into the system well before all the fuel has been used.

You will need a container large enough to catch all the spillage you will cause now, or have someone else there who can empty it. Go to the first filter in the system and loosen off the nut on the exit side of the pipe, allowing fuel to push its way down the pipe, through the filter, and into your container. When you are sure there are no more air bubbles coming through, tighten up the nut. Now go to the next filter and do exactly the same. If there is another filter repeat the performance. When you get to the fuel pump, disconnect the outlet and crank the engine, so that fuel is dragged through, and keep doing so until there are no bubbles in the fuel.

When you get to the injectors, loosen off their retaining nuts and crank the engine to force any bubbles out. After a little while, tighten up the nuts and try the engine again. If it still doesn't work, slacken the nuts and force more fuel out. You will have to keep doing that until the engine starts. If it doesn't start after two or three tries at the injectors, go back to the beginning and go right through the system again. It is most unusual, in my experience, to have to make a second run at it. Now the engine is ready for starting.

Starting

If the engine will not crank at all, the first thing to do is ascertain whether the fault is electrical or fuel. Get the can of ether you have in your store and fire a quick burst into the air cleaner while somebody else presses the ignition. Stand back when you do this because the engine may well spit at you. If it fires the fault is fuel. If not, see whether the starter motor is moving.

At this stage of its working cycle nearly every diesel has to rely on electricity to start, although some surprisingly large ones will start by hand cranking. Only the checks most likely to succeed are listed here. If they do not work, turn to the more detailed electrical checklist in the section on petrol (gasoline) engines on page 233.

BATTERY

If the starter does not move check the battery. If there is absolutely no noise or indication of action when the starter button is pressed, the first and most common fault is that the battery is absolutely flat and dead. Not just weak, totally empty. Nevertheless, it may be the connections on the battery. Check to see if they are really tight, which they should be. If they are not, or perhaps broken, or very heavily corroded, clean them up, put a light coating of petroleum jelly over them, and tighten the connections very strongly. Any of these conditions would so reduce the amount of power available that the battery would appear flat and thus prevent any reaction from the starter motor. If the battery is in bad condition, recharge it to full capacity, or replace it if necessary. If the battery is in good order you will have to check the whole electrical starting system, but first see whether you have fuel, and whether the throttle is opening. If these two conditions are met, check the wiring to the starter motor and the solenoid.

SOLENOID

Sound is a helpmate here. When the jolt of electricity to the solenoid is powerful enough, it makes the solenoid shaft engage with a distinct 'thunk'. If the jolt is insufficient the shaft will manage only a click or a series of clicks. This is a good indication that the problem is in the battery, not the solenoid, although it is possible that the solenoid contacts are corroded. A visual check will soon see if that is so. If it is, clean them up. If there is absolute silence from the solenoid it may have a short in it, or may have burned out. In either case, you will have to replace it as it is unlikely you will be able to repair it.

IGNITION SWITCH

Before you give up hope on the solenoid, try the ignition switch which may be faulty. The best way to check is to bypass the switch's circuit. Take a short piece of wire of about the same dimensions as the wiring in the circuit and take it across the live wire from the battery to the solenoid. If the solenoid engages, the fault is in the switch. Remember you will have to disconnect the wire when the starter motor engages.

STARTER MOTOR

If you have not been able to isolate the fault in the switch or the solenoid, it may be in the starter motor. If a diesel cranks slowly, you have to remember that they are harder engines to start than petrol (gasoline), and thick oil in cold weather can make a great difference to their starting capacity. Also, if the engine cranks but seems reluctant to start, one or more of the decompression levers may be sticking open, preventing the proper compression of the fuel from taking place. Decompression levers are handy things to have because if you are finding the engine a bit hard to turn over with the compression on, you can take it off by letting off the lever(s), swinging the engine up to good revolutions with the starter, then quickly cutting in the decompression lever so that the fuel compresses, the engine fires, and you are away.

If you cannot make the starter motor work check that the mountings are tight. If they are loose they can throw out the alignment of the pinion and shaft and the flywheel, so that the starter cannot engage with the teeth on the flywheel. While you are about it, check that there is no dirt around the motor as even a small amount will upset the electrics, and surprisingly little will upset the mechanics.

If the starter is getting plenty of power, and can be heard rotating, but nothing is happening, you probably have a serious fault. The Bendix spring may be broken or bent, there may be teeth missing from the flywheel, or the clutch may be broken. The second is the only condition you can recover from, unless you carry a spare starter motor or you can start the motor by hand.

Follow the instructions for starting the motor when decompressed and fire the ignition switch for a very short time, so that the section of the flywheel without teeth moves away from the starter motor. Then keep trying the ignition until you hear the teeth engage and the engine begin to turn. Keep going long enough to start the motor.

As an aside, do not persist if the starter motor can be seen to be labouring when trying to turn the engine. Not only do you take the risk of flattening the battery, and then have the monumental, self-made problem of not being able to recharge your batteries, but also insufficient power to the starter motor can cause serious damage through overheating, which at best will shorten its life and at worst will burn it out.

If, after all these checks, you still cannot get the motor to start, and you are satisfied the starting system is satisfactory, you will have to carry out the check to the fuel system set out in the section above on engine failure.

LUBRICATING OIL

Let's say that we are now satisfied that the starting system is working, and the engine has started but is sluggish. You will have to check the oil to see that there is, first of all, enough, and second that it isn't thick and viscous. In some climates, it may simply be that the engine oil is too cold. In this case the diesel will be fitted with heaters which warm up the cylinders to help the injected fuel atomise. These won't warm up the engine oil, but because they make starting easier, they indirectly help the oil, which rapidly heats up once the engine moves. If the oil is black and thick, it must be replaced, but it should not have been allowed to get to that state in the first place.

SMOKE

A handy symptom to aid in the diagnosis of a running engine's faults is smoke or at least the colour of it. Normal exhaust from a marine diesel is almost colourless, so that discolouration indicates something wrong with the engine. The discolouration will be black, white or blue. What each indicates is listed below, but each colour has one indication in common with both others, they indicate that the wrong fuel, or lubricating oil, or both, is being used.

Black smoke is most common, particularly when the engine is being run by a careless skipper, as it denotes overloading, or starvation of air. In the case of overloading, dropping the engine revolutions usually will remove the offending trail of smoke. If air starvation is the problem, a thorough cleaning of the air filter, or replacing it if need be, will work. There is a third cause of black smoke, which is excess or dribbling fuel. This can be rectified only by adjustment to the injectors, which will certainly have to be done on shore. Luckily this is not a serious fault so it can be tolerated at sea.

White smoke indicates misfiring, which again will need to be fixed on shore and again is not a serious problem at sea.

Blue smoke indicates that lubricating oil is getting into the cylinders and being burned. If this is because of a crack in the block, or overheated oil, it may be serious, as the oil may have got into the combustion chamber. While you could still run the engine, you would want to keep a very good eye on it and get an expert to attend to it as soon as possible.

The less serious problem could be that the rings on the piston have worn, allowing oil past them into the combustion chamber. The engine would lose some power, and would use a lot of oil, but would be safe to use. If blue smoke indicates that the engine oil might be overheating, check the temperature gauge, if you have one. If not, pull the cover off the engine and see whether the usual signs are there—a smell of hot paint, a strong oily smell, greater than usual radiation of heat.

If the heat being radiated is very great, stop the engine at once and go straight to the cooling water pump. Dismantle it (see diagrams 11.2–11.3) and see whether the impeller is damaged. The usual damage is that the base of one of the impeller's flexible 'legs' is fractured. Replace it from your spares. Water pump impellers are the prime **musts** to be carried as spares. For even a short journey there should be one in the pump, a spare, and another spare. The longer the journey the more spares should be taken. Without an impeller you can't use the engine, and you can't charge your batteries, and your refrigerator won't work, and you will not be able to use your Satnav **or your radio**. Need I say more?

Even if the new impeller works satisfactorily and there is now a good flow of water to the engine (which you must not start again immediately in case

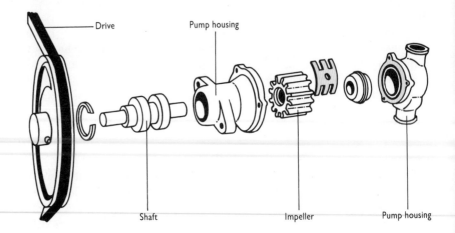

Drive   Pump housing

Shaft   Impeller   Pump housing

Diagram 11.2 *A typical cooling water pump for the engine.*

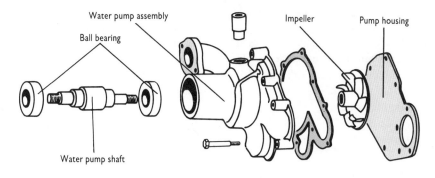

Water pump assembly   Impeller   Pump housing

Ball bearing

Water pump shaft

Diagram 11.3 *An impeller type cooling pump.*

the cold water cracks the hot engine block), check out the rest of the cooling system. You should do this particularly if, when you have started up again, the flow is sufficient to cool the engine a little, but not to its proper temperature. The pump may be pushing water through cooling galleries which have been narrowed by years of deposits on their walls from impurities in the water. Some can be checked at sea, such as the main pipes to the engine, and even some of the easier to get at pipes in the block itself, but usually this is a job to be done on the slips. If you suspect the cooling system needs flushing you will have to nurse the engine until you can do it. But you can still check to see whether any other pipes between the sea and your engine are restricting the flow of water.

I remember one case where the flow of water to an engine was insufficient, but the pipes turned out to be clear. It wasn't until somebody realised that the heat exchanger for the refrigerator cooling system ran from the same inlet, and that it had clogged, that we understood why the engine was being starved of cooling water. If the pump is satisfactory, and the flow of water, check the thermostat.

THERMOSTAT

The easiest way to check the thermostat is to remove it and replace it with a plug. Let the coolant run through and watch the engine temperature. If it drops to anywhere near normal the thermostat is the problem. You can carry a spare thermostat if you want, but I don't believe it is necessary. The engine will run indefinitely without one, even though it would rather not be too cool. If the thermostat checks out as operating satisfactorily, and the pump is working, and the engine is still overheating, the problem may be outside the boat.

WATER INLET SKIN
(THROUGH HULL) FITTINGS

Most skin (through hull) fittings have a grille over them to keep out the smaller items that can block the inlet pipe. But that modern scourge, the plastic bag, has an incredible ability to cling just where it is not wanted, or the inlet may be blocked by weed, or something else. The only way to tell is to send a diver over the side, or if you are alone, do it yourself. All way will have to be taken off the vessel and the diver properly kitted with goggles, weights, and a knife. He should be attached by one line, and have another over the side with loops in it, to help him climb back on board. If you have a big crew you can rig a boarding ladder and detail one crew to watch out for the diver, otherwise you are relying upon yourself or one other. The diver has to clear the inlet, if it proves to be blocked. (The traditional reward for a diver when his or her task is completed, is rum.) If you still haven't solved the problem, you may find that a hose has been kinked, or a tiny hole has worn in a pipe and water is escaping. You will have to check everything until you find the cause.

OIL

Do not overlook the oil system, which as well as lubricating the engine, cools it. So if you have been running the engine for a long time, it may well be that the oil level has dropped too low. You **must** carry spare oil, so top up to the dipstick level and see whether that brings the temperature down. If you haven't any oil, which is a sin, you can use cooking oil, preferably mineral rather than vegetable, and it works very well.

Marine engines do not like being at too great an angle of heel for too long. If you check the manufacturer's handbook you will see that it recommends a maximum angle of heel for that particular engine. It is a good idea to stick rigidly to the recommendations. When an engine is heeled for too long the oil follows the level of the sea surface and important sections of the engine are left without oil. They become overheated and temperature distortion can take place through the engine. This distortion can be irreversible.

INJECTOR OR VALVE TIMING

The last possibility for overheating is the timing and little can be done at sea to correct that. The only possibility is to nurse the engine—to use it only when absolutely necessary and then shut it down again when it starts overheating.

There is one nasty habit that diesels have that doesn't confront the owner of a petrol (gasoline) engine. They can run away, and nobody really knows what makes it happen. It is useless to shut off the fuel because they can consume their own gases, even their own lubricating oil, and run up to such a speed that they cause severe damage. The only way to stop them is to block their air supply by taking off the filter and holding something strong and slightly flexible over the air intake, then covering with cloth or something else that will completely block the air. Do not try putting cloth over the intake first as it will probably disappear down the pipe.

PETROL (GASOLINE) ENGINES

TOOLS YOU WILL NEED

This will depend on the job you have to undertake, so check with the master list on page 271. At the least you will need:

- Full set of spanners (wrenches) for the engine
- Electrical tools (screwdrivers, pliers, strippers)

- Adjustable (shifting) spanners (wrenches)
- Vice grips
- Set of screwdrivers

- Allen keys
- WD-40 or similar product
- Plug spanner

SPARES YOU WILL NEED

- Spark plugs
- Points
- Coil
- Solenoid
- Fuel pump
- Gaskets
- Gasket sealant
- Impellers for pumps
- Injector(s)
- Fuel filters

- Oil filters
- Plug for thermostat socket
- Can of ether
- Grease for water pump
- Hose clips (clamps) (various)
- Drive belts
- Fuel pump (or diaphragms, seals or impellers)
- Set of feeler gauges
- Engine oil

The petrol (gasoline) engine has two disadvantages as an auxiliary installation. It relies on an electrical ignition system all the time it is running, and the fuel is explosive. But they have one great advantage. The technology is used and understood worldwide, and there is nowhere so remote that there isn't a mechanic available who can handle even the most major of repairs.

The need for constant electrical ignition is its major weakness. Salty air, the usual boat environment, is inimical to electrical circuits. Even boats which are used exclusively on freshwater lakes suffer from damp, which the electrics do not like. So the most common area for faults to be found is the electrical circuit, which includes the batteries, starter switch, the starting solenoid, the starter motor, the distributor, the points, the condenser, the spark plugs, the breakers and the generator or alternator.

ENGINE FAILS TO START

The first task is to discover whether the fault lies with the electrical system or the fuel system, and then to follow the logical sequence of conditions which must exist in either system to see where the fault lies. Because petrol (gasoline) and diesel engines both rely on an electrical ignition system to start (the diesel does not use electricity once it has started running) the checklist is the same for both up to the point of engine starting. To prevent readers having to skip backwards and forwards through the book, we will repeat here the relevant steps from the section on starting diesel engines. First see whether the starter motor is turning the engine. We will assume that it does not, and that the fault therefore lies somewhere in the starting circuit.

BATTERY

If the starter does not move check the battery first. If there is absolutely no noise or indication of action when the starter button is pressed, the first and most common fault is that the battery is absolutely flat and dead. Not just weak, but totally empty. Nevertheless, it may be the connections on the battery. Check to see if they are really tight, which they should be. If they are not, or perhaps loose or broken, or very heavily corroded, clean them up, put a light coating of petroleum jelly over them, and tighten the connections very strongly. Any of these conditions would so reduce the amount of power available as to make the battery appear flat and thus prevent any reaction from the starter motor. If the battery is in bad condition, recharge it to full capacity, or replace it if necessary. If the battery is in good order you will have to check the whole electrical starting system.

Solenoid

First check the wiring to the starter motor from the solenoid. Sound is a helpmate here. When the jolt of electricity to the solenoid is powerful enough, it makes the solenoid shaft engage with a distinct 'thunk'. If the jolt is insufficient the shaft will manage only a click or a series of clicks. This is a good indication that the problem is in the battery, not the solenoid, although it is possible that the circuit is open between the battery and the solenoid—in other words the wire has broken or is not making a good enough connection. If there is a break, replace with equivalent heavy duty wire. If you have a short circuit, which is much less likely, you will know immediately from the vicious, almost sparkling flash. A short circuit within a high tension circuit is highly dangerous.

A further reason for silence at the solenoid is that the solenoid contacts are corroded. A visual check will soon see if that is so. If it is, clean them up. If there is absolute silence from the solenoid it may have a short in it, or may have burned out. Experts with a great deal of experience put a heavy, insulated screwdriver across the terminals, without causing sparks. If the motor then starts, the solenoid is faulty. A safer way to check a petrol (gasoline) engine is to use the trouble light. If it shows a light the current is getting through the solenoid and the problem will be further on, in the starter.

It is unlikely you will be able to repair the solenoid if it is faulty, which is why it is listed as a spare that should be carried.

Ignition Switch

Check the ignition switch which may be faulty. The best way to check is to bypass the switch's circuit. Take a short piece of wire of about the same dimensions as the wiring in the circuit and take it across the live wire from the battery to the solenoid. If the solenoid engages, the fault is in the switch. Remember you will have to disconnect the wire when the engine starts. If you have not been able to isolate the fault in the switch or the solenoid, it may be in the starter motor.

Starter Motor

If you cannot make the starter motor work check that its mountings are tight. If they are loose they can throw out the alignment of the pinion and shaft and the flywheel, so that the starter cannot engage with the teeth on the flywheel. While you are about it, check that there is no dirt around the motor, even a small amount will upset the electrics, and surprisingly little will upset the mechanics.

If the starter is getting plenty of power, and can be heard rotating, but nothing is happening, you probably have a serious fault. The Bendix spring may be broken or bent, there may be teeth missing from the flywheel, or the clutch may be broken. The second is the only condition you can recover from, unless you carry a spare starter motor or you can start the motor by hand.

Fire the ignition switch for a very short time, so that the section of the flywheel without teeth moves away from the starter motor. Then keep trying the ignition until you hear the teeth engage and the engine begin to turn. Keep going long enough to start the motor.

As an aside, do not persist if the starter motor can be seen to be labouring when trying to turn the engine. Not only do you take the risk of flattening the battery, and then have the monumental, self-made problem of not being able to recharge your batteries, but also insufficient power to the starter motor can cause serious damage through overheating, which at best will shorten its life and at worst will burn it out.

If, after all these checks, you still cannot get the motor to start, even though the starter is functional, you will have to turn your attention to the fuel system.

FUEL SYSTEM

First check to see that you haven't run out of fuel which is very easy to do if the fuel gauge is inaccurate. Next see whether the fuel tap (shut off valve) is open at the base of the tank. If there is fuel, and the tap is open, check along the fuel's path to the engine. The filters may need changing, there may be water in the fuel, which would show at the bottom of a glass bowl filter, but would have to be tested for with other filters. The method of testing is to catch a little fuel in a small container and see if there is water below the fuel.

FUEL PUMP

Somewhere in the modern engine's fuel system there is a fuel pump which must be tested as would any other pump, using the trouble light. If the pump checks out as being satisfactory electrically, take it apart, noting the sequence of steps if you do not have a manual, and see whether the diaphragm is damaged or the impeller. If necessary replace the part.

AIR LOCK

If the pump seems satisfactory, the last possibility is that there is an air lock in the system. This is particularly likely on very hot days. You will have to bleed the system in exactly the same way as a diesel fuel line is bled.

Starting from the tank, make sure there is fuel at the first filter, crank the motor to draw petrol (gasoline) through until there are no bubbles, and go right along the line until you have satisfied yourself that fuel, without air, is getting to the carburettor.

SPARK

Once you are satisfied fuel is reaching the carburettor, and the engine still won't start, you will have to check for spark. Whatever size engine you are trying to kick into life, the next test applies to them all. Disconnect the high tension lead between the coil and the distributor, at the distributor end. Get someone to crank the engine while you hold the lead about a centimetre (quarter inch) from the engine block. If there is a healthy spark it will leap from the high voltage wire to the engine casing. The coil transforms the electricity from the battery into a short surge of high voltage which goes through the distributor and on to each spark plug. If there is no spark the coil will have to be replaced. It cannot be repaired. Assuming you have spark, or have replaced a faulty coil, check each plug in turn. If each is getting its proper 'hot' spark, check next whether the plugs are clean and the gap setting is accurate.

SPARK PLUGS

These must fire at their own precisely timed moment for the engine to run properly. The correct gap will be in your manual and you should have a set of feeler gauges on board. Take each plug, clean between the points with some very fine sandpaper, or wet and dry, or even the emery board you use for your fingernails, and gently rub until you get bright metal. Set the gap to its proper amount and replace the plug. Do the same for each plug. If they look badly pitted, replace them with the model recommended by the engine manufacturer.

When you take the plugs out, have a good look at them. They can tell you a lot about the way your engine is running, even if it is not causing any immediate problems. An expert will diagnose many more conditions than we will discuss here, but the simplest indications are these: **Damp, black carbon deposits on the plug**. The condition is known as 'oiling up' and indicates oil is getting on to the plug, either in the fuel or through the piston rings. **The plug is carbonised, but dry**. Plug is too cold and the gap needs adjustment. **The plug is dry and abraded looking**. Good news, this is a normal plug. **Crack in the porcelain (inside or out)**. The spark will almost certainly be 'jumping' and firing out of sequence.

Your engine should now start. If, when you checked for spark with the lead between the coil and the distributor, there was a spark, but the plugs did not show a spark when shorted against the engine casing, the fault lies in the distributor.

DISTRIBUTOR

The most common fault is moisture in the distributor cap. Check that the distributor cap is intact as even the smallest of hairline cracks will let in enough moisture to ruin its delicate insides. The only possible way of remedying this fault is to cover the outside of the crack with a two-part epoxy glue like Araldite and hope it works. Otherwise you are going to need a new cap. Next, take all the components, breaker points, rotor etc. and put them into a 'slow' oven for 10 minutes or so to thoroughly dry them out.

The breaker contacts can be very, very gently rubbed with fine abrasive paper to smooth them so they make better electrical contact. When everything is dry, spray a water repellant such as WD40 over the components of the distributor, as well as the cap itself, inside and out. It is a good idea now to check for proper breaking of the current by the distributor. Its function is to send the bursts of high voltage to each spark plug in turn at precisely the right moment for it to fire the petrol and begin the power thrust of each cylinder. If the timing is wrong the engine will run roughly, or perhaps not at all.

The way to check is to connect a simple 12 volt bulb (with a 12 volt system) between the wire into the distributor from the coil and the engine block. It is easiest to have such a test light permanently placed in the electrical kit, with leads soldered to each of the bulb's base contacts, and small crocodile (alligator) clips (clamps) on the end of each wire. It is then a simple matter to connect the wires as described and, while the engine is cranked, watch the bulb. If there is a regular flickering of the bulb, each flicker representing one burst from the coil, the timing is correct. If the flickering is erratic, the timing is off and will have to be corrected. This is not a job for the inexperienced and should be undertaken only by someone confident of their ability. Luckily, bad timing usually will not prevent a motor starting, it will only prevent it from running efficiently.

Now comes the good news. Modern electronic ignition systems give hardly any trouble at all. The best preventive maintenance is to have one of them, not the old-fashioned sort we have just dealt with.

LUBRICATING OIL

If the engine has started but is sluggish, check the oil to see that there is, first of all, enough, and second that it isn't thick and viscous. In some climates, it may simply be that the engine oil is too cold. Some sort of general heating will have to be applied to the engine to warm the oil sufficiently for it to thin a little. If the oil is black and thick, it must be replaced, but it should not have been allowed to get to that state in the first place. The chief area of neglect in maintaining boat engines is in changing the oil regularly, yet neglect will lead to much inconvenience.

Remember that the oil, as well as lubricating the engine, cools it. So if you have been running the engine for a long time, it may well be that the oil level has dropped too low. You **must** carry spare oil, so top up to the dipstick level and see whether that brings the temperature down. If you haven't any oil, you can use cooking oil, preferably mineral rather than vegetable.

Marine engines do not like being at too great an angle of heel for too long. If you check the manufacturer's handbook you will see that it recommends a maximum angle of heel for that particular engine. It is a good idea to stick rigidly to the recommendations. When an engine is heeled for too long the oil follows the level of the sea surface and important sections of the engine are left without oil. They become overheated and temperature distortion can take place through the engine. This distortion can be irreversible.

SMOKE

A handy symptom to aid in the diagnosis of a running engine's faults is smoke or at least the colour of it. Normal exhaust from a marine engine is almost colourless, so that discolouration will be black, white or blue. What each indicates is listed below, but each colour has one indication in common with both others, they indicate that the wrong fuel, or lubricating oil, or both, is being used.

Black smoke is most common, and indicates that the mixture is too rich, so that the carburettor setting needs adjusting, or the choke has jammed. In general the air/fuel mix is not correct.

If the engine has only just started it may not be warm enough to take a heavy load. Diesels start full work immediately, but petrol (gasoline) engines need a little time to get going. Dropping the revolutions, or waiting before applying load, will usually work.

If air starvation is the problem, a thorough cleaning of the air filter, or replacing it if need be, will work.

White smoke indicates misfiring, which will need to be fixed on shore and is not a serious problem at sea.

Blue smoke indicates that lubricating oil is getting into the cylinders and being burned. If this is because of a crack in the block, or overheated oil, it may be serious, as the oil may have got into the combustion chamber. While you could still run the engine, you would want to keep a very good eye on it and get an expert to attend to it as soon as possible. A less serious problem could be that the rings on the piston have worn, allowing oil past them into the combustion chamber. The engine would lose some power, and would use a lot of oil, but would be safe to use.

OVERHEATING

If blue smoke indicates that the engine oil might be overheating, check the temperature gauge, if you have one. If not, pull the cover off the engine and see whether the usual signs are there—a smell of hot paint, a strong oily smell, greater than usual radiation of heat. If the heat being radiated is very great, stop the engine at once and go straight to the cooling water pump. Dismantle it and see whether the impeller is damaged. The usual damage is that the base of one of the impeller's flexible 'legs' is fractured. Replace it from your spares. Water pump impellers are the prime **musts** to be carried as spares. For even a short journey there should be one in the pump, a spare, and another spare. The longer the journey the more spares should be taken. Without an impeller you can't use the engine, and you can't charge your batteries, and your refrigerator won't work, and you will not be able to use your Satnav **or your radio**. Need I say more?

Even if the new impeller works satisfactorily and there is now a good flow of water to the engine (which you must not start again immediately in case the cold water cracks the hot engine block), check out the rest of the cooling system. You should do this particularly if, when you have started up again, the flow is sufficient to cool the engine a little, but not to its proper temperature. The pump may be pushed through cooling galleries which have been narrowed by years of deposits on their walls from impurities in the water. Some can be checked at sea, such as the main pipes to the engine, and even some of the easier to get at pipes in the block itself, but usually this is a job to be done on the slips. If you suspect the cooling system needs flushing you will have to nurse the engine until you can do it. But you can still check to see whether any other pipes between the sea and your engine are restricting the flow of water.

THERMOSTAT

If the pump is satisfactory, and the flow of water, check the thermostat. The easiest way to do that is to remove it and replace it with a plug. Let the coolant run through and watch the engine temperature. If it drops to anywhere near normal the thermostat is the problem. You can carry a spare thermostat if you want, but I don't believe it is necessary. The engine will run indefinitely without one, even though it would rather not be too cool. If the thermostat checks out as operating satisfactorily, and the pump is working, and the engine is still overheating, the problem may be outside the boat.

WATER INLET SKIN
(THROUGH HULL) FITTINGS

Most skin (through hull) fittings have a grille over them to keep out the smaller items that can block the inlet pipe. But that modern scourge, the plastic bag, has an incredible ability to cling just where it is not wanted, or the inlet may be blocked by weed, or something else. The only way to tell is to send a diver over the side, or if you are alone, do it yourself. All way will have to be taken off the vessel and the diver properly kitted with goggles, weights, and a knife. He should be attached by one line, and have another over the side with loops in it, to help him climb back on board. If you have a big crew you can rig a boarding ladder and detail one crew to watch out for the diver, otherwise you are relying upon yourself or one other. The diver has to clear the inlet if it proves to be blocked. (The traditional reward for a diver when his or her task is completed, is rum.) If you still haven't solved the problem, you may find that a hose has been kinked, or a tiny hole has worn in a pipe and water is escaping. You will have to check everything until you find the cause.

T R O U B L E S H O O T I N G
T H E   H E A D

Perhaps the most unpleasant thing that can go wrong at sea, which is why it always does, is the head. You really must have the manufacturer's manual for this job because although examples of two basic types of head are illustrated here in diagrams 11.4–11.5, there are literally hundreds of designs to meet the regulations in each country concerning pollution, holding tanks, pumping stations, and so on, which differ greatly.

For some reason the job of fixing the lavatory always seems to fall to the skipper. That's probably because if you have to dismantle the installation, and it is done wrongly, there can be a risk to the boat's safety. The skin fittings obviously must be closed off, because the sensible thing to do if the head is blocked or defective in any way is to dismantle it completely, and clean and flush the system. It becomes a sort of forced maintenance rather than just fixing a fault.

In any case, a head installation should be dismantled and thoroughly cleaned in an enzyme-based liquid at least once a year. In colder climates, where the installation needs to be winterised, it should be cleaned at least twice a year. This is not just to keep it working properly, but also to keep the system sweet smelling.

The best way to keep a head and its surrounding areas sweet smelling is to have a properly educated crew and intimidated guests. There should be a large notice at eye level specifying how the head works and what should not go into it. Even when you do have such a notice, people will ignore it, either through ignorance or stupidity or both. Each person should be asked if they have read the notice, and then the rules should be explained to them. This can be done in a pleasant, but firm, manner. Everybody should know that they are responsible, when they use the head, for leaving it exactly as they found it, and abiding by the rules. The longer the voyage the more important this hygiene is. Explain to everyone just how inconvenient it is going to be if the rules aren't followed. In educating crew and passengers, try to instil one basic fact—going to the lavatory ashore is what you might call a one stop operation. At sea it should be a three-phase operation. There's nothing more likely to clog the lavatory than to have the normal amount of effluent, plus probably twice this amount in paper, in the bowl when flushing starts. It is much more sensible to pump two or even three times while seated on the bowl so that the system has to deal with less mass in one go. However, if a blockage occurs despite all these precautions, here is what you do.

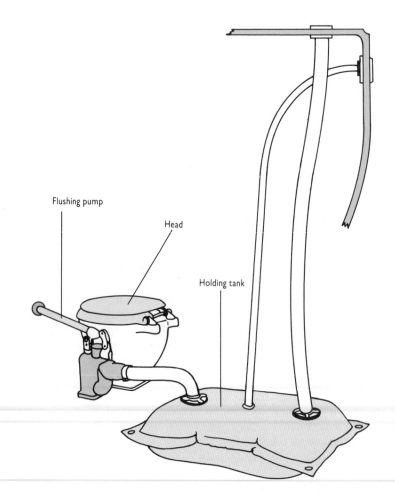

Flushing pump

Head

Holding tank

Diagram 11.4 *A common style of marine toilet (head) installation, incorporating holding tanks which are demanded almost world-wide.*

Diagram 11.5 *Another style of marine toilet (head) installation, which also incorporates holding tanks.*

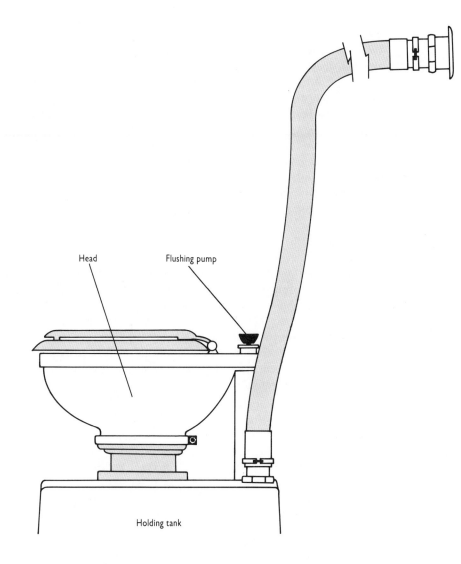

Head   Flushing pump

Holding tank

THE BASIC HEAD

All lavatory systems operate on the same basic principle: the system starts off clean and fresh and ready for use, the inlet and outlet valves are opened, the lavatory is used, the waste matter is pumped out, fresh water flushes the system, and the inlet and outlet skin (through hull) fittings are closed off so that the installation is safe and clean and ready for use again. Where the systems vary is in whether they pump straight into the sea, or into a holding tank, or into a chlorinator (a sort of small on-board sewage treatment plant), or into a chemical tank. A further variation is whether it is pumped electrically or moved by means of air pressure or a vacuum; and whether the system is flushed with fresh water from within the boat's own system, which is the case with some large boats, or from lake or sea water from outside.

If any section of the installation is going to be below the waterline at any angle of heel, then a U-bend needs to be put into the pipe to raise the pipe at least six inches above sea level to prevent siphoning and also flooding of the system.

In Australia, where the anti-pollution laws are less strict than overseas, although they are changing, not many vessels are fitted with an outlet for pumping soil from a holding tank into a land station. Likewise in European coastal waters where the anti-pollution laws are less strict than on inland waters. But it would be prudent for anyone building a boat to install such a facility, because the anti-pollution laws are due to be tightened in the near future.

Some systems have an inlet valve which is part of the pumping handle and which acts automatically. Others have a separate valve on the side of the bowl. It is a little right-angled lever clearly marked to show where it should be positioned to pump the bowl dry or to flush it. Yet others have virtually automatic systems which are engine driven. The basic valve assembly is the same on all.

When doing the sort of maintenance or unblocking work on facilities of this kind, use the manufacturer's manual. If you don't have one, take notes of each step as you dismantle the system and be thorough because you are going to have to put it back together again. Inlet valves can be assembled the wrong way, but you'll soon know when you try to use the system, so all you'll have to do then is dismantle the valve and turn the valve part so that it is the opposite of what it was.

Some people customise their installations by slightly offsetting the holding bolts in the base in such a way that there is only one way they can be installed, preventing wrong installation.

Tools You'll Need

- Standard plumber's wrenches
- Medium screwdriver
- Shifter
- Pump grease
- Light oil

Spares You'll Need

- Return spring
- Flat valves
- Spare parts kit from manufacturer

Stripping Down the System

We'll start by looking at one of the world's widest-selling lavatory systems, the Simpson Lawrence SL400. It is small and cheap, it fits into almost any boat, and it is very simple. Diagram 11.6 shows that there are not many parts. Once you understand how this one works you can handle virtually any model.

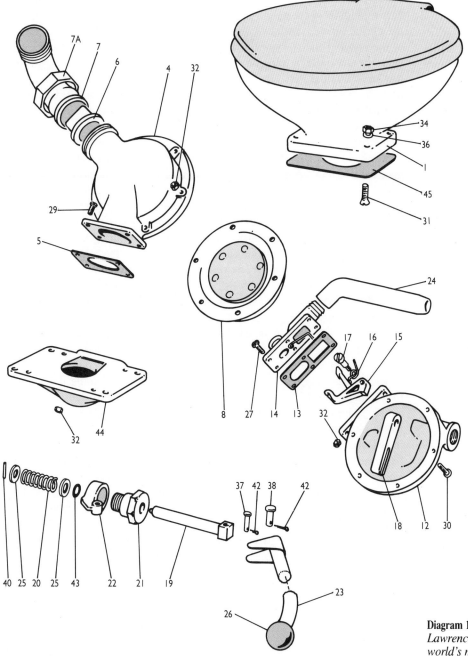

Diagram 11.6 *The Simpson Lawrence SL400 head, one of the world's most popular.*

First remove the pump/discharge operating handle (No 23). This is held by two clevis pins with washers and split pins (42). One of the clevis pins is larger than the other, which helps prevent mixups when reassembling. This model head may be mounted on a sub-base on the floor. If yours is, then it needs to be taken off the sub-base by undoing four stainless steel hexagonal-headed bolts which are captive. When you lift it off the sub-base, the soil outlet base moulding (2) comes into sight. The entire plastic-moulded assembly is held on to the ceramic basin (1) by four brass countersunk head screws with washers and nuts (31, 34, 36). The neoprene gasket (3) seals the plastic base moulding where it joins the basin. Work becomes easy now as you remove the plastic pipe (24) which connects the fresh water inlet housing to the back of the basin. This inlet nozzle housing is pushed into a hole in the basin and over the neck of the moulding. Next, the base (2) has to come away from the large circular soil chamber (4) by removing four stainless steel round-headed screws (29) with nuts on them. This brings into view the flat neoprene soil valve (5) which prevents the soil from returning into the pan. This type of flat valve will be found in almost all systems and will also be somewhere in the dry bowl and flush bowl systems. This is where you need to look very carefully to see how the valve is mounted and to make sure that when it goes back together it goes back the way you took it off.

In this model, the open side of the flap must go towards the back of the lavatory, otherwise back pressure may force soil through the valve seat. There is a fresh water inlet nozzle assembly (14) which has two flat valves (13). One allows the diaphragm to draw water into the pump chamber and then closes, and sideways pressure on the handle during the stroke of the pump opens the other valve and sends water into the basin with a strong flush. Six stainless steel roundhead screws (27) hold this inlet nozzle which houses the flat valves. Two of these stainless steel screws have captive nuts, but the others are not captive (32).

Now that you have reached this stage of dismantling the lavatory, make sure that all the time you're looking out for any signs of wear and tear, or even fatigue problems where the synthetic stiffener backs the flat valve. But, generally speaking, not much goes wrong here. The soil outlet pump fits on to this moulding (7) and inside is a one-way valve, not so laughingly called a joker valve (6). This prevents pumped soil from returning to the soil chamber, but in unusual circumstances water can seep back if something solid remains in the slit of the joker valve. This is why it's good practice in all cases to have an anti-siphon bend in the system. Another reason for having an anti-siphon bend is that if the joker valve should rupture and the lavatory is below the waterline, the boat can sink very easily if the sea-cock is not closed off (a nasty habit of landlubbers). There really is no circumstance where an anti-siphon bend should not be fitted.

When you have this part of the assembly separate, look carefully at the moulding, which has a recess to take a flange on the joker valve body. The valve has to be seated correctly before reassembly.

Soil Chamber

Now we come to stripping down the soil chamber. Remove six stainless steel roundhead screws and their nuts (30, 32). This is a nice piece of manufacturing, because when you reassemble them there is only one way the holes line up. But when you come to reassemble it, don't overtighten the screws; they need to be finger tight, plus one more full turn only, and that will seal the chamber.

When you have taken that cover off, you will see that the diaphragm (8) comes into view. This side of the chamber, the side you can see now, is what pumps the soil from the system. If you push the screws back and peel the diaphragm out of its housing, you'll be able to see the other half of the chamber, which is used to pump the fresh inlet water. The shoulder pin (17) which you unscrew, acts as a pivot for the inlet flat-valve operating lever (15). It also retains a small return spring (16) and this works when the pump handle is pressed inwards while being operated. The return spring (16) causes the lever to swing clear of the inlet valves and lets them work as simple flaps.

The operating lever is not difficult to remove, and it can be replaced in only one way. The return spring is trickier. The straight leg fits against the inside of the housing, and the crank leg goes into a depression in the operating lever. The shoulder pin has a brass captive nut moulded into the plastic body. This spring is a potential cause of trouble, although it has been strengthened on later models. If there is any galvanic corrosion, or an impurity rots the wire, the spring can rot right through and then the system won't prime.

Non-Priming

If non-priming is the symptom you have, go straight to the spring to check it out. When you pump the handle, the strokes are transmitted to the rocking lever (18), and that operates the diaphragm. There's a spring-loaded return to the horizontal. To remove the spindle you undo the gland nut (21). But when you put it back don't overtighten it—and put a small amount of water pump grease on the spring and threads. You'll have to make sure that the square shank on the end of the spindle correctly fits the slot on the rocking lever. The error you can make is 90 degrees. The bronze swivel ring (22) is an extra support for the pumping handle and is something to push against when actuating the flush, so if your head installation squeaks, a touch of grease between the ring and the gland nut should stop it. When you're reassembling the large coil torsion spring (20), fit the pivot pin in its assembly first and then screw in the gland nut. We're now in the core of the system, and if this pivot pin is not correctly seated or not screwed home properly on reassembly, it can cause one of the nastier symptoms of a sea-going head—recirculating soil.

The pivot pin, if it is loose, can press against the diaphragm, which then rubs against the reinforcing disc, and obviously once this gets thin the high pumping pressure will burst the diaphragm. Nowadays these diaphragms are likely to be made of neoprene or some other synthetic, which means they are much stronger.

Simpson Lawrence, like many good pump manufacturers, make kits for those parts of their system that can perish through disuse or too much use, and if you are going on a long cruise you would naturally want at least one packet of these parts.

Reassembly is the reverse of the process described above, but before reassembly, thoroughly wash every part.

Holding Tank System

Here is an example of a typical system with a holding tank. Some of these operate with the ship's own pressurised water system, and others have a hand-operated pump. Diagrams 11.4–11.5 show a typical arrangement.

These systems really are no different from what we've described except that the holding tank connected to the lavatory holds the effluent until the vessel reaches a dockside pumping station. Maintenance is simple. They should be cleaned thoroughly, preferably with an enzyme solution. In those countries where it's not yet illegal to pump directly into the ocean, there are very efficient heads in use which work on the basis of making a vacuum in the bowl. With this system, the lines have to be able to take very strong pressure, and again it's essential to have an anti-siphon bend in the pipe. The operating instructions for the vacuum-type pump, where the lid of the bowl is put down on to the seat and held firmly while a handle is pumped vigorously to create a vacuum, specify that there should be 15 to 20 strokes and then a pause, and then another 10 strokes or so. They really do mean that. It's pointless to try to work it on fewer pumps than are recommended, particularly as the system gets older. So, once again, follow the manufacturer's instructions. When you come to the pause, you'll actually hear a slight hissing, and then when you pump again the whole of the effluent is sucked through the system and over the side. Once again, maintenance is very simple—it's just a matter of flushing it clean every time the system has been used. Allow the cleaning fluid (enzyme solution) to stand in the tank for up to half an hour, and then pump it out and rinse thoroughly with fresh water.

CHLORINATORS

On larger vessels, where space is not at such a premium, there may be more than one head and there will be more power available to drive a more sophisticated system such as a chlorinator. Several heads can pump to one chlorinator, where the effluent is finely chopped with a macerator and then broken down with household chlorine—sodium hypochlorite. It is a miniature sewage plant. It depends entirely on the effluent being completely chopped and can only be fully efficient when it is so. There is no need to clean the system as the chlorine does this all the time. Properly maintained, this system can be treated exactly as is a land-based toilet.

WINTERISING

Winterising, in cold climates, is removing liquids which might freeze and break equipment (toilets, engine blocks etc.) or adding anti-freeze chemicals to the liquids. Do not use alcohol based solutions as these are unkind to some of the internal parts. Ethylene glycol products are usually satisfactory, but in any case follow the manufacturer's recommendations. The standard bowl fitting does not need winterising.

S M A L L   P E T R O L
(G A S O L I N E)   E N G I N E S

The trouble-shooting paths outlined for diesel and petrol (gasoline) auxiliary engines hold good for small engines, such as outboards and generators, but the smaller petrol (gasoline) power plants have idiosyncracies which mean they need an additional checklist of their own. Diesel is less commonly used for smaller engines, but the checklist for the large engines will cover them as well. (Just follow the instructions starting on page 225.)

Tools You Will Need

As for a full-size engine (listed on page 225).

Spares You Will Need

As for large engine, plus:

- Electronic ignition
- Propeller
- Shear pins, split pins, cotter pins

General Rules

Before going into the detailed checklist, there are some rules to follow. First, if you are replacing any parts they must be of the same material and dimensions and strengths as the ones you are replacing or you will cause more trouble than you started with. Bolts, particularly, must match. Sometimes there are special locking nuts on the bolts and you have to be certain that the right ones are used and that they are tightened only to the tension they had before. If you are replacing bent, or cracked, or broken bolts, it is more than usually important that the right part replaces them. After all, they would not have broken unless they had been subject to too great a stress, so replacing them with an inferior part won't solve anything. The new ones will almost invariably break.

Second, remember that just because the engine is smaller than an auxiliary does not mean that it is not as dangerous. When refuelling, if there is even a little spill of petrol (gasoline), a spark can ignite it and it can explode. So be very careful.

Now to troubleshoot the small petrol (gasoline) engine.

The Electrics

Use the same checks of the electrical wiring and high voltage leads that you would for the larger engine. Generators and outboards however rely on screws and nuts to hold various sleeves and shields and boots in place and to prevent sparks flying from the ends of wires by holding them firm. So check all such fittings as they might be preventing the current from getting through.

At the same time see that the sleeves and other covers aren't displaced, or torn, or cracked. Carefully check that the spark plug boots are firmly pushed on. All too often they are loose, the engine doesn't get enough kick to start, and when the owner investigates to see what is wrong, he gets a hefty jolt from the leaking electricity.

On outboards, in particular, there are wire clamps and tie straps which keep the wiring away from mechanical parts which can abrade them. It is very important that any of these parts, if being replaced, should be replaced by exactly the same thing and in exactly the same way.

Spark plugs need to be checked often, because any crack or other fault in the ceramic part of the plug can allow the spark to jump and to interrupt the timing sequence. Electronic ignition systems have taken away much of the worry about small engine starting, but all high-tension systems have to be carefully handled.

The following checklist will uncover all but the most deep-seated faults, so if you are unable to get the motor going using these methods, you will have to seek professional help.

You are trying to start the engine with an electric starter and it simply won't kick. Check for loose wiring and/or corroded connections, and particularly for corrosion around the battery terminals. If the battery seems to be weak and does not give enough kick to the starter, you may have charging problems. The electrical check system for large petrol (gasoline) engines on page 233 will give you the sequence of checks to make. If the electrics seem to check out, try the fuel system. Again, the big engine checklist on page 268 will cover most faults here, but not all.

Air Vent

Make sure the air vent on the fuel tank is open. If it is not, the fuel cannot flow. Check also to see whether the flexible fuel lines have any kinks in them, a common fault with small installations. With a moveable fuel tank lines can get caught under the tank quite easily and fuel will not flow. Sometimes the hand priming pump near the fuel tank needs squeezing to return a good flow of fuel to the engine. Check the fuel filters at the tank and the motor, particularly with a generator, and make sure there's no water or dirt in the system.

Starting Procedure

Have you choked the motor? Did you prime it, if that's required? Is the connector locking into position properly on the engine housing? Have you squeezed the bulb in the fuel system? Have you checked the distributor cap? Is the rotor cracked, broken, or worn? Is the spark plug gap correct? Are they tightly seated? Are their leads firmly clipped on? Are the breaker contacts operating properly? We are now starting to get out of the realm of do-it-yourself and into the expert's field, but on page 236 we do give some rudimentary checks for breaker points that could be tried here. If you have not solved the problem yet, you are in grave difficulty and will need to find your engine's symptom in the list below and try to solve it.

Intermittent Running

First check that the fuel is properly mixed to the manufacturer's recommendations. It may not contain the correct oil, or oil in the right proportions. Usually it will be enough to add some more, correctly mixed fuel, but in extreme cases the tank may have to be drained and the fuel replaced.

Check that the diaphragm of the fuel pump is not holed. If it is, the diaphragm will have to be replaced. Check the ignition switch, as the electrics may not be properly connected. If there is any problem, bypass it, but remember you will have to remove the bypass before the engine will stop.

Motor Misses at High Revs

The spark plugs are the most likely culprit in this case. Check the gap and if necessary adjust to the maker's specifications. Also, make sure the plugs themselves, and the leads, are clean. The breaker points may be at fault, or the engine may need retiming.

There could be water in the fuel, so check the filters. If the motor coughs or spits or slows when running at any speed, the idle or high speed needles may be set for too lean a mixture, or the carburettor may not be synchronised. Once again, fuel is the most likely problem here, so check lines for obstructions, check the diaphragm in the fuel pump to see that it's not damaged and see whether perhaps there's a leak in the fuel connector somewhere, which could mean that the mixture is changing.

EXCESSIVE VIBRATION

If vibration is accompanied by rough running and a lot of smoke it may be that the needle valves in the carburettor are set for too rich a mixture or there's too much oil in the fuel, which would certainly smoke. The smoke would tend to be blue.

Other possibilities are that the carburettor isn't synchronised, the fuel float level is too high, the choke isn't opening properly, or the air flow through the carburettor is obstructed and therefore the mixture is wrong.

If the problem is not in the fuel system, it may be that there are problems with the engine mounting bracket, which could be too loose, or the propeller might be out of balance, or the angle of incidence of the shaft may be wrong.

If the engine has run for a while after you started it and then it slows down and stops, there may be quite a serious problem, particularly if the water intake is blocked and the engine begins to overheat. If this is the case, clear the blockage as soon as possible so that cooling can resume, or if that might take too long, stop the engine.

The overheating may not be from shortage of coolant. It may be that the propeller has weeds or other restrictive agents around it that are increasing the friction, and therefore the load, to such an extent that the extra work makes the engine labour and overheat. Check there is not dirty fuel, that the tank vent is fully opened, and that there is lubrication getting to the shaft of the engine.

Finally, the spark plugs may be igniting too early and therefore need cleaning, or the slow speed adjustment may need rotating until the idle is as low as possible without causing the engine to stall.

BACKFIRING

This normally is caused either by spark plug leads being led to the wrong cylinder, or by the engine being in sore need of a tune-up. If it is neither of these things, it may be that the flywheel gear has sheared off. If that is the case, only a spare can solve the problem.

LACK OF ACCELERATION

If the motor starts but won't reach proper revolutions or won't accelerate, the engine may need a timing check or tune-up, or the carburettor may need adjustment. Certainly check out the ignition, in case the plugs or breaker points or ignition wires are wrong. See whether the fuel line is being choked off in some way, and check whether the oil mix of the fuel is satisfactory, also whether anything is restricting the turning of the propeller.

If the engine overheats, check first of all that the oil/fuel mixture is correct (you can see by how often this check comes up in our fault-finding system that correct fuel mix is vital for small engines). Another strong possibility is that the thermostat is faulty, so check it. Also make sure that the engine is set deep enough on the transom for the propeller to be biting into the water properly, rather than revving too high. Check the water intake on the lower unit, too, to make sure there is sufficient water coming through. Also check the impeller and the gasket round the water pump in case there is a leak which would reduce water pressure.

If, despite all this, you can't find the fault it will almost certainly be the engine timing and the engine should be tuned. If the motor runs well at one speed, but still won't accelerate there may be a problem in the fuel delivery system, such as the choke jammed closed or partly closed, dirt in the needles, or even too lean a mixture coming from the carburettor. You'll need to organise a tune-up if you can't do it yourself.

No Power Under Load

Once again, check that the oil/petrol (gasoline) mix is as the manufacturer specified, and that the fuel lines aren't obstructed or restricted. Make sure spark is being delivered to the cylinders. Check that the right propeller is attached or that the hub is not slipping. See that the propeller and lower unit are not hampered by weeds or some other handicap like the ubiquitous plastic bag. Again the breaker points may be pitted or out of synch.

Sudden Stop

If a motor has been running perfectly well and suddenly stops, the first likelihood is that it has run out of fuel, but once more it may be the fuel mix. Check also that the water pump is supplying sufficient cooling water and that the lower unit is well lubricated. Check the drive belt, which may have come off its proper tension, or even have broken.

If the motor has not only stopped, but seems to have set solid, there may be a much more serious problem, such as a broken or bent part of the piston or crankshaft system, or even the drive or propeller shaft. These cannot be repaired, normally, at sea.

Engine Knocking

Proper fuel mixture is the first thing to check, again. Make sure all the mechanical connections are tight, so that power is being delivered smoothly. Check that the flywheel nut isn't loose. If none of these measures works, get professional help.

Idle Speed Adjustment

If on checking through your trouble shooting list you find that the idle speed of the engine needs adjustment, you can do that by yourself, but you have to make sure that the accelerator is set at the slow position and the motor is at its normal operating temperature. The idle speed is **increased** by turning the knob (see diagram 11.7) clockwise and **decreased** by turning it anti-clockwise. You may decide you want to do something with the carburettor if it shows up as one of the symptoms in the checklist, but you must bear in mind that the factory calibrates and sets the high-speed and low-speed needles and it is pretty rare for them to need adjustment. Certainly you should never have reason to adjust the high-speed needle.

CARBURETTOR
NEEDLE ADJUSTMENT

While the low-speed needle is factory preset, there is provision to make adjustments when you get fuel of different quality, or the climate is different from normal. Even changing from warmer to colder weather can make a difference.

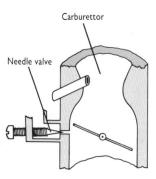

Diagram 11.7 *Idle speed adjustment.*

The way to get a leaner mix at the low-speed needle is to rotate the valve clockwise, and do the opposite to enrich the mixture. First, stop the motor when it is at normal running temperature. Take off the cover, and use a screwdriver to turn the needle valve clockwise until it seats. Do this gently, because it is a delicate mechanism. After you have felt it seating, turn it back one and a quarter turns and then start the motor again and run it up. Drop it back to normal idling speed, and adjust the valve in either direction until you get the level of low-speed running that you consider best. Once you have done this, you can stop the motor and replace the cover, and that setting should hold for quite a considerable time.

IMMERSED ENGINE

Despite the utmost care, chains holding motors for instance, and all the precautions one can think of, outboards do sometimes fall overboard. More often, outboards clamped to the pushpits of ocean wanderers get soaked by following seas and become thoroughly wet.

In the first case, the motor must be recovered as quickly as possible and serviced within three hours. In the second case, the problem is more serious because proper service facilities may be hundreds of miles away. The highly machined engine parts, such as the crankshaft and con-rods and bearings, will become pitted and scored once they are taken out of the water and exposed to the air.

If you are unable to get the engine serviced within three hours, the thing to do is remove the motor cover, rinse the motor thoroughly in fresh water, then disconnect the spark plug leads and take the plugs out. Put the motor on its side, with the spark plug openings facing down, and use the starter cord to rotate the flywheel until all the water is worked out of the cylinders. This will be **at least** 25 rotations of the flywheel. If the flywheel sticks at all when you rotate it to get the water out, this indicates that there is a bent con-rod. In that case, under no circumstances should you start the motor, and you must get it serviced as soon as possible.

Next put the motor upright, remove the high-speed needle valve and drain the carburettor. Obviously, you must dry everything you possibly can, at the very least all those things that have been dismantled. After drying, spray them all with water-repellant spray like WD-40 and squirt small amounts into the cylinders.

Reassemble the motor, making sure that you have replaced the fuel (if the tank went overboard too). Use your normal method and try to start the motor and see whether it will start. If it will, run it for at least half an hour so that everything can dry out. If you are at home and you have a test tank (say a large drum of water), then run the engine in that with the test wheel on in place of the propeller. If it still will not start, check the plugs thoroughly, or put in new plugs.

If you haven't been able to start the motor, and you can't get it serviced, resubmerge the engine in fresh water. It's not so much the water that's damaging, although that's bad enough, as the mixture of air and water afterwards that causes trouble. Even though this is a drastic step, if you do not take it you will face expensive and extensive repairs. You still might if you resubmerge the motor, but the chances are less.

G A L L E Y
E Q U I P M E N T

The choice of cooking fuel on a boat, motor or sail, is yet another of boating's compromises. The really safe fuels don't deliver much heat, and those that deliver the cooking power can blow up your boat. The safest is the **alcohol burner** but it will hardly fry a steak let alone cook a turkey in the oven. And even alcohol burners can spill and cause very dangerous fires. So generally speaking, it doesn't rate very highly. The next step upwards is the **pressurised kerosene stove** which can be very efficient. But you will only get a two-burner stove available for frying or boiling, they can smell, and they are not at their most efficient when they have too much, or too little, fuel in the reservoir. The kerosene heater probably is halfway between safe and efficient, with one exception, which we shall see later in this section. The next level is **LPG** (liquid petroleum gas), or **butane** which cook as well as any shore gas cooker, have an oven as well as four top burners, and will grill beautifully. However, these gases are heavier than air and when a burner is left on, or the whole stove is not switched off when not in use, the spilling gas drops to the bottom of the boat bilges and waits until it makes a perfect 'bomb' mix with air, or petrol, or both and then will explode with the slightest provocation. The best development so far is compressed natural gas, or **CNG**, which is called **SAFGAS** in Australia and the US, which both have great reserves of natural gas. **CNG** is not widely available in Europe and Asia or the Pacific yet. It has all the efficiency of LPG or butane and it is lighter than air. This means that any that escapes will most likely be blown away by the natural air flow in the cabin. But don't take it that gas that escapes upwards doesn't have dangers too. Gas that's caught in a corner of the cabin, or behind a locker, can still be lethal. On one voyage I undertook I could not understand why I woke after every four hours off watch with a splitting headache. I don't usually get headaches. We finally realised that this boat's beautifully snug quarter (navigator's) berth, was trapping gas and that was causing the headaches.

Let's take the systems one by one, so that whatever you have, you can get it going again if it gives you trouble at sea.

Tools You Will Need

- Basic plumber's kit
- Plumber's tape
- Screwdrivers

- Set of Allen keys
- Files
- Sandpaper

Spares You Will Need

- Pricker
- Pressure valve

- Burner
- Washers

Alcohol Burner

Diagram 11.8 shows a typical burner. It is a simple mechanism, but like all mechanisms must be kept clean to work properly. Most alcohol stoves have a pricker system, so that if the fuel inlet nozzle becomes blocked the main control knob can be turned sharply anti-clockwise, which pushes the pricker through the aperture and cleans the inlet jet, and then it's turned back clockwise so that the flame keeps going. If it goes out, relight it. Not much goes wrong with these heaters, and as long as they are maintained properly they'll give good service for many years. Many alcohol systems increase their heat output by incorporating a pressure system. A simple pump pressurises the fuel inside the tank and it is fed under that pressure to the burner, where as it heats

Diagram 11.8 *A two burner alcohol stove.*

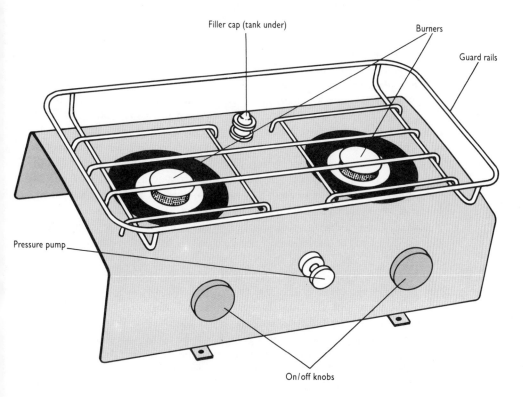

Filler cap (tank under)

Burners

Guard rails

Pressure pump

On/off knobs

it becomes a gas and provides a hotter flame. But these burners, and the fuel outlet nozzles which go through the centre, must be preheated to start the system going.

Raw methylated spirits (alcohol) is poured from a special container with a little bent tube coming from it, so that it can reach into the cup under the burner. Fuel is poured into the cup, lit and allowed to burn away. Practice will tell you how much you need to put in the cup. When you are experienced you will be able to open the gas knob at just the right moment for the fuel from the tank to ignite and give you a lovely cooking flame, but until then you'll have to let the spirits burn away, then open the gas jet and light it with another match.

The most common fault with these stoves happens when you are trying to pressurise it with the pump. The handle jams and can't be pushed through its full travel. This is because the check valve has stuck. The only cure is to replace it.

The second most common problem is lack of efficient preheating. This has many causes but the most usual is that rubbish such as spent match ends and spilled, dried-up food is in the preheater cup. They interfere with the preheating because they catch fire and take away from the alcohol in the cup. If they catch fire thoroughly, they add to the heat in the cup which is dangerous. If the heat becomes too high the fuel will catch while it is still liquid, it will run all over the place, and you will have an out-of-control fire on your hands being fed by a steady stream of fuel from the stove. The preheating cups should be kept scrupulously clean to avoid flare-ups.

As part of the general good husbandry of the vessel, any leakage that is noticed around the stove should immediately be fixed, so that it cannot cause a more serious problem. There may be holes in the tank, or leakages from the burner spindle or the burner connections, the connections may be loose, or the fittings may be damaged. As soon as you see any sign of leaking fuel, make sure that any fittings that are worn are replaced, everything that can be and should be is tightened and check whether the burner spindle or the burner connections need new packing.

Sometimes there is a yellowish, not very hot, flame on the burner and it flares. This is mostly because the fuel hasn't been preheated sufficiently, but it may also mean that more pressure is needed, in which case the pump should be used a few times. Otherwise, the nipple may be loose or dirty, or carbon may be baked on the burner, which comes down to a matter of cleanliness. If the burner won't shut off, then the needle is maladjusted, and the needle assembly should be closely looked at and, if necessary, a new needle put in, following the manufacturer's recommendations.

A weak flame will mean that insufficient fuel is getting through. The nipple may be blocked, or the cleaning needle may be blocked, and again you'll have to check that. Perhaps low pressure is the problem, in which case see whether you can get more by pumping. If you can't, very often putting more fuel in the tank, even if it is not empty, will do the trick. Whatever the manufacturers might say, these burners work best when the tank is between a third and two-thirds full.

If, after refilling, you still don't get enough pressure, you must be losing air somewhere in the system. Check the seals, and the gasket on the screwtop at the filler, and the fuel lines and its joins. Tighten everything up and, almost certainly, the flame will come back to full strength.

KEROSENE
PRESSURE STOVES

The Swedish company Primus so dominated the market for this type of stove that for decades they were known as 'Primuses'. They work on the same principle as the alcohol stove, but use kerosene which burns with a hotter flame under pressure. When used often, these systems need little maintenance and the same troubleshooting steps that apply to the alcohol burner apply to kerosene. The fuel is smelly, although some brands nowadays have overcome that problem. Both systems have the advantage that their fuels are readily available in some of the less developed parts of the world which is where the cruising sailor usually wants to be.

BOTTLED
GAS SYSTEMS

We have discussed the relative safety aspects of LPG and CNG and, to my mind, CNG wins hands down. The only drawback is that the gas is not as widely available as LPG and they use different fittings because they burn at different heats (CNG is hotter). The systems can be converted, but it is a job for a tradesman. The technician who comes up with a system which can be adapted for either gas, by a sailor, at sea, will make a lot of sales.

Other advantages of the gas systems are that they require little maintenance and they store considerable amounts of fuel in one pressurised tank. A vessel on a long voyage can use large tanks and can carry several replacements. They can be changed over easily, using at most a shifting spanner (wrench) of suitable size.

Gas bottles should be stored in separate, vented compartments, preferably on deck, where the natural flow of air will dispose of any leak. The only real enemy of these systems is vibration, so that it's prudent to paint a soap and water mixture around all the joints every now and then to see if any bubbles indicate that gas is escaping. It goes without saying that you don't search for a gas leak with a match. But if you do find a leak, you are supposed to find a gasfitter to make it good. It is illegal to do it yourself.

With these stoves one of the major hazards is that, because they need so little maintenance and because the fuel supply is kept away from the stove itself, they're not very often cleaned. The top may certainly be cleaned, and the oven less often so, but over only a few months there will be a build-up of spattered fat, since the flames from these burners are quite hot enough to fry steaks and other fatty foods, and so build up quite a thick skin on the hull or fittings around the stove. If this is the case, and a fire breaks out, it can take hold through the fat catching, turning a small danger into a life-threatening hazard.

One final word on gas and safety. The system must make provision for the gas to be turned off at a position close to the stove itself, as well as the standard position at the gas bottle. In most countries it is required to have a large permanent sign beside the appliance saying: 'Remember. Turn off gas at bottle.' It's a good idea to train the crew so that the person who has finished using the gas appliance calls up to the people on deck for the gas to be turned off at the bottle.

P U M P S

Tools You Will Need

- Plumber's wrenches
- Shifting spanners (wrenches)
- Electrical screwdrivers
- Plumber's tape

Spares You Will Need

- Washers of all sizes
- Impellers
- Diaphragms
- Manufacturer's spare kit
- Universal clips

Diagrams 11.9–11.10 show the types of pump found on most sailing yachts and motor boats. Quite small boats nowadays have pressurised on-demand water systems. They are quite simple. An electric motor pressurises the system so that if a tap is opened water flows through it until the tap is closed and pressure is built up again. These can include hot water systems as well as cold, and can also incorporate a flushing system for the head or heads. It's not very often that the on-board maintenance man can do much with an electric motor that fails on a pumping system, unless he has a spare. If he does have a spare, he has only to note which wires go where before he removes the old one, and then reconnect exactly as before. If he does not have a spare electric motor, he must either have a hand pump in the line as a fail-safe, or must put one there. Otherwise he will be carrying water from the tank as if it were a well.

Quite often with pressure systems the pump will not come on when a tap is opened, which is very irritating, and denotes a serious fault. It is not one which can be fixed at sea, but luckily that doesn't matter. The fault is that the switch's sensing device, which should turn it on, has failed. But the pump itself operates quite satisfactorily. Isolate the pump's switch and bring the wires of the circuit to the pump near to the sink that is most used. You probably will have to use quite a bit of wire for this extension. Tape the wires so that they are held firmly in position, but when moved deliberately can touch each other. Then bare the ends. When you want water you simply bring the bare ends together, the circuit closes, and the pump pumps.

In the same way that leaks from the outside of the boat into the boat are the last thing a skipper wants, so leaks in the water system inside the boat

Diagram 11.9 *A typical impeller pump with the impeller itself highlighted.*

Impeller

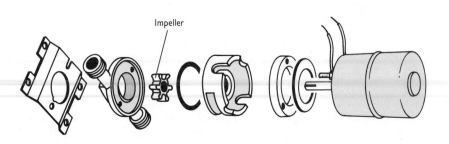

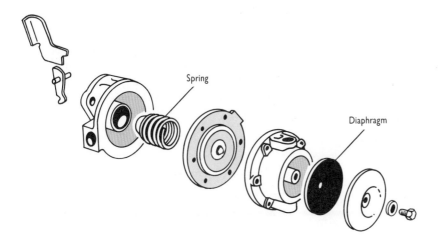

Diagram 11.10 *Diaphragm type water pump.*

Spring

Diaphragm

are bad news. Boats carry a limited amount of water, and even when the proper amount has been stored before departure there's not much margin for error, so any leak, however small, must be stopped. For this reason it is imperative to have on board enough spare washers of the right dimensions to be able to stop a leak in a tap anywhere. The chapter on safety, page 171, explains that water tanks should be split into at least two sections, which can be individually sealed so that if a bad leak develops and can't be stopped, at least it can be isolated and some of the water saved. For really long voyages, I believe there should be at least two main tanks, each of which can be split into two and isolated if necessary. There should also be a rubber emergency tank, rubber because it can be stowed almost anywhere, as it will follow the shape of the hull in out of the way places. This should be used only in emergency. It will most likely taste vile when used, but it's a small price to pay for being safe. It's much the same as drinking car radiator water in the desert, it tastes rotten while it is saving your life. In any case, water conditioning tablets added to the emergency supply when it is needed go a long way towards making the water potable.

F A U L T   F I N D I N G —
P R E S S U R I S E D   S Y S T E M S

The first thing that will make you realise there is something wrong with your system is when little or no water comes through a tap when it is opened. If there is no flow, the fault probably lies with the electrics, but it may be that there is a leak. Check first that there is a flow somewhere even if it is not reaching the outlets. If you discover a leak fix it quickly. When the leak starts it will be under pressure, and you could lose a lot of water, apart from a considerable amount sloshing around in the boat. The leak will slow once the pressure equalises. If there is water in the tank, check the fuse or circuit breaker. If the circuit is broken, use the checking systems listed on page 60 and isolate and correct the fault before installing your spare motor. It is quite pointless to replace a bad motor with a good one and have it, too, burn out because the underlying failure hasn't been overcome. If there appears to be nothing wrong, use the trick above—isolate the pump's sensor or switch. If the tap spits and rattles, there may be some restriction somewhere in the plumbing, or the vents or filters may be blocked. A common fault is that the little wire-mesh screens that aerate the water flow are clogged. I'm not sure that these screens have a place on a boat. They seem to give nothing but trouble in return for a very small benefit.

FAULT FINDING — NON-PRESSURISED SYSTEMS

These are the most common installations on sailing boats. They may still have an electric pump to push the water around, but they are much simpler to check in case of a fault. If the pump isn't priming and there is therefore no water at the tap, use the same checks as for the pressurised system. Check whether there's enough water in the tank, whether there are any kinks in the lines, whether vents are blocked or whether the hoses are leaking. If they are leaking, tighten up all the connections and/or replace any faulty sections of pipe. If the pump still won't prime, try doing it by hand, which is possible with some types. If it still won't work, check out the fuse or circuit breaker and the electrical connections. Last, take the pump apart and see whether the diaphragm is holed or worn, or, if it is a pump with an impeller, see if the impeller is broken. You should have spares, whichever part your pump uses. If you still cannot get the pump to work, you have a fault which needs to be rectified on land and you will have to resort to the emergency hand pump you should have somewhere in the line.

BILGE PUMP

The best bilge pump in the world is two frightened sailors with a bucket, but, luckily, one can usually make use of more conventional pumps. It seems to me only a little while ago that bilge pumps were enormous wooden handles jutting from a brass box as big as my head, which took more strength than a youth had to move, let alone effectively pump. They leaked, they were green with corrosion, they were inefficient, and they blocked all the time. Now, throughout the world, there are extremely efficient pumps, such as Whale, Henderson and Guzzler, which can throw great amounts of water with relatively little effort and which, being almost entirely made of plastic, have few corrosion problems. Actually, the part most likely to corrode is the universal clip (clamp) which holds the rubber diaphragm on to its mounting. It is in open view and can be changed when it is clear it is on its last legs. For those internal parts that can corrode, the manufacturers sell replacement kits. If you are going on an extended cruise you should carry one kit, at least, for each pump.

On the matter of pump numbers, you should have at least two, one of which can be operated from the cockpit. This may seem elementary in those countries where a cockpit pump is required, but there are many countries in the world which do not demand it. The value of a deck pump is clear when you imagine trying to pump out a boat where the only operating pump is under water!

These modern pumps, like the old-fashioned monsters, can block, but they are so easy to dismantle that it does not take long to find the problem and remove it. But prevention is very much better than cure in the matter of bilge pumps. The limber holes through the floors, which allow water to run from either end of the boat and collect at the deepest point, should be checked immediately water collects anywhere except where it is meant to. Obviously the suction end of the main bilge pump should be at this deepest point, and there should be a strum box (strainer) or filter to keep out any debris which might block the pump.

It is increasingly the fashion to have a large main outlet into which flow drain pipes from the sink, the shower, any handbasins, and the bilge pumps and engine water cooling outlet. They come together in a kind of Christmas tree and all flow out through a single skin (through hull) fitting, which simplifies the isolation of faults and reduces the risk of leaks through skin (through hull) fittings.

It is good to have the handle of each pump attached to a nearby fixed strongpoint, as is required in major ocean racing events, so that it is readily found.

Always remember, in an emergency, that the engine can be converted to a far more efficient pump than manual ones by closing off the cooling water inlet skin (through hull) fitting, detaching the pipe, and putting its open end into the water in the bilge (see diagram 11.11). But let's hope you never have to do that.

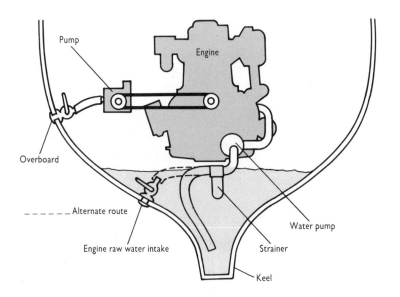

Diagram 11.11 *The conversion of an engine into a pump in an emergency.*

REFRIGERATION

A eutectic or holding plate is the most common type of refrigeration plate on most vessels, although some of the larger ones work on 240 volts and therefore have virtually standard household refrigeration. The eutectic plate contains chemicals and water through which runs a copper pipe containing the refrigerant. A compressor driven by the auxiliary engine compresses and therefore cools the refrigerant gas, which is pumped through the plate, turning the mixture in it to ice. The ice box comes down in temperature as the ice begins to melt, on the principle that it takes energy to melt the ice, for example it takes 144 British Thermal Units to change a pound of ice into a pound of water. It is this need for heat that produces the refrigeration, because the insulation of the box forces the plate to take the heat from the box to make the ice melt. As the box gets colder the ice melts more slowly and the box gets still colder. In the end a state of balance is reached between the insulation and the melting ice, and the ice box is at its lowest temperature. From then on the box warms up until the engine needs to be run again to cool it down.

The only difference between 'household' refrigeration and a eutectic plate is that there are no chemicals in the ice box. The refrigerant passes through coils of tubes in the cabinet and the heat caused by the cooling of the cabinet is radiated from a web of pipes on the back of the cabinet. Most of the rules for troubleshooting apply to both systems.

TOOLS YOU WILL NEED

- Trouble light
- Ohmmeter
- Voltmeter
- Two small electrical screwdrivers, one a Phillips head
- Small shifting spanner
- Plumber's sealing tape
- Electrical tape
- Pliers
- Insulation strippers
- Set of Allen keys
- Soap (for leak testing)
- Pressure gauges
- Vacuum pump

SPARES YOU WILL NEED

- Filter/driers
- Capillary tube
- Compressor
- Copper piping to match installation
- Electronic Unit
- Thermostat

INSTALLATION OF PLANT

The plate type of refrigerator is extremely simple and when properly installed very effective. But the key words are properly installed. The aim is maximum comfort for minimum inconvenience, that is, the shortest possible engine hours for the maximum possible cooling. Obviously, the cruising power boat sailor has less objection to the engine running to provide refrigeration than a person who would rather sail, a quiet pastime. There has to be a compromise reached, and noise is only one of the factors to be taken into account. Another major

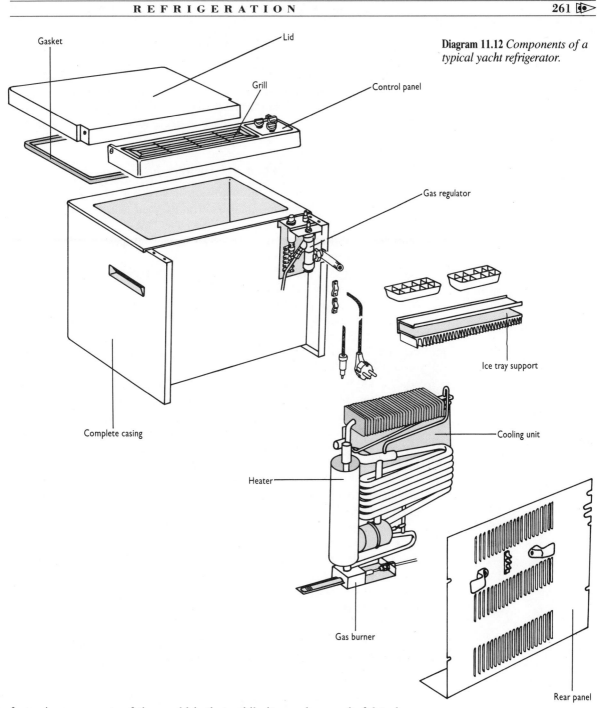

Gasket

Lid

Grill

Control panel

Diagram 11.12 *Components of a typical yacht refrigerator.*

Gas regulator

Ice tray support

Complete casing

Cooling unit

Heater

Gas burner

Rear panel

factor in many parts of the world is that, while it may be wonderful to have lumps of ice to put in the evening's cocktails, it is not so nice if everybody has been cooked all day with the heat given off by the engine when cooling the refrigerator.

One of the most effective refrigeration systems I have ever seen is on a not-so-young Australian vessel that has covered a lot of ocean miles. The plate refrigerator is a fairly standard top-opening device driven by a compressor, but above it is a small day locker, also cooled. What is wanted for the day is taken out and put into the day locker. The obvious saving is that the main refrigerator is opened far less often, even if something has been forgotten, with a consequent saving in engine time.

Another system which is very effective is to have two plates, one each side of the ice box. The resultant cooling capacity is so great that, provided the box is cooled down when empty and then loaded with the perishables, a mere 10 minutes a day will keep it cold enough to freeze foods solid if you want.

TROUBLESHOOTING

When you have no cooling and you want to find out why, first check the two pipes which run from the compressor to the plate. These will most likely be accessible in the box itself, near to the plate. One should be cold and the other hot. If this is not so the refrigerator cannot refrigerate. If it is so, and the contents of the box are not cold, it may be that the refrigerator is overloaded, something has damaged the insulation, or the box was not made cold by cooling while empty and before loading up.

If the refrigerant pipe is not cold, and the refrigerant therefore not running into the plate, suspect loss of gas. Nearly every fault in refrigeration is caused by loss of gas, and this applies to all forms of refrigeration. The following description of how to check and, if necessary, restore gas pressure to the system comes with a strong warning.

All connections in commercial refrigeration units have been factory tested before being sent out, so if any components are broken or fractured or loose, it is likely to have happened during transportation or installation, or through damage when the boat is sailing. Any gas installation or repairs done on board are required by government regulation in many parts of the world to be done by a certified mechanic, who has to provide you with a document that certifies that the regulations have been followed in making the repair or installing the appliance. Your insurance company would certainly be interested in the history of repairs in case of any claim you make.

At sea, a different set of imperatives will go through a skipper's mind when there is no refrigeration or cooking flame. Some of those may not be to the liking of either the government or the skipper's insurer, but it won't change his attitude. The refrigerator may be not working because when sailing through a patch of bad weather, the boat has fallen off some waves, and the piping has started and come loose. Or it may be that the electrics have come adrift, as is so often the case. If the same happens to you, you will have to investigate to see which is the fault, the gas or the electricity. Because regassing is such a major job it is more practical to start by checking the electrics.

ELECTRICAL CHECKS

First, do the simple checks. Look along the whole circuit for loose or wobbly wires, crossed wires, or plain disconnected or broken ones. Some skippers may have an ohmmeter and/or a voltmeter, and if they know how to use them they can be very effective.

Check the fuses or circuit breakers, there may have been some surge that overloaded the circuit temporarily. Put in a new fuse if needed (make sure it is the right amperage). If the fuse blows again, check the polarity of the battery. If that is functioning check the circuit with a trouble light.

Trouble Light

An indispensable test system on a boat is the simple twin circuit trouble light, as shown in diagram 3.5, which is powered by torch batteries and with a two-way switch to convert from one circuit to the other.

To check the refrigerator circuit, isolate it from the rest of the ship's systems and see whether there is a glow when the tester is connected across the positive terminal of the battery and the wire leading to the plate when on the out circuit. If there is a glow you have a short circuit, which you'll have to track down.

If the compressor seems abnormally hot, there may be problems with it. Put the trouble light across the compressor itself. If the trouble light does not glow, there is a problem with its circuit. This is a major problem, because the pressure on space in boats may have persuaded the skipper not to have brought a spare compressor, and generally a sea-going repair is impossible. Whether to carry a spare compressor would have been decided before the boat left port, but for something as important as keeping your food edible and safe, there is a very good argument for having a spare compressor.

Electricity Supply

If the circuit checks out as being in good order, but the compressor cuts out after only a short time, the quality of the electricity from the house battery system may be the cause. The electronic unit which controls every refrigerator will not work properly below a specified level, usually about 11 volts. If the batteries have been allowed to get too low, or are faulty, the voltage will drop below the required level and the electronic unit will cut out. This again shows the need to keep batteries in tip-top order, because if this fault isn't rectified the unit will become damaged and will have to be replaced.

If the compressor is running for a short cycle and the battery is OK, another possibility is that the capillary tube has become blocked, or the filter/drier is congested, causing the unit to overload and cut out. The method of dealing with this fault is not electrical, and is listed on page 265.

Thermostat

A faulty thermostat can cause the refrigerator to overfreeze, or not to freeze enough. It will be obvious which problem you have if the unit is covered with a lovely white frost, but more difficult to determine if it is not letting the unit get cold enough, as other faults can cause this symptom. First check that the setting is correct. If the thermostat is functioning properly but turned too high or low the ice box will follow its 'instructions'. Turn it anti-clockwise for a warmer ice box, and vice versa. If the unit still does not cut out, and the box ices up, test for an electrical fault in the thermostat. Short out the terminals and if the unit still runs the thermostat has an open circuit and must be replaced.

A less likely fault, but one which does occur, is that incorrect wires were used in installation. On page 264 is a table showing the size of wire needed to carry electricity various distances from the battery to the electronic unit without causing any voltage drop. We have already shown that if the voltage drops below a specified level the electronic unit will cut out and may be damaged.

VOLTAGE DROP WITH DISTANCE		
FLEXIBLE WIRING METRIC (CROSS-SECTION MM²)	**CURRENT RATING DC** (AMP)	**VOLT DROP AMP/METER** (ʍV)
.5	3	85
.75	6	55
1.0	10	45
1.5	15	30
2.5	20	19
4.0	25	10
SINGLE CORE CABLES (CROSS-SECTION MM²)	**CURRENT RATING DC** (AMP)	**VOLT DROP AMP/METER** (ʍV)
1.0	10	40
1.5	13	25
2.5	18	15
4.0	24	10

If, despite the most thorough checks, the fault does not appear to be electrical, the mechanical side of the system will have to be investigated, usually by a certified technician. What he would do would be to pressurise the system and use a bubbly solution of soap and water to test for leaks. Having found the leak he would repair it and retest with the soapy solution. He would also put in a new filter/drier and recharge the system with gas.

This is a major job. To regas a system is for qualified mechanics only. One reason for this is government regulations insist on it, another is that refrigerators use only a small amount of gas, and overcharging can cause serious damage to the compressor. The third is that a high vacuum pump and gauges are needed to evacuate the system before it is regassed.

REGASSING PROCEDURE

The appropriate gauges are attached to the inlet and outlet pipes so that the state of vacuum or pressure can be read. The first step in regassing is to make sure there are no leaks in the system. This is achieved by pumping the lines out for at least 30 minutes to get a full vacuum. Gas is then allowed back in the system at 105 kPa (15 lbf per sq in), using the nominated gas. The unit is then started, and pressure reduced to zero when the unit is stopped again. If the pressure then equalises the capillary tube is not blocked. After equalisation has taken place let the gas out of the system, apply the vacuum pump, and pump again until a full vacuum is achieved. Next close the vacuum unit down and open the gas bottle fully, making sure the bottle is upright so that no liquid can get into the pipes. After five minutes close the gas bottle and turn the unit on. The gas pressure on the gauges will continue to drop towards zero, so it must be maintained by letting in more gas at around 28 to 35 kPa (4 to 5 lbf per sq in) pressure.

Frost Line on Pipes

The amount of gas let into the system is adjusted according to the position of the frost line on the refrigerant tubing where it leaves the evaporator. There should be no frost line on the suction line back to the compressor, as that would indicate there is too much gas in the system. It is most important when gas is released that no vacuum is showing on the gauge.

Filter and Capillary Tube

It may be that during the check on the gas pressure in the system as described above, the pressure did not equalise after repressuring and stopping. This would indicate that the capillary is blocked and it should therefore be blown clear or replaced. The gauges are the only way to tell whether equalisation has taken place. After the tube has been blown and a new filter/drier fitted the system must be recharged.

Compressor

If the compressor is not pumping, and you don't have a spare, you have a real problem because it is rare for the head gasket or valves to be faulty on a compressor. There are a couple of checks you can perform. First try the drive belt. Even a slight loss of tension in the drive will destroy its efficiency. If the belt seems loose, tighten it so that it pushes in about a half to a quarter of an inch under the pressure of one finger. Next, see whether the compressor's own circuit is shorting, as described on page 263 under the heading Trouble Light. Once again, you want to hope there is nothing wrong, as it is almost certain you will not be able to fix it at sea, unless you are an electrical expert.

BOAT CHECKLISTS

HULL CHECKLIST

- Are the through hull fittings sound, easily accessible, fitted with seacocks, and with plugs near them?
- Are there spare hose clips (clamps) of the right size for every hose that goes to a skin (throughhull) fitting?
- Are there tools on board to adjust the stern gland (stripping box), or any rudder fitting?

SAILS CHECKLIST

- Are there storm sails, in good condition, and with the appropriate sheets? Will the slides fit into the track?
- Are all the reefing lines led, and has their operation been checked at sea?
- Are the sail bag zippers free to run?
- Are the sail bags clearly marked with relevant sail number?
- Are the tacks, heads, and clews of sails marked?
- Are the hanks, if they are used, free operating and recently oiled?
- Are the bolt-rope ends that go into a Gemini, or similar tracked forestay, tight, not frayed?
- Are all the sheets aboard which are needed—for **all** the sails?
- Is the sail repair kit aboard?

DECK CHECKLIST

- Are lines (jack stays) rigged the full length of the vessel, on each side, to clip harnesses to?
- If there is a mechanical or electrical anchor winch, does it work? Even if it does, can the anchor be handled without it?
- Are there at least two anchors of the right size for the vessel?

- Are the correct lines/chains rigged? (Sizes are on page 96.)
- Is the chain securely connected to the anchor?
- Is the inboard end of the warp (anchor line) attached to the vessel?
- Is there a secure cover for the hawsepipe?
- Can the warp (anchor line) be slipped easily?
- Is there a suitable position, preferably below, to secure the anchors at sea?
- Is there a large cleat, or Samson post? If there is, will the anchor warp (line) fit over it?
- Is there a Scotsman (chafing gear)—a piece of rubber or plastic hose, split along its length—which can take chafe if the vessel is anchored for long?
- Are there storm covers for any large windows?
- If the boat rolls through 90 degrees, will the forward hatch be above water?
- Are there slides, or storm boards, for the companionway hatch which can be removed from inside or outside the boat, but are secured against falling out if the boat capsizes?
- Are the drainage holes in the cockpit big enough to drain the cockpit quickly if it is filled with water?
- Are the lifelines well mounted, with backing plates, and will they take the weight of a big man thrown violently against them?
- Are the lifelines high enough (a metre/two feet six inches) and are there two of them?
- Is there a bilge pump which can be used from the cockpit?
- Test any hydraulic systems.
- Check that spare hydraulic fuel is on board if needed.
- Have one anchor at ready in bow until clear of port.

INTERNAL CHECKLIST

- Are there properly tapered softwood plugs next to each skin (through hull) fitting in case the fitting carries away?
- Is there a medical kit on board?
- Can all doors, lockers be shut so they cannot open in a gale?
- Are the leecloths in good condition? (They should be strong enough for the crew to feel safe using them.)
- Are there at least two stout buckets, with strong lanyards attached?
- Is there a freshwater hose which can be adapted to different sizes of outlet?
- Are there deck cleaning materials—scrubbing brush, deck soap, mop etc.?
- Is there a safety belt for the navigator, and another for the cook, so that they can carry on with their work in rough conditions?
- Are all supplies stowed and below decks secured for sea?
- Are the water tanks full? Check that each section of a compartmented system is full.
- Is there sufficient cooking fuel? Is there any emergency system?

NAVIGATION CHECKLIST

- Has the compass been swung (adjusted)?
- If necessary, is there a deviation chart for the boat? (Method on page 137.)
- Is there an accurate hand-bearing compass on board?
- Is there a second compass, not a hand-bearing compass?

- Are all the charts, and plans, required for the voyage on board and stowed in a dry, accessible place?
- Are there enough pencils, erasers and navigation tools (sextant etc.)?
- Is there a barometer? (For a long voyage there should be.)
- Are the tide tables, tidal atlas, star charts, *Nautical Almanac*, sight reduction tables, Pilots, International Rules for the Prevention of Collisions at Sea, list of signals, ship station radio manual, *Ship Captain's Medical Guide* and any other required books on board?
- Are the Portland Plotter, protractor, parallel rules, sextant, hand-held programmable calculator, dividers, pencils, erasers on board?
- Are the binoculars in good order?
- Is there a battery operated radio for checking the weather?
- Has long range weather forecast been obtained?
- Has barometer reading been taken?
- Has the relevant sea safety authority been notified of the voyage?
- Has log been calibrated and reading taken as voyage commences?
- Is ship's log on board?
- Is satellite navigator switched on and initialised?

E N G I N E C H E C K L I S T

- Is there a loop in the exhaust system to prevent water flowing into the boat through it?
- Are the engine manuals on board?
- Is there some way to record the engine hours? (An instrument is best, but a note can be kept in the log, although this is less reliable.)
- Is there a separate bilge compartment under the engine, and if so, does it have its own drip tray?
- Is there sufficient spare engine oil, of the correct type, available for the voyage? For an extended cruise, several complete changes may be needed.
- Are the required spares and tools (see lists on pages 225, 232 and 247) aboard?
- Is the fuel tank full?
- Is there fuel for any auxiliary (generator, outboard etc.)?
- Is there spare packing for the stern gland (stripping box) and rudder stock?
- Run engine and check temperature, oil pressure and temperature. Are batteries charging?
- Test engine controls.
- Are engine hours noted?

S A F E T Y C H E C K L I S T

- Are lines (jack stays) rigged the full length of the vessel, on each side, to clip harnesses to?
- Are the navigation lights in working order?
- Are there sufficient strong points for the crew to clip to, particularly when entering or leaving the accommodation?
- Is there a heaving line within reach of the helmsman?
- Are there the regulation two horseshoe liferings with lights, dan (tall) buoy and stain (dye marker) attached, within reach of the helmsman?

- Are the bilges clean, limber holes unblocked, and strum boxes (strainers) on pump hoses clear?
- Are the bilge pump handles retained by a lanyard so that they cannot be lost?
- Is the steering mechanism sound and free of corrosion?
- Is there a spare set of pre-cut cables on board (wheel steering)?
- Is there an emergency steering mechanism, and if so, where is it stowed?
- Is the liferaft of sufficient capacity to carry the crew you propose for this voyage?
- Are there sufficient lifejackets for all on board? (Children need their own sizes.)
- Is there a safety harness for every crew member of a yacht? (Only two are required for a motor boat, but some jobs may take more than two people, so a couple of extras would be sensible.)
- Is the regulation number of flares on board and are they stowed both where they are handy, and where they are safe? (Near the gas bottle is a poor idea, for instance.)
- Is there a radar reflector, and can it be rigged in a hurry? It should be up every night in any case, and in poor visibility.
- Are there boltcutters on board, strong enough to cut the thickest stay on the vessel with one bite?
- Are there several batteries for flash lights?
- Are the batteries secure against coming adrift?
- Is there a pressure-powered fog horn on board, and plenty of reserve pressure cans?
- Is there a lead line? (Yachts don't need one that is too cumbersome, and only need the depth marked about every three metres (10 feet).)
- Check that there is a satisfactory light for the compass at night.
- Has an emergency rudder (not tiller) been made up of a spinnaker pole, two U-bolts and nuts and a locker cover (see page 171)?
- Are emergency navigation lights tested and stowed within easy reach of deck crew?

ELECTRICAL CHECKLIST

- Are batteries the sealed type which do not need topping with distilled water (preferred)?
- If not, can they be reached so that the level of water can be checked?
- Are the terminals free of corrosion, as tight as they can be, and lightly greased?
- Is there a hydrometer on board, to check the batteries?
- Is there a wiring diagram for the boat, or failing that, are the circuits marked?

BERTHING/UNBERTHING CHECKLIST

- Are there enough fenders, of the right size, handy and in good condition?
- Is there a plank for tying alongside at unfriendly berths?
- Are there sufficient mooring lines? Remember, you can need six to secure you to a berth, and then more if someone comes alongside you outside. In extreme cases, as in a pen (slip) where there is a heavy surge, you can need 10 or more lines.
- Is there a towline on board, or two good lines that could be joined for the purpose?

TOOLS AND SPARE PARTS

General Tools

- Boltcutters
- Bench vice
- Two power drills, one that can be run from the boat's electrical system or a 240V generator, and a rechargeable battery-powered model
- One hand drill
- Two sets of drill bits
- Counter-sink and drills for steel 12 mm (½ inch) size and shank to fit hand drill, to be used for wood or soft metal
- Set of Allen keys
- Set of taps for self-tapping screws
- Set of dies
- Knife with multi-purpose blades
- Small wood saw
- Two hacksaws with 12 extra blades
- Screwdriver set (hard plastic handle) with a range of accessories
- Phillips head screwdriver set
- Rivetting tool and various rivets
- Flexible shaft screwdriver, with socket for various heads
- Socket set 6–19 mm (¼–¾ inch)
- Chisel set, including cold chisel
- Pliers (single joint, side-cutting type)
- Punch
- Claw hammer
- Tack hammer
- Metre rule (extending tape type which shows millimetres and inches)
- Adjustable spanner to open up to four centimetres (1½ inches)
- Large adjustable spanners (wrenches)
- Set of open ended spanners (wrenches)
- Set of ring spanners (wrenches)
- Pair of multi-grips
- Grease gun
- Wire brushes

Rigging And Sail Repair Tools

- Swaging tool and various swages
- Wire cutters
- Rigging knife
- Marlinspike
- Hollow fids for splicing
- Serving wire
- Serving mallet
- Splicing vice
- Wire cutters for largest size of rigging
- Sailmaker's palm
- Needles in various sizes
- Grommet tool
- Longnose pliers
- Pliers to hold cloth

Sail Repair Spares

- Bosun's chair
- Beeswax
- Hot knife
- Sailcloth in a variety of weights
- Dacron sail twine, plain and waxed
- Sail hanks and slugs
- Ripstop
- Leather
- Thread (various sizes)
- Rolls of marlin
- Two rigging screws (turnbuckles)
- Spare halyard
- Coil of wire
- Lashing
- Shock cord (various sizes)
- Rope for halyards and sheets
- Wire, the length of the longest stay
- Blocks
- Shackles (more than you think you'll need)
- Cotter and clevis pins
- Monel seizing wire
- Plastic adhesive tape
- Winch repair kit and grease, pawls and springs

ELECTRICAL AND PLUMBING TOOLS

- Tube cutter
- Pipe wrenches
- Wirecutters
- Insulation stripper
- Crimping tool
- Soldering iron
- Test meter and light
- Hydrometer

ELECTRICAL AND PLUMBING SPARES

- Fuses
- Flashlight batteries
- Batteries for instruments
- Bulbs (globes), especially for compass and instrument dials
- Solder
- Copper hose joiners
- Hoses and clamps
- Diaphragms for bilge pumps
- Insulation tape
- Connectors
- Light oil
- Spray (WD-40)
- Nylon jointing tape
- Gasket material
- Plastic hoses
- Plumber's tape
- Repair kit for heads
- Switches
- Navigation light globes

ENGINE AND MECHANICAL TOOLS

- Starting spray (ether)
- Oil can
- Hand pump for engine oil
- Set of engine tools
- Tappet, ignition, fuel line, carburettor wrenches
- Feeler gauge
- Bottle gas torch
- Vice grip pliers
- Slip joint pliers
- Files (rat-tail and flat)

ENGINE AND MECHANICAL SPARES FOR PETROL (GASOLINE) ENGINE

- Gasket set
- Points
- Condenser
- Coil
- Distributor cap
- Ignition leads
- Plugs
- Water pump
- Belts
- Filters
- Engine oil
- Hydraulic fluid
- Transmission fluid
- Grease

ENGINE AND MECHANICAL SPARES FOR DIESEL ENGINE

- Filters
- Belts
- Injector(s)
- Longest needed high pressure pipe
- Water pump impellers
- Belts
- Engine oil
- Transmission fluid
- Hydraulic oil
- Grease

OUTBOARD SPARES

- Propeller
- Shear pins, split pins

MAINTENANCE EQUIPMENT

- Silicone sealant
- Penetrating oil
- Spare engine oil
- Timber in blocks and ply sheets
- Tubes of Locktight
- Tins of epoxy jointing compound
- Araldite (quicksetting and normal)
- Vaseline for battery terminals
- Oil stone
- Waterproof grease
- Packing for stern tube/rudder post
- Exhaust patches
- Six sheets each of various sandpapers, wet and dry

HULL REPAIR MATERIAL FOR FIBREGLASS

- Fibreglass mat
- Cloth
- Polyester resin
- Activator (catalyst)
- Expanded metal sheet
- Epoxy resin
- Epoxy resin putty

HULL REPAIR MATERIAL FOR WOOD

- Sheet plywood
- Sheet lead
- Fastenings
- Bedding
- Caulking compound

HULL REPAIR MATERIAL FOR METAL

- Quick-drying cement
- Epoxy
- Under-water epoxy
- Primer paint

THE LANGUAGE OF THE SEA

A

Aback. Behind. Of the sails, pressed against the mast when the wind is on the wrong, inefficient side. Deliberately sailing aback is useful in close quarters sailing, such as when leaving a jetty or mooring.

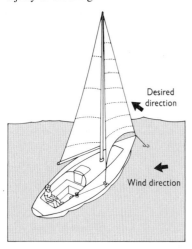

Diagram A2.1 *Holding a sail aback can turn the boat's head in a wanted direction when leaving a mooring.*

Abaft. Behind, towards the back.

Abaft the beam. More behind a vessel than in front of it. Bearing more than 90 degrees on either side from dead ahead.

Abeam. At 90 degrees to the vessel's direction or fore and aft line.

About. Having changed tacks, to have all sails full and drawing on the new tack.

Above. To pass or steer to windward of a mark or vessel.

Abreast. Similar to abeam, but usually applying to one or more other vessels travelling on the same course and with a relative bearing of approximately 90 degrees.

Accidental (Chinese) jibe (gybe). An involuntary jibe which occurs when the helmsman allows the wind to get under the mainsail when running either by carelessness or by a major wind shift to which he doesn't react in time. The result can be extremely dangerous, especially in heavy weather. The mainsail will slam across to the other side. If a preventer is attached it will hold the boom in and create severe heeling of the vessel. If the vang is applied the boom may break. In extreme cases the vessel may lie on its side in the water for many minutes before being brought back under control.

Aclinic line. The imaginary line where the compass needle does not dip due to the earth's magnetism.

Adjustment of compass. Compensating for a ship's magnetism by placing correcting magnets near the steering compass in such a way that the compass reads as though there were no error.

Admiralty anchor. An anchor which can be folded for easy stowage. The shank and arms do not move, but the stock moves up to right angles to the arms.

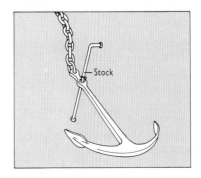

Diagram A2.2 *An admiralty pattern anchor.*

Admiralty hitch. See Marlinspike hitch.

Admiralty sweep. A large, cautious turn made to approach a gangway or to come alongside a vessel or jetty in a boat.

Aft. Towards the back of the boat, in the after part of it, for example the after cabin is the cabin in the stern of a boat.

Age of the tide. The interval between full moon or change of the moon and the highest high tide. In Australia, where there is no age of the tide the highest high tide occurs on the day of full moon or change of moon. In northern Europe the interval is between 1½ and 2½ days.

Agonic line. Lines on the earth's surface joining points where there is no magnetic variation.

Ahull. Lying almost beam-on to strong winds and being driven before them while under bare poles (without sails). The helm is lashed so as to point the boat into the wind, but it continually falls away because of the pressure of the wind. It is a technique for riding out storms.

All aback. With all sails filling from the opposite side from which they are trimmed.

All-round light. A light showing an unbroken light over an arc of the horizon of 360 degrees. An anchor light (riding light) is an all-round light.

Almanac (nautical). Annual publication of astronomical data for the use of navigators.

Altazimuth. Instrument for establishing the altitude and azimuth of stars and planets.

Alternating light. A light that shows different colours alternately.

Altitude. The angle a heavenly body makes with the horizon.

American whipping. As a normal whipping except that the ends are brought up at the centre and reef (square) knotted.

Amplitude. In navigation, the arc of the horizon between east and a body when it is rising, and west and a body when it is setting.

Diagram A2.3 *Amplitude showing the ascent and descent of a star.*

Anchor bed. Chocks which hold an anchor in place either in a locker or on deck.

Anchor bell. On large vessels a bell near the bows which is tolled at regular intervals during fog. The in-

terval denotes the kind of vessel that is at anchor.

Anchor buoy. A small buoy used to mark the position of an anchor. It is attached to the base (crown) of the anchor and can be used to recover the anchor if it has to be cast adrift, or to trip it if it has wedged itself.

Anchor light (riding light). An all-round white light, mandatory when anchored, which indicates that a vessel is anchored.

Anchor watch. When anchored in heavy weather, or where wind direction may change dangerously, it is prudent to mount an anchor watch of people who specifically check to see whether the anchor is dragging. They do this by taking bearings or transits of objects on shore.

Anemometer. Device of three or more cups on a spindle which measure the strength of the wind. Usually at the masthead of racing yachts.

Angle of heel. The number of degrees of list a vessel has. The first indication that a sailing vessel may need to reef is too great an angle of heel.

Annual variation. The amount by which variation changes up or down each year in a particular area. The annual increase or decrease is printed in the compass roses on each chart and may make a significant difference over a number of years.

Anticyclone. An area where the barometric pressure is high, usually indicating light, variable winds and fine weather.

Antitrade. Wind that blows in the opposite direction from trade wind in an area where trade wind would normally be expected to occur.

Apparent wind. The wind that results from the interaction of the true wind and the forward motion of the boat. When running at a speed of 8 knots with the wind blowing at 18 knots, the apparent wind speed would be 10 knots.

Arbour (Aust.), Hole cutter (U.S.). A collection of saws, usually with a drill bit in the centre, which will drill

holes of various sizes when attached to a power drill.

Arc of visibility. The sector(s) marked on a chart and showing where a light is visible from the sea.

Aries. The star which for purposes of navigation is taken to be stationary in the sky. While this is not strictly true, the star has moved considerably in the past 1000 years, it is sufficiently true to allow the movement of all other heavenly bodies to be taken as relative to Aries, which is the constant of celestial navigation.

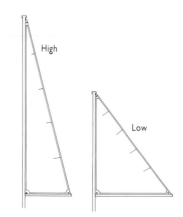

Diagram A2.4 *The aspect ratio of sails.*

Aspect ratio. The relationship between a sail's height and length along the foot. High aspect ratio means a sail that is tall and narrow, low aspect ratio is a short, squat sail. The phrase can also apply to centreboards and rudders.

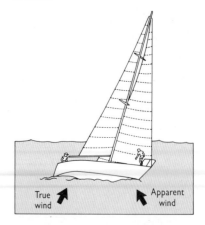

Diagram A2.5 *The boat's motion brings the true wind forward, making it the apparent wind.*

Astrolabe. A precursor of the sextant, an old navigational device for checking the angle of stars in the skies.

Aurora Australis. Southern lights, the display of shimmering ghostly lights caused by light refraction through clouds over ice.

Aurora Borealis. The northern hemisphere version of polar lights.

Azimuth (Zn). The bearing of a heavenly body from an observer's position.

Azimuth angle (Z). The angle a star makes to the northern or southern points of a meridian.

Azimuth circle. On a compass, a mirror and prism which enable bearings to be taken. These are fitted usually only to hand-bearing compasses.

Azimuth compass. An old-fashioned instrument for finding the bearing of a heavenly body.

B

Baby stay. An intermediate forestay which supports the leading edge of the mast. Often hydraulic on racing yachts, the baby stay can be used to flatten the mainsail as wind strengths increase.

Back splice. A crown knot is made in the end of a piece of line and the ends are tucked at least three times into the standing part of the line.

Backing a sail. A sail is backed when it is held out against the wind and fills in reverse on the windward side of the boat. It is a useful technique when leaving a mooring, when the wind is very light, or when trying to complete a tack when in irons, or when heaving to.

Backing and filling. Alternately letting the sails draw, then spilling wind so as to keep a vessel more or less on station until space is available, marking time. It has come to mean being indeterminate, indecisive.

Backspring. A line taken from well astern of the vessel to midships to prevent it from moving forward. Also known as the 'after' spring.

Backstay. Fixed wire standing rigging to support the mast in a fore and aft direction. On light modern racing masts further support is often needed and is provided by 'running' backstays or runners which are changed at each tack. Their adjustment is often critical to the tuning of the mast.

Backwind. The turbulent air flowing off a sail. This wind can affect either the mainsail of your own boat (when the backwind comes from your own headsail) or can interfere with the flow of air onto the sails of a following boat, when on the wind. One of the techniques of tactical sailing is to position your boat, on whatever point of sailing you may be, so that your backwind hits your opponent's sails, cutting their effectiveness.

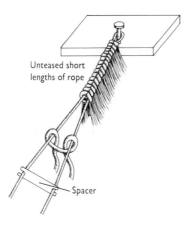
Unteased short
lengths of rope

Spacer

Diagram A2.6 *Baggywrinkle to reduce chafe.*

Baggywrinkle. 'Mops' of teased-out line, yarns etc. which are lashed around chafe spots such as spreaders to prevent wearing through the sails.

Balance (of the boat). The characteristic shown in the boat's behaviour when it has been tuned. A perfectly balanced boat, when not being steered, would try to remain on a perfectly straight course. A boat with weather helm would tend to edge up into the wind, a boat with lee helm would tend to fall away to leeward.

Balanced rudder. A rudder where the stock divides the blade so that the pressure on the forward part and the after part balances out. Such a rudder is easier to use than one where the stock is the leading edge, and they are more sensitive to steer.

Barge (to). At the start of a yacht race, to reach in to the windward end of the line with no rights over boats to leeward.

Barograph. An instrument with a circular drum and an inked needle which constantly records barometric pressure as a graph.

Barque. A multi-masted vessel with fore and aft sails on the after mast.

Barquentine. A multi-masted vessel with square sails only on the foremast.

Basic speed figure (BSF). A figure developed from a yacht's rating which is the theoretical time that yacht will take to sail one mile. It is used in distance handicapping, usually inshore, where the boat with the fastest BSF is put on scratch and other boats are given a time allowance corresponding to their BSF.

Batten-pockets. Recesses in a mainsail or sometimes jib which take the flat, flexible battens which hold the leech stiff.

Battens. Nowadays usually fibreglass, they were formerly of wood or cane. They fit into the long, narrow batten pockets on a mainsail or jib and are used to adjust the flow in a sail, if fully battened, or to hold the leech tight. If full length they will run from the luff to the leech. Some classes use foot battens in the jib to gain extra area.

Beacon. (1) A mark on the sides of a channel as an aid to navigation. In North America they are often called daybeacons, and if they have distinguishing topmarks they are called daymarks. They may have lights, and/or radar reflectors. (2) Radio signals emitted by shore stations which allow a ship to find her position by taking bearings of two or more.

Beam. (1) The widest part of a vessel. (2) A strong support, as for the deck in a timber boat. (3) A strong ray of light, as from a lighthouse. (4) The stock of an anchor. (5) The sides of the boat around its widest point, hence port beam and starboard beam.

Beam-ends. Excessively heeled, knocked down so that the vessel is almost flat in the water. Unable to sail efficiently.

Beam-on. The wind is beam-on if it is coming directly across either beam. Also, any object which can be sighted directly across either beam is described as being 'beam-on'.

Beam reach. Sailing with the wind on either beam—the fastest point of sailing unless the boat has broken its skin friction and is surfing.

Beam sea. A sea at right angles to the vessel's course.

Bear away or off (to). Steer away from the wind, come off the wind. The tiller is pulled towards the steerer, the wheel is pulled down in the direction wanted.

Bear down on (to). Approach from windward.

Bearing (to take a). Check the direction of a particular point from the boat or of the boat from the point. Bearings are given as true, magnetic, or relative. Sometimes, as with lead lights, bearings are given from seaward and to seaward, depending on whether you are entering or leaving port.

Bearing light. A light with one source above the other so that when they are in line an accurate bearing is available without using a compass.

Beat (a). A boat is on a beat when it is tacking into the wind. The whole distance it travels while doing this is called the beat. To sail as close to the wind as is efficiently possible, close hauled.

Beaufort Scale. A scale of wind speed, sea state, and sailing ability devised by a British admiral in the 18th century.

Becket. A bar across a block so that it may be shackled to a pad eye or similar fitting. An older meaning was a loop, or small eye on the end of a line.

Before the beam. Ahead of 90 degrees to the boat.

Belay (to). Secure a line to a cleat or pin.

Bell buoy. A buoy containing a bell, which sounds through the motion of the buoy in the seaway and so warns even when the buoy cannot be seen.

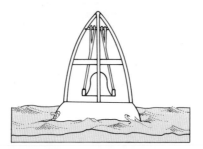

Diagram A2.7 *A typical bell buoy.*

Bend (to). Attach anything securely, as sails, or sheets. They are said to be bent on.

Bend. A knot used to join two lines, or tie a line to a fixed object, and which can be easily untied.

Bermudian rig. The modern rig of triangular foresail and mainsail.

Beta light. Small radioactive cell which glows, producing faint green light suitable for instruments, compass etc.

Bifurcation buoy. Buoy which indicates a preferred channel when more than one is available.

Bilge keel. In small yachts a vessel which has two small fin keels on her bilges instead of the deeper central keel which is more common. Bilge keel vessels have shallow draft and are able to run up on a beach, sitting on the twin keels.

Bioluminescence. Light emitted by living organisms, such as that often seen in tropical waters at night, particularly in the Great Barrier Reef when it is regenerating.

Bitt. Specially strong timbers for mooring or towing. Sometimes called a king post. Often found in pairs called bitts.

Blackwall hitch. A quick way of attaching a line to a hook.

Blanket (to). To position your boat so that its backwind interferes with

a competitor. If it happens to you, the term is that you have been blanketed.

Block. A nautical name for a pulley. Lines run through the blocks on rollers called sheaves. A block can be single purchase (one sheave), double purchase (two sheaves) and so on.

Block and tackle. Any arrangement of blocks which gives mechanical advantage, the most common on yachts being the system used to control the mainsheet.

Blooper. Offshore racing sail near the size of a spinnaker, but set on the opposite side and without a pole. It is tacked at the stem, outside the pulpit and not hoisted to the top of the mast. The sail is sheeted to the stern of the boat and trim is achieved by a crewman at the mast rapidly hoisting the halyard to clear the sail from the water.

Blue Peter. (1) The code flag 'P' in the International Code of Signals, which is a blue flag with a white rectangular centre and which indicates that a vessel is sailing within 24 hours. (2) In a yacht race, often used as an indicator of time, as the 5-minute gun.

Boat boom. On large vessels, a boom swung outboard to which the ship's boats are attached when not in use. A convenient way to tow a dinghy in a big following sea is to swing out a spinnaker pole, or the main boom, and attach the dinghy to the outboard end so that it floats parallel to the larger vessel.

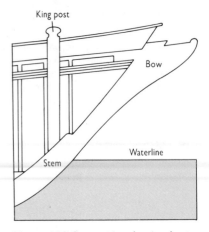

Diagram A2.8 *Cross section showing the bitt.*

Bobstay. The stay from the bowsprit to the bow just under the water to take the upward pull of the forestay.

Bobstay piece. A timber supporting the bowsprit at the stem.

Bold sheer, or strong sheer. A pronounced curve from the middle or stern of the boat to the bow.

Bollard. (1) A large solid column of metal to which vessels can moor in port. (2) The same when constructed on the deck of a ship. (3) A strong vertical timber on a yacht, as a bitt.

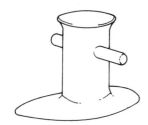

Diagram A2.9 *A bollard.*

Bollard eye. A large eye in the end of a hawser.

Bolt rope. The rope sewn into the leading edge of a sail. This rope slides along the groove in the mast, holding the sail firmly in place.

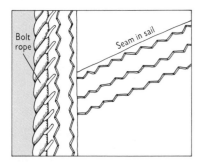

Diagram A2.10 *The boltrope is attached to the leading edge of a sail.*

Boom. A spar used to extend the foot of a sail.

Boom vang. A strong purchase or hydraulic ram to hold down the boom and control the twist in a racing yacht's mainsail.

Boomkin. A stern sprit or spar extending from the stern.

Booster. A large, double, lightweight headsail which projects equal shape

and area either side of the forestay and is good for running, with or without a main. Suitable for long distance running.

Boot top (U.K.), painted waterline (U.S.). The band of paint, usually of a different colour, between the anti-fouling paint on the bottom, and the topsides.

Bosun's chair. Originally a stave of wood and a rope sling for hoisting a man aloft. Now more likely to be of sailcloth with a strut in the seat and pockets on the side to take tools needed aloft. For bowmen on 12 metre yachts, a sort of nappy, permanently worn, to enable the crewman to be lifted to the outboard end of the spinnaker pole for some manoeuvres.

Bottle screw. A central female screw which accommodates two male screws, one each end, and which when tightened will tension or shorten rigging. Commonly used on yachts, they are locked in position by locknuts, but to be properly secure should still be wired or taped.

Bottom boards (U.K.). See Floor boards.

Bottom line. In large vessels, a chain permanently rigged underneath and from side to side to haul round a collision mat when required.

Boundary layer. The layer immediately next to the hull or a sail in which the water or air is affected by friction. The greater the friction the wider the boundary layer.

Bouse (bowse) (to). Haul down on a line, to tighten a halyard or line by pulling out sideways then taking in the slack.

Bow. (1) The leading edge of a vessel, its stem, the narrow pointed end. (2) Of a shackle, the rounded part opposite the jaws, or open end.

Bow (stem) fitting. Metal shaped to a particular boat's profile where the boat comes to a point, where the forestay is secured. There is usually a bolt through the bow fitting for the forestay to attach to. The fitting spreads the load.

Bow wave. The wave formed at the bow of the boat by its forward motion

and growing backwards on each side. Small vessels need to be wary of the bow wave of large, fast, commercial vessels.

Diagram A2.11 *The bow wave affects the amount of hull that is in the water and therefore the boat's speed.*

Bower anchor. The main anchor; the most secure, best-fitted anchor, usually with an all-chain line (warp) on large vessels, and at least some chain on smaller ones.

Bowsprit. A spar projecting horizontally, or slightly above horizontal, from the bow of a boat and taking one or more headsails.

Box the compass (to). Call all the headings of the compass from north through south and back to north. No longer valid since the 360 degree notation, but still a useful skill to keep an eye on the wind.

Brace. (1) The line controlling the outboard end of the spinnaker pole, usually containing wire on larger racing yachts. (2) In square-rigged ships the line used to control a yard; each yard has two braces, secured near the yard arms, to give as much horizontal trim as possible. When sailing into (on) a wind, the braces are nearly fore and aft and are described as 'braced up'. When running (off the wind), with the yards square, the braces are described as 'braced in'.

Break off, or to be broken off (to). Be so headed by the wind that one must sail lower, more to leeward.

Breast, breastline, breastrope. A line taken at right angles or nearly at right angles from the ship to anything to which it is being moored or fastened.

Breech. That part of a block opposite the swallow.

Breeches buoy. Formerly a circular lifebuoy with canvas breeches in which a person being rescued could sit. Nowadays part of the equipment used to transfer people from wrecks close to shore.

Bridgedeck. In a catamaran the crosspieces which join the forward sections of the two hulls together and on which the mast is stepped.

Brig. (1) A ship's prison. (2) A two-masted sailing vessel with square sails on both masts and a gaff mainsail.

Brigantine. A two-masted sailing vessel with schooner rig on the main mast and square sails on the foremast.

Bring by the lee (to). Alter course when running so that the lee side is brought to windward. It is highly dangerous, especially in strong winds, and should not be attempted by the inexperienced.

Bring up with a round turn (to). (1) Snub a line. (2) Bring to an abrupt halt.

Broad on the bow. Slightly aft of 45 degrees from the ship's heading.

Broad reach. A reach where the wind is coming from about 15 degrees either side of beam-on.

Broken. A yacht is said to be broken when, while sailing on the wind, the wind changes direction enough to force the yacht to sail further from the wind.

Bruce anchor. Modern lightweight British design with great holding power in sand and mud.

Brummel hook (U.S.). See sister clip.

Buck the wind (to). Leave harbour heading into strong contrary winds.

Bulkhead. Any cross-ship wall, particularly those which are strong and watertight.

Bull ring, Panama lead. A large steel ring fitted transversely on the bow to lead headropes through or for a towing hawser.

Bulldog grips, clips or clamps. A U-shaped steel rod with threaded ends over which a bar is placed and clamped tight with nuts. Good for joining wires or repairing broken rigging.

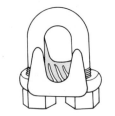

Diagram A2.12 *Wire passes through the hole in the bulldog grip.*

Bullivant's nippers. Steel appliances for temporarily controlling wires under great load.

Bullrope. A line from a bowsprit to a buoy to keep it clear of the stem in slack water.

Bull's eye. (1) A wooden block or fairlead without a sheave, but able to take a strop. (2) Thick glass or a prism let into the deck to admit light but not water below decks.

Bullwanger. A strop on a yard, to which a sail may be attached.

Bumpkin. A small bowsprit on little yachts.

Buoy. A floating container anchored to the sea bottom so that it remains in position. Buoys can be used to mark a channel, the position of a boat's mooring, a wreck, or the turning points in a race course. There is an international system of designs, colours, shapes and lights so that buoyage is standard throughout most of the world.

Buoy room. The space demanded by, and due to, a racing yacht when it has right of way.

Buoy rope. Any rope used to mark anything on the bottom when attached to a floating marker. It is good practice to make the line heavy enough to retrieve the object.

Burdened boat. The boat which, under the Rules of the Road, does not have right of way and must behave in prescribed ways to avoid a collision.

Butterfly block. A small snatch block fitted with a strop and a long tail. A butterfly block used to snub down a spinnaker sheet is called a snotter.

Butterfly nuts (U.K.), Wing nuts (U.S.). Nuts with flanges on them to allow easy tightening and untightening by hand.

Buttock. The underneath of the ship's stern out of the water, usually between the transom and the rudder post.

Buttock lines. In boatbuilding, lines on the plan which are a series of fore and aft sections taken at equal distances from each other.

By points. In boxing the compass, those points which are between the intermediates and the cardinals and half-cardinals. They get their name from always having 'by' in them, such as south by west.

By the head. A vessel that is down by the head has been trimmed so that the bow is lower than the stern in the water.

By the lee. When the wind is coming across the boat from the same side as the mainsail.

By the stern. Opposite of by the head.

By the wind. Close hauled, sailing as close to the wind as the vessel is capable.

C

Cable. (1) Coaxial or other type of electrical or electronic wiring for the transmission of data from instruments, computers etc. (2) The chain or line (warp) attached to the anchor. (3) One tenth of a nautical mile, 158 m (520 ft, 173 yds).

Cable buoy. Buoy marking the position of a telegraph or cable buoy beneath the surface.

Calculator navigation. Navigation by programmable hand-held computer, which stores data normally held in sight reduction tables and will plot position from observations of time and sextant altitudes.

Caliper hooks (clip hooks, clove hooks or clasp hooks). Flat metal half-hooks opposed to each other on a hinge. When closed they form one complete hook. They are used as boom topping lifts and in other cases where ease of attachment is important.

Camber. (1) The curvature of either a sail or keel. (2) The curve of the deck, usually being higher in the centre so that water will run off. (3) A small sloping slipway, as in modern launching ramps. (4) A small dock for loading and unloading.

Can buoy. A flat-topped cylindrical buoy. (See pages 120-121.)

Cap. A fitting at the head of one mast to receive the foot of another, higher mast.

Cap a rope (to). Cover the end of a rope with a canvas dolly and whip it into place for the protection of the rope end.

Cap rail. The rail under the toe rail, an extension of the hull above deck line on a wooden boat.

Cappen. The thin wooden covering on top of the gunwale. Like the rubbing strake, it can be replaced easily if damaged.

Capstan. A usually power-driven revolving drum for hauling cables and anchors or drawing a ship in to a wharf.

Cardinal marks. The IALA international system of marks, lit and unlit, which delineate major channels and dangers entering and leaving port.

Cardinal points. Of the compass, the four main headings, North, South, East and West.

Careen (to). Run a vessel on to a suitable beach so that she heels to one side and work on the underwater section of the opposite side can take place.

Carlins. Structural fore and aft timbers between beams to strut them.

Carpenter's stopper. A portable clamp and wedge which when shackled to an eyebolt or pad eye will hold any wire in control.

Carrick bend. The knot to join two hawsers that will allow them to pass around a capstan after joining.

Carrying helm, or rudder. A vessel carries helm when a constant application of helm is necessary to get it to sail a straight line.

Cat (an anchor). Raise anchor from the sea surface to the cathead.

Catamaran. Fast sailing vessel with two hulls of similar shape and length separated by beams. The hulls have very little wetted surface and so are faster than a monohull of similar length.

Catboat, or cat-rigged boat. Originally, a one-masted vessel carrying one sail only, with the mast well forward. The design is very popular in the United States.

Catch a turn (to). Rapidly take a turn around a post or bollard so as to be ready for strain coming on the line.

Catenary curve. Curve of anchor line (warp) from bow of vessel to the anchor. Also the curved tow from one vessel to another. The curved tow acts as a spring and absorbs shocks, for instance from sudden changes in speed.

Celestial equator. The equivalent of the earth equator projected on the celestial globe. The prime great circle which is at 90 degrees to the celestial poles.

Celestial fix. An accurately timed observation of the angle a heavenly body makes from an observer's position. By the use of nautical tables a navigational position can be made from two or more observations.

Centreboard (or centre plate). A board or metal plate lowered through the bottom of the boat to prevent the wind forcing the boat sideways. It may also increase the size of the keel.

Certificate of registry. The legal identification of a vessel, which must be kept on board at all times. It records the vessel's radio call sign, identification number, name, tonnage, method of construction, and the names of the people holding shares in it. The British convention is that

there are 64 shares in all vessels which are registered.

Chafing batten (or rubbing strake). The strip of wood which runs the whole length of the boat on the outer section of the gunwale and absorbs the shock and scars of any object coming into contact with the boat. It is easily replaced when badly worn.

Chain stopper. A short chain used to secure wire under load.

Chain swivel. A join which can rotate, preventing wire or chain from kinking. A large version of the swivels used in fishing lines.

Chainplates. The whole arrangement that transfers the load from the shrouds through to the hull, or even the keel. The term includes the rigging screws, the actual plates on or in the hull and any further fittings which continue from the hull to the keel.

Characteristics (of a light). A description of the number of times a light flashes, occults, etc., its range, height and other information of use to the navigator.

Chart. A compilation of all the up-to-date knowledge of the coastline of a particular area. Included is information on latitude and longitude, conspicuous land objects, currents, tides, navigation lights, water depths, composition of the sea bottom and any other constant information of use to navigators. They are corrected weekly by Notices to Mariners.

Chart datum. The baseline of tidal height in use on a particular chart. It is the basis of the survey of the area, and tides are unlikely to fall below the datum in any but the most unusual circumstances.

Chart factor. The ratio of a fixed interval of longitude to the same interval of latitude expressed in nautical miles. The factor allows for the world not being a perfect sphere.

Charted depth. The distance between the sea bottom and chart datum.

Cheater. A small headsail of low aspect ratio often set under a spinnaker on large boats. Its purpose is to use the clear air under the spinnaker without interfering with the spinnaker.

Cheek block. A block flat against a deck or spar.

Chine. The angle formed when two non-curved sections of a boat's hull join. On a boat where the topside meets the bottom at an angle, it is said to leave a hard chine or be hard chined. On a boat where the topside meets the bottom in a curve it is said to have a soft chine or be soft chined.

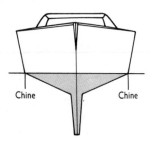

Diagram A2.13 *A chine-built boat.*

Chinese jibe. See Flying jibe.

Chocks. Small wedges used to adjust the mast position on skiffs and dinghies. They control the amount of bend or rake in the mast. In larger boats the chocks hold the mast firmly in the collar and prevent unwanted movement.

Choker. A pulley for pulling down a spinnaker sheet to take the rolling moment out of the sail. It usually consists of a cheek block on the end of a line which is then led through another block on to a winch so that it can be loosened or tightened to adjust the downward pressure on the sheet.

Chronometer. The time measuring device used solely for navigation. Because time and distance relate in the measurements used at sea, the more accurate the chronometer the more accurate the ship's navigation. Nowadays, satellite navigators update the time at each satellite pass.

Claw ring. A metal ring with rollers on each jaw, used mostly nowadays to take the mainsheet or vang or preventer on boats with roller reefing.

Clearing line or circle. A line or circle drawn clear of a danger to give

the vessel a safety factor when passing it.

Clearing mark. A charted object which provides one end of a clearing line. Two clearing marks are needed to create a clearing line, whereas one will allow a clearing circle to be drawn.

Cleat. (1) Traditionally, a low, flat, T-shaped piece of wood with the upright very wide and very short. The wooden piece is screwed or bolted to the deck and used to fasten sheets, halyards, etc. (2) A jam cleat is one where the line is led into a tapering V-shaped channel with vertical grooves which is narrower at the end facing the load so that it jams as it is pulled into the cleat. (3) The latest form of jam cleat is one with a pivoted arm which has a grooved semi-circle on its end. When the arm is moved through its arc it pushes on to the line until it is so tight it jams in position (cam cleat).

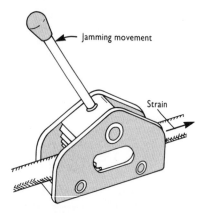

Jamming movement

Strain

Diagram A2.14 *A jam cleat, which allows one winch to tension many lines.*

Clench (to). Bend the pointed end of a nail at right angles to its shaft when it has come through the wood, thus preventing it pulling out when loosened.

Clew. (1) The lower corner of a sail. With spinnakers, both lower corners are clews; with fore and aft sails, only the corner from which the sheet is led is a clew. (2) To clew up is to pull up a sail when furling it to a yard.

Clip hooks. See Sister clip.

Clipper. Normally these ships had a fine entry, fine lines, relatively

narrow beam and highly raked masts. They were used in the tea trade, and sometimes carried wool.

Close-hauled. To be sailing as near to the wind as possible.

Close reach. A reach when the wind is well forward of the beam.

Close reefed. (1) When all the reefs of a sail have been taken in. (2) Dressed for the sort of conditions one gets when a boat is close reefed.

Club (footed). A spar fitted to the bottom of a triangular sail, hence a club-footed, self-tacking jib. It allows the sail to tack under control without a crewman going forward.

Club hauling. Although this technique once allowed sailing vessels to get out of dangerous situations, it is now used mainly for swinging an anchored vessel so that bearings can be taken from a fixed position while swinging the compass. The vessel is anchored and a line passed from the stern and secured to the cable. By veering cable and heaving on the line the vessel is pulled around under control. When it has been done from one side it is done from the other to complete the circle of observations.

Club topsail. A large topsail with clubs at the foot.

Coast Guard. (1) U.S.: the para-military sea-going force entrusted with the security of the coast, with customs activities, and with enforcing the law of the sea. (2) U.K.: a body with similar functions, but now disbanded. (3) Australia: a band of voluntary coastwatchers who provide surveillance of the coast.

Coastal quick release (CQR anchor). This anchor is very popular with small vessels as it has good holding power for its weight and as its name implies

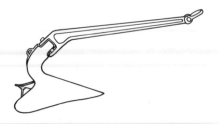

Diagram A2.15 *A CQR anchor.*

is generally easy to break free from the sea bottom. Also known as a plow anchor (U.S.) because of its shape.

Cocked hat. In navigation the triangle formed when three lines of bearing or three position lines cross. Ideally lines would intersect at the same point. The centre of the triangle is by convention taken as the yacht's position, but if near a danger it is safer to take the point closest to the danger as the position and make allowances for it.

Coffee grinder. On large racing boats, these great, two-handed winches are used for trimming sheets. More than one coffee grinder can be linked together for greater power.

Coil. A single loop of line, otherwise known as a fake. When several coils are put together, each overlapping the other, the line is said to have been coiled. As each succeeding turn is placed on another the line should be given a half twist against the lay to prevent it kinking when being uncoiled. This applies even to modern braided (woven) lines, and particularly to kevlar lines, which are hard to coil satisfactorily.

Collar knot. A special knot for use when making a jury rig which leaves two lines each side of the new mast to act as shrouds.

Colregs. International rules for the prevention of collisions at sea (72 colregs). The navigation rules or rules of the road.

Come about (to). Change the vessel from one tack to another.

Come to (to). Point up closer to the wind.

Compass. The instrument which indicates the position of north and thereby any relative position. A magnetised needle is pivoted on an upright post slightly above a card on which the points of the compass are graduated. The whole is encased in watertight materials to contain a special liquid to dampen the movements of the needle. The whole is mounted on a binnacle.

Compass adjustment buoy. Specially laid buoy where the compass can

be swung to produce a deviation chart, or to correct the compass.

Compass card. The graduated card showing the points of the compass.

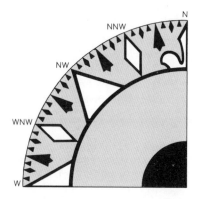

Diagram A2.16 *The old-fashioned compass card with directions instead of the 360 degree notation.*

Compass correctors. Small magnets placed to counteract the effect of a ship's magnetism on its compass.

Compass error. The total a compass needle is deflected by variation (due to local anomalies in the earth's magnetic field) and deviation (due to the magnetism of the vessel itself).

Compass rose. The equivalent of a compass card printed, usually twice, on a chart. It can be used to read off bearings and to note local variation.

Complimentary (courtesy) ensign. The small courtesy flag used when visiting a foreign port. It is a miniature of the ensign of the visited country. It is worn from the main shroud on yachts and from the foremast on large vessels.

Composite group flashing light. A group flashing light with two distinct and different groups.

Composite group occulting light. A group occulting light with two distinct and different groups.

Composite group occulting. A light where the occultations are combined in alternate groups of different numbers.

Cone. A black conical shape used for weather warnings at land stations.

Continental shelf. The area of comparatively shallow water extending around the coast, running usually about 16 km (10 miles) out to sea but sometimes much further.

Continuous light. Lights which flash continuously and are split into three speeds, quick, very quick and ultra quick. Quick is about 50-60 flashes a minute, very quick about 100-120, and ultra quick about 240-300.

Coordinated universal time. The world standard for time which replaced Greenwich Mean Time. Also called Zulu.

Coordinates. The intersection of two lines on a grid system to identify position. A simple example of coordinates is latitude and longitude, where the first gives a position north or south of the equator and the second one east or west of the prime meridian (Greenwich). The intersection of the two is the vessel's position.

Corange lines. Lines along which the range of the tide is the same.

Core temperature. The internal temperature of a human being, which, if lowered, leads to hypothermia and possibly death. How to maintain core temperature, or slow its reduction, when immersed in the sea, is an important part of survival technique.

Coriolis effect. The deflection of the wind or currents to the right in the northern hemisphere and the left in the southern hemisphere due to the rotation of the earth.

Counter. An overhanging stern, or the underneath of that overhang.

Cow hitch. A method of joining two soft eyes.

Cowl. A cover over a ventilator. On large vessels they often have a wind vane on them to ensure they swing to the wind.

Cradle. (1) The structure on which yachts or commercial vessels are hauled out of the water on to the land on a slipway. (2) The structure that supports a vessel while she is being built. (3) Any structure over the side of a vessel for performing work on her.

Cranse iron. A circular hoop fitted to a bowsprit to take the standing rigging.

Cras protractor. A protractor developed by the French which allows bearings to be plotted without sliding across the chart. It has some similarities to the Portland plotter.

Cringle. A loop of rope, or a hole with a grommet, let into sails to take reefing lines and hooks, Cunningham fittings, and other forms of control.

Crinolines. Lines lead from the lower block of a purchase to steady the whole.

Crooks. Pieces of timber which have been steamed, or selected, so that the natural grain follows the curve of the piece.

Cross bearing. A two position line fix. Nearly simultaneous bearings of two objects are taken, corrected, then laid off on the chart to give a position.

Crosstrees (spreaders). Metal or wood set at an angle to the mast and attached to the mast and shrouds to keep the mast under tension, counteract the sideways pressure of the shrouds, and force open the slot between headsail and main.

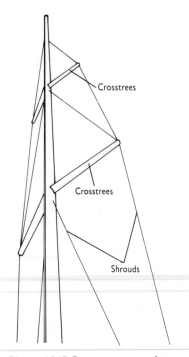

Diagram A2.17 *Crosstrees, or spreaders.*

Crowd sail; crowd on sail (to). Set extra sails to press the vessel faster and faster.

Crown. That part of an anchor where the arms and shank meet.

Crown and wall. A wall knot made on a crown knot.

Crown knot. A knot made in three-stranded line as the first part of a splice, or as the base for more intricate knots.

Cruiser. A private motor vessel covering a wide range of styles and sizes.

Crutch. (1) Any arrangement of timbers to support the boom of yachts when not in use. (2) A cradle-like apparatus to support a yacht.

Cunningham eye. A moderately powerful pulley device which tightens the luff of the mainsail when the sail is to be flattened.

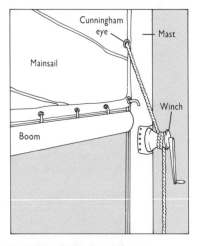

Diagram A2.18 *The cunningham eye controls the shape of the sail.*

Current wind. The wind created by the movement of a vessel through the air when in the grip of current. This movement therefore becomes a factor of apparent, or modified true wind.

Cut splice. A splice to put an eye at a desired spot along a line.

Cutter. A sailing vessel which carries two jibs.

Cutter rig. Setting a staysail inside a genoa on a vessel which would normally be too close-winded for two

headsails. Used just before a spinnaker can be worn on racing yachts.

Cutting. A cutting tide is one between springs and neaps, when they are becoming successively lower in height.

D

Dagger boards or plates. Very high aspect ratio centreboards, such as those used by skiffs and catamarans.

Dagger knees. Supports set at an angle between beams and timbers.

Dan buoy (U.K.), Tall buoy (U.S.). Originally a small buoy used as a marker, but now part of the safety equipment of racing yachts. A metal weight is fixed at the end of a long pole. In the middle is flotation, and on top a flag and sometimes a light activated by a mercury switch. The buoy is used as a marker, particularly when someone has fallen overboard. In some cases the central pole of the apparatus is a whip aerial for use if the main aerial is lost or damaged.

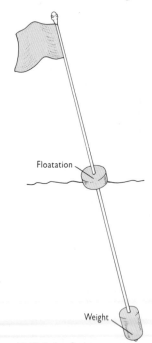

Diagram A2.19 *A dan buoy.*

Danforth. A very popular form of anchor in which the stock passes through the crown suitable for holding power in most types of bottom.

Davits. A pair of davits, from which a boat is suspended, or from which hoisting can take place. They are most commonly used for the dinghy on large yachts, or for lifeboats on commercial vessels and passenger liners.

Day's work. A record, usually taken each half hour, of a vessel's speed, and course, and of estimated leeway and set and drift. This record is used by the navigator to calculate the vessel's estimated position at any moment. It is the basic navigational information available to the navigator.

Dead eye, or dead men's eyes. On old sailing vessels, flat wooden timbers with holes drilled through them to take the shroud lanyards.

Dead flat. The central flat sections of a hull between the bow and stern, but not including either.

Dead on end. A vessel presenting her stern to an observer so that it is in line with the observer's track.

Dead reckoning. Keeping track of a vessel's position through recording its speed and direction and any external factors which may affect its course. The basic information of a navigator. The estimated position arrived at is actually only an educated guess, which has to be verified by observation of land-based objects or celestial objects.

Dead (or proud) run. A run when the wind is directly behind the boat.

Dead water. The churned up water immediately behind a moving vessel, but not the wake.

Deaden a ship's way (to). Reduce speed by sailing too high, so luffing the sails, or by any other means. The technique is often used in yacht racing when a competitor is approaching the starting line too fast and is in danger of being over early (before the starting gun).

Deadrise. The height between the bottom of a vessel and its widest beam, not to be confused with draught, which is to the waterline only.

Decca. A system of hyperbolic coastal navigation beacons where the accurate measurement of differences

in time signals from three stations gives a position.

Deck watch. A watch used on deck to time lighthouses to ensure their accurate identification.

Declination (Dec.). Distance north or south of the celestial equator. The equivalent of latitude on the celestial sphere.

Declinometer. Instrument for measuring astronomical or magnetic declination.

Demise. The legal condition of having chartered a vessel for a period and during that time having no control over her.

Departure. (1) The last accurate position, normally taken of land objects, before losing sight of land. From it the navigator plots the vessel's course, having the departure as a certain point. (2) The aggregate result of the various courses steered by a vessel during a fixed period. Therefore a vessel will have made good a distance between its starting point and finishing point, that distance being its departure.

Depression. (1) The amount by which an object is below the horizon or horizontal plane expressed as an angle. (2) An area of low barometric pressure and the system of winds around it.

Depth. The distance from the gunwale of a vessel to its keel.

Depth of a sail. Of a fore-and-aft sail, the length of the leech; of a square sail, the distance from top to bottom. Sometimes also refers to the curvature of a sail when filled by the wind.

Depth of the sea. See Chart depth.

Deviation. The amount of deflection of a compass needle caused by the magnetism of the vessel itself. The deviation varies according to the vessel's heading.

Deviation chart. A chart of a vessel's deviation on each point of the compass which is obtained by heading the vessel on each point and recording the compass bearing of the same object on each heading. This action is called swinging the compass.

Deviation curve. The curve obtained by smoothing out the observations from swinging the compass. The result gives the deviation for courses other than the points of the compass.

Devil. The outboard plank on the deck. The closest to the gunwale.

Devil to pay (the). To pay is to caulk, and the devil (see above) is the most difficult plank to caulk because each deck plank is let into it at a different angle. Hence to pay the devil was often given as punishment.

D.F. Direction finder.

Diagonal planked. Of a wooden boat built with two layers of planking, the first laid at 45 degrees to horizontal and the second at right angles to the first. If a third layer is used it is usually horizontal. Another method is to have two diagonal-planked layers, an inner and an outer, with a filling of some light substance, such as end-grain balsa to give tremendous strength and rigidity to a hull. The method has largely been overtaken by the use of exotics for racing boats but is still greatly favoured for cruisers.

Diamond knot. Used when a knot is required in the length of a line.

Diaphone. The most powerful sound signal which warns of fog.

Diaphragm pump. Pump in which a flexible diaphragm replaces the piston. These pumps suck in and expel water simultaneously and are more efficient than the older type.

Difference of latitude. The north and south difference in the position of any two places.

Difference of longitude. The east and west difference in the position of any two places.

Dip. (1) Apparent depression of the horizon due to observer's elevation. In calculations, as of distance and in making astronomical observations, corrections have to be made to allow for dip. (2) The 'nod' in the point of a compass when pointing towards the nearest pole. If the compass is large enough and dip is a problem it has to be countered by small weights. In small compasses it is unusual for dip to be a great problem.

Dipping needle. A needle used to measure magnetic dip.

Direction finder. A device for making bearings of the source of known radio stations' signals so that a position can be found.

Displacement. The volume or weight of fluid displaced by solid floating or immersion in it (e.g. a ship with a displacement of 11,000 tonnes).

Distress signals. Those signals recognised legally and internationally as indicating that the vessel making them is in need of urgent assistance. (See page 174.)

Dividers. Pointed arms with a hinge, allowing them to be spread apart for measuring distances on charts, or for reading off the latitude and longitude of a position or a landmark.

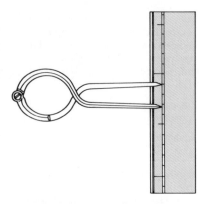

Diagram A2.20 *Dividers measure distances on charts.*

Dodger. Any shelter specially constructed so as to break the force of spray or small waves on a vessel.

Dog. A clip which applies increasing pressure as it is rotated until it forces watertight doors tight shut.

Dog (to). When ending a splice, to dog the strands is to take half of each strand and bind it to its neighbour.

Dog Star. Sirius, the brightest star in the heavens.

Dog watches. The watch from 1600 to 2000 is split into two, the first and second dog watches, to allow an uneven number and therefore that no crew will work the same watch day after day. On racing yachts a more

common method is to work three-hour watches between 1800 and 0600 and four-hour watches for the rest of the day, achieving the same result.

Dog's lug. That part of a reefed sail which is between the tack point and the reef cringle, the part no longer being used.

Doldrums. Zones where the winds are fitful, light and unpredictable.

Dolphin striker. The perpendicular strut, usually metal, which tensions the martingale under a bowsprit.

Dorade. A ventilator leading into a box with baffles, allowing the entry of air but not water. Invented by the U.S. naval architect Olin Stephens for a yacht called *Dorade*.

Dory. A flat-bottomed, flat-sided boat with high bow and stern. Very strong and seaworthy and often used in whale hunting in the past.

Douane. French or diplomatic name for customs, or the customs house.

Double. To double a point is to round it, to double back is to return along one's course.

Double bottoms. Of a hull which has an inner and outer bottom.

Double bowline. The bowline in the bight (see diagram 1.28, page 19).

Double ender. A boat with the bow and stern both pointed.

Double luff. A purchase having double blocks top and bottom, and the standing part secured to the upper block. Often used on racing yachts for preventers, vangs etc.

Doubling. (1) A strengthening piece sewn into a sail. (2) The edge of the sail where the boltrope is secured. (3) The extra layers of sailcloth where they lead into a Gemini track on the forestay.

Doubling the angle on the bow. In navigation, finding the distance off a point by taking a bearing and later taking another which is twice the angle of the first. By plotting the course and distance travelled between where the bearings were taken the boat's position will be known. This method does not allow for the effects of current.

Doublings. The overlapping portion of a mast built of more than one spar.

Douglas Scale. The International Sea and Swell Scale, notations being figures.

Dowel. Headless pin of wood, metal, etc. for keeping two pieces of wood in position.

Down at the head. Said of a vessel that is lower than her lines at the bow.

Down helm (to). Push the helm away and so bring a vessel up into the wind.

Downhaul. A line which controls the upward motion of a spar, hence the spinnaker downhaul, or kicker. It can also mean a line to bring something down from high in the rigging.

Drabbler. Extra sailcloth laced to a sail.

Drag sheet. A makeshift sea anchor of a sail laced to a weighted spar.

Draught. (1) The distance between the waterline, in smooth water, and the bottom of the boat when unladen. (2) The belly, or curvature, in a sail.

Draught marks. Painted graduations on the side of a ship which indicate her depth in the water, used, with the Plimsoll line, for loading.

Draw. (1) A vessel of 4 metres draught is said to 'draw' 4 metres. (2) Said of a sail when it has filled into its proper shape from the force of the wind.

Dries. See Drying height.

Drifter. (1) A race in which there is very little wind. (2) An extremely

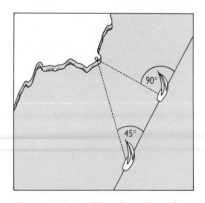

Diagram A2.21 *Doubling the angle on the bow.*

light headsail sheeted wide so as to catch the slightest of airs.

Driver. The mizzen, or spanker.

Drogue. Any friction causing agent, such as a bucket or conical canvas tapering tube, which will tend to hold a vessel head to wind when streamed over the bow. Drogues are also attached to liferafts, and liferings and horseshoes to prevent them drifting too fast from anybody who is overboard.

Drop. The length of a sail in its middle.

Drop astern. To divert from one's course to pass astern of another vessel. To sail more slowly than another vessel and so 'fall' astern.

Drop keel. (See also Centreboard.) A keel, with mechanical advantage or not, which can be lowered through a casing to increase the stability of a vessel.

Drying height (features). Those parts of the shoreline, or more rarely the ocean, which dry out at low tide. Such features are shown on the chart as, say, 'Dries to 1 metre'.

Dumb compass. A compass dial without gimbals or cover, usually fixed to the deckhouse in small vessels, or on a pedestal, and used to take bearings of objects ashore for navigation.

E

Earring. Any line that ties a sail to a spar beyond those normally fitted. Most often used to tie down the reef cringle if the standard gear seems insufficient for the job.

Ease the helm (to). Lift into a head sea, then fall away slightly down its back so as not to fall off it.

Easting. Aggregate distance made good to the east over a number of courses.

Echo sounder. A system where pulses are sent from a transducer in a vessel's hull to the sea bottom and returned. The time taken by the impulse is translated into depth. The mechanism can be set to give an alarm at any given depth of water.

Eight bells. The number of strokes of the ship's bell sounded at the start of each four-hour watch (4 o'clock, 8 o'clock and 12 o'clock).

Electronic navigation systems. Navigational method where the traditional chart is replaced by a display on a VDU. Research is continuing, but there are reservations among hydrographers about the system in its early stages.

Elevation. The angle a heavenly body makes with the horizontal; the height above chart datum of an object.

Elongation. The angular distance of a planet from the sun or of a satellite from earth.

End for end. To change rigging over with one end taking the place of the other, reversing it. This is done with galvanised rigging to move areas of excessive load or chafe.

Entrance, or entry. The forward shape of a vessel. A fine entry is gradual and narrow, a blunt entry is wide.

Ephemeris (plural, ephemerides). Astronomical almanac or table of predicted positions.

EPIRB. Emergency Position Indicating Radio Beacon. Small floating radio transmitter for emergency use which emits a signal for up to 5 days on emergency frequencies.

Equation (personal). In navigation, the allowance made for a person's speed at making observations.

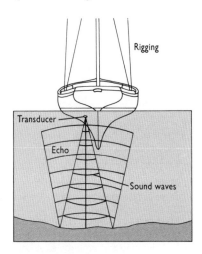

Diagram A2.22 *Echo sounding.*

Equator (magnetic). Aclinic line on which magnetic needle has no dip.

Equinoctial. (1) Of equal day and night; happening at or near time of equinox (e.g. equinoctial gales); at or near terrestrial equator. (2) Celestial equator.

Equinox. The two occasions each year (around March 21 and September 23) when the length of the day equals the length of the night. Hence it is the beginning of the change of seasons, and noted for the gales that come at that time—the equinoctial gales.

Escutcheon. Middle of ship's stern where name is placed.

Estimated position. In navigation that position between dead reckoning and an observed position which is the navigator's best estimate allowing for leeway currents, winds and other modifying factors.

Evening star. Planet, especially Venus, when seen in the west after sunset.

Eye. (1) The loop formed in an eye splice. Also the metal hoop on a flat base which is fixed to the deck to take blocks etc., a pad eye. (2) Of a tropical revolving storm, the cloudless, windless centre, where a calm may last for many minutes before the wind strikes again from the opposite direction, often with greater force. (3) The eye of an anchor is the hole which takes the ring.

Eye splice. Splicing the strands of a rope to form a loop. If a metal thimble is inserted to reinforce the eye it is hard, if not it is called soft (see diagram 1.43, page 20).

F

Faint sector. That sector of a navigation light which is relatively faint.

Fair wind. A wind that allows a straight course to be set for one's destination, without course changes.

Fairlead. A pulley or fixed block which changes the direction of a line so that it leads fairly to a winch or work station.

Fall. The line between the pulleys on any purchase, but in particular the lines which lower or hoist lifeboats on large vessels.

Fall down, away (to). Sag to leeward, to sail less well to windward than the optimum.

Falling off. Dropping to leeward of the required course.

Fathom. A measure of depth. A fathom is six feet and many older charts record depths in fathoms. The more modern ones use metres. A fathom is 1.8288 metres.

Feather (to). (1) In strong winds, to sail too high into the wind so that the leading edge of the headsail stalls slightly. It takes delicate helmsmanship and the effect is to depower the sail sufficiently for the boat to continue on its course without excessive heeling. More commonly used in dinghies than anywhere else. (2) To roll an oar face upwards when rowing to lessen drag and reduce the chance of splashes. (3) To smooth adjoining surfaces of different height to the same height.

Feeder. Rotating balls or narrowing section of tube used to feed the luff rope of a headsail into the track of a modern forestay fitting such as a Gemini.

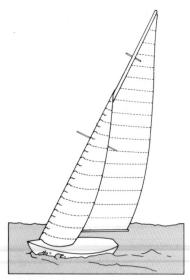

Diagram A2.23 *Feathering the jib, by stalling the leading edge, allows a fractional rigged yacht to carry a larger sail in heavy winds.*

Fender. Usually plastic tubes containing elastic material and suspended by a lanyard. Any material suspended against a ship's side to prevent damage or chafe.

Ferrocement (U.S.), Ferroconcrete (U.K.). The generic term for vessels framed up in metal and covered with a hull of many layers of chicken or similar wire. The wiring is then filled with a mix of special cement which can be smoothed and faired. Vessels built in this way are as strong as steel and much lighter but there are limitations to the amount of curvature the material will stand.

Fetch. (1) The distance a wind or seas can have travelled without obstruction. So that a westerly sea at Cape Horn could have travelled 10,000 miles (16,000 km) without let. (2) To fetch something is to lay it accurately. One fetches a mark, or a port. (3) A fetch is laying a mark without having to tack.

Fid. (1) A long cone with a relatively sharp point. They come in various sizes and are used to separate the strands of rope so that they can be spliced. (2) The pin which wedges a bowsprit or topmast in place.

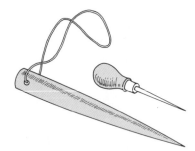

Diagram A2.24 *Two versions of a fid.*

Fiddle block. Two blocks, one above the other.

Fife rail. A rail with belaying pins and used for securing running rigging, usually halyards.

Fine on the bow. Forward of 45 degrees on either bow.

First point of Aries. The vernal equinox, the intersection of the sun's orbit and the celestial equator as it begins its south declination.

First watch. On large vessels, the first of the night watches, from 2000 to 2400.

Fisherman's anchor. The shape of an anchor with a fixed stock at right angles to the shank. It is best used over a rocky bottom because it hooks in easily yet normally will clear without trouble.

Fisherman's bend. A knot for attaching a line (warp) to an anchor.

Fishing lights. Those lights displayed by fishermen by international convention to indicate their course and the type of fishing they are carrying out.

Five fathom line. (Or 10 fathom, 20 fathom etc.) Lines on a chart indicating depth and marked by numbers of dots or dashes.

Fix (to). Fixing position is to take bearings of coastal landmarks, or reduce celestial observations. Where the bearings intersect, or nearly do so, is the ship's observed position.

Fixed and flashing light. A fixed light with an intermittent flash of greater strength.

Fixed and group flashing light. A fixed light with two or more intermittent flashes of greater brilliance.

Fixed light. A light that does not vary and is permanently alight.

Flag of distress. The national flag of a vessel, hoisted upside down, either at the full or half mast.

Flake (to). (1) To coil a line and lay it flat; a mat coil. (2) To stow the mainsail by hanging equal amounts on both sides of the boom, each hanging loop is called a bight.

Flare. (1) Pyrotechnics of various colours and characteristics some of which, when fired into the sky, erupt to attract attention in an emergency. Others emit coloured smoke or glow brightly when hand-held. (2) The V-shaped entry on fast vessels which first cuts the water and then pushes it to one side.

Flat. (1) Of a sail, its shape when the halyard and outhaul are tightly on, taking the curvature out of the sail so that it spills the wind efficiently in heavy weather. (2) A bank of mud or sand which uncovers at low tide and is low and even in surface.

Flat bottom. A boat without curves on its bottom and with a hard chine.

Flat coil. Sometimes called a Flemish coil or mat coil, the end of a line is made into a small coil and the balance of the line coiled around the first and so on until it is all used. The result is a series of concentric coils lying close to each other.

Flemish eye. This can take the place of an eye splice when the eye is wanted to fit a particular size. The line is unstranded and the yarns tied successively around a spar of the required size. The whole is then bound, tapered and served.

Flinders bar. A soft iron bar in the binnacle of every ship to overcome the magnetism of the ship itself. Matthew Flinders, the 18th century marine explorer of much of Australia, first recognised that every ship had its own induced magnetism and the bar is named after him.

Float drop. A spinnaker drop system where the pole is taken off and the spinnaker kept aloft and filled (floating) as the boat jibes at a mark and, with headsail up, hardens up on a windward leg of a race. The spinnaker is dropped as the boat fills on the new course.

Floating light. Lights, particularly safety lights, which are attached to lifebuoys and float when thrown in the water to direct rescuers. They usually have a mercury switch so that they come on as soon as they are upright.

Floor boards (U.S.), Bottom boards (U.K.). Duck boards shaped to fit in the bottom of dinghies and small row boats and outboards, or in the cockpit of cruising boats to spread the weight and protect the hull.

Floors. Vertical timbers which join the bottom of the frames to the keel. They are important transverse strengtheners of the framework of a boat.

Fluxgate compass. An arrangement of solenoids through which a current is passed. The earth's magnetic field

affects the current in the solenoid. The compass is linked to a satellite navigator which translates the output from the solenoids into a compass heading.

Flying jibe. The same disastrous sort of jibé as a Chinese or standing jibe.

Fog buoy. Any buoy fitted with a bell.

Fog signal. A bell, whistle or horn used to sound regularly during fog to warn approaching vessels. Though usually sounded from other ships, they can be sounded at lighthouses or anywhere else that is likely to prove a danger.

Folding tiller (U.K.). A two-part tiller with an extension, often used on dinghies.

Fore. Towards the front of the vessel, such as foremast, foredeck etc.

Fore and aft rig. A vessel that has no square sails.

Fore course. The front, lowest sail on the foremast.

Fore guy. Any line led forward to hold something in place. For instance, the modern spinnaker kicker is in fact a fore guy. The brace is an after guy.

Fore horse. A traveller arrangement to control a foresail.

Fore sheets. Lines used to control the foresail if it tacks automatically, i.e. if it is club-footed and fitted with a traveller.

Forecastle (now called the fo'csle). The foremost part of the vessel. Now usually the crew's accommodation.

Forefoot. Where the stem and keel join.

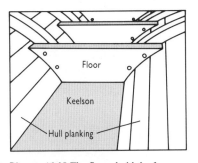

Diagram A2.25 *The floors hold the frames in place and tie them to the keelson.*

Forelock. A flat pin which fits into a slot in an anchor stock, shackle pin etc., to prevent its loss.

Forenoon watch. The watch from 0800 to 1200.

Foresail. Any sail set forward of the mast, except a spinnaker. A foresail on the forestay is a genoa if it overlaps the mast and a jib if it doesn't. A foresail set on a stay inside the forestay is a staysail, and a vessel carrying a foresail on the forestay and a staysail is said to be cutter-rigged.

Forestay. The main support for the mast from the bow. The stay goes from a strongpoint on the bow to the top of the mast and takes the genoa or jib.

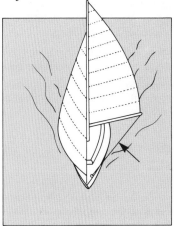

Diagram A2.26 *A fore guy.*

Foretriangle. The triangle formed by the mast, the forestay and a line from the stem to the mast at the deck. It is used in calculating sail sizes and handicaps.

Fractional rig. Any yacht with the forestay extending only part of the way up the mast, hence three-quarter

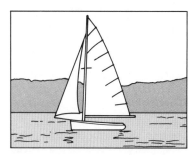

Diagram A2.27 *Fractional rig.*

rig when the forestay attaches 75 per cent of the way up the mast, also seven-eighths rig.

Franchise. A proportion of the value of a vessel which will not be paid in an insurance claim. It is applied to every claim.

Free. A boat is said to be free if the wind moves aft when sailing a fixed course, allowing the vessel to sail free. When climbing to windward a vessel that had been freed (lifted) would sail closer to its destination.

Freeboard. The distance from the waterline to the deck.

French bowline. Like a bowline except with two bights.

Full and by. Sailing as close to the wind as possible while maintaining top speed and not pinching.

Futtock plate. A metal plate to take the deadeyes for the topmast rigging.

Futtock shrouds. The wire or chain securing the futtock plate to a band on the mast.

G

Gaff. (1) The spar hoisted up the mast on old-fashioned sailing boats to extend the top of the mainsail. (2) A wooden pole with a hook on the end for gaffing fish (hooking them and lifting them aboard).

Gaff topsail. A triangular sail which fits between the mast and the gaff.

Gale. A wind averaging more than 30 knots. When it exceeds an average of 50 knots it becomes a storm. Force 7 to 10 on the Beaufort Scale.

Gallows. Crossed legs of timber, bolted through, to support the boom when a topping lift is not used.

Gammon iron. The iron band which fixes a bowsprit to the stem.

Gantline. A line, used for hoisting, which runs from the deck to the top of the mast, through a block, and back to the deck.

Garboard. The garboard strake is the first plank after the keel. It has compound curves and is both difficult to form and hard to keep watertight.

Gaskets. Small line or woven straps used to lash sails to booms, or to tie anything to secure it.

Gennaker. A cross between a genoa and a spinnaker, it is hoisted without the use of a pole, with the tack attached to the bottom of the forestay. Developed in America's Cup sailing, it has become very popular with cruising boats because it is easy to handle.

Genoa. Any headsail, attached to the forestay, which is large enough to overlap the mast. The most common form of headsail on racing and cruising yachts.

Geographical position (GP). The point on the earth's surface through which a line joining the centre of the earth and a heavenly body passes.

German eye splice. An eye splice with the first tucks with the lay instead of against it.

Ghosting. Sailing in very light conditions, with the apparent wind so light as to seem almost non-existent. It is now recognised, on well-sailed racing yachts, that a boat can reach a speed of, say, 3 knots in an apparent wind strength of 5 knots when the true wind may be less than 3 knots. The technique for achieving this is described in the section on sailing theory (see above page 21).

Gimbals. A double suspension which allows galley stoves, lights etc. to remain relatively steady while the boat 'moves around them'.

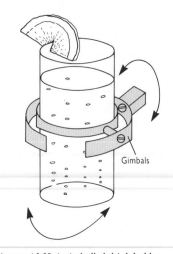

Diagram A2.28 *A gimballed drink holder.*

Gin block. A large single sheave block with a skeleton frame.

Gong buoy. A buoy equipped with a gong which sounds either permanently, or in fog.

Gooseneck. The joint which joins the boom to the mast allowing lateral and vertical movement of the boom.

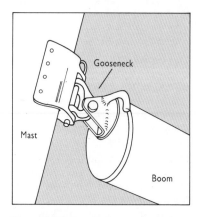

Diagram A2.29 *A main boom gooseneck.*

Goosewing. When running, to have the headsail filled on the opposite side of the boat to the main.

G.P.S. Global Position System.

Gradient current. Current formed when there is a slope between waters of different salinity or temperatures or both, or through the action of the wind. The current starts in the direction of the slope but is deflected by the Coriolis effect.

Graveyard watch. The middle watch.

Graving dock. A dock where graving (cleaning and anti-fouling the bottom) can take place.

Grease the ways (to). Readying a slipway for a launch.

Great circle. Circles on a sphere whose planes pass through its centre. So, the equator is a great circle, and so is a circle through both poles. It follows therefore that any circle between those two is also a great circle. A circle at, for example, latitude 30 degrees north, does not pass through the centre of the sphere (earth) and is known as a small circle, as are any others like it.

Green sea. A large sea which lands on a vessel without having broken.

Greenwich hour angle (GHA). The angle at the pole made by the meridian of a heavenly body with the Greenwich meridian. It is always measured west.

Grid compass. Compass with a rotating arrow which can be turned to the boat's course. The arrow consists of a head and parallel arms, through which the compass needle can be seen. The needle has merely to stay within the arrow for the boat to be maintaining course.

Gripes (U.K.), Slings (U.S.). Wide bands of canvas or woven, reinforced material on which boats sit while in davits, or while being lifted by mobile hoists in marinas.

Grommet. (1) Metal eyelets let into sails to take the Cunningham fittings (also known as a Cunningham eye), reefing lines and other controls. (2) A rope ring made from one strand wrapped twice around after making a loop.

Group flashing light. Two or more flashes shown at fixed intervals.

Group occulting light. A fixed light which goes out twice or more at fixed intervals, with the period of darkness never being more than the period of light.

Gudgeon. The female fitting at the stern of a vessel which takes the pintle of the rudder.

Gunter rig. Similar to gaff rig, except that the spar hoisted up the mast is pulled almost vertical, instead of at an angle of about 30 degrees as with a gaff.

Gunwale. Pronounced 'gunnel'. The lengthwise timber which ties the hull and deck together, stiffening the framework.

Guy. Any line used to control a spar. Hence, foreguy, afterguy.

Gybe. See Jibe.

Gyro compass. A rotating wheel with a free axis which, if undisturbed, will maintain a fixed direction.

Gyro repeater. A compass card which repeats the heading on the master gyro.

H

Half cardinals. The points halfway between the cardinal points of North, East, South and West—North-east, South-east, South-west and North-west.

Halyard. A wire or rope for hoisting sails, flags etc.

Hank. (1) A metal clip sewn to foresails with a piston arm that opens to allow the clip to attach to the forestay. (2) A small length of line or wool.

Hard alee, hard to lee (U.S.). See Lee Ho.

Hard aport, hard astarboard, hard over. (1) The instruction for the person steering to turn as fast as possible to port or to starboard. (2) To move the helm as far as possible in its current direction.

Hard chine. That method of building which joins relatively flat sections of the hull together at an angle instead of in curves.

Hard down. The order to put the helm down as far as possible.

Hard eye. An eye splice fitted with a thimble.

Harden up (to). Sail closer to the wind.

Hawe line. A line which zigzags between a forestay and an inner forestay and prevents a spinnaker wrap.

Hawse. The area where the anchor cables pass through the hawse holes.

Hawse holes. Large holes in the bow which take the hawse pipes, through which the anchor chain passes.

Hawser. The heavy rope used to moor large vessels, or to tow them.

Head. (1) The bow of a ship. (2) The top part of a sail. (3) The top part of a spar. (4) A lavatory on a boat or ship.

Headboard. Metal or composite strengthening plate at the head of mainsails.

Header. See Lift.

Headsails. Any sail that is set forward of the mast.

Headstay. The same as the forestay.

Heave to (to). Deliberately bring the vessel to a slow speed. With sails, to back the headsail and put the tiller down so that the forces counterbalance and the vessel forereaches very slowly.

Heaving down. Pulling a vessel over on its side by a line taken from its masthead to another boat or the shore. Used most often to drag a boat off when it has grounded, or for careening.

Heaving line. A light line with a small weight or large knot on one end which can be thrown considerably long distances. A heaving line is sent over first and a line too heavy for heaving then attached to it and pulled across to the wharf or other vessel.

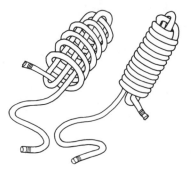

Diagram A2.30 *A heaving line, given this treatment, will throw further and more accurately.*

Heel. (1) The angle of list of a boat under sail. (2) The lower end of any vertical spar, derrick, outrigger etc. (3) The joining of the keel and the sternpost.

Heel brace. The iron support at the bottom of a rudder.

Heeling error. An error induced in a compass when a vessel heels greatly. The heeling distorts the magnetic field compared with that created by a stable vessel.

Height of the tide. The distance between sea level and chart datum.

Helm. (1) All the apparatus that goes towards the ship's steering; the wheel, the tiller. (2) That degree of pressure, or lack of it, that a sailing ship's rudder transmits through imbalance of the rigging or sail setting. A properly set up boat will have just enough weather helm (tendency to turn into the wind) for the helmsman to feel it, without the rudder being applied so much that it is acting as a brake.

Helm amidships. Applying no helm.

High focal plane buoy. A particularly high light on a buoy, used for landfall or fairway buoys.

Hike out (U.S.). See Sit out.

Hiking stick (U.S.). See Folding tiller.

Hiking straps (U.S.). See Toe straps.

Hitch. Those knots which work by jamming under load, but can be easily undone (see above page 20).

Hole cutter (U.S.). See Arbour.

Hollow seas. Overfalls. Waves which become 'tripped' by shoal bottom or countercurrents and become very close together and exceptionally steep.

Horn timber. The angled piece of wood joining the keel and transom.

Horse. A track or bar on which the mainsheet traveller can move as required when the wind freshens or lightens.

Horse latitudes. Zones of high pressure and therefore light and variable winds.

Hounds. The part of the mast where the shrouds attach.

Housing. The part of a mast below decks.

Hovercraft. Craft supported on a manufactured cushion of air and propelled by one or more aircraft-type propellers. They can travel, skimming the sea surface, at up to 80 knots.

Hull speed. The theoretical maximum speed of a hull. The formula 1.5 times the square root of the load waterline expresses the speed. No vessel can exceed this speed unless it breaks into a plane, or surfs on a wave. Physically it is the time when the wave cycle equals the hull length.

Hydrolant, hydropac. Long range navigational warnings, similar to Navarea warnings, issued to mariners by the U.S. hydrographic authorities.

I

In ballast. Carrying ballast, but no cargo.

In irons. Inadvertently caught head to wind while trying to tack and so unable to move or to fall on to either tack. Not to be confused with sailing deliberately head to wind for tactical reasons.

Inboard. In the ship away from the sides or ends.

Inclinometer. A pivoted pointer set on the centreline of a vessel and showing on a scale the degrees of heel.

Diagram A2.31 *An inclinometer, to indicate angle of heel.*

Inland Rules. Rules of the Road for vessels operating in the navigable waters of the U.S. inside the established navigational lines of demarcation including the Great Lakes.

Inshore traffic zone. A zone, usually on either side of a traffic separation scheme where local traffic travels to keep away from the 'through' traffic.

Intercept. The difference in distance between the true and calculated altitudes of a heavenly body. The distance is measured in nautical miles towards or away from an assumed position.

Intermediate points. The points between North, North-east, East etc. Hence, North-north-east, East-north-east.

International Code of Signals. Letter flags which are universally used, also combinations which have specific meaning and are used ship-to-ship, and ship-to-shore.

International port signals. Internationally agreed system of virtual traffic signals controlling vessels entering or leaving different ports.

Interrupted light. One which flashes rapidly but has long periods of darkness. They are split into quick, very quick and ultra quick.

Irishman's reef. The head of a sail tied or knotted to reduce its size. Quite handy with a jury rig in heavy weather.

Iron wire rope. Rigid wire used for standing rigging.

Isobars. Charted lines joining positions of equal barometric pressure.

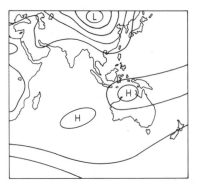

Diagram A2.32 *Isobars on a weather map indicate points of equal barometric pressure.*

Isochrone. Charted lines of equal time, or occurring at the same time.

Isolated danger. One which is clear of the coast and in deep water and therefore a particular hazard. It is marked with a buoy.

Isophase light. A light of equal durations of light and darkness.

J

Jackstay. Strong wire led the length of a vessel so that harnesses can be clipped to it in heavy weather. Some racing boats prefer silver rope because it is strong and more elastic.

Jawrope. The line joining the jaws of a gaff or gunter and preventing the jaws sliding off the mast.

Jaws (of a gaff or gunter). The curved arms that fit on the end of a spar and around the mast.

Jib. A triangular sail, set to the fore-stay and not overlapping the mast.

Jib club. A boom along the foot of a foresail.

Jibe. To change course when running before the wind so that the apparent wind comes across the opposite quarter. If a spinnaker is up, it too must be jibed.

Jumper. The highest struts on a mast, supporting the very top section of the mast, usually strutted forward.

Jury rig. Any temporary arrangement to replace a failed mechanism on a vessel, but more commonly accepted as an arrangement of the maximum rigging and sail area possible to replace the vessel's designed rig.

K

Kedge. A small anchor used for lighter duties than the main anchor(s). Usually used to haul forward in a tideway, or as a stern anchor in yachts or power boats. The action of hauling a boat forward or around is called 'to kedge'.

Keel. The main strength of any vessel, the fore and aft timber which is laid down first in building, and which takes all the frames that shape the boat. In the case of a yacht, the weight protruding below the hull which counterbalances the force of the heeling of the boat and so produces forward motion.

Keelson. A fore and aft timber fitted on top of the keel which also binds together the frames and floor timbers.

Ketch. A two-masted yacht with the after mast (mizzen) stepped in front of the steering position.

Kevlar. A material used in the sails of racing yachts which has great stability and will hold its shape in changing wind conditions. It is,

weight for weight, stronger than steel. It is also used in sheets which take great load but care must be taken with leading it through turning blocks and around winches as it dislikes being in anything but a straight line.

Kicking strap (vang). A purchase for holding down the boom so that the power of the sail is more efficiently translated into forward motion.

Kingpost. See Bitt.

Kite. Slang for a spinnaker.

Knees. Right-angled pieces to support horizontal or vertical joints. Hanging knees are vertical and lodging knees horizontal.

Knot. The speed of one nautical mile per hour.

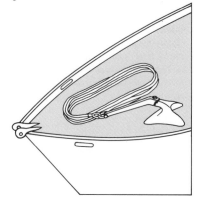

Diagram A2.33 *Preparing a kedge.*

L

Lanby. Large automatic navigational buoy. Very large, up to 12 m (40 feet) diameter, usually automatic, floating base for a light and/or fog signal.

Landfall buoy. An exceptionally high buoy, often miles to seaward, marking landfall at a port.

Landing strake. The uppermost but one strake on a wooden boat's hull.

Lanyard. A small line used to join to anything or on a sling.

Lateen. A large triangular sail set across the mast on an angled yard so that the sail is partly in front of and partly behind the mast.

Lateral mark. Buoys used under the IALA system.

Lateral resistance. The resistance to leeway, or sideways drift, given by the keel. One of the major components of a yacht's motion.

Latitude. Lines of latitude divide the earth horizontally from the equator to both poles. They cover 90 degrees each in each hemisphere. Each degree represents 60 nautical miles. The sides of each nautical chart are marked with degrees of latitude and because they are constant are used to measure distance. Lines of longitude, which divide the world horizontally taper near the poles and therefore are not constant and cannot be used to measure distance.

Layline. Particularly in racing, the line along which a close-hauled yacht would have to sail to round a mark or obstruction. To tack before reaching a layline would mean the mark was underlaid and the yacht would have to tack again. To tack after reaching the layline would mean the yacht had sailed too far. Obviously if the wind changes during the approach to a mark, the layline will change. Because a yacht can approach a mark on either port or starboard tack, there is a port layline and a starboard layline.

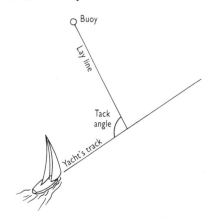

Diagram A2.34 *The layline to a mark will depend on wind strength, the boat's pointing ability, and the skill of the helmsman.*

Lazy (guy, brace, sheet). In double systems, as used for a dip pole jibe, the control not being used.

Lazyjacks. Lines rigged so that the mainsail will gather in them when being dropped. They can run from the mast to the boom or from standing rigging higher than the boom. Quite common on large cruising boats that don't have self-furling.

Leading lights. Lights one above the other but well separated in distance so that when kept in line they provide a bearing to enter a harbour.

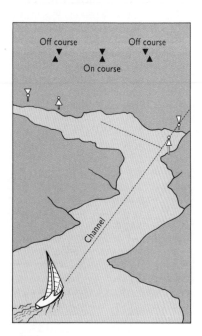

Diagram A2.35 *Leading lights and beacons. When the approach is accurate the diamonds look as in the centre illustration. If the approach is too far to the right, the first misalignment will show; if the approach is too far to the left the second misalignment will show.*

Leading marks (beacons). Like leading lights, but unlit and so can be used during the day only. They are usually triangular shapes, the bottom pointing up and the top down, with the points meeting in the centre.

League. Three nautical miles.

Lee bow. In an ocean race, when close-hauled and in a current or tide, to choose the tack which will put the current on to the lee bow of the yacht. The effect is that the current will push the yacht to windward and so shorten the distance to the next mark. To go

on the opposite tack would mean the wind and the current pushing the yacht further to leeward, making it sail further. The tactic can also be used in shorter races but is more difficult to apply in big fleets and short legs.

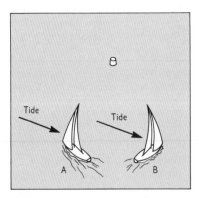

Diagram A2.36 *To lee bow a yacht is to choose the tack where the tide is pushing the lee bow towards the mark as in yacht A. The yacht on tack B is pushed away from the mark and has to sail further to get there.*

Lee edge. See Leech.

Lee helm. The latent intention of a boat to sail to leeward if not corrected by pointing up into the wind (applying lee helm). Not desirable in a racing boat.

Lee Ho (U.K.), hard alee, hard to lee (U.S.). The second of the two commands from the helmsman when tacking. This he gives after 'Ready about' and when the crew is ready. As he says 'Lee Ho' he pushes the tiller away or turns the wheel to begin the tack.

Leeboards. Formerly boards dipped vertically into the water on the side of flat-bottomed trading boats to act as a sort of inefficient keel. Also, boards on the lee side of a berth to stop the sleeper sliding on to the floor when a boat heels excessively.

Leech. The trailing edge of a sail, the edge between the head and the clew.

Leech line. The line through the trailing edge of the leech and often led down the luff, for tensioning the leech so that it does not flap.

Leeward. Away from the wind, in the direction the wind blows, on the sheltered side.

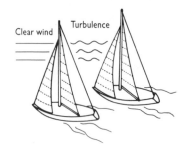

Diagram A2.37 *The leading yacht is in the safe leeward position and is directing turbulent air onto the sails of the other yacht.*

Leeward (go to). Move the weight of the crew to leeward, as when there is little wind, to keep the boat on its lines and so sail faster.

Leeway. The difference between where a boat aims across the surface and where she actually goes. For navigational purposes it is expressed as an angle and added into the corrections made to the compass when arriving at a course. It is an inexact amount and its measurement is part experience and part instinct.

Leeway meter. A simple way to measure leeway quite accurately in all conditions is to place an ordinary protractor on the stern with the arc facing the sea. A line attached at the middle of the protractor and going into the sea for a few feet with a small weight attached will give the angle.

Lifeboat. Any vessel, whether ashore or afloat, which is equipped with lifesaving equipment. International standards are set as to the qualities the boat should have and the equipment it should carry. Boats designated for lifesaving purposes are subject to inspection to see that the standards are being observed.

Lifeline. Like a jackstay, the line rigged for crew to attach to in heavy weather.

Liferaft. Inflatable rubberized nylon craft used in emergency. They have regulation safety stores and equipment packed with them. They should be used only as a last resort as the vessel itself is a safer refuge unless actually foundering.

Lift. A wind shift in which the wind moves further behind the boat. Sailing to windward this allows the yacht to head more directly towards its objective.

Lifting sail. Any sail, such as a jib or spinnaker, which tends to lift the bows. Such sails are important when running before heavy seas.

Lifts. Any line which supports a spar or pole, such as a spinnaker topping lift or main boom topping lift.

Limber holes. Holes drilled through the floors alongside the keelson so that bilgewater will drain to a low point and not collect in pockets throughout the vessel. From the low point the water can be pumped clear. It is important to keep limber holes open.

Line. (1) The old definition of line was anything under 1 inch and all the rest was rope. (2) The equator, hence crossing the line.

Line of position (LOP). A bearing or other indication that a vessel is on a particular line. The intersection of two or more lines of position gives a fix or observed position.

Line of transit. A line drawn on a chart which will avoid all dangers without deviation.

Line squall. Sudden acceleration of wind speed with the passage of a cold front, occurring in temperate zones of the westerlies. In South America it is called the Pampero, and in southern Australia the Southerly Buster. Classic line squalls are relatively easy to see as the front shows as a cigar-shaped roll of cloud, either grey-white or black. The barometer often gives no warning.

Lizard. A wire or line with an eye in the end for another line to be attached or rove through, or for a block to be attached. Technically speaking, a spinnaker choker is a lizard.

L.O.A. Length overall.

Local hour angle (LHA). The distance of the local celestial meridian west of Greenwich.

Local magnetic anomaly. A local effect added to the earth's normal field. It can be dramatically large.

Lodestar. The pole star, Polaris.

Log. Any device, mechanical or electronic, for measuring the speed of a vessel. To log something is to enter it in the ship's log (book).

Log (book). Any book which records the working of the ship or a department of it, and which is filled in regularly. A rough or deck log is kept, ideally every half hour, and the fair or smooth log is filled in later by the navigator or captain. On large vessels each major department keeps its own log so that there is a detailed record of the functioning of the whole ship.

Long fetch (to). Be able to sail a long distance while close-hauled without having to tack. It is a fetch because the mark can be laid without tacking.

Long flashing light. A navigational light which exhibits for at least two seconds, followed by a longer period of darkness or less strong light.

Longitude. Any great circle passing through both poles measured in degrees east or west of Greenwich, which is taken as 0 degrees and is the prime meridian.

Loom. (1) The first sighting of a navigational light when it is seen as an area of light rather than as a point. Usually the loom, when first seen, will show against clouds, or the land behind a lighthouse. Noting the point

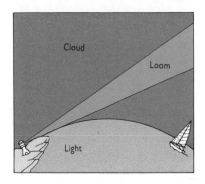

Diagram A2.38 *The loom of a light is the diffused reflection in clouds etc. The moment the light can be seen as a clear pinpoint the distance off can be calculated.*

at which the loom changes to the actual light, and simultaneously the height of eye of the observer, can give a navigator a rough idea of the distance to the light. (2) The diffuse glow of lights from a city against the clouds. (3) The part of the oar the rower grips.

LORAN. Acronym for long range navigational system. Loran C covers most of the northern hemisphere and extensive areas of the Pacific. The system measures the differences in the time of radio signals from widely dispersed stations and because of the distances involved is accurate to about 200 metres.

Lubber line. White painted post in the compass, which when the compass card is lined up against it, indicates the ship's heading.

Luff. The leading edge of a sail. To luff a boat is to turn directly into the wind so that the luffs on each sail stall and flap.

Luff groove (track). Grooved aluminium rod, usually double, which fits over the forestay of racing yachts and allows one sail to remain hoisted while another is hoisted in the other groove to replace it.

Luff zipper. A plastic zipper which runs vertically down the luff of the mainsail of some large yachts, particularly 12 metre yachts. When opened they increase the area of the sail.

L.W.L. Load waterline length.

M

Magnetic bearing. A bearing taken without corrections made to it for compass error, but including variation.

Magnetic course. An uncorrected course taken directly from the compass, but including variation.

Magnetic meridian. Where a compass needle points if there is no deviation, or the deviation has been counteracted.

Magnetic north. The area in the northern hemisphere to which all compass needles point. It is the area of greatest magnetic attraction in the earth.

Magnitude. The system of classifying stars according to their brightness, stars of the first magnitude being the easiest to see, and of the seventh being the dimmest the naked eye can pick up. The navigational stars are of the first or second magnitude.

Main boom. The boom holding the mainsail.

Main mast. The tallest, most important mast on the boat.

Main sheet. The line controlling the mainsail.

Main stay. The line supporting the main mast.

Main yard. On old vessels, the yard to which the mainsail is attached.

Mainsail. The largest sail, attached to the main mast.

Marconi rig. The standard fore and aft rig of the modern ocean racer.

Diagram A2.39 *The marconi or bermuda rig.*

Marl. (1) Shingle as marked on charts relating to the sea bottom. (2) To marl something is to whip or serve it so that every turn is knotted.

Marline. Tarred light line for serving or whipping.

Marling hitch. The hitch most commonly used when tying down a sail, particularly the mainsail. The line is tied off at one end, led part of the way along the sail, and secured

around it in a half hitch which is then tied off with an overhand knot. This continues until the whole sail is secure.

Marlinspike. A gradually tapered, pointed spike of wood or iron, used to separate the strands of a rope when splicing.

Marlinspike hitch. A hitch with a marlinspike through it which gives leverage.

Mast boot. Canvas or rubber fitted around the area where a mast goes through the deck to its step below decks. It is lashed around the top, or has a large jubilee clip around it top and bottom. It then prevents water running down the mast.

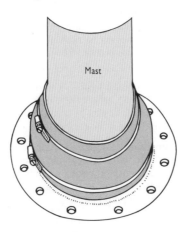

Diagram A2.40 *A typical mast boot, with metal jubilee clips tightly compressing rubber against the mast.*

Masthead. The top of the mast, the area for electronic wind sensors, VHF aerials, halyards etc.

Masthead light (U.S.). A white light placed over the fore and aft centreline of the vessel showing an unbroken light over an arc of the horizon of 225 degrees and so fixed as to show the light from right ahead to 22.5 degrees abaft the beam on either side of the vessel. See also Steaming light (U.K.).

Masthead rig. A yacht with the forestay reaching to the top of the mast. Hence masthead sloop, masthead cutter.

Matthew Walker. A very useful development of the wall knot.

Mean. The mean is the average, so for instance, mean low water springs translates as average low water when the tides are largest.

Measured mile. Areas marked on charts which denote precise distances of one nautical mile, usually between two transits or two buoys. There is usually at least one in any major harbour, and there are many coastal measured miles at sea. They are used for calibrating logs.

Mediterranean berth. See page 101.

Meridian. (1) A line passing through both poles and intersecting the equator at right angles, known as longitude. (2) The meridian of a planet or star is its highest point in its orbit, hence meridian passage for the sun near midday. (3) The prime meridian is that of Greenwich (0 degrees).

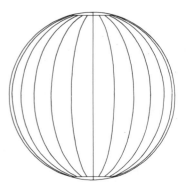

Diagram A2.41 *Meridians of longitude. Each is a great circle.*

Messenger. A line passed over the anchor cable to try to snare a fouled anchor by the stock. If this is successful the anchor cable is buoyed and slipped and an attempt made to free the anchor by pulling on the messenger from a different direction.

Metacentre. The point upward and away from the centreline of a boat which is heeling. The metacentre is at the intersection of a vertical from the now moved centre of buoyancy and the centreline. As long as the metacentre is above the vessel's centre of gravity the boat will right itself, but as it moves further outboard and therefore lower, the heeling moment increases and, unless it can be corrected, the boat will capsize.

Mid latitude. A method of calculating a course to make up for the fact that the representation of a sphere on a plane surface is distorted in high latitudes.

Middle ground buoys. A buoy marked in a special way to indicate that there is middle ground. (See pages 120-121.)

Middle watch. From 2400 to 0400.

Minute. A measurement of time, arc or latitude which is 60 seconds in time, and one-sixtieth of a degree when applied to arc and latitude. Distances are invariably measured off charts on the latitude scale, where one minute equals one nautical mile.

Mizzen. The triangular sail hoisted on the aftermost mast. On older vessels, where the mizzen could be square, although still fore and aft, it was also called a spanker or driver.

Modified true wind. True wind as modified by outside factors such as current, motion of a vessel etc. Apparent wind.

Monkey's fist. An especially heavy knot on the end of a heaving line to help it cover more distance.

Monohull. A single-hulled vessel, not a catamaran or trimaran.

Mooring buoy. A buoy of any size to which a vessel can moor, or which denotes that there is a mooring below the buoy.

Morning star. Usually, but not necessarily, Venus, rising just before dawn.

Morning watch. 0400 to 0800.

Morse code fog signal. A sound signal in Morse code warning of reduced visibility.

Morse code light. A light which flashes Morse code character(s).

Motor sailer. A boat with characteristics of a yacht and a power boat; a good engine and fair sailing qualities.

Mouse. (1) A light line reeved ready to lead a halyard over its sheaves if required. (2) To mouse a knot or line on a cleat is to tie it so that it cannot come undone. (3) To mouse a hook is to tie across its upper part so that a sling or line cannot come free.

Multihull. A vessel with more than one hull, such as a catamaran or trimaran.

Mushroom anchor. Anchor with a mushroom-shaped heavy head for anchoring in mud or other soft ground.

Diagram A2.42 *A mushroom anchor.*

Mylar. A light but very strong material useful for sails such as 100 per cent lightweight genoas and some spinnakers.

N

Nadir (Na). The point on the celestial sphere which is an extension of the line from vertically above an observer drawn through the observer.

Name. When latitude and declination are the same they are said to be of the same name. They are contrary when they differ.

Nautical mile. One minute of latitude at the equator, 1852 metres (6077 feet).

Navarea warnings. Warnings of danger to navigation promulgated by the Worldwide Navigational Warning Service. The world is divided into 16 Navareas for which an appointed authority is responsible. The local authority also gives coastal warnings which are of a more parochial nature, and port or pilotage authorities give local warnings.

Navigation lights. Lights exhibited when required by international regulations, which by the arrangement and colours required show the existence of the vessel, its type and its course.

Navigation Rules. The Rules of the Road in the United States.

Navigational triangle. The spherical triangle formed by the pole, the observer's assumed position and the geographical position of a heavenly body.

Navtex. The beginnings of a worldwide telex warning service being developed by the International Maritime Organisation. The service broadcasts maritime safety messages, weather information and distress messages.

Neaps (tides). The lowest range of the tidal variation.

Negative surge. Occasions when weather conditions cause the level of the sea to be below predicted height. This can happen in bays when strong prevailing winds bank water up at one end, lowering it at the other.

Nip (to). (1) Take a quick turn around a winch. (2) A small kink in a line which prevents it passing through a block.

Non-directional beacon. A beacon broadcasting its signal in all directions, not one particular direction.

Noon sight. The sextant sighting taken to establish the highest point through which the sun passes at noon. From this, corrections can be applied to arrive at the latitude of the observer.

North star. Polaris.

Nun buoy. Two cones, base to base, anchored so that one cone points upwards.

O

Observation spot. A position of precise latitude and longitude.

Observed position. A position arrived at by observation; a fix.

Occulting lights. A light interrupted by periods of darkness. The opposite of flashing.

Off the wind. With the wind free, not close-hauled.

Omega. Very low frequency navigation system which gives worldwide position fixing to an accuracy of one mile by day and two at night. Can be interfaced with satellite navigation systems.

On the wind. Sailing close-hauled, close to the wind.

On the beam. Abeam, at right angles to the vessel.

On the bow. Towards the bow, not abeam.

On the quarter. Towards the stern, not abeam.

One two three rule. More usually called the rule of twelfths, this is a handy way to remember the approximate strength of a tide that has no unusual characteristics. Proportionate to the range for the day the tide will fall or rise in the time ratio 123:321. The rate of flow can therefore be seen to be at its greatest in the third and fourth hours of the six hours between high and low, and at its least in the first and last.

Outhaul. The control line which loosens or tightens the foot of a sail, particularly the mainsail. It is very important as it matches the shape of the sail to the strength of the wind.

Outpoint. To sail closer to the wind than another boat and so get to a weather mark sooner. A highly desirable quality in a yacht.

Outrigger. A float on one or both sides of a main hull to prevent capsize. A second or third hull near the size of a main hull is not an outrigger.

Overfall. A dangerous, steep wave formed where a current meets an opposing wind, or at shoal grounds, or where a tide rip forms.

Overhand knot. The simplest knot of all—make a loop near the end of a line and pass the end through it.

Overhangs. The area forward and aft on a boat which projects beyond the waterline.

Overlap (to). To have begun to overtake another vessel so that one's bow projects over a line drawn at right angles to the fore and aft line of the boat being overtaken.

Override, overrider. To have a turn around a winch caught under a later turn which jams increasingly tightly as the load grows. If not taken out the line may have to be cut off. The usual method is to take the free end of the line to another winch and pull it free. Sometimes a stopper knot can be put on the line under strain, transferring the strain, and the override cleared when the line is not under load.

P

Painted waterline (U.S.). See Boot top.

Painter. The mooring line for a small boat or dinghy.

Parallel rules. Two similar, flat oblongs joined by pivoted arms so that wherever one goes the other will follow and will stay parallel. Largely superseded now, they were once indispensable for the navigator for transferring bearings from the compass rose. A plotter with a floating compass rose is better because it can be read from any part of the chart provided it lines up with a latitude and longitude, or any other square line.

Parallax error. That error which comes from not viewing the compass, an instrument etc., from directly in front. The amount of error varies with the different angles of viewing. In celestial navigation parallax is the difference between the true altitude of a heavenly body and its observed position.

Parrot beak. The hooked jaw with a sliding barrel on the spinnaker end of a spinnaker pole. The brace is slotted into the beak. When a jibe is required the pole is lowered and moved forward and the lazy brace replaces the old brace.

Pelorus. A rotating pointer over a fixed compass dial for taking bearings of the land.

Perigee. The point when the moon is closest to the earth, increasing the gravitational pull on the ocean and so causing perigee tides which are greater than normal.

Personal Flotation Device (PFD) (U.S.). See Lifebelt.

Pinching. Sailing a boat too high into the wind so that it stalls and falls away.

Pintle. The male part of the rudder fittings, it is attached to the transom or sternpost and slides into the gudgeon which is attached to the rudder.

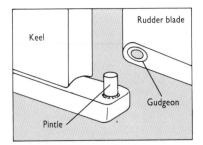

Diagram A2.43 *A rudder pintle.*

Pivoting beacon or tower. A spar or tower with a light or topmark which can be tilted by wind or current because it is anchored to the sea bed.

Planing. A vessel planes when its bow lifts, the wetted surface decreases greatly, and it exceeds its hull speed.

Plimsoll line. The lines drawn on the side of merchant vessels showing their legal draught in different conditions.

Plow (plough). Ursa Major, or the Great Bear constellation.

Plow anchor (U.S.). See Coastal quick release (CQR anchor).

Point (to). (1) Sail as high as possible to the wind. A boat that points well sails closer to the wind than others. (2) A point of the compass is 11¼ degrees.

Polar performance curve. Plotted graph of ability of yacht under various sailing conditions. Many observations are put into a computer program and 'smoothed' to give a benchmark performance against which the vessel can be sailed.

Points of the compass. The 32 points which make up the 360 degrees of the compass. The degree notation is the only one used now.

Pole star. Polaris.

Poop. The stern deck of a vessel.

Port. (1) A safe harbour. (2) The left hand side of the boat.

Port and starboard. The Rule of the Road that says the port tack boat must give way to the starboard tack boat. The basic rule of sailing.

Port hand buoys. Under cardinal system A of marking channels those red buoys that must be left on the port hand when entering port, or with the flood tide. Those countries in area B use green markers for port.

Port tack. Sailing with the wind coming over the port side first.

Port watch (starboard watch). See Watch.

Position doubtful. Marked on a chart as PD if there is any reason to suspect a position.

Position line. Any line on a chart which gives one indication of position such as distance off, bearing, celestial observation. At least two are needed to give an observed position.

Positive surge. An unpredictable increase in depth of water through weather conditions. See also negative surge.

Pram (dinghy). A small tender with a bow cut off like a transom.

Preferred channel buoy. A buoy which indicates the better of one or more channels in a harbour, or which the port authorities prefer to be used.

Preventer. A purchase taken from the main boom to the gunwale or toe-rail when running so that the main is unlikely to jibe.

Prime meridian. The meridian of longitude through Greenwich.

Prolonged blast. Under the Rules of the Road a whistle lasting at least six seconds.

Propeller allowance. An allowance in yacht handicapping for propeller arrangements which have varying amounts of drag. A small-bladed, folding propeller would have a

smaller allowance than a fixed, broad-bladed propeller.

Protest flag. Code flag B, or in emergency any red square, attached to the backstay during a yacht race by a vessel that claims to have been fouled by another.

Pulpit. Stainless steel or other guard-rail around the bows of a yacht or motor boat.

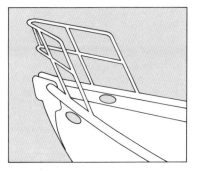

Diagram A2.44 *A pulpit.*

Pushpit (U.K.), Stern pulpit (U.S.). Stainless steel or other guardrail around the stern of a vessel.

Q

Quadrant. The metal section of a circle attached to the rudder stock and taking the control cables in wheel steering.

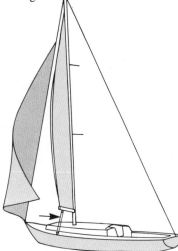

Diagram A2.45 *A preventer, which protects against the accidental jibe.*

Quarter. The after section of a vessel on one side. To be on the quarter means to be at 45 degrees aft of the beam, or thereabouts.

Quick flashing light. A light which flashes 60 or more times a minute.

R

Racon. A radar beacon which emits its signal when triggered by beams from a radar set.

Radar clearing line. A radar range to provide a safe distance off when travelling along a coast where accurate fixes are impossible or unlikely.

Radar reflector. Metal apparatus with many surfaces which reflects radar signals on structures or vessels which otherwise would be difficult to detect.

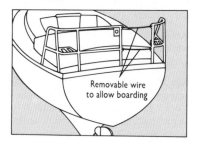

Diagram A2.46 *A stern pulpit or pushpit.*

Radio beacon. Radio station on shore emitting a fixed signal which can be used, with other beacons, or other navigational aids to get bearings and from them, a position.

Radio direction finder (RDF). Radio receiver used to determine the direction of a radio wave source. Navigation system of finding position from the intersection of several radio bearings from transmitters in known positions.

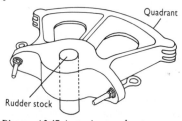

Diagram A2.47 *A steering quadrant.*

Radio fog signal. Signals from a radio beacon in times of low visibility.

Rake. The angle out of the upright of a mast. Ideally a mast would rake slightly aft going to weather and slightly forward running.

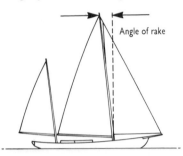

Diagram A2.48 *Rake of a mast.*

Range. (1) The North American equivalent of transit. (2) The difference in height between high tide and the next low tide.

Ratio of ranges. A factor for calculating the tidal range offshore.

Ratlines. Small lines across the shrouds to form footholds when going aloft.

Reach (to). Sail across the wind: acutely is a head reach, at right angles a beam reach, and with the wind from slightly behind a broad reach. A beam reach is usually the fastest point of sailing for any vessel.

Reef (to). Reduce sail so that a boat is not overpressed in heavy weather.

Reef cringles. Strengthened thimbles in a sail to take the reefing lines.

Reef points. Short lines which can tie around a boom (with reef or square knots), or through eyes in a loose-footed sail, so that sail not required after a reef can be neatly stowed.

Reefing line. Lines led ready to pull in a reef quickly when necessary. The quickest system is to put a hooked line into the first reef cringle against the mast and pull it down as the halyard is lowered. At the same time the reefing line permanently through the first reef cringle is winched tight so that the whole slab is removed in one operation. Properly done the boat need not lose any speed (see diagram 2.5, page 30).

Reeve. Run a line through a block or ring, lead it to the sail etc. which it has to control.

Reverse sheer. Sheer the reverse of normal. The sheerline rises above the straight line from stem to stern instead of curving below.

Rhumb line. A course which intersects each meridian at the same angle.

Riding light. Anchor light.

Riding sail (U.K.), Stability sail (U.S.). Any small sail, such as storm jib or mizzen, which will help a vessel hang in a particular direction during heavy weather. A vessel which has lost its steering can be controlled by the use of riding (stability) sails.

Roach. The curve in the trailing edge of a triangular sail.

Roaring Forties. Between 40 degrees and 50 degrees south where the prevailing westerlies circle the earth with little obstruction.

Roller furling. Means of furling a jib by winding it on a spring loaded stay. Used on cruising boats.

Roller reefing. A system for reefing the mainsail where the boom rotates and winds the sail in.

Rope. Classically cordage above one inch in diameter made of any number of vegetable fibres, now almost completely superseded by man-made fibres of nylon, polypropylene, mylar, kevlar etc. Some are woven and without stretch, some made in the classical manner.

Rotating pattern radio beacon (radio lighthouse). A beacon emitting a signal containing time markers so that a navigator can, from tables, arrive at a true bearing.

Round bilge (soft chined). The term used to denote a bilge without sharp corners, as is a chine bilge.

Rubbing strake. A strip of buffer wood along the length of the outside of the hull just below the gunwale.

Rudder chains. Chains fitted on each side of the rudder to allow steering to continue if the wheel mechanism or tiller fails.

Rudder post. The post which carries the rudder and to which the tiller or wheel is attached.

Rules of the Road. The international regulations governing the behaviour of vessels in close proximity by day and night.

Runners. Double or single adjustable stays which run from the mast to the quarters of the boat and are pulled on on the weather side to support the mast. They are now very sophisticated in that they bring the final tune to the mast rather than act simply as a support.

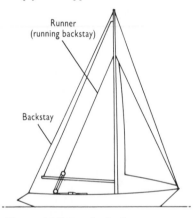

Diagram A2.49 *Running backstays or runners.*

Running bowline. A normal bowline with the other end passed through the loop forming a constricting loop. Because it constricts it is dangerous to put around people.

Running fix. Two bearings are taken of one object with a reasonable time

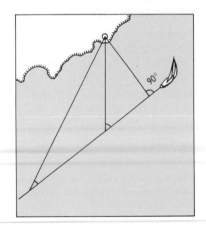

Diagram A2.50 *A running fix.*

between them depending on the vessel's speed. The distance travelled, and the course and first bearing are transferred giving the position of the vessel at the time of the second bearing.

Running rigging. Everything that isn't fixed, such as sheets, halyards, lifts, guys etc.

S

Safe overhead clearance. The distance which must be left between the top of the mast and overhead hanging electrical cables to prevent electricity arcing from the cables to the mast.

Safe water mark. Mark, under the IALA system, which indicates safe water.

Sail track. A groove or slot which takes the luff of a sail. Double tracks such as Gemini allow sails to be changed without going bareheaded as one can be raised on a separate halyard while the first stays up.

Sailing directions. Books issued by hydrographic offices which list the characteristics of a coastline, its dangers, harbours etc.

Sampson post. A strong post, usually on the foredeck, to take a tow, to secure to, or to moor.

Scantlings. Timbers or other material used in the construction of a vessel. For racing under the International Offshore Rules (IOR) or other international rules the scantlings must meet certain safety standards and size of scantlings as set out by the American Bureau of Shipping (ABS).

Scend. (1) The depth below mean water level that the trough of a wave descends. Calculating scend can be important when travelling over shallow water in a sea, and particularly when entering a river over a bar. A rule of thumb is to add the estimated height of a wave to the boat's draught to allow for freak conditions. (2) The severe downward movement of a ship's bow when crashing into a deep trough.

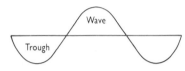

Diagram A2.52 *Scend.*

Schooner. A fore and aft rigged vessel with two or more masts and the second mast taller than the first.

Screw. The propeller. Screwing up in a controlled way is the ideal way to race to windward so that the vessel performs a series of shallow scallops maintaining top speed while pointing high.

Scuppers. Holes in bulwarks or toe rails to allow water to escape.

Sea anchor. Any combination of weights or drogues which will have the effect of holding the ship towards the sea (when streamed from the bow), or slowing it down (when streamed from the stern).

Sea cock. A valve fitted through the hull of a vessel which allows liquid into or out of a hull under control.

Sea mark. A beacon clearly visible from the sea.

Sea mile. The length of one minute of arc along the meridian at one's latitude. The length varies with the latitude.

Secondary port. In the tide tables a port for which daily predictions are not given, but variation in the time of high and low water are given relative to a standard port.

Sector, of a light. That portion of a circle, marked on a chart, from which a light can be seen, or, if there is more than one light, the characteristics of each can be seen.

Separation zone or lane. A congested area where shipping is directed to travel in opposing directions in separate lanes, with a space between, as does motor traffic on a highway.

Serving mallet. A grooved mallet which applies serving under pressure to keep it tight.

Set. The movement of current or tide which diverts a vessel from its chosen course. The calculation of set is one of the most difficult parts of a navigator's duties. Set is described by its direction of movement; if it is flowing from North to South it is a southerly set and it sets to the South.

Sextant. A navigator's instrument for measuring angles, vertically, as of stars, lighthouses etc., and horizontally, of landmarks.

Shackle. A U-shaped rod of steel with holes in each of the ends, one threaded and the other slightly larger and unthreaded. They come in many shapes and sizes and are used as connectors.

Shank. The part of an anchor connecting the flukes and the stock.

Shear pin. A sacrificial pin attaching a propeller to the shaft of an outboard motor. When the propeller hits an object the pin breaks preventing further damage to the propeller.

Sheave. The wheel inside a block, grooved so that a line will fit in it.

Sheepshank. A knot used to shorten a line.

Sheer. The curve between the bow and stern at the gunwales.

Sheer legs. Two or more spars resting at a common apex to hoist heavy weights.

Sheer strake. The plank which follows the sheer of a vessel.

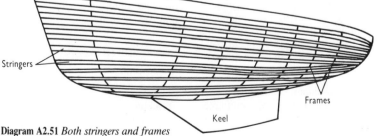

Diagram A2.51 *Both stringers and frames are scantlings.*

Sheet. Any line attached to the clew of a sail and which controls how it is trimmed.

Shorten sail (to). Reef, or put up smaller sails, or both.

Shrouds. The wires or rod standing rigging that supports the mast. The usual rig is cap shrouds (the main shrouds that run from the chainplates to the top of the mast) (the uppers), intermediates which run from below the top spreaders to the chainplates, and lowers, which run from the chainplates to below the bottom spreaders.

Side lights. A green light on the starboard side and a red light on the port side each showing an unbroken light over an arc of the horizon of 112.5 degrees and so fixed as to show the light from right ahead to 22.5 degrees abaft the beam on its respective side. In a vessel of less than 20 meters in length the side lights may be combined in one lantern carried on the fore and aft centreline of the vessel.

Sidereal hour angle (SHA). The Greenwich hour angle of a star, minus the GHA of Aries.

Sight reduction tables. Tables containing mathematical information relative to the position of heavenly bodies which, when used with a sextant and time observations, allow the calculation of a position.

Single buoy mooring (SBM). A large mooring buoy in open water.

Sister clip (U.K.), Brummel hook (U.S.). Easy to use clips, basically a flat circular piece of metal with a hole in the middle and a tapered slot in one side. Each slips into the other and can only come undone by hand manipulation.

Diagram A2.53 *Sister clip.*

Skeg. Any metal plate which supports something outside the hull such as the rudder, the propeller shaft.

Skin. The outside of a boat, particularly if it has been moulded.

Slant (U.K.), Lift (U.S.). A favourable shift in the wind.

Slings (U.S.). See Gripes.

Small circle. A plane which intersects a sphere but does not pass through its centre.

Snatch block. A block which can be opened on one side to be quickly put over a line already under strain or without having to pass the whole line through the block.

Soft eye. An eye splice without a thimble.

Sound signals. Those signals required by regulations for use in harbours to indicate a vessel's intentions, or in fog to indicate its presence.

Soundings. The depths marked on charts. To sound is to take the depth either by handline or electronic means.

Spar. Any mast, spinnaker pole, boom, gaff, gunter.

Spar buoy. A buoy with a spar on top so that it can be seen from afar.

Spherical buoy. A buoy of spherical shape denoting particular hazards. (See pages 120-121.)

Spider band. An iron band with rings welded to it which goes around the base of a mast and takes shackles on the end of running rigging. Also often fitted with extended T-heads to take the lines themselves.

Spilling the wind. See Feather.

Spindle buoy. Tall conical buoy.

Spinnaker. A racing sail, usually of nylon or mylar, which is cut very full and sets on the opposite side of the boat from the main when running or reaching. Specially flat cut spinnakers are used for reaching. Large boats carry several spinnakers of different weights of material to use in different conditions.

Spinnaker boom, pole. The spar used to extend the foot of a spinnaker and take the topping lift and downhaul. The spinnaker brace (guy) is slotted into the parrot beak so that

the clew can fly free when the sail is being dropped.

Sponson. A permanent platform on the outside of the hull of a vessel.

Spreaders. Arms horizontal to a mast which push out the shrouds, helping them support the mast.

Spring lines. Mooring lines which prevent a vessel moving forward or backwards. They run from the stern to a bollard or cleat well forward of the bow, and from the bow to a bollard or cleat well aft of the stern. When two vessels tie up alongside the spring lines can only run to the bow and stern of the longer vessel.

Spring ship. A technique often used when swinging compass. A line is passed over the stern and attached to the anchor cable. When the cable is let out the boat gradually swings through a circle.

Spring tides. The largest height between high and low water, taking place just after a full or new moon, when the sun, earth and moon are almost in line and the gravitational attraction is the greatest.

Square rig. A ship with square sails set across its mast. A true square rigger carries nothing but square sails on every mast except the mizzen.

Squat. The lower attitude taken by a ship in the water when travelling at speed compared with when stationary. The effect is heightened in shallow water and becomes a serious problem for vessels with little clearance.

Stability. Ability of a boat to sail stiffly when under full canvas, also not to roll badly when running. Capacity to handle what it was designed to do competently.

Stability allowance. In handicapping, an allowance for gear (engine, masts etc.) which is heavy.

Stability sail (U.S.). See Riding sail.

Stand of tide. Longer than usual high water; a 'double tide'.

Stand on (to). Maintain one's course and speed. It is particularly important to understand when one has the obligation to stand on under the Rules of the Road. The privileged vessel in a meeting situation.

Standard compass. The ship's main compass which may have repeaters elsewhere. It usually has an all-round view for taking bearings.

Standard port. A port included in tide tables with a full listing of the predicted times and heights of high and low water for that port. The time difference in tides at smaller ports (secondary ports) in the area of the standard port are listed and from these differences the tidal height at the smaller ports may be calculated.

Standing rigging. Those parts of the rigging such as shrouds, stays, etc., that are set up permanently and do not move, except for tensioning.

Standpipe. A vertical pipe containing a water supply; a water tower.

Starboard. The right-hand side of a ship looking forward.

Starboard tack. Sailing with the wind coming across the starboard side of the boat first.

Starboard watch. See Watch.

Starboard-hand buoys. Those that mark the right hand side of a channel seen from the entrance to harbour, or going with the main stream of a flood tide. Green in IALA area A, red in area B.

Station pointer. A graduated circle or square with one fixed and two pivoting arms used in navigation. Their prime function is to transfer horizontal sextant angles or other bearings to the chart.

Stays. The forestay, backstay and intermediate or baby stay. Wires, part of the standing rigging, which support the mast fore and aft.

Staysail. A triangular sail set inside another headsail so making a sloop into a cutter. Also a special sail set under a spinnaker to catch the air under it. A tall, narrow such sail is a tallboy and a short, low aspect ratio one is a plain spinnaker staysail.

Steaming light (U.K.). The white light or lights to show that a vessel is under power. See also Masthead light (U.S.).

Steerage way. Each vessel has its own minimum speed below which the rudder will not work effectively. Steerage way is speed just enough for the rudder to begin working.

Step. Any socket into which the foot of the mast is inserted. It is also known as the mast step, and the act of standing the mast into a step is called stepping the mast.

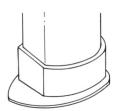

Diagram A2.54 *A mast step.*

Stern. The after part of a ship or boat.

Stern light. A white light placed as nearly as practicable at the stern showing an unbroken light over an arc of the horizon of 135 degrees and so fixed as to show the light 67.5 degrees from right aft on each side of the vessel. (See pages 122-129.)

Stern pulpit (U.S.). See Pushpit.

Sternpost. The after vertical timber which supports the transom.

Stiff. Not easily heeled, a boat which heels only slightly when carrying full sail. The opposite of tender.

Stock. The bar or cross-beam through the upper part of the shank of an anchor.

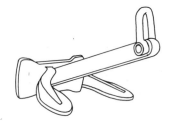

Diagram A2.55 *Stockless anchor.*

Stopper. A short rope, chain, or fitting used to take the strain from another rope or chain temporarily.

Stopper knot. A figure eight, or two round turns and loop, or any other knot to end off a line (see diagram 1.33, page 19).

Storm jib. The 'spitfire', the smallest, strongest jib on board.

Storm sails. The spitfire and trysail. The trysail is attached to the mast and sheeted loose-footed so that heavy seas will not break into it. The spitfire usually has a fairly long strop below it for the same reason.

Storm signals. Shapes, flags, lights or other warning displayed at shore stations to indicate a storm is due.

Stringers. Long fore and aft timbers to join together the frames and add rigidity to a hull.

Strongback. Any strong temporary support when extra strain is being taken on a vessel such as carrying an anchor, towing etc.

Strop. A doubled length of wire or rope. Strops can be used at the head and tack of small jibs to make up the balance of their hoist. Also for peeling a spinnaker, when it is sometimes known as a stripper. Serious racing boats make up a peeling strop to the required length and have a snap shackle at the upper end to hold down the second spinnaker's tack when peeling.

Stuffing box. A through-hull fitting for the drive shaft or rudder post.

Strum box. A perforated container fitted to the end of a bilge pump hose to exclude debris.

Swing the compass (to). Turn through the compass to different headings while taking bearings of one object. The bearing is noted at each heading and plotted on a graph paper and the different headings smoothed out to form a curve. The smoothed out curve is a deviation card and is used to record the amount of deviation to be allowed for every heading.

Swinging circle. The circular area a ship at anchor needs to be able to swing freely through 360 degrees.

T

Tabernacle. A hinged upright, supporting frame to house the foot of a mast. Tabernacle mounted masts are useful when taking sailboats under fixed bridges.

Tack. (1) The forward bottom corner of a sail; the lowest part of the leading edge. (2) To tack is to bring the wind on to the other side of the boat when going to windward; to go from one tack to the other. A boat is on the port or starboard tack depending on which side the wind crosses first.

Taffrail. A rail around the stern of a vessel.

Tall buoy (U.S.). See Dan buoy.

Tender. (1) A motor vessel which acts as the link between a larger vessel and the shore. (2) A vessel is said to be tender when she heels greatly in the slightest breeze and has to be reefed early to remain on her lines.

Throat or head. The upper fore corner of a fore and aft sail.

Thumb cleat. A small cleat with only half the cross piece. Useful for jamming.

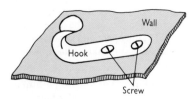

Diagram A2.56 *A thumb cleat.*

Tidal atlas. Chartlets published by hydrographic authorities which show the direction and rate of flow of tidal streams.

Tiller. A wood or metal arm attached to the rudder for steering.

Tiller extension. An extra length attached to a swivel at the end of the tiller to allow the helmsman to hike out or to steer from a position where he can see ahead. See also Hiking stick.

Time correction factor. A decimal figure arrived at from a yacht's rating and which is applied to its elapsed time in a race to find its corrected time for the race.

Time on time. The handicapping system which applies a time correction factor to a yacht's elapsed time in a race to arrive at a corrected time. The yacht with the lowest corrected time wins.

Time zone. Areas of the world, each 15 degrees of longitude, which have different local times.

Tingle. A temporary, thin metal patch put over a hole or leak in a boat in an emergency. A flattened out food can is ideal. A more permanent-shaped wooden capping can be placed over the leak when more time is available.

Topping lift. Any line used to support the end of, or raise, a spar.

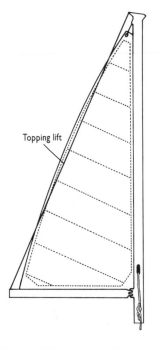

Diagram A2.57 *The topping lift supports the boom when the mainsail is not hoisted.*

Topsail. A sail set over a mainsail, or above the course.

Topsides. The area between the water level and the gunwales.

Towing light. A yellow light having the same characteristics as the stern light.

Trade winds. Winds which blow from a consistent direction at certain times of the year. So called because they allowed trade to expand throughout the world as sailors followed them.

Trailing edge. The leech, the leeward edge of a sail.

Transducer. The electronic apparatus which sends and receives sound signals and converts them to electrical impulses for instruments such as depth sounders, logs etc.

Transit. Two objects in line are in transit. Two transits will give a position which can be returned to, as a fishing spot.

Transom. The flat area at the stern of a vessel.

Transom knee. The knee angling the hog and sternpost.

Traveller. A metal car which slides along a track and takes the pulley controlling a sheet, as a mainsheet traveller. Also the car which carries the spinnaker bells on the forward side of the mast.

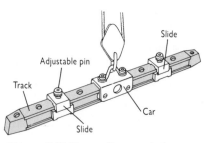

Diagram A2.58 *The traveller controls the shape of the mainsail and the balance of the boat.*

Traverse. A traverse is the resultant of the courses sailed by a vessel during a given period. So, if a vessel covers equal distances to the North and the East, the resultant will be North-east.

Traverse tables. Tables which reduce various traverses to a latitude and longitude, given a departure.

Triatic stay. The stay from one mast to another, as from main to mizzen, at their heads and spreading the load between them.

Tricoloured light. The masthead light on sailing yachts and some trawlers which contains the port and starboard and stern light. (See pages 122-129.)

Trimaran. A vessel with three hulls, usually a large centre hull and a smaller but equal-sized hull on each side.

Tropics. The tropics of Cancer and Capricorn are 23 degrees 27 minutes

North and South respectively of the equator and the area between them is the tropics.

True wind. The direction from which wind blows when it is not deflected. The wind as caused naturally.

Trysail. A very strong, loose-footed sail attached to the mast along the luff but not to the boom at all. Used in storm conditions.

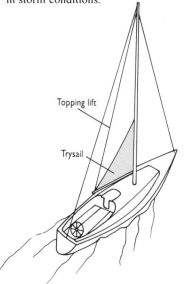

Topping lift

Trysail

Diagram A2.59 *The trysail is loose-footed and sheets to a winch.*

Tumblehome. The outward bulge of some yachts between the waterline and the gunwale. Brought to its extreme about 1975 this trend in racing design was intended to give a yacht greater stability and a longer-heeled water line without penalty under the I.O.R. rules. Superseded when lighter boats used flared topsides and crew weight to achieve the same.

Turn turtle (to). Do a 360 degree turn. Turn completely over horizontally.

Turnbuckle. Screw arrangement set at the base of the shrouds so that tension can be applied to them. Also called rigging screws.

Turtle. A bag of sailcloth which can be clipped to the rail of a yacht, near the bow, and used to launch a spinnaker, blooper or gennaker. The sails are specially packed beforehand to ensure clean hoisting.

Tweaker. A choker used on a spinnaker to pull down on the windward luff when it falls in.

U

Under bare poles. Without sails set.

Under the lee. In the shelter of any object sufficiently big to reduce the power of the wind.

Under way. Any vessel not anchored, tied up, rafted up, aground or connected to the shore is defined as being under way, although technically it may not be moving.

V

Vang. A strong purchase or hydraulic ram to hold down the boom and control the twist in a racing yacht's mainsail.

Variable pitch propeller. A propeller where the pitch can be altered mechanically by the crew from inside the boat while it is moving.

Variation. The amount by which a compass needle points away from true north, through deflection by the earth's magnetic field, if there is no other distortion. The angle between the magnetic and the true meridians.

Veer (to). (1) Let out a line or cable. (2) Of the wind, to change direction clockwise.

Vertical circle. A great circle which passes through the zenith and nadir of the celestial sphere. The celestial equivalent of longitude.

Vertical clearance. The distance between chart datum and the highest part beneath a bridge, or the lowest part of an overhead cable.

Very light. Flares fired from a Very pistol and accepted as alternates to other pyrotechnics for safety purposes.

Very quick light. A navigational light which flashes at between 100 and 120 times a minute.

VMG. Velocity made good. As distinct from boat speed through the water, VMG takes into account current, tide, leeway, boat speed, course sailed and any other factor which may affect the speed with which a yacht is aproaching a mark. It is sometimes also known as speed over the ground.

VPP. Velocity prediction program. The computer program which correlates all the past performance factors of a yacht and applies that information to a situation. It then produces data which indicates how the boat should be sailed for optimum VMG (velocity made good).

V sheet. Large plastic sheet with a large black letter V, signifying 'I need assistance', on it. The sheet has lanyards attached so that it can be tied in a position easily seen from the air.

W

Wake. Disturbed water extending from the stern of a vessel when moving to considerable distances behind it, depending on its speed. Very close to propellers on large ships there may be areas where the rudder of a small vessel will not respond, and whirlpools and strong currents (undertow) that toss it about. A wake at sea can cause large waves to trip and break where otherwise they would not have, creating some danger. The wake also consists of waves formed at the bow and stern and these can be seen at very great distances from the source in flat water.

Diagram A2.60 *Wake indicates the angle of leeway and is useful in navigating.*

Wall knot. A knot used as a collar or stopper.

Watch. (1) A division of the crew. Because ships must be worked day and night the labor fource has to be divided so that one works as the other sleeps. Two is the normal division, usually called the port watch, and the starboard watch. (2) The amount of time that a watch stays on deck, or below, is also called a watch, normally four hours. Racing yachts normally work three-hour watches between 1800 and 0600 and four hours for the balance of the day, which means the times of keeping watch alter for each group each 24 hours.

Watch buoy. A buoy marking a special position which can be watched by a vessel which needs to maintain its position.

Waterline. (1) The design waterline is that at which the vessel theoretically will float. (2) The actual waterline is where a vessel floats under different loads. The painted waterline is the boot top.

Waterline length. The length of the boat along its waterline, is important in handicapping because the hull speed of a vessel depends upon its waterline length.

Weather helm. A vessel which tries to sail closer to windward unless corrected is said to have weather helm. A little weather helm is desirable as it gives 'feel' to the boat but too much means the application of consistent counteracting rudder, so braking the boat. The position of the mainsheet traveller or the sail trim should be adjusted to balance the helm.

Weaver's knot. The single sheet bend.

Weight the cable. Lower a weight part of the way down the anchor rode. This moves the catenary and improves riding in waters that are not fully sheltered.

Well. (1) Open spaces between, for instance, the focsle and the bridge (the well deck). (2) For fishermen or lobstermen, the hold, open to the sea at the bottom, where fish are kept live.

West. A cardinal point, 270 degrees on the 360 degree notation.

Whip. A simple tackle of one rope and a single block.

Whip (to). To wrap turns of light line round the end of a rope to prevent it coming apart. The result of this action is called a whipping (see diagrams 1.39 and 1.40, page 20).

Whistle buoy. A buoy with a whistle incorporated.

Wind shadow (back wind). The cone of disturbed air to leeward of a yacht for up to 10 lengths and which can be used to 'blanket' a competitor which cannot sail as efficiently in the cone.

Windlass. A drum driven by manpower or machinery which when it rotates winds in wire or rope and so hauls or lifts.

Windscoop. (1) A wide funnel facing the wind and hoisted so that it directs fresh air below decks. (2) A metal scoop which juts out behind portholes and catches air which enters the compartment to cool it.

Wing and wing. Hoisting two headsails when running before the wind.

Wing nuts (U.S.). See Butterfly nuts.

Woven line. See Braided line.

Y

Yacht. A non-commercial vessel larger than a boat and smaller than a ship used entirely for the pleasure of the owner, whether it be cruising,

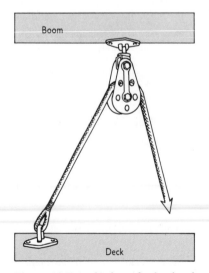

Diagram A2.61 *A whip has a fixed end and a direct purchase.*

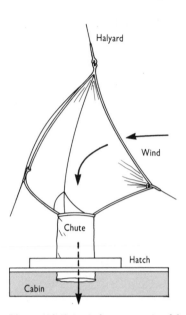

Diagram A2.62 *A wind scoop, very useful in the tropics.*

racing or voyaging, either power or sail.

Yard. A spar on a mast for attaching and extending sails.

Yard arm. The outboard end of a yard.

Yawing. A vessel with the bow swinging from side to side is said to be yawing. A good example is one at anchor on too short a rode.

Yawl. (1) A two-masted vessel with the mizzen only a little shorter than the main and the tiller or wheel aft of the mizzen mast. The mizzen of a yawl is much larger than that of a ketch.

Z

Zenith (Z). The point of the celestial sphere which is exactly overhead.

Zenith angle (distance) (z). The angle between the zenith and a heavenly body.

Zephyr. A gentle breeze; the slightest movement of air.

Zulu. Coordinated universal time, formerly Greenwich Mean Time.

FURTHER REFERENCES

Beaumont, Richard. *The Yachtsman's and Boatowner's Handbook.* Arlington Books, London, 1963.

British Admiralty. *Admiralty Manual of Seamanship.* HMSO, London, 1964, 2 vols.

Brooke, Lieutenant Commander G.A.G. and Dobell, Captain S. *Radar Mate.* Adlard Coles Ltd, London, 1986.

Brown, Captain Charles H. *Deviation and Deviascope.* 8th ed., Brown, Son & Ferguson Ltd, Glasgow, 1961.

Brown, Charles H. *Nicholl's Concise Guide to the Ministry of Transport Navigation Examinations.* 10th ed., Brown, Son & Ferguson, Glasgow, 1966.

Bruce, Erroll. *Deep Sea Sailing.* Rev'd ed., Stanley Paul, London, 1967.

Coles, Adlard K. *Heavy Weather Sailing.* Adlard Coles Ltd, London, 1967.

Conner, Dennis. *Comeback.* St Martin's Press, New York, 1987.

Couper, Alastair (ed.). *The Times Atlas of the Oceans.* Angus & Robertson Publishers, Sydney, 1983.

Dahl, Norman. *The Yacht Navigator's Handbook.* Ward Lock Ltd, London, 1983.

Dalton, Teki. *Sea Safety for Small Craft.* Australian Government Publishing Service, Canberra, 1988.

Davis, Murray. *Australian Ocean Racing.* Angus & Robertson Ltd, Sydney, 1967.

Department of Trade. *The Ship Captain's Medical Guide.* 20th ed., HMSO, London, 1967.

Fagan, Brian M. *Anchoring.* International Marine Publishing Co., Camden, USA, 1986.

Fletcher, Mike and Ross, Bob. *Tuning a Racing Yacht.* 2nd ed., Angus & Robertson Ltd, London, 1978.

French, John. *Electrics and Electronics for Small Craft.* 2nd ed., Adlard Coles Ltd, Granada Publishing, London, 1981.

Garrett Smith, Hervey. *The Marlinspike Sailor.* Wren Publishing Pty Ltd, Melbourne, 1973.

Gibson, Charles. *Knots and Splices.* Rev'd ed., Granada Publishing Ltd, London, 1979.

Heaton, Peter. *Sailing.* 4th ed., Penguin Books Ltd, Middlesex, 1970.

Holford, Ingrid. *The Yachtsman's Weather Guide.* Ward Lock Ltd, London, 1979.

Hollander, Neil and Mertes, Harald. *The Yachtsman's Emergency Handbook.* Rev'd ed., Angus & Robertson Publishers, Sydney, 1989.

Hooper, Rosanne (ed.). *The Sailor's Handbook.* Marshall Editions Ltd, Pan Books, London, 1983.

Hoyt, Norris D. *Seamanship.* Rev'd ed., Darton, Longman & Todd, London, 1962.

Hunter, Dr T.A.A. *Yachtsman's Medical Companion*. Nautical Publishing Co, Lymington, UK, 1969.

Institute for Advancement of Sailing. *Best of Sail Trim*. 7th ed., Adlard Coles Ltd, Granada Publishing, London, 1975.

Johnson, Peter. *The Encyclopedia of Yachting*. Angus & Robertson Publishers, Sydney, 1989.

Jorgensen, Eric. *Powerboat Maintenance*. Clymer Publications, Los Angeles, 1975.

Layton, C.W.T. *Dictionary of Nautical Words and Terms*. 3rd ed., Brown, Son & Ferguson Ltd, Glasgow, 1987.

Mate, Ferenc. *The Finely Fitted Yacht*. Albatross Publishing House, Vancouver, 1979.

McEwen, W.A. and Lewis A.H. *Encyclopedia of Nautical Knowledge*. Cornell Maritime Press Ltd, Centreville, USA, 1953.

Meisel, Tony. *Nautical Emergencies*. W.W. Norton & Co., New York, 1984.

Meteorological Office. *A Course in Elementary Meteorology*. HMSO, London, 1962.

Meteorological Office. *Meteorology for Mariners*. HMSO, London, 1967.

Miller, Conrad. *Your Boat's Electrical System*. 2nd ed., Hearst Books, New York, 1981.

Nicolson, Ian. *Surveying Small Craft*. International Marine Publishing Co., Adlard Coles Ltd, Camden, USA, 1974.

Pardey, Lin and Pardey, Larry. *The Care and Feeding of the Offshore Crew*. W.W. Norton & Co., New York, 1980.

Postal and Telecommunications Department. *Handbook for Radiotelephone Ship Station Operators*. Australian Government Publishing Service, Canberra, 1978.

Rogoff, Mortimer. *Calculator Navigation*. W.W. Norton & Co., New York, 1979.

Royal Life-saving Society. *Manual of Water Safety and Life-saving*. 6th ed., Royal Life-saving Society, Melbourne, 1976.

Schult, Joachim. *The Sailing Dictionary*. Adlard Coles Ltd, Granada Publishing, London, 1981.

Street, Donald. *The Ocean Sailing Yacht*. W.W. Norton & Co., New York, 1973.

Westfall, Fran. *Basic Seamanship and Boat Handling*. Lansdowne Press Pty Ltd, Melbourne, 1967.

White, Reg and Fisher, Bob. *Catamaran Racing*. Cassell & Co. Ltd, London, 1968.

Zadig, Ernest A. *The Complete Book of Pleasure Boat Engines*. Prentice-Hall Inc., Englewood Cliffs, USA, 1980.

A C K N O W L E D G M E N T S

Illustrations

Pages 65, 66, 67, 71, 72, 79, 80, 81	Adapted from *Meteorology for Mariners* with the permission of the Controller of her Majesty's Stationery Office.
Pages 119, 122–129	Marine Board of Queensland, *Small Ships Manual.*
Pages 130–134	Reproduced from Admiralty Publications with the permission of the Controller of Her Majesty's Stationery Office.
Page 243	Reproduced with the permission of Simpson Lawrence, Glasgow, Scotland.
Line drawings and illustrations	By Russell Jeffery, except for 'The Language of the Sea' by Leonie Bremer-Kamp.

Photography

Cover	Sextant, compass, snap shackle supplied by Bias Boating Warehouse. Yacht photograph supplied by Volvox—Australian Picture Library.
Page iii	Philip Quirk, Wildlight Photoagency
Pages vi, vii, ix	Malcolm Clark
Page x	Oliver Strewe, Wildlight Photoagency

INDEX